THE EXPERTS

The Experts

BY SEYMOUR FREIDIN
AND GEORGE BAILEY

NEW YORK
THE MACMILLAN COMPANY

COLLIER-MACMILLAN LIMITED
LONDON

FIRST PRINTING

The Macmillan Company, New York
Collier-Macmillan Canada Ltd., Toronto, Ontario
Printed in the United States of America

For Joshua *and* Nicholas Freidin

and Ariane Bailey

The New Generation

CONTENTS

viii   CONTENTS

PREFACE

A S foreign correspondents, we two have lived with the obsession for expertise in foreign affairs from its beginnings. Over more than twenty-five years we have watched and, indeed, lived with the experts in the sense that we have seen how they operate and what impact they make. Their persuasions and prejudices have, we believe, coalesced into an arrogance that menaces clear thinking and uncluttered policy and action.

An age of hope to restore reason, to make the world safe for parliamentary democracy, has been brushed aside to make way for an era dedicated to instant specialization as a corollary of the pragmatic approach to world problems. The new pragmatism sank roots just before and during World War II and has flourished ever since—nowhere so much as in America and at no time so proudly as during the Kennedy Administration. Thus the cult of expertise was spawned, and the expert, with or without quotes, became a household word.

But the term and the concept are ambiguous and self-contradictory. There is an essential connection between the know-nothing and the know-it-all, between the man who knows very little about everything (the universalist) and the man who knows everything about very little (the specialist). There is also a connection between the experienced veteran and the dilettante, if only because of the confusing similarity between style and facility. Inevitably a certain style, a flair, attaches to the exercise of ability. For the American, perhaps, the best definition of style is the image in motion. There is a smoothness, a neatness, an unwavering relevance that is the chief attribute of the American ideal of the genre: the efficiency expert, the man who steps in, puts his finger on the trouble, and steps out. There is also a mystique that surrounds the man who performs minor miracles as a matter of course.

ix

By reverse association, articulate expertise is confused with poise and style. The uninformed public believes that the late John F. Kennedy was an unusually effective President because he unquestionably had style. To complicate matters further, there are fields where the dividing line between style and expertise is indistinct. Personality, charm, wit, and social grace are attributes in the practice of diplomacy that are certain to weigh heavily in favor of the possessor. But style itself, far from being a guarantee of ability, is more likely to serve as the camouflage of its absence.

In America the experts—real and imagined—form the only elite. Since wealth is the single criterion of success and the only basis of status, the wealthy are presumed to possess ability. Moreover, the very wealthy can buy expertise or even, like Robert Kennedy, assemble and maintain staffs of experts. The rich used to play polo; now they play politics—and not for sheer love of the game. Nor is it primarily a question of prestige: There is a strong element of social compulsion in the modern penchant of the rich for politics, of the very rich for diplomacy. It is not only that diplomacy is at once the most occult and arcadian field of human endeavor: The world has shrunk and America has grown. It is more and more the duty of every American with an inborn or acquired sense of political responsibility to occupy himself with foreign affairs. There is a rush to serve. It is widely assumed that only highly qualified professionals have any business in the field, and it is taken for granted that anybody who happens to be in the field is a highly qualified professional. With this there is the broad tendency of the public to leave decisions affecting the fate of nations to the experts—the workers of minor miracles. It is this complex of interrelating opposite extremes, deceptive similarities, and confusions that accounts for the presence of a few widely dispersed qualified practitioners in the midst of a legion of dilettantes ("dilettante" is diplomatic parlance for fraud). Wrote George Kennan:

> . . . you could make much more effective use of the principle of professionalism in the conduct of foreign policy; . . . we could, if we wished, develop a corps of professional officers superior to anything that exists or ever has existed in this field. . . . However, I am quite prepared to recognize that this runs counter to strong prejudices and preconceptions in sections of our public mind, particularly in Congress and the press, and that for this reason we are probably

condemned to continue relying almost exclusively on what we might call "diplomacy by dilettantism."

Men and women, by virtue of living in a foreign country, enjoying election to high office, or having the gift of journalistic, academic, or even managerial gab, have felt called upon to pass judgment on the welfare of peoples and the fate of nations. These are the experts. By reason of their fluency, status, and specialized interests they hand down tablets of their findings and conclusions. They expect millions to listen to their comments, to allow their dissent, and to approve their subjective distaste. Their expectations are fulfilled.

A handful of these experts, due to a ripe, old age and rear area comfort and safety, have disposed of a special influence. Theirs is the most uninterrupted cult of personality. They contrive the persuasions and erect the standards by which they themselves are accepted.

Theirs is a self-perpetuating, incestuous world. They either scoff at criticism as nonintellectual or disdain it as "reactionary." A rebuff is not taken lightly. Any critic of the experts always runs the risk of being consigned to pariahdom in his own milieu. "The difference between an intelligent man and an intellectual," said Stanley Baldwin, "is the difference between a gentleman and a gent."

Those who preen when they hear themselves described as intellectuals have often tapped great reservoirs of initiative and energy and harnessed the resultant power for the institutionalized belief in patent, primary evil. It may, in their view, exist in a political personality, in economics or an abrasive philosophy. But the need to believe in something or someone has brought strange and invidious acceptances. Where a political system is called "socialist," for example, their willingness to believe in the ultimate good of the experiment moves them to pardon or ignore the most monstrous crimes against humanity.

The experts of intellectual compulsion have shown by act and word that they have somehow lost faith, or never had any, in their own society. They have fancifully led themselves to believe that parliamentary society is corrupt and easily corruptible. Yet a misnamed "socialist" society can rarely be so corrupt.

The intellectuals, endowed with special insight by a regime that calls itself socialist but is totalitarian, yield to the total power and usually serve it willingly. They feel flattered being courted by autocrats, and their passions and talents flow toward power. They become the cronies of politicians who mistake fashion for reality, the compeers of men of state ready to make a deal in the name of pragmatism. Recruited and recruiting, they are annexed by the dilettantes to generate public support for the dilettantes.

There are the poly-historians, who comment from the sagacity acquired in their own, often veteran, roles as observers of the world and domestic scenes. They have lately been emulated by a youthful crop whose stamp of authority in expertise is the benign approval of their seniors.

Within the last twenty years we have developed an army of these most specialized "experts." Often they lack even the elementary qualifications to pass judgment on a given area, personality, trend, or conflict. Just as frequently, they write and speak in quite articulate and plausible styles. Few have ever been conversant for any stretch of time with the subject at home and abroad that they hold up to the public at large as their special field.

Some—a small minority—may handle a foreign language or two acceptably or even fluently. They even try to outdistance their competitors with expertise in travel to corners of the world. The swift visits endow them with a little extra expertise. What they assess and present, however, is no different from conclusions circulated from home bases in Washington or New York.

Another little cluster of experts has spent decades abroad but never managed to absorb enough of the local foreign tongue to use it themselves, except in restaurants to impress visiting firemen. This little group passes its own judgments: contrary in many cases to those of the intellectuals, the crypto-historians, and the soft-sell Establishment career diplomats. It is regarded as expertise, of course, but simple exposure to a strange land, its customs and political habits, can just as easily be acquired by reading straightforward histories. Little and inadequate knowledge of a foreign tongue is likely to be an inhibiting factor. But these novitiates and tyros are taken seriously, too.

Often, in late middle age, men who have made their marks as business specialists or troubleshooters find a craving to disperse their expertise for the benefit of government and the public. Delighted to use their experience and their names, the government puts them to work. They lead delegations to international conferences, debate with such opposition as trial and corporation lawyers or business personalities, haggling with trade unions or their own lower echelons over a new model.

Invariably, a career specialist paid by the government is at the sudden expert's elbow, advising, persuading, and usually convincing his latter-day superior that the ideas were his very own. With a few brilliant exceptions the hidden persuader also runs affairs of state for the noncareer ambassador appointed for his largesse and support of one of the political parties.

Professional careerists in foreign affairs for the United States— as in most government foreign offices—built up with our State Department a mutual protection society. It is often denounced today, in crude oversimplification, as the "striped pants set." What was, for example, an "original" American diplomatic expedition into Soviet affairs before and just after United States recognition in 1933, is still largely controlled by these pioneers.

They have risen to high career prominence. Their expertise is predicated on fluent knowledge of Russian, the Soviet Union, and the Russian Communist party apparatus and its approaches to the outside world. Their assessments, as experts, have been rather appalling, since they were supposed to be as much on the inside of events as any Westerner could hope to be. One such expert, Charles E. ("Chip") Bohlen, for instance, was dead wrong on twenty-two of twenty-five major Russia–United States issues. Bohlen, fluent in Russian and several other languages, also translated for President Roosevelt. For the last few years he has been ambassador to France. Another adviser to American Presidents speaks bad Russian. He is Llewellyn E. ("Tommy") Thompson, back in Moscow on his second tour as ambassador.

Nevertheless, these experts have achieved a continuous built-in objective. They have safeguarded their specialized roles in Sovietology for their immediate associates and themselves. Without their approval, younger, more energetic and imaginative career men cannot ascend the ladder. Too often these gifted younger men find themselves either stymied or shunted far away from the area for which they have been trained.

More pernicious in the short run are the experts who always manage to accentuate the positive in Communist countries. They manipulate a galaxy of writers and reporters, known disparagingly to their own craft as "visa writers." The "visa writers" are always prone to condemn some misfeasance in their own society,

but they rarely rise to criticize known totalitarian brutalities
and inequities. Pinpointing deficiencies and inhumanity means risking expulsion. A "visa writer" prefers to take no risks. For years,
while millions of Russians suffered under summary arrest, long
prison mistreatment, or wanton execution, a prominent American
journalist called Stalin a "benign grandfather." He must have
known many of these horrible stories, but he didn't care to emphasize them. His name is Harrison Salisbury, an Assistant Managing Editor of *The New York Times.*

Many others before and since this outstanding case similarly
took the easy way out. They reported the bland side of the seamy
life in Eastern Europe or other totalitarian communities. Their
word pictures were—and quite a few still are—singular distortions
that befuddle an already upset public. Some even made the adjust-
ment from a bland diet under a Fascist or right-wing authoritarianism to Communist rule. The irony has been that they came
under scathing attacks by the poly-historians and intellectuals for
antiseptic reports about the far right, but got cordial mention for
blandness toward Communists.

Full-blown into the network of experts have arrived men who
thought they should make amends for amassing fortunes. Unusually they are the most naïve-minded, compulsive do-gooders extant. Their efforts are rewarded with laudatory comments about
their desire to ease tension. One of the best known, a genial
gentleman who built a fortune in railroads and various capital
investments, steadfastly claims that he asked Russian and East
European power practitioners if they killed people. When they
replied *no,* his attitude amounted to: See, I asked and they answered.

So he underwrites great conferences of scholars and self-made
experts, West and East, to sound each other out on the problems
besetting today's society. Never would he accept the thesis that
those from Communist-governed nations sound a regime line even
when confronted with testimony from those who bolted from their
governments.

On the other side of the business line are the men who pride
themselves on being hardheaded, tight-fisted operators. They tell
the world that they aren't soft; they are only interested in a good
deal—for money. The result is deliberate inquiry into grandiose
transactions. When they find the other negotiating set will deliver

a contract for a fat bribe, their consciences are clear. You can buy most things and people, they declare solemnly. What they have never clearly seen, however, is how transactions of this kind are planned regime exercises, either for a desperate need at the time or for making an outside industry dependent on the regime's orders. Once satisfied, the same regime calmly refuses to renew contracts, and an enterprise in the West is badly dislocated. As for bribery, it is poisonous in non-Communist communities but unbelievably ignored by experts when it comes to totalitarian nations. The tough, cigar-smoking caricature of a big businessman therefore becomes an expert too. His advice on how to deal with "those people" is eagerly solicited and patronizingly provided.

The rise of the expert on Soviet affairs to public esteem inevitably assures eminence for those with expertise on developing stretches of the world—Africa and Latin America—and latterly, the mystical science of Sinology. We have, for example, China watchers battened on to Hong Kong, watching the mainland presses and monitoring reports of upheavals and gyrations inside Red China. These experts, some of whom have steeped themselves in Mandarin Chinese, decipher hidden meanings—so they tell us —from among the arcane passages of dreary monographs. Occasionally, they glean telltale snippets from frightened refugees.

On a daily basis our press contains expertise from the Sinologists who also have spread their wings to interpret the scene in Vietnam. Very few have ever been to China even for a brief visit, as difficult as it is to obtain a visa. They usually speak to each other, view with disdain perplexed inquiries from outsiders. They regard as semiequals young career diplomatists who are determined to absorb outside China what they can of the principal language, history, customs, and political lines.

None of them—and this is remarkable—ever forecast the cataclysm that rocked the archipelago of Indonesia. This was Red China's single greatest setback in the battle with the Soviet Union for control of party apparatus around the world. The fact that both Communist giants were rejected has all but been ignored. Our policy toward Vietnam became the obsessive single factor for the critics. Scant attention has been paid to the planned terror catalogue of the Viet Cong and North Vietnamese expansionist ambitions. At a minimum, critics demand neutralization which substantively means neutralization of ourselves.

The Africanists, more veteran than other experts in the star-studded realm of nonalignment, often reach hard to explain why African leaderships follow the slippery path to "socialism." The Soviet example is the comparison usually cited. Historically, they twist the case or are ignorant of some simple facts. Czarist Russia, that feckless despotism, was in 1912 the world's greatest wheat exporter, had vast rail trackage, a developing industry and, most important to the experts, a splendid heritage of literature, music, and culture. These assets are nearly nonexistent in emergent Africa. But the Soviet so-called "example" is held high as Africa's hope.

We, the authors, have known the overwhelming majority of the experts about whom we undertake to write. We are also acquainted first-hand with their works and rise to eminence. The rapid growth of the expert in American life has, as we have briefly outlined thus far, proliferated in most key areas of our lives.

In most recent times we also see the rise of the young super-specialists who pronounce on customs and governments. They do not hesitate, where their more veteran sponsors have exercised more prudence, to set out deliberately to destroy someone or something. Why? Because they have decided well in advance that elimination is the only solution to a specific problem. They undertake the crusade, are abetted by being heard and cited by other experts, and quickly exude the charisma with which they have endowed themselves. That this is a pernicious form of nihilism goes almost unnoticed. And the practice has become more extensive in the last few years.

There are few heroes in this book; there are a few more villains, and a great many fops, dupes, and dolts. It is obviously impossible to cite all the glaring examples of expertise in the age of the expert. We have endeavored to lift the veil that conceals the experts from their audience and delineate the provenance and attendant circumstances of their actions. The great and horrible gaffes of modern foreign policy—the Treaty of Versailles, the doctrine of Unconditional Surrender, the Morgenthau plan—are the results of collective obsessions, the hangovers of the mass hysteria generic to war.

But the gaffes of the later postwar period, say from 1955 on (whether they were minor or major, horrible or laughable, remains to be seen), were conditioned and caused by deliberate, programmatic deception. The *leitmotiv* of American inaction in the face of Soviet or Soviet-inspired aggression and aggressiveness—the Berlin blockade, the crushing of the East German uprising in 1953, the crushing of the Hungarian uprising in 1956, the construction of the Berlin Wall in 1961, the arming of Arab nations for war against Israel—is demonstrably the result of the United States government's unswerving determination to conciliate, accommodate, cooperate, and otherwise come to terms with the Soviet Union. And this virtually in spite of the Soviet Union.

The motivations of the experts—groups and individuals—in ceaselessly plumping for this consummation are diverse, but they converge in the goal of *detente-cum-entente* with the Soviet Union. To do this has involved a policy and practice of euphemism, an insistence that cancer is a mere heat rash, the invention and refinement of a vocabulary for concealment and disguise of the hideous truth. This institutionalization of pious deception has been adopted and complemented by the Soviet Union for its own subversive purposes.

The result is an artificial superstructure of international relations within the context of which is being carried out the life and death struggle of two opposing systems. The surface of this carapace is so far removed from the underlying realities that the truth sounds like sheer madness, while folly takes on the appearance of sweet reason. The deception is abetted by the nature and circumstances of the dupe. It is extremely difficult for the citizen of Western industrial society, living in relative affluence, to grasp the steady intent of a foreign power to encompass the destruction of life as the Westerner knows it.

The most telling result of this curious conspiracy is the manipulated appearance of the struggle in Vietnam—in reality an integral part of the ideological Armageddon, since it is the struggle of the American government to contain a local application of the Communist strategy of conquest by terrorism—as a simple piece of naked imperialist aggression on the part of the United States. In attempting to expose the experts, it is the hope of the authors to bid halt—at least on our side—to career duplicity, to reveal these manifestations of Communist aggression in their true light—the better to oppose and end them.

Chapter 1

MASS COMMUNICATIONS AND
COMMUNICATORS: PART ONE

THE hothouse atmosphere in Washington produces the biggest and most diffuse crop of experts in foreign affairs in the world. This is logical, if rather unnatural, given the annual growth of the capital into the greatest citadel of power on earth. Young men on the make gravitate toward Washington, where with some deference and a little effort they can consult with Presidential advisers, listen sometimes to the President of the United States, dine with high court judges, senators, glib lobbyists, assorted diplomats, sonorous intellectuals, academicians on loan to the government, and their own kind. Never in any one capital in contemporary history has such an assemblage of real and fancied expertise on what is wrong with us and the world been gathered.

In Washington the deliberate leak is regarded as a deft art. It may come from a Cabinet Secretary, occasionally the President; usually from men within the inner workings of government, who provide shards of information edged with gossip when they are supposed to clam up on something important. The appearance of television cameras and microphones has been, in large measure, responsible for advancing expertise by a generation. It also provided the medium necessary for an expert to get into millions of living rooms. Therefore, the oddity today is an expert unwilling to participate on some TV program.

Walter Lippmann, for instance, resisted for some years. Now he appears on well-billed programs with a big-name commentator. Rare indeed are the experts who only print views or shape phrases for delivery at a lecture or in the sanctity of the Congress or some lower legislature. TV has diversified the quality of the leak. The experienced practitioners have a point of view they want to get across before it appears on a memorandum or a proposal. To maintain their share, the less experienced and articulate like to blurt things out before a camera or, if wary, pass them on to selected, attentive friends.

Expert practitioners of the leak are usually protected by the traditional and hoary anonymity. They almost never hesitate to use someone who is sworn by legend never to reveal the original fount. Many of the sharper governmental experts will rely on a person of some probity, who is regarded as "solid," even if he cannot be accepted as an equal. Then, when it is most useful and profitable, they rely on the silence of the solid man to comment publicly.

A couple of years ago Roger Hilsman, an outgoing Deputy Undersecretary in the State Department, did the trick with some nimble footwork. Hilsman, regarded by his friends as a modern-day soldier-statesman-intellectual and a sound authority on the perils of guerrilla warfare, may have stretched his authority. He was the author of a message to Saigon advising procedural policies contrary to Defense Secretary McNamara's. It is unclear to this day whether this message was properly cleared. He was offered a post on the Columbia University faculty, which he accepted. Brooding briefly on his departure from government, Hilsman wrote an article, not about Vietnam, but about the Cuban missile crisis, of which he had some inside knowledge.

His piece appeared in *Look* magazine. The man centrally involved, a hard-working reporter for the American Broadcasting Company, remained mum. He is John Scali, former Associated Press reporter, who since 1959 has covered the State Department. In the hectic late autumn days of October, 1962, when the tension over Soviet missiles in Cuba was coming to the eyeball stage, Scali was approached by a ranking officer of the Soviet Embassy. Had he high-up contacts in the American government as the Russian thought? Sure, said Scali. In this neo-Byzantine way the Soviets prefer to handle many delicate problems. Scali became the transmission belt for the first series of the gravest messages. With the knowledge of his company, he was sworn to secrecy. To his credit and dignity, he kept his word, only to see the episode published by Hilsman.

Scali is not regarded as an expert by experts. That part of the Establishment, particularly under President Johnson, is considered fair game. Its complaints usually are disregarded or held up to public scorn as clumsy efforts to gag opinion-makers. The tribal habits of the experts in Washington are rather uniform. They feel compelled to have their names seen on all imposing invitation lists. In turn, they offer cocktail and dinner parties of their own, at which a Cabinet member, a ranking diplomat, and a couple of Senators are on hand. The host normally is flanked by a couple of agreeable fellow-experts. Views are expounded, soundings are taken, and the experts usually hog whatever conversation they can to impress their views on listeners.

The authors have attended some of these dinner parties through the years. Some are notable for their hosts' bad manners—badgering a political personality about an issue, or searching for information. It is like singing for your supper. Chiefly the experts like to talk to each other. We were at a dinner recently where the host derided a leading congressman for supporting the government role in Vietnam. His friendly expert on international affairs, from a prominent newspaper, pushed a half-filled glass of red wine next to the lady beside him. He adjusted horn-rimmed spectacles firmly on his nose and leaned forward, elbows on table.

"You don't know what you're talking about," said the expert. "I believe you are going about this back-asswards. You'll never learn."

The congressman, a veteran of long years of service, turned crimson. He replied that the critic should state his case and not make sweeping judgments at table. The expert pulled a pipe from his pocket, stuffed it with tobacco, set fire to the mixture and blew great clouds of smoke at the congressman. It was a most extraordinary exhibition, hailed by the host as "plain talk." The cabal-like togetherness of the majority of experts predominates in Washington. They really prefer talking to each other. At the United Nations in New York, a goodly share of expertise has become part of the scene. Collectively, UN experts make far less impact on the American public than do their counterparts in Washington, or abroad, where they report with the solemnity of ex-officio American delegates. Newspapers and TV, on news merit, long ago deemed UN news as largely a bore. Emergency sessions of the Security Council or the Assembly, amid a crisis like Suez or missiles in Cuba, get sudden treatment. Normally the UN arouses little excitement or sustained interest even for an expert.

Abroad it is a much different story. A correspondent becomes an expert by staying long at a given capital, by self-promotion, and by being seen with personalities in power, literary and artistic figures, and diplomats of the same vintage. There is, in assignment in the foreign field, a greater tendency towards incestuous accommodation. Diplomatic and journalistic couples see, talk, and play together with great exclusivity. A wife, in her devotion to duty in this smart set of experts, will be a hostess even to the point of dropping with fatigue. She is a lioness, out to help her husband. The husband—lunching, drinking, and dining with the kings of policy—rarely keeps tabs on what else is going on in the community about which he reports. A reverse attitude prevails, alarmingly, among a sizable bloc of our national legislators. Many are suspicious of our own diplomats and foreign affairs generally, although they hold a veto power on budgets. Congressman John Rooney of Brooklyn for years, in the name of economy, has slashed willy nilly at State Department fund requests. Yet he does not hesitate to take tours, at government expense, for on-the-spot inquiries. Equally debilitating is the parochial indifference about the outside world still shown by congressmen who pass on our material involvement in difficult and far-flung communities.

Most experts-at-large still chortle over a bizarre incident involving a veteran House of Representatives' colleague of foreign affairs expert Senator J. William Fulbright. The mission, headed by a senior congressman, was to check on spending at assorted East European missions. As the plane took off from Vienna on the short flight to Budapest, the touring congressman beckoned to his escorting officer. "Tell me, son," he asked plaintively, "why they sometimes call this Budapest, sometimes Bucharest and sometimes Belgrade?" It was a hair-raiser, of course, but in the same class we must place some regional experts who are respectfully regarded for their supposed knowledge of specific places and situations.

One of the most prominent is Drew Middleton, now chief of bureau for *The New York Times* at the UN. Middleton, a facile writer, for years was bureau chief in London. He had covered the war in Europe. Then, between the end of the war and his UN assignment, Middleton served in Germany and the USSR, and for a while, he was in Paris. Middleton cannot speak even a modicum of any foreign language. Concededly, this can be a grave handicap. There have been unique figures who had such transcendent political perspicacity that they could overcome a linguistic short-coming. Invariably this occurs in action situations—wars and civil wars. Middleton, naturally, felt most comfortable in London. He could handle the language.

But he effected many of the outer trappings of the proper Eng-lishman—maintaining carefully a New York voice—so that he became generally known to locals as "Sir Drew." He also preferred Conservative party people, which was his right, even as successors on the same paper have gone overboard for the Labour party. But then the Conservatives were in power, as Labour is today.

On his German assignment it was remarkable that Middleton could write so knowledgeably—rise of neo-Nazis, Adenauer's tech-niques—without grasping more than a phrase or two of the local language.

In France Middleton had the same language problem. It didn't deter him. George Lichtheim, in his study of *The New York Times,* probably was unaware of Middleton's language deficiency when he wrote: "Mr. Middleton used to be based in London and has always tended to be an admirer of all things British. De Gaulle's exclusion of his favorite country hit him hard, and he has not been the same man since it happened."

Lichtheim examined some of Middleton's reports on de Gaulle. In June, 1965, Middleton went to Lille, de Gaulle's birthplace, to sample opinion about the French President. Lichtheim quoted from a Middleton article: "When an American remarked at a dinner party that de Gaulle was a 'Lilleois,' the hostess sniffed and pointed out that the General had been born here only because his father had been teaching here at the time."

Archly, Lichtheim made this observation: "No prizes are offered for guessing the identity of the American." What remains unknown, of course, is whether the hostess was English-speaking or there was an interpreter at Middleton's elbow.

In much the same manner, Middleton toured cafes to get reac-tions. He concluded that the people of Lille were all for European integration and unimpressed by de Gaulle's insistence on national sovereignty. For a nonspeaker of French it wasn't a bad tour de force, except that a man like Lichtheim, with an abiding knowledge of the area, was taking a jaded look at the article.

During his years in Britain, Middleton enjoyed a special role. He was chief of *The New York Times* bureau, which automatically endowed him with a privileged position. The *Times* is, for some reason, viewed as either an ex-officio branch of United States government, or the most authoritative voice for all America. Middleton, whose Anglophilia was duly noted, soon was recognized by the government as a spokesman for his countrymen. Nobody appointed him or agreed in advance that he should be so selected. Briefings—those strange background sessions provided for selected correspondents by most Western governments—were usually accorded the average American reporter, if he was part of the "Middleton group." The practice in London has since been pursued in the name of other successors.

Middleton, as an expert on Europe in general and on Britain in particular, competed for preference and preferment over the years with Sydney Gruson. Gruson began his career as a cub foreign correspondent in London, later in *The New York Times* London Bureau, as considerably junior and more or less subordinate to Middleton. Gruson has proved to be competition for Middleton in every sense. Although he has spent more than two decades abroad covering the Benelux countries, Mexico and Central America, Poland, Germany, and France, he is a foreign correspondent of truly outstanding linguistic inability. Despite his long residence abroad, particularly in Germany and Poland, it is doubtful that Gruson could put together a sentence in any foreign language if his life depended on it. In 1964 Gruson took over *The New York Times* London Bureau, ending Middleton's twelve-year tenure, while Middleton took charge of the Paris Bureau. In 1965 Gruson became foreign editor of *The New York Times,* overseeing and controlling its motley array of talent, the largest corps of newspaper correspondents in the world. This was a corps—under Gruson—to which Middleton abruptly ceased to belong. Middleton was transferred to the United Nations in New York shortly after Gruson's assumption of the new position. A new breed of foreign correspondent has developed—with foreign language talent—but they are still mostly in subordinate posts.

Two noteworthy exceptions are in London, where language is usually no barrier for an American. *The New York Times* chief of bureau is a smallish man, Anthony Lewis. He had been in the Washington bureau before coming to Britain, which was his first overseas assignment. Lewis, an expert on the United States Supreme Court and civil rights, became an expert on Britain. It was swift, but in the *Times* tradition.

About the same time that Lewis turned up in London, the Washington *Post* sent over a new chief correspondent. Karl Meyer, a pipe-smoking man with a mass of disorderly hair, has been obsessed with British live-a-day customs, music, fashions, and political party abberrations. He is an avowed champion of the Labour party, a trait shared by Lewis, although more mutedly.

Meyer, who knows relatively little about Europe or the rest of the globe, finds Britain generally better than almost any other nation in all complex forms of human endeavor. He uses a broad brush bemoaning the inadequacies in the United States of, say, chamber or symphony music compared with what he says he found in Britain. For the Labour party Meyer finds almost uncritical favor. He analyzes the twists and turns of Prime Minister Harold Wilson with undisguised admiration. When the human disaster befell the little Welsh mining community of Aberfan, Meyer ignored what certainly was one of the most wrenching news stories of 1966. Obviously the catastrophe didn't fit within his scope of expertise on the British scene. Meyer's reports, of course, are distributed by the Washington *Post*-Los Angeles *Times* combined news service, with international circulation.

Both Meyer and Lewis, as the newest representatives of the more important American daily publications, are searchingly scanned and cultivated by government officials. They caused a miniature uproar in Britain with dissimilar reports on swinging London, the mini-skirt, and the country's feelings in general. Meyer assessed the mini-mood with enthusiasm. He found it fresh and exhilerating. Lewis was glum. There was no real concern among the young, he felt, for encroaching economic disaster. Swinging London, Lewis thought, was an unhappy distraction from reality.

As soon as the reports of the two leading younger experts on Britain appeared, follow-up pieces cascaded from magazines and local papers. TV had a field day with associated live shows. The British government was generally unhappy. Its efforts are to show great seriousness. The swinging atmosphere mars the image. In truth, swinging London amounts only to a minority of Chelsea— the area which is roughly equivalent to New York's Greenwich Village or the Left Bank in Paris. The Left Bank swings far more than the Village or Chelsea. As a matter of fact, John Crosby, American commentator who lives in London, first wrote about swinging London in 1964—as a gag. Meyer and Lewis rediscovered the swinging set and established a vogue for a mini-mentality.

After he had been in London nearly two years, to our knowledge, Lewis came to the conclusion that Wilson, his local hero, had misled Britain on Rhodesia. That had been written before, on the spot, by Donald Loucheim of the Washington *Post*. After the shipboard meeting between Wilson and Rhodesian Prime Minister Ian Smith got nowhere, Lewis found frustration and depression in Britain's governmental setup. The country couldn't do much, so it went to the UN. When Wilson haughtily declared that he would be able to bring down the white supremacist regime by April, 1966, Lewis and Meyer reported the prediction as something sure to happen. April, 1966, came and passed. They didn't note the prediction's inaccuracy. Nor did they note, in more than an annoying offhand way, public opinion polls that showed a public distaste for the whole Rhodesian affair and belief in a hands-off policy.

Although the Washington *Post*—now that it has near-joint ownership, with John Hay Whitney, of a European edition—is acquiring experts, it doesn't come close to *The New York Times*. It bought into the foreign-based edition after folding an opposing money-loser. Growth and development come naturally to publications bent on a worldwide image and with money to spend. In a few years the Washington *Post* appears certain to compete with *The New York Times* in expertise. Presently the *Times* is unchallenged. As a result, it performs like a medieval hierarchy, passing along expert edicts to the faithful. It has made a fetish of criticizing the Johnson Administration on nearly all major foreign policy issues. No government operating in a substantive parliamentary society should escape criticism or examination. But the way *The New York Times* has aimed its shots and exploited techniques is open to serious demurrer.

For example, its criticism even engaged the person of Johnson and his record in World War II. It was not contained in a regular news report but in *Times Talk,* a house organ. The monthly periodical is distributed much more widely than just among *Times* employees. Thus a bitterly critical article on L.B.J. appeared in the November, 1966, issue of *Times Talk*.

The magic circle of the experts on foreign affairs has been given free rein, which speaks rather well for top editors and publishers. Or, it might well be that supposed superior judgments are never exercised out of ignorance or indolence. Higher judgment was invoked, however, by "Punch" Sulzberger for the edition of Monday, November 28, 1966. The lead editorial of the first edition commented on the subject of a Christmas truce in Vietnam.

"Kill and maim as many as you can up to 6 o'clock in the morning of December 24 and start killing again on the morning of December 26," began the editorial. "Do your damndest until 6 a.m. December 31 and again after January 1, 1967, when it will be all right to slay, to bomb, to burn, to destroy crops and houses and the works of a man until 6 o'clock on the morning of December 24, 1967." It was perhaps the most ferocious *Times* editorial in memory. Punch Sulzberger called for a toning down—a rare thing for a *Times* publisher. So, it was cut in subsequent editions to start reading: "By all means let there be peace in Vietnam for a few hours or a few days. . . ."

The man who wrote the original editorial was Herbert L. Matthews. He was the first prominent journalist to have found Fidel Castro a progressive, balanced reformer. The *Times* supported the Matthews theme for a long time. Matthews was intrigued with European authoritarian rule.

In a *Times* column a week after Matthews's editorial, James ("Scotty") Reston wrote about a crisis of confidence. He lamented what he believed was a widespread doubt about our principal leaders and institutions. Reston thought there was an issue of veracity in statements from the White House and terrible cynicism about the Congress. Then, he observed in alarm: "The disbelief in the press is a national joke. ('It's just a newspaper story!')." Reston would do well to look over reports he should easily remember from the Truman and Eisenhower Administrations. As for disbelief in newspapers, Reston's own is a good place to begin.

Reston, a pleasant writer and an amiable personality, tries hard to avoid expertise. As associate editor of the *Times,* with responsibility primarily for his three-a-week column stint, he stumbles into the twilight land of the expert more frequently. He is unhappy about the pursuit of United States policies in Vietnam, and he quite frequently is upset with the state of the nation. His natural pursuits of inquiry, however, do not endow him with the gleaming shield of an expert.

In *The New York Times* that place is reserved for Harrison Salisbury, a tall, thin man with the wisp of a mustache and spectacles. Rising to assistant managing editor, he has branched into many fields.

Salisbury writes of juvenile delinquency and East-West problems without pausing for breath between articles or books. From 1944 to 1946 Salisbury was Moscow bureau manager for the United Press, today United Press International. He served in Moscow for the *Times* for some years and has revisited the U.S.S.R. and Eastern Europe a good number of times. But Salisbury's talents—including a fluent grasp of Russian—show an unerring instinct for making flat assessments of the Soviet Union that are either dead wrong or wishful thinking. Some years ago it did not require any special insight into the U.S.S.R. to realize that Stalin's rule was one of terror. Of Stalin, Salisbury wrote: ". . . not the kind of executive you cannot speak up to . . . His manner with inferiors is fatherly and benevolent."

There was a memorable passage in one of Salisbury's books, *Russia on the Way,* which said of the NKVD (now the KGB): "Most people think of the NKVD as a sinister secret police which carts off Russians in the dead of night and sends them packing to Siberia. Well, there is something in that impression, of course. The NKVD does things like that, occasionally . . ."

When Salisbury contributed that gem of information, the NKVD had decimated most of the political, intellectual, and diplomatic elites of the U.S.S.R. and its satellites. Stalin had launched another purge, which struck at nearly every family. It was well-known at that time. Salisbury believed that the terror was distorted by his colleagues. After the death of Stalin and the change of the security agency's initials, Salisbury suggested that the renamed MVD was just another force of tough cops. Hardly. Soon another name replaced MVD, but the old apparatus was scarcely altered.

In mid-May, 1967, when a new Middle East crisis was triggered by Arab armies closing a ring around Israel, the outside world paid little attention to a switch of prime importance in the U.S.S.R. A veteran Soviet party higher-up and troubleshooter became head of the KGB, dread three-letter super-security agency.

There is nothing in terms of power and influence anywhere in the world to match the KGB. Its initials stand for *Komitet Gosudarstvennoy Besopasnosti,* Committee for State Security. Our more publicized, often leaky CIA cannot compare with its militant adversary for funds, influence, or imposed inscrutability.

The KGB commands—from all the estimates supplied by defectors and British, French, and West German intelligence, as well as our own CIA—unlimited financial resources. It employs the biggest staff of secret agents in the world and has its own armed forces. Most Soviet embassies abroad contain a KGB officer who pursues policy. Sometimes he is masked as an ambassador, as Nikolai Federenko—delegate to the UN, but a career-long officer of the KGB with the rank of major-general.

Today the KGB is headed by fifty-two-year-old Yuri Andropov, who bears a startling physical resemblance to Lavrenti Beria. It was Beria who, under Stalin, widened the apparatus of terror. He was removed and executed by a military court in 1953 by officers who feared him and his vast powers. Ironically, Andropov has even more might at his command than did Beria.

Andropov is a member of the all-powerful eleven-man secretariat of the Soviet Communist party. He is the closest comrade in the hierarchy of party secretary, burly Leonid Brezhnev. His appointment, announced in a terse eight-sentence message by Tass, came as the KGB managed to win domination over GRU, Soviet military intelligence. Even under Stalin, Beria never achieved that power *coup*.

Not since Beria has there been any Soviet politician of the standing and experience of Andropov at the KGB. His appointment enhances the role of Brezhnev in maneuvers for power. Andropov has at his disposal today the single most important, organized body inside the U.S.S.R.

As a troubleshooter, Andropov had liaison with all Communist parties outside the Soviet Union. He accompanied Brezhnev on all his trips to confer with comradely leaders. When Premier Kosygin visited Nasser in Cairo, the trip was followed up with an unheralded one by Andropov to both Nasser and Syria.

Andropov was at the side of brutal ex-security chief General Ivan Serov in Budapest, during the uprising. That was when the Russians tricked the Hungarian revolutionary command into a meeting. Serov, flanked by Andropov, entered a meeting and arrested the late Hungarian Defense Minister, General Pal Maleter, and others.

When Andropov took over, out went Vladimir Semichastny, protégé and pal of Aleksander Shelepin, youngest member, at forty-eight, of the Politburo and former head of the KGB. Semichastny ran the KGB for five years. It had been, after Stalin, officially truncated but unofficially ran its own show with worrisome counsel from above.

Under Semichastny's direction there had been some notable

failures. They were disclosed through trials, intended as a warning. The KGB, unlike the CIA, forbids, under pain of death, public scrutiny inside the country. No public outcry is allowed to accompany its failures or demands for funds.

One of the most glaring of the KGB deficiencies was the case of Colonel Oleg Penkovsky. He supplied Russian rocket secrets to the West. When trapped, he was tried and subsequently shot. The defection of Svetlana Stalin and exposure of Soviet espionage rings have been among recent KGB difficulties. It also was slow to deal, as it did later, with restive writers and intellectuals. And there were the political rebuffs from free-wheeling Communist-led Romania and the dismissal of Tito's heir, Aleksander Rankovic, with whom the KGB had been working under cover.

Andropov's job is to overhaul the KGB, retread its far-flung operations, and provide hard-nosed leadership at the top. Soviet diplomats say so freely to Westerners eager to pursue the course of conciliation and bridge-building with the U.S.S.R. Yet Andropov, before and since his appointment, has declared publicly: "The United States is the real enemy. We must never relax, and we must be eternally vigilant."

Both the authors know Soviet writers who detested the roughhouse methods of Andropov. They have told us about his cold contempt for them and other intellectuals. In her written protests Svetlana Stalin has complained bitterly of KGB intrusion into creative work and thought. Now Andropov is in a position to pull KGB wires—and therefore policy—on a worldwide front.

Salisbury still insists, in his writing and lectures, that the instruments of brutal authority are gradually atrophying in the U.S.S.R. No matter what strain is imposed on either internal Russian life or external association by party *diktat,* Salisbury sees progress. In a more sad than angry commentary, Abraham Brumberg wrote in 1962 that he was "left with the nagging impression that Mr. Salisbury's approach to the Soviet Union has not changed very much after all."

Brumberg has been writing about Soviet and Communist affairs for years, basically dealing with documentation. He briefly mentioned Salisbury's compulsion for writing an analysis of a situation immediately after arriving in a given place. This could be explained by his earlier wire service training, which requires that a correspondent shoot off an immediate dispatch, to show he has reached his assignment and to give his service a dateline for the public before the competition gets one out.

Salisbury astounded many *New York Times* colleagues by arriving in Hanoi and filing his first dispatch on a highly complicated situation the following day.

The New York Times columnist C. L. Sulzberger does not feel so charitable about the U.S.S.R., in spite of the many experts in favor of building East-West bridges. In an article on June 27, 1966, Sulzberger wrote about the conduct of governmental and departmental Soviet affairs.

> Sixty percent of the approximately 6,000 Soviet officials stationed outside the USSR today are actually career officers of either KGB or GRU (military intelligence). The proportion is even higher among accredited Russian diplomats. The entire Ministry of Foreign Affairs in Moscow includes only some 1,300 people, and among them at least a third are intelligence professionals. The Moscow staff of the KGB approximates 6,000.

Looking at the extension of the Soviet diplomatic apparatus, Sulzberger added:

> Almost half of Russia's 75 envoys to non-Communist countries today are affiliated with the KGB or GRU. The present Soviet Ambassador to Havana, who uses the name Alekseyev, is actually a full colonel in the KGB, named Shitov, originally sent to Cuba to organize clandestine security. Four out of five Soviet diplomats in Cameroon are intelligence agents, thirteen out of sixteen in Ethiopia, seven out of eight in Senegal.

The Sulzberger article goes into more detail. It seems strange that the expert Salisbury, with his super-specialized knowledge of Soviet affairs, never saw fit to comment on these points. Obviously the *Times* publishes both men—Salisbury less, because these days he is usually involved in higher planning—to prove that it strikes a balance. The reader, should he manage to wade through the vast swamp of daily news, rarely manages to find time for adequate comparisons.

The American wire services, Associated Press and United Press International, try with some degree of success to avoid having experts. They offer services and features around the world as objective news disseminators. Their reports are sold to Communists and non-Communists—the best price, so to speak, without political prejudice. Rather than have an expert view, these services use "analysts" to provide background and comment. They are, on balance, pallid. Veteran of them all is Henry Shapiro, a dapper little man with a mustache, who spent most of his adult life working in Moscow.

As a veteran reporter and bureau chief for the UPI, Shapiro has about as good contacts with locals as a Westerner on the scene can obtain. He was born in 1906 in Romania and became a naturalized citizen of the United States in 1928. Shapiro became a lawyer but has spent more than thirty years in Moscow for the same agency. He speaks virtually letter-perfect Russian and is married to a Russian woman. As a writing stylist, his copy is toothless. Shapiro is scrupulous about staying out of trouble with Soviet officialdom. He runs a tight shop.

He is a unique expert. Never inclined to engage in any controversy with Soviets of any standing, Shapiro rides hard on his staff to perform the same way. Shapiro's curious expertise on Soviet and Communist matters is another factor. While his reports are an almost official presentation, he imparts his views with alacrity to important visitors and diplomats. They generally add up to an emphasis on the need for understanding Soviet tactics, whether practiced by Stalin or his successors.

At best, this is a bloodless, standoffish behavior pattern. Because Shapiro has been in the U.S.S.R. so long, he also is in demand to lecture—on holidays or sabbaticals—in the United States and European centers. At these meetings he is introduced and regarded by audiences as an expert, which Shapiro does nothing whatever to deny. His lecture themes rarely differ from the points he makes in private conversations with touring personalities. In his view the United States always seems to be responsible for the most egregious errors and to lack tolerant insight into Soviet behaviorism.

In a grander manner, but with studied humility, Cyrus L. Eaton has sought American understanding and even ratiocination about Soviet habits. He launched conferences, bringing together scientists from East and West, first at his home in Pugwash in Nova Scotia. An enormously wealthy industrialist and free enterpriser, Eaton has made Pugwash conferences financially possible, beginning in 1957. The authors were at the airport in Paris, when Nikita Khrushchev flew in for a de Gaulle-sponsored state visit. Eaton was there, too, and a Soviet diplomat whispered the news to Khrushchev. Before entering his car, Khrushchev made a point of going over and shaking Eaton's hand. Then he turned to reporters to say: "My favorite capitalist."

Eaton beamed. His conferences always carry the slogan of peace and understanding. But it is important to understand how Eaton became interested in a field so vastly different from his own previous interest and business background. Professor Eugene Rabinowitch, founder and editor of the *Bulletin of the Atomic Scientists* published in Chicago, described Pugwash's origins:

> Again it was the initiative—and prestige—of Bertrand Russell that overcame stagnation. He interested Cyrus Eaton, the Canadian-born American industrialist, in supporting a new conference. Mr. Eaton offered for this purpose his home in the old clipper-building town of Pugwash on the Northumberland Straits in Nova Scotia.

Lord Russell, as we have seen, has been the sponsor for various and often conflicting conferences and movements.

Today Eaton is an expert by sponsorship of the call to coexistence, understanding the U.S.S.R., and all the thorny problems of peace and disarmament. It's quite different from running railroads as he has in the past.

Seeking light in the Communist-run world, particularly in Eastern Europe, has become something of a latter-day fashion for many prominent people in our business world.

A group, which included New York Stock Exchange President Keith Funston and Henry Ford, traveled throughout Eastern Europe in the autumn of 1966. They chartered a jet and touched down in five countries in less than a fortnight. It was magic carpet travel, and they met top regime people, including Tito, wherever they went. The programs had been worked out in advance. The private trip had the benign approval of our government, which deploys a rather amorphous project, called "building bridges," to find accommodation with Eastern Europe. All the well-heeled junketeers did not return home as experts, but many began to sound as if they had spent a great deal of time studying the problems on the spot.

This is a premonitory note of experts-in-the-making. One of the more macabre features of this trip was their arrival in Budapest on the tenth anniversary of the uprising that rocked the world, and which the Russians so savagely repressed. The timing could not have been more exquisite for any expert bent on creating new traditions and legends.

Chapter 2

MASS COMMUNICATIONS AND
COMMUNICATORS: PART TWO

TELEVISION, with its mass production of photo-facts and introduction of living color, is made to order for the professional
expert. He can engage in a high-flown colloquy with a usually
deferential questioner or participate in a panel discussion certain
to tranfix millions in their living rooms on a Sunday. Young commentators with an appealing presence have grown, in the public
mind, into uncertain experts. Most people are unsure of what TV
newsmen stress so emphatically by the expedient of reading prepared news bulletins freshly ripped by a news staff off wire service
machines.

Political personalities, from the President of the United States
down, constantly pump messages or trial balloons via TV. Today a
Presidential TV address is common in the East as in the West.
But we spend more time, money, and effort. This may be because
television in the United States is run on a competitive, profit-
making level. Within even the most serious electronic presentation,
a whiff of the ham exudes. Take Eric Sevareid's monographs on
the state of the world, nightly on the news show managed by
Walter Cronkite, a serious and fine journalist. "Walter?" inquires
Sevareid quizzically, from Washington usually. "And that's the way
it is," replies Cronkite, somewhat self-consciously, as he gives the
date. It isn't the way it is; only the way Cronkite, his team, and
CBS have pulled the show together. This probably stems from a
commingling of the human instinct to preen before a camera, to
sound important, and the desire to reappear quite soon.

Television and television news are part of everyday life for
Americans. The printed word may have more lasting qualities for
the reader and writer, but they have both come to believe almost

absolutely that TV is what the second newspaper once was. Repeated appearances of prominent people and fixed program news specialties provide instant identification for the public. It is something no byline in a newspaper or other publication can effect no matter how gifted the reporter.

The result has been, as *Time* magazine reported from an Elmo Roper poll taken in 1965, that 58 per cent of the American public obtains most of its news from television. The magazine also noted that the impact of TV is not lost on any politician. Senator Robert Kennedy has said that he would prefer to appear for thirty seconds on an evening program than be treated to extensive coverage in every newspaper around the world. Still, the Senator does not pass up the newspapers, either.

According to Bill Moyers, ex-White House Press Secretary for L.B.J.: "President Johnson feels that television offers him the most direct, straightforward, and personal way to communicate with people. It is not someone else's attitude or interpretation of what the President said. It's the purest form of communication, and I think the most desirable."

Moyers' point may be well taken—as far as delivering a speech or conducting a press conference. TV has hardly been pure, for example, on coverage of places, people, and problems. It is almost impossible to tell in two minutes, or thirty seconds, why a person defected from a tyrannical regime, or why we were increasing military power in Vietnam. True, documentaries of personages and countries, along with specific issues, are made and shown. Many are excellent reports. They take lots of time and money. The movies used to do them, too.

It is, of course, more comfortable to lean back and let someone tell you what he believes, rather than mull it over in a publication. Certainly, it is more rousing to see someone and something in action, with commentary, than to read the account. The effect does not normally provide for reflection. It leaves the viewer, consciously or not, rooting for or against the personality commenting on the TV screen. There are tricks of the trade in TV reporting and expertise, controlled directly by pictures. If the film is good, then it must be shown. This is what frequently occurs in Vietnam.

The war and searing tragedy in Vietnam, the most intensively covered conflict ever, has been described by television reporters and crews as a "TV war." As we have seen, producers, correspondents, and great caravans of equipment with attendant technicians go into areas like the vast armed hosts of old. Flaming action is sure-fire for the TV programs. Thus, in Vietnam episodes like those reported by Morley Safer of CBS are shown and stir sharp controversy.

Safer's big spot, which caused a bellow of rage and despair from critics of American involvement, came from a hamlet called Cam Ne. The film sequence, made in the summer of 1965, showed United States Marines burning a Vietnamese village. Safer and his crew risked their lives as did the marines in combat. "This is what the war is all about," declared Safer excitedly. His camera sequence also swung over weeping old men and women. Safer had a story, but it was far from what the war was about. Yet the pictures from Cam Ne made all the difference. They appeared with Safer's comments on the regular news show of Walter Cronkite. Inside CBS the Safer sequence still stirs fierce controversy. Among the smoldering arguments about the film, we have heard complaints of angled shots—deliberately contrived, so to speak. We also listened to TV editors contend that the "Safer show" proved that we never had any business in Vietnam. Critics in the field of anti-Vietnam expertise have naturally evoked the Cam Ne film as additional proof of their arguments.

Tragically, there are only few film shots of refugees wantonly struck down by the Viet Cong. Terror tactics, leaving dead and maimed strewn near the now-familiar rice paddies, only provide corpses for TV. The camera crew cannot film from the other side, so the whole pattern of power becomes one-sided and most macabre. Besides, what does the terrible wake of a Communist raid leave for the commentators? A one-line mention and photos of the dead.

But Cronkite, a giant in a field overgrown with pygmies, didn't glibly seize on the film and comment to induce shock. He puzzled and worried over it for a long time. We happen to disagree with the distorted impact of the sequence. But Cronkite, rather unique among TV commentators, behaved like the editor-reporter he always has been. Rather than rush on the air with the report, Cronkite studied the film and its narration. Then he consulted with his top editors who help prepare his news show. Queries went out for further explanation to men in the field and to the CBS Washington Bureau. Cronkite sought holes in the story. When he satisfied himself there were no major mistakes, he ran the controversial report. It is strange that the younger generation in television, trying to come of age, prefers the "blood-on-the-moon" daily shocker as General "Slam" Marshall said, to the thoughtful and perceptive report. Eager and ambitious to be acknowledged as regional experts, the majority of younger TV correspondents believe they can only get on the air with something abrasive, if not brutal.

For NBC, Chet Huntley, who with David Brinkley makes up the competitor team pitted against Cronkite, has been frankly upset by that trend. He feels that too many TV reporters in Vietnam emphasize Saferlike reports. They believe it guarantees showing with alacrity at home. Another radio-TV veteran like Cronkite and Charles Collingwood, also of CBS, Howard K. Smith of ABC strives for a balanced view. When Buddhist demonstrations were in vogue in Vietnam, said Smith, "television gave the impression that the whole country was rioting, instead of two thousand out of seventeen million." The demonstrations were cited by Senator Fulbright, among others, as added evidence of our wrongdoing there.

Except for a handful of TV commentators like Cronkite, Smith, Ed Morgan, and Huntley, the TV tendency is to accentuate the expert view even when the medium denies anything but objectivity. Electronic journalism has not yet produced its own cadre of TV-trained reporters and correspondents. It has relied principally on recruiting newspapermen. The first corps of television journalists will shortly get its chance to comment, edit, and counsel on programs. Its move, from the training and proving grounds that are peculiarly TV's own, concentrates on the framework of the expert.

The reasoning is logical for this fresh corps in the ever-expanding and rather self-important medium. A regional expert in, say, Vietnam, acquires a name and something of a reputation. Expansion simply requires more expert judgment. There is a predilection among the up-and-coming TV journalists to become young stuffed shirts. They see, alas, too many of their veteran colleagues go places in their business by sounding sententious. It also leads to a competitive know-nothingism, compelling a would-be expert to try to get ahead with the first idea.

That kind of compulsion led CBS into a red-faced fiasco in a plot intended to unseat "Papa Doc" Duvalier, dictator of Haiti. The network denied it contributed any money to the anti-Duvalier war chest. A CBS correspondent in the Haitian capital, Port-au-

Prince, broadcast that an invasion had taken place. It hadn't, but then the embarrassing details unfolded. CBS thought it had sewed up the invasion story. Its rivals learned that the network was on the inside track. They tried to make up for lost ground. Expert opinion on what was to come next in Haiti was given lots of air time.

When the "invasion" broadcast was made, the rival networks felt deflated and out-maneuvered. When it turned out to be a nonevent, they smugly mentioned the fiasco. CBS, discomfited, revealed how for six months it had been let in on the conspiracy. It reported rather lugubriously: "We filmed the preparations and began filming in the field in early October, 1966. We were standing by for the potential invasion, and as everybody now knows, it never happened." It was a wretched nonevent kept alive like a bad act by sponsors.

The tragicomedy was, in effect, an attempt by an agency totally outside government to help create foreign policy. It falls in line with the enthusiastic prediction of TV producers that they could envisage the day that the Vietnam war, if it lasted, would be brought into everyone's home. So much progress has been made in the direction of TV war that it can be discussed in terms of a household program. None of this incongruity, masked as another phase of expert knowledge, seems to have bothered personalities who regularly appear on TV as experts in their own right. Senator Fulbright, wearing special spectacles to cut the glare of the lights, never objects. But he commends attention to any usurpation, as he sees it, of Presidential intrusion on making and breaking foreign policy.

He can count, even during the lowest peak watching periods, on several million listeners tuning in to catch his hearings when they are presented for television. It was on TV that he first made his "manifest destiny" statement about the Johnson Administration and Vietnam. Walter Lippmann subsequently followed up the observation with references to "messianic megalomania," which is alliterative, if not especially accurate. The remark has been quoted so often by other experts supporting Lippmann's views that it will not be of merely transitory interest. They leap, when opportunity is offered, to air their views on network panel discussion shows.

So intent are they to be heard and seen that few even demur about having pancake makeup applied so they will look better.

The technical expert in this case is chief counselor. Because these worldly experts are involved with their views for the edification of millions, the aberrations of show business are discounted. But the coordination of TV, written journalism and monographs, books and lectures, have become the synthesis of the all-around expert. TV leaves him ample room in which to juggle his views, repeat them if they find receptive ears, and emphasize them.

None of the earnest arguments take refuge in the old prewar form of introspection. TV is more urbane, with philosophical preachments that command instant attention. A senator can be interestingly indiscreet on TV, in full knowledge that what he says will be picked up by some expert. So Senator Fulbright could play the whole range, even to summoning two psychologists to analyze United States foreign policy for the Senate Foreign Relations Committee. Their assessments, Fulbright suggested, showed that our political leaders were unwise and ignorant. "We don't know enough; we just aren't wise enough," sighed the senator. In his compassion, Fulbright overlooked the possibility that the psychological analysis might have included him.

To Senator Fulbright's defense have sprung specialists in dazzling fields, turned passionate experts in foreign affairs. They are of recent growth and emerge out of diverse fields from the study of geriatrics to baby care. Most prominent in the anti-Vietnam clamor is the internationally known baby specialist Dr. Benjamin Spock. His interest in matters global had previously been confined to well-bred New York salon conversation. Vietnam and the Fulbright-Lippmann tandem set the springboard for Dr. Spock. He had the arguments of these two experts for reference. His eminence in his own field provided ready-made access to hearings before TV sidewalk commentators, their cameras, and the press.

Acclamation of the experts by Dr. Spock, and advertised proponents of peace in Vietnam and worldwide accommodation with all, may sound superficially reasonable and plausible. They ignore the stresses of power behavior, especially motivations behind Soviet tactics, the Chinese Communist drive to superpower, and the invocations of Mao Tse-tung's Red Guards for the "cultural revolution." What the accepted pro-Lippmann experts propose is rather subtle and even sophisticated. It adds up, nevertheless, to withdrawal from power responsibilities and retreat into a wordy world of neo-isolation. This is not the blunt, grass-roots Middle Western aversion of forty years ago to the outside world. Its urbanity also draws on a special European veneer to make the arguments seem insuperably logical.

Newspaper headlines, columns, TV reports, senatorial debates, street demonstrations, expensive advertisements, and now a plethora of books are underwriting what has become fashionable neo-isolationism.

In a book by Edmund Stillman and William Pfaff, *Power and Impotence,* the authors essentially accept the findings of so supreme a universal expert as Lippmann. They use terms like globalism and internationalism, in regard to United States foreign policy, as dirty words. The specter of abject failure for what American policy makers seek runs through the pages of this book like a funereal theme. Errors ascribed to "defects of the national style and intelligence" might well be read in a like vein in much of Lippmann or in Fulbright's sentiments.

Amazingly, Messrs. Stillman and Pfaff refuse to concede any worthwhile credit to American policies anywhere in the world. One of their contentions is that Indonesia's upheaval against its surging Communist party would have happened anyway. Maybe so. But they charge that American meddling only delayed reaction. One must ask whether the authors either know nothing of Indonesia and Southeast Asia or they have permitted enchantment with their own views to cloud their vision.

"Meddling" was the lamentably amateurish manner in which Bobby Kennedy tried to make a fast deal with President Sukarno. The Indonesian army, anti-Communist in the main, waited on the best timing. Communist over-eagerness provoked the army into retaliation. Moreover, the army's counterstroke, giving China her worst black eye in diplomacy and foreign policy yet, might not have happened had there not been an American commitment in Vietnam. We have heard this explanation from present day Indonesian leaders who insist on a public attitude of nonalignment. Stillman and Pfaff reflect the neo-isolationist style of the experts of the late 1960's. The temperamental company they keep swings from the magic circle of Lippmann and Fulbright to Senator Frank Church of Idaho, who is on Fulbright's committee, and the altitudinous, articulate Professor John Kenneth Galbraith. Bobby Kennedy, his perspectives prepared, seems ready to join hands, if the trend can prove majority favor.

Senator Robert Kennedy, whose grasp of foreign affairs is tenuous, got burned with one prepared formula for Vietnam. But the scorching did not prevent him from making an emotional declaration to a student audience at Berkeley, California. He did not personally believe the people of South Vietnam wanted Marshal Ky as their ruler. This could be so. But how would Bobby Kennedy or anyone else really know? Would the people of Burma want General Ne Win? Or, how about Brezhnev and Kosygin in the U.S.S.R.? Or, for that matter did the Americans in 1960 go all out to opt for his late brother? His audience in Berkeley, where a student political faction has practiced modern nihilism to riddle a great faculty, got what it wanted to hear from Bobby. This is scarcely statesmanship.

His explanation, as delivered to British writer Anthony Howard, was in keeping with his rapier approach to issues. "Look, I'm not going to give a crowd of students like that a bunch of crap just because it's the politic thing to do. I've got to be honest with them—and I don't give a damn what LBJ or anyone else thinks." It was not a matter of what anyone else thought. Bobby personally sought to suppress the reports of the incidents on campus. When that proved impossible, he had one of his entourage call a well-known editor asking for the story to be toned down. In journalistic parlance, this was asking for it to be buried around the truss ads. As it turned out it was displayed deadpan in the news length it was worth across the country.

A more sympathetic view of Bobby and his insight into foreign affairs turned up in an article by Richard Starnes of the Washington *Post*. It was an interview, ranging from poignant personal reflections to Vietnam. Said Senator Robert Kennedy in the Starnes' piece:

> No, I don't see any immediate hope. None at all. Militarily, we're doing weil but I don't believe that's the solution. I think the first step has to be a civilian government in Saigon, one that will negotiate with the Viet Cong.
>
> And I don't think that the war can end in total surrender, nothing like the business on the deck of the battleship Missouri. I don't think the bombing has seriously hurt morale in the North. We've solved the unemployment problem for them, putting them to work repairing bridges and roads. . . . Counting Viet Cong dead isn't the way to do it.

Bobby's presentation to Starnes was an admixture of Fulbright and Lippmann, topped by the show he made at Berkeley. The offhand reference to the Japanese surrender in 1945 was his modern contribution to contemporary history. But the mosaic taken apart, simply does not square with the actual picture. Despite North Vietnamese scorn for the air raids, their own ideological journals have warned against manifestations of defeatism. They have, in the tortuous language of party verbiage, conceded dislocations because of the raids. There is, in short, no effort by Bobby Kennedy to acknowledge the entire role of the Americans, even to the briefest mention of terror and murder by the Viet Cong.

The interview was widely distributed. Ironically, it followed by a few days the press conference in Saigon of the most senior Viet Cong officer yet to defect to South Vietnam. He was thirty-seven-year-old Lieutenant Colonel Le Trung Chuyen. Before he defected, Colonel Chuyen commanded the 165A regiment of the Viet Cong in the Mekong River delta. For twenty years he had been a member of the Communist party. He spoke of dissatisfaction because of domination of political cadres infiltrated from the North. Further, in clear terms, Colonel Chuyen doubted that this was civil war. To him it was a North Vietnamese prepared and sponsored conflict to win total domination.

His interpretations, however subjective, are as worthy of consideration, perhaps more so, as Senator Kennedy's, except for one fact of life: Bobby can, within minutes, command a huge audience and put forth his ideas as a communicator via mass communications, and Colonel Chuyen cannot. Chuyen's ideas, which have to be translated, hold only the briefest interest at large. Bobby's or those of the Fulbright–Lippmann tandem are in the realm of the expert. Nobody has suggested that Colonel Chuyen could know more than they.

Rising fast in the swelling group of experts on many-faceted foreign affairs is Senator Church, once the champion boy orator of Idaho. He is of the same age group as Bobby Kennedy, and has Fulbright's paternal benevolence in the foreign affairs committee. Church, a most pleasant and articulate man, has read and studied foreign affairs. But his living, actual contact with them has been minimal. In the spring of 1966 he took a trip to Europe to sound out political leaders. His findings were mostly included in an article that appeared in *Foreign Affairs,* a scholarly quarterly. This made Church, at long last, an expert.

Interviews for his brand of expertise, which had not been hard for Church to secure in the past, proliferated. He had arrived as a mass communicator, and he was to be taken most seriously. His evaluations might just as well have spared him the trip abroad. The quintessence was largely Lippmannesque. There was, to be sure, the marked deference to de Gaulle—a Lippmann favorite. Not a line was used to mention the illegality with which de Gaulle came to power in 1958 and toppled the Fourth Republic. There was only admiration for the ways and means he exercised to produce what Church believes is a vibrant, prospering France. The pressures used by de Gaulle, abetted by the army at the time of his drive to power, are anathema to the experts when they talk of our own affairs. Abroad, of course, they look at France and wonder rapturously what hath de Gaulle wrought.

The experts collectively suggest as mass communicators that American efforts abroad are hindered and rendered ineffective by, at best, clumsy, overbearing, and officious behavior. Often they claim the worst—that we are intolerably brutal or cruel. These emotive declarations ignore that United States policy persuasions have been deterred frequently by clashing moral and humane scruples. Thus, we have now reached the staggering conclusion that the Soviet Union—despite Vietnam—really wants to go from deterrence to *detente,* especially in Europe.

In the shifts among East European nations and the rise of new nationalism—sound there, say experts, but bad in Germany—the American government is to blame for stalling with the Russians. Senator Church in this area speaks of "dogmatism" in the State Department. Interestingly, dogmatism is an integral part of the expert attitude, which scathingly rejects criticism of any of its ideas and attributes inflexibility to doubters. Secretary of State Rusk cautiously suggested a step-by-step probing of Soviet intentions as well as declarations—he has observed that the climate of East-West relations might sour very swiftly. If they do, rebut the critical experts, it's up to us to keep trying. Their claim is that we can't go Red— just red in the face.

Latterly, there is the big increase in the Soviet military budget. The reason, the regime declared, was United States escalation of the war in Vietnam. But the war had nothing whatever to do with the Soviet decision to take the initiative for a new arms race. The Russians, after Secretary McNamara decided against such a step for us, went ahead with a costly antimissile defense belt, beginning with Leningrad and Moscow. They earmarked capital investment for the project, even as they discussed a treaty with the United States to eliminate military bases in outer space. The Russian high command and party regime leaders were never afflicted with doubts about their arms system as they tore at McNamara (who has since resigned and been elected president of the World Bank) and his team. Premier Aleksei Kosygin defends the anti-ballistic-missile system. It is defensive, he says.

The concept of *detente* from deterrence is largely a daydream. President Johnson, in a major speech given a month before the interim elections of 1966, appealed for the "broader vision of peaceful engagement." He urged: "Where possible we shall work with the East to build a lasting peace. We do not intend to let our differences on Vietnam or elsewhere ever prevent us from exploring all opportunities." A sound theory, but only a theory, unless actively practiced and implemented by two sides. The "bridge-building" appeal has, in fact, been eroded by the action of the East European nations to which engagement is addressed. In Vietnam, the Viet Cong and the Northern regime use weapons provided by the U.S.S.R. and Eastern Europe. Experts reply, why not? Because if Eastern Europe were primarily concerned with a cherished *detente,* we would see less logistical supply and more actual accommodation with the United States, might well be the logical answer.

The ready-made argument that the Communist-ruled nations must give tangible support to another comradely country is filled with loopholes. Many of these nations have not hesitated to effect trade deals with West Germany, ignoring complaints from the sordid regime of the East Germans that they are being let down. Arrests of creative talents in literature, art, and the theater persist in spite of protests by colleagues inside and outside the area. The European regimes, bankrupted by insistent Soviet-type planning, seek new underpinning with outside cash and credits, ours in particular.

Detente is neither an overnight occurrence nor a one-way street. From the sound of the experts, who professed grudging interest in the Johnson approach, our policy-planners are dragging their feet in coming to rapid accommodation. Their own guided missives directed through mass communications show them ready to make agreements across the board with Communists. It's their way of opting out of responsibility and of arrogantly assuming that freedom is not indivisible in the topsy-turvy world of today.

Such a retreat from the world, no matter how elegantly embellished, is an expert's objective. Lippmann, as usual setting the pace for his cult, wrote a column that appeared on November 16, 1966, following an extended visit to Europe. It was headed: "Modern Isolationism and America." If any doubts lingered about his views, they were dispelled with the flat declaration: "Modern men are predominantly isolationist." He went on in the body of the article to say: "The differences between capitalism and communism are ceasing to be ideological and are becoming increasingly managerial and technical."

Lippmann's assertions are so simplistic that they point up starkly his indifference and paucity of study of Communist behaviorism. To say that modern men are predominantly isolationist ignores the immediate interest and curiosity of people about others' moods, creations, and developments, as transmitted instantly by mass communications. These are the same media Lippmann himself uses so adroitly to convey his beliefs. Were modern man indeed isolationist, Balkanization of beliefs would be prevalent. Instead, the tendency is to try to keep from heading toward a splintering process.

But Lippmann's terse explanation of modern-day communism is as untrue as it is thoughtless. The Russians and the Chinese would dispute the analysis, let alone Yugoslavs, Romanians, Hungarians, and Poles. When the ideological cement cracks, the party in power withers with the decay. A Communist party in power must perpetuate itself or vanish. Lippmann loftily assumes that reforms in economies are sufficient proof for his conclusions. They are within the same context with the judgments Lippmann passed on Hitler as an authentic voice of revolution in Germany back in 1933. But Lippmann bristled when President Johnson, in awarding a soldier a Medal of Honor for bravery in Vietnam, criticized his critics. Johnson's was a scalpel-sharp remark about the soldier's courage. That bravery, he said, "far outweighs the reluctance of men who exercise so well the right of dissent, but let others fight to protect them from those whose very philosophy is to do away with the right of dissent."

Lippmann's reply in another column—since he felt singled out anonymously—was to charge that the President was toying with "stirring up a war fever." In private, roving Presidential emissary W. Averell Harriman, who owes nothing to any man, swore up and down that Lippmann was performing a deliberate public disservice. Harriman, wedded for years to public service, has never been challenged by Lippmann on his quests for peaceful settlements. Yet Lippmann, the elder expert, is rebuffed by the elder counselor on the important issue of veracity. Lippmann, without qualification or any documentation, accused L.B.J. of trying to restore lost popularity by inducing a war crisis.

So grave is the charge that Lippmann, were he any other newspaper writer, would have been challenged by editors to show proof. As the senior expert on the American scene, and perhaps the world, he went unchallenged. For good measure, Lippmann added a warning that President Johnson and his Administration are "living in a glass house and should be careful about throwing stones." Any White House is framed in glass, sometimes made deliberately opaque by admirers. Lippmann's establishment is rarely made translucent through the protective devices employed by his cultists. Theirs is a very simple iron maiden: Lippmann is right, and therefore unchallengeable. Thus he serenely went on to comment on the fissures splitting NATO. The military arm of the organization was finished, contended Lippmann. "The main consideration is that the cold war with the Soviet Union has thawed out to a point where coexistence is an accepted fact, where the beginning of detente and collaboration are in sight."

These values were presented by Lippmann the day the U.S.S.R. announced an expanded arms budget. The mauled word *coexistence* is only an accepted fact to Lippmann and his school of experts. He totally overlooked—perhaps never knew—the fact that the structure of regime power in the U.S.S.R. remains unaltered. Brezhnev, for example, was in Stalin's Politburo; Kosygin, was a responsible minister at the time of the Hitler-Stalin pact. The most glaring omission Lippmann and his associated experts make is that the most profound upheaval in Russia centers on the protest against imprisonment of writers Sinyavsky and Daniel. The complaint was signed with the complainers' own names. It was an intellectual uprising and the first real sign of any public opinion in the U.S.S.R. since the revolution.

But the unassailability of the expert's stand is promoted and perpetuated by imitators. As communicators for home and foreign consumption, theirs is a presentation of combined and often collective views. More balanced, even openly doubting and differing attitudes, are in a substantial minority today. While they can be read and heard as communicators too, they draw only condescension as observers and reporters. They are not accorded the "experts" cloak. In the last few years some earnest attempts have been made to try to achieve more equilibrium from communicators and mass communications. To date they have been futile. The most tragic of these attempts caused the elimination of the New York *Herald Tribune,* which went under in late summer of 1966. John Hay Whitney, the wealthy owner, is a man of enormous goodwill, possessed of a deep feeling for public responsibility. His credo for the paper was simple and penetratingly direct: "Ferociously fair." Years of dry rot before Whitney bought the paper and excessive trade union demands and strikes compelled even a rich man to seek surcease. In addition, Whitney got terrible business counsel which he accepted, knowing nothing of the field in which he desired only to be "ferociously fair."

Chapter 3

GERMANY: PART ONE

❦

THE world around us today is generally not a happy haven for Americans. Where he is not actively disliked, suspected, or considered an encroaching enemy, the American is only tolerated. A whole epoch of built-up togetherness with Europeans, and later efforts for active association with Africans, Asians, and Latin Americans, has vanished. In areas where we have expended blood, treasure, and interest—even dedication—a composite picture of the American has emerged that can only dismay an American. It is not the wholesome package Madison Avenue customarily presents. We are held to be a government exercising a policy varying from crude to primitive in terms of superpower; naive to ultra-innocent in judging national feelings and sensibilities; grasping to insatiable in commercial expansion; and domineering for self-interest.

Obviously, we cannot be all things to all foreigners. The way they and their governments consider our approaches and efforts are sometimes real, often fancied, and largely confused.

The United States undertook to draft a long-range foreign policy in the passions of World War II. Torn from self-willed isolation, it was compelled to participate in a shattered world, riddled with unrest, devastation, fear, hunger, and most important the quest for a future. In an affluent condition, unmarked within the continental limits by the ravages of war, the United States set about putting the global house in order.

But emerging from World War II, the United States found a wartime ally—the Soviet Union—turned a fierce adversary, and a brutal wartime enemy—Germany—an ally. The pleasant vision of one more or less cooperative world was in shreds. On the other side of the world—the Far East—America suddenly awoke to the grisly spectacle of restoked civil war in the vast stretches of China.

A Communist organization and armies were on the march. And the one-time occupier of much of China, and enemy of the United States—Japan—was in the process of becoming an ally. The United States possessed a monopoly, it thought—the atom bomb—a deterrent to Stalin and certainly to Mao Tse-tung. It was the American dream.

There were, as policy plans for American entrance into foreign affairs took vague shape, articulate and skilled defenders of Soviet policies. Some were in government and many in peripheral councils. There also existed advocates of Communist Chinese aspirations and those of the Nationalist Chinese. They argued cases on high, as did Alger Hiss; or defended China for specialized interests, as did the China Lobby. Prominent personalities took sides and found themselves propelled into policy-making affairs. Many were lawyers of internationally reputed firms. Others were businessmen who ran giant corporations successfully. They were expert in their fields. Therefore, the reasoning in government ran, they would adjust quickly and become expert in affairs of state.

The accent in the United States was on expertise. In regional fields it was reduced to know-how. But an expert had charisma. It enabled him to become part of an elite establishment, to plan objectives and programs that could possibly have an enduring impact. They were carefully instructed in the demonology of the uncertain outside world by a special elite in affairs of state, our career diplomats. Having spent years abroad, speaking foreign languages, they represented a cadre of mandarins. In our formalistic, isolationist days, politicians in Washington sneered at them as "cookie pushers." The label still crops up occasionally, but the infinitely more important description, *expert* has become the accepted, permanent term of approval.

To grapple with our overnight thrust into the affairs of the world, we gratefully accepted experts and their expertise. They had been around more than almost anyone at home; they were acquainted first-hand with foreign machinations and applications of power. With them emerged a proliferation of experts in an associated field. These were the foreign correspondents, who reported from far-flung crisis areas. Theirs was a role that provided daily, eyewitness, expert judgment on people and places.

In the Congress a similar development occurred. Senators and congressmen who were directly concerned with appropriations for foreign places became—by virtue of their required approval—experts, too. Once their ascension into the stratosphere of foreign affairs was universally hailed, lesser-known and more junior colleagues sought to turn to more profound studies of world problems. In time they managed to have their pronouncements heard with respected attention. For confirmation of their evaluations, our officialdom turned to the academic world. Academicians in economics, history, and the various cultures were possessed of a special expertise. They were usually of a "liberal" persuasion, regarded as a special sophistication.

The bouillabaisse of expertise was heady stuff. It could not be a satisfactory dish for all the people and governments—especially ours—for whom it was intended. Too many cooks, claiming special expert privileges, got into the act. As a result, many directives, lifted from the concoction as policy tidbits, left those in the field perplexed or revolted. Intergovernmental conflicts became intense, and deliberate "leaks"—so dear to the American psyche—revealed clashes of personalities and conflicts of policies.

In wartime this went nearly unnoticed. The pell-mell introduction of experts into foreign affairs and their recommendations also were kept confidential or secret while hostilities raged. Thus the infighting over the partition of Germany was not generally known until the war was almost over. The Battle of Berlin, at which one of the authors was an eyewitness, was won by Soviet arms. But General Eisenhower has conceded that he could have taken Berlin. It was his command decision, in view of high-level political arrangements among Britain, the United States, and Russia, not to do so. In the same context our fighting units could have reached Prague before the Soviet armies, with Soviet-sponsored Czechoslovak units, entered that ancient, Central European city.

The division of Germany had been hammered out in the West by an agglomeration of experts with contrary motives and concepts. Many of the opinions were fired by deeply riveted hate, for which there is no logical panacea. Others were sparked by desire to accommodate the Soviet Union as soon as possible. These won over colleagues who urged detachment and future self-interest. The Russians never budged. The division of Europe, devised at wartime international conferences, was as Stalin principally envisaged it. In the Soviet scheme of *Realpolitik,* this left East Europe, including large chunks of prewar East Germany, under Soviet domination.

What else can we do, thundered various governmental voices. Besides, the Russian armies are in East Europe.

They certainly were. Moreover, they brought with them, in ranking Red Army officers' uniforms, many of the veteran apparatus comrades who took political control in East Europe. Stalin had a set pattern for implementing political aims. We did not. We had only ruminative expertise, which passed as policy. Thus, in the division of Germany, Berlin was left as a permanent hostage. It, too, was divided.

Soviet consolidation in East Europe was implemented over the prostrate forms of opposition; conservative, social democratic, and center. It was only when Winston Churchill, in his ringing phraseology, called attention to the Iron Curtain that the experts were called upon to make a rush assessment for future policy. It left the United States with a split—containment and an avowed "rollback," driving communism back to the old U.S.S.R. frontiers.

In all the postwar years the authors happened to be observers, reporters, and eyewitnesses in the areas affected: Germany and all of East Europe. In an amazingly short time the expert, drawn from disparate fields, usually had his predictions aired first and then drafted into a policy paper or directive. An abundance of them made quick trips abroad called fact-finding tours. The mandarins made sure they were housed, well fed, well transported, and systematically briefed. On balance, the self-perpetuating foreign policy elite at home and abroad worked in tandem: theirs was the counsel and guidance. It was up to the highest levels to consent and implement. Supporting the mandarins were the now-accepted "expert" correspondents. It was a sort of one-two punch that beat out policy.

That way, the acceptance of the indefinite division of Germany came to be known as practical because it already existed. To make a change meant war, and nobody wanted war. It was a thesis that ran through Democratic and Republican administrations. And both used political proponents of the other party to raise a bipartisan sense of understanding for the American public. The rollback, fraudulent in its conception because none of the architects ever really intended to put it into practice, became a rowback.

This joust at policy, however, produced tragicomic episodes. Self-important congressmen always turned up on tours for a firsthand view. They could also pass judgment on appropriations after so arduous a trip. The "Iron Curtain" was for years a number one tour. A senator or congressman could lecture on what he witnessed after he got home.

In spite of budget-conscious congressmen and over the ultra-cautious reservations of the mandarins, General George Catlett Marshall went ahead with his plan. It was perhaps unequalled in contemporary times, both for the money allocated and the scope of rehabilitation foreseen for Western Europe. We were in the Old World to stay. Marshall's program was the more remarkable because his role in trying to devise an accommodation between the Nationalists and the Communists in China was already attracting fire.

A basic irony, however, was built into the European Recovery Program. As NATO followed later to protect France, the principal lines of the Marshall Plan envisaged the portion of Germany that was under Western supervision. The Soviet intention, clearly stated by Stalin and successors, was to prevent that if possible. If not, it was to cling to East Germany and maintain there not only a despised regime but the presence of Russian troops. The center of gravity for all European policy, American and Soviet, was Germany.

Advice from experts cascaded on how much, or how little, a restored West Germany should command in continental restoration. East Europe was frozen, so the calculation—almost always in good faith—was that it could never change from marching in lockstep to Moscow time. There was in this evaluation a large element of caution, a whiff of arrogance, and the despair that suffused Europe between the wars. Mandarins didn't want to be caught wrong; theirs was a career conditioning. If asked flat out by a superior, they would answer couching appraisals in subtleties. These they communicated to prominent or rising politicians, held up as experts. They were not inhibited by any thought of racing breakneck into opinions that conditions were subject to sudden or gradual change. The frustration of elitism has only begun to tug at politicians in the last few years. It causes them to wonder often about the advisability of exploring differences and tactical switches in East Europe.

The experts in the elite establishment of business and journalism are even less nagged by inhibition or doubt. What is haphazardly described as a "thaw" in East-West relations, the overwhelming majority of journalists abroad call a definite development. It has glamour, the appeal of quick settlement, and it is calculated to get rid of that tired blood feeling. Businessmen sense vast and golden opportunities, and what's good for them is good for the country. It is not an issue of sound prediction, good advice, or poor counsel. All of these were meshed together in policies launched in 1945 and expanded on an *ad hoc* basis later.

After twenty-odd years in the first row of global affairs, America has not managed to recast affairs of state into substance that, at least, provides for soundness and common sense. Reliance on the expert has become overwhelming. In the past we were bailed out by the living fact that the Soviet Union, then Red China, committed egregious errors, bound as they are to certain dogmas and outlooks. The have-not areas in Africa and Asia play their hand more realistically than the greater powers. They try to use foreign policy to implement their own self-interest. Inexperience, unfortunately for many of them, leads to constant convulsion. In turn, this produces hasty, harried overreaction from the United States.

The way we propel ourselves into some topsy-turvy situations is prompted by a desire for stability; stopping trouble, so to speak. Our actions have caused many experts to lament the moves. They prefer in these trials to offer ex post facto counsel and formulae. Little of it takes into consideration the essence of foreign policy, the intentions and objectives of self-interest. The criticism takes the form of name-calling and labels, like "policemen of the world," which the world doesn't want. As a nation we are scarcely policemen; auxiliaries might be a more apt term. The genuine policemen are the experts, who tell us how to do things and why—but never beforehand or even on time. Then the mandarin with his soft-sell expertise slips through and gets priority.

We have for some years been engaged in a great crisis—many would feelingly call it a crisis of conscience—over Vietnam. That single interval of policy and involvement has produced more experts and expertise than some of the great issues in Latin America, which we have neglected in cavalier fashion. Our obsession with Vietnam has also compelled a do-nothing attitude toward Europe, where a spiraling crisis of movement is certain to command our attention, and that of our main adversaries.

The problem is fixed in the center of developed Europe, in Germany and its eastern approaches, not with General de Gaulle and his *grand stratégie*. A coalition government of conservative Christian Democrats and Socialists rules the enormously rich and potentially powerful part of Germany known as the Federal Republic. On their own, they have begun to outflank Soviet-sponsored East Germany, in arrangements with East Europe. Many experts never even deigned to look into the origins of the maneuver and the reasons behind it. But the approaches began seriously back in 1964. Most experts took a brief time off to call attention, with alarm, to a neo-Nazi, or ultranationalist minority share of provincial votes in late 1966. A worldly man of state, with reason to be more prejudiced against Germans than most, scoffed at the consternation as superficial and silly. His name is David Ben-Gurion. Examine deeply, he recommended, the structure of present-day Germany before raising all the specters of the past. He was speaking, of course, of the Federal Republic. In Europe the center of gravity—or *schwerpunkt* as the Germans say—remains for the foreseeable future in Germany. That goes for East and West. It didn't seem so at the end of World War II.

The collective of authors who wrote the book *Germany Is Our Problem,* published in the summer of 1945 under the signature of Henry Morgenthau, Jr., state that "the Germans are hated with a virulence unknown in modern times because it has never been so richly deserved!" Still, the Germans' deservingness of virulent hatred is by no means its only provenance nor the main reason for its undiminished continuance. The hatred of Germans, Germany, and things German is a curious phenomenon. Germanophobia came to be accepted in America as the basic criterion of expertise and the cachet of the expert on Germany (not only American expertise—the German-hating German is a common subspecies of the phenomenon), the *sine qua non* of valid political judgment concerning Europe, and in British and Anglophile circles generally, the hallmark of good form. Germany has long played a signal role in American foreign policy, because the American attitude toward Germany is characterized by two distinct alignments for and against; ever since Germany's emergence into nationhood, with relatively few exceptions liberals have been anti-German, while conservatives, with almost equally few exceptions, have been more or less pro-German. The reason for this alignment is simple enough: Germany is the classic conservative nation of modern times. Its conservatism has always been the well-spring of its virtues—"Germany is of the stuff that endures," sang Heine in his alternately pro-German mood, "it is healthy to the core." But it was also the source of Germany's vices; deeply ingrained in German conservatism was the instinct and urge for order, the ethic of labor and frugality, the drive to organize methodically.

Germany's arrival on the international scene was singularly inauspicious. A late child as a nation, her sudden simultaneous emergence as a world power (particularly since it involved the defeat of France and the annexation of the ore-laden German-speaking provinces of Alsace and Lorraine) destroyed the continental balance of power on which Britain depended. Germany thus posed an intermediate threat to the United States, since American foreign policy —such as it was before the First World War—depended on the primacy of Britain in world affairs.

The nucleus and dominating element of the new nation was Prussia, a state with a military tradition comparable to that of ancient Sparta and with an army which even then was generally acknowledged to be the strongest in the world. "Other states have an army," said Count Mirabeau, "in Prussia the army has a state."

But most important, the German Reich was the fastest growing nation in the Western world. Its population almost doubled within sixty years (from 1850 to 1910). By 1914 Germany had roughly twice the population of France and half again that of Great Britain. Most alarming, however, was the fact that Germany rapidly became the industrial state par excellence. In thirty-two years German coal production increased by 600 per cent (overtaking that of England in 1912). In twenty-two years German steel production rose 450 per cent (overtaking that of Great Britain in 1902). At the outbreak of World War I German steel production was approximately twice as great as that of Britain. But most alarming was the fact that Germany had become the second greatest trading nation in the world by 1893 and proceeded to gain steadily on Britain thereafter. It was the commercial genius of the Germans that disturbed most, the excellence of German craftsmanship, the quality guaranteed by the label "Made in Germany," and the great names of German industry; Bosch, Krupp, Bayer, Mannesmann, and the rest. As Franz von Papen put it in his memoirs describing Germany's situation on the eve of the First World War: "Our only interest was to protect our markets and to win new markets through the expansion of our colonial possessions." (Germany's chief prewar frustration was its comparatively minute piece of the world colonial pie.) This was the specific meaning of the Kaiser's famous demand for "a place in the sun," and it was more than enough to excite the animosity of the traditional colonial powers—Great Britain, France, Belgium, and the Netherlands.

The Austro-Hungarian Empire was destroyed by the First World War, leaving Germany, in the ill-fated form of the Weimar Republic, to bear the brunt of international sanctions and restrictions as the putative aggressor. Germany was not the initiator of World War I, but her march through neutral Belgium in accordance with the preliminary stages of the von Schlieffen Plan ("Belgium put the kibosh on the Kaiser") and the very fact that she was by far the greatest of the Central Powers earned her the onus of Western democratic censure.

Probably of even greater importance was the fact that during and immediately after World War I an emotional attitude on the part of the West was generated and deliberately as well as inadvertently cultivated by official and unofficial Allied propaganda. There were, for example, the postcards depicting German soldiers raping Belgian and French women. The German prototype was created and converted into a stereotype by Hollywood and the budding international movie industry in general. This stereotype was the brutal, arrogant, indeed almost fiendish "Boche," the "Hun." In short, the German was not only branded, he was also popularized by the tremendous and growing machine of the Western democratic entertainment industry as the chief culprit and archdisturber of international peace. Anglo-Saxon (and French) distaste of the German both drew from and added to the pariahdom of the Germans. George Kennan cites as a grotesque case of social snobbery the fact that as late as 1927 a German could be prohibited from using the golf links at Geneva, the seat of the League of Nations.

With the development and perfection of electronic mass communications media, especially television and the wide screen and technicolor, the exposure accorded the German bogey became more effective than ever. The stuff the Nazis provided for sensational, lurid, political horror films became a staple of the Hollywood *B* picture and thence infected the consciousness of two generations throughout the world. Movie houses in the English-speaking world had scarcely stopped showing Nazi films of the late thirties and early mid-forties, when the whole series was taken up again and repeated on television. In Communist countries the Hollywood Nazi films were bought and shown to fulfill a propaganda purpose that was and still is anti-Western in its ultimate intent. Parallel with this process and reinforced by it was the British tradition of anti-German intellectual snobbery. This tradition is epitomized in the published comment of Philip Toynbee that "Dr. Jung (the eminent Swiss-German psychologist of the University of Zürich) never quite managed to achieve intellectual respectability in Britain." But one of the most curious aspects of the Western anti-German prejudice is its extension into the field of linguistics. Expressions of this extension are not always to the point. In discussing the nature and structure of the ancient Greek language, so eminent and discreet a scholar as H. D. F. Kitto remarks that the Greek language was incapable of "the imprecision and the lack of immediate perspicuity into which English occasionally deviates and from which German occasionally emerges."

More typically, the novelist Geoffry Household makes a much more serious charge. This is an excerpt from his novel *Fellow Passenger,* first published in 1955:

> I don't wonder that the speakers of that insensitive language feel outlawed from the rest of Europe. *Treasure, treasor, joya*—all have syllables which lend themselves reasonably to a term of endearment. But *Schatz,* though meaning the same, sounds like a small piece of machinery. It must, I think, be one of the reasons for the peculiar complexes of the Germans—that they are continually using words the meaning of which contradicts the primitive emotional value of the sounds.

The German word *Schatz* apparently reminds Mr. Household of the English words *slots, pots, knots,* etc. Mr. Household forgets that Germans, or those non-Germans who speak "that insensitive language" well, are not reminded of English or other foreign phonetic equivalents when they use the word *Schatz,* just as Hungarians are concerned only with treasure or a loved one when they use the word *kincs,* which rhymes with and reminds one of *flinch, clinch,* and the singularly unlovely American slang term, *ginch.* All that Mr. Household's charge reveals is his inferior knowledge of the German language. But the charge is by no means confined to the ethnic camp of provincial Anglo-Saxons.

George Steiner, a literary critic fluent in three languages, particularized the charge in the February 18, 1960, issue of *The Reporter* magazine:

> For let us keep one fact clearly in mind: the German language was not innocent of the horrors of Nazism. It is not merely that a Hitler, a Goebbels, and a Himmler happened to speak German. Nazism found in the language precisely what it needed to give voice to its savagery. Hitler heard inside his native tongue the latent hysteria, the confusion, the quality of hypnotic trance. . . . A language in which one can write a "Horst Wessel Lied" is ready to give hell a native tongue. (How should the word "spritzen" recover a sane meaning after having signified to millions the "spurting" of Jewish blood from knife points?)

While the seat of the passion operative in this passage is obvious enough, it is a typical if extreme example of the self-perpetuating hysteria the Germans inspire in the world about them.

There were ethnic and geographical attributes that conspired to constitute an ominous reality. German expansionism was always nationalist, its nationalism always militarist and in a literal sense fascist—the binding together of separate elements. It was hence far more terrible than, say, the militarist expansionism of Napoleonic and post-Napoleonic France, which plagued Europe for seventy years and almost broke the hegemony of England.

Permanently embattled by the lack of natural borders east or west, German colonists moved over land instead of over seas. Instead of forming colonies on foreign continents, the Germans formed minorities in foreign countries.

The overland colonization east and west by Germany was innocent enough in the beginning, because the Germans played so enthusiastically the role, approved by Goethe, of dispersed bearers of civilization from the thousand and more duchies and principalities that made up the German lands in the Middle Ages. But when the German lands were unified into a centralized Reich, the overland colonies of the Germans became embattled colonies of civilized Germans among the primitive peoples of Eastern and Southeastern Europe—"justified" goals of German expansion— and laid the basis for the drive to annex the colonies to the heartland. The German expansionist movement launched in World War I and again in World War II, and labeled by the Nazis *Heim ins Reich* (home into the Reich), was actually *Reich ins Heim*

(Reich into the foreign home). France was the revolutionary bearer of the idea of the Enlightenment, the inspiration of the youth of Europe, while Germany was the arch-opponent of the Enlightenment. Germany was the heavy authority of the beer and pretzel bourgeois, the scene of the inglorious pratfall of 1848—which enraged every liberal and radical in Europe—and the consequent ascendancy of Bismarck, Blut, and Boden, and the repressive era of the *Kulturkampf.*

The spark struck by German liberal intellectuals in the midnineteenth century, and all but stamped out in Germany itself, jumped eastward to kindle the holocaust of the October Revolution more than half a century later.

On November 13, 1917, Lenin sent his first official message to the revolutionary proletariat of the world: "Comrades! Greetings from the first proletarian republic. We call you to arms for the first international social revolution." For the first time in modern history an active ideological alternative to German conservatism was offered. The liberal had finally found a home. As far as liberal disappointment with Germany was concerned, worse was yet to come. After the October Revolution, Trotsky was assigned the task of spreading the revolution to Germany. The plan that was worked out and approved by the Soviets turned on the assassination of the Kaiser. But the Kaiser had to be assassinated by a German. After a year's search Trotsky was forced to admit that it had proved to be impossible to find a German, regardless of political persuasion or lack of one, who was willing to assassinate the Kaiser—not out of fear, it was understood, but out of inborn reverence for authority and propriety.

But worst of all was the piddling Spartacus revolt in Germany in 1919. Lenin had proclaimed what every revolutionary had almost taken for granted since 1850: Germany would be the proving ground of world revolution—as Germany fared so would fare the cause of the world proletariat. But the main chance in Germany was never what it seemed. The Spartacus Union mounted the barricades in pompous mummery for a few days in Berlin and then collapsed. Rosa Luxemburg and Karl Liebknecht, the darlings of the European intellectual left, were murdered by minions of the extreme right, and the Social Democrats, split a dozen ways, stood by and earned themselves an undying reputation of being far more German than Socialist.

That tug-of-war between Western liberals and conservatives for the soul of Germany continued in a new form after the First World War. There was the Messianic drive that produced the Fourteen Points and the outraged puritanism that withheld them from application to Germany. There was the Treaty of Versailles that sowed the dragon's teeth of World War II (Alexander Kerensky regards the whole period as "a two stage war—1914–1945"). There was the liberal campaign to bring the German nation to trial for its crimes—or at least the Kaiser and several hundred of the worst offenders. A special international commission was formed to set up the necessary criteria, gather proof, and classify data. This was to have been the first war crimes trial. The commission found that "all persons belonging to enemy countries, however high their position might have been, without distinction of rank, including chiefs of states, who have been guilty of offenses against the laws and customs of war or the laws of humanity, are liable to criminal prosecution."

But the American delegation to the commission dissented from the finding (along with the Japanese delegation), on the grounds that there could be no legal prosecution of chiefs of state, whose responsibility had never before been established in municipal or international law, and "for which no precedents are to be found in the modern practice of nations.". The American delegation based its refusal to prosecute the Kaiser on Chief Justice Marshall's decision in 1812 in the case of *Schooner Exchange v. McFadden and Others,* which held a sovereign to be exempt from judicial process.

"Despite the disagreement of the Americans and Japanese," wrote Louis Nizer in 1944 in his book *What to Do with Germany,* "the Peace Conference adopted the majority report of the Commission that there was no reason why rank, however exalted, should in any circumstances protect the holder of it from responsibility when that responsibility has been established before a properly constituted tribunal. This extends even to the heads of states." In an earlier passage Nizer explains the make-up of a "properly constituted tribunal": "The Versailles Conference began brilliantly," he wrote. "It was the first treaty of peace in which an attempt was made by the victorious belligerents to enforce against a defeated adversary the principle of individual responsibility for crimes committed during the war."

The peace conference having accepted the majority report of the commission, Article 227 of the Treaty of Versailles provided that "the Allies and Associated Powers publicly arraign William II of Hohenzollern, formerly German Emperor, for a supreme offence against international morality and the sanctity of treaties." The Allied and Associated Powers addressed a request to the government of the Netherlands for the surrender of the ex-Emperor to a special tribunal, to be constituted for the trial. The Dutch government refused to surrender the Kaiser, pleading that it could not "admit any other duty than that imposed on it by the laws of the kingdom and national tradition." This episode was to have a curious repetition in the immediate aftermath of World War II.

Holland's refusal to deliver up the Kaiser for trial constituted the first breach of the Treaty of Versailles. After this the peace conference decided to settle for the prosecution of fifteen hundred accused war criminals, the issue having become an extremely controversial one: Liberals in the West felt that the list of accused should have numbered in the "tens of thousands," while conservatives expressed their incredulity that the prosecution of "war criminals" was to be taken seriously.

Understandably (for conservatives) the Germans were extremely reluctant to extradite their militarists, "chiefly of the Prussian military caste," to an international court. After various delays, counterproposals (one of which was the offer of the Crown Prince to substitute himself for the number—since shrunk to 896—of those listed for extradition), and flat refusals, it was finally agreed to allow the Germans themselves to try the culprits, whose number had finally been reduced to fourteen. In the end, two and a half years after the war ended, four people were actually tried (the Allies prepared cases against seven, but three of these could not be found). Of these, one, a general, was acquitted, one received six months, and two were sentenced to four years (both escaped shortly afterward).

Thus the pattern was set. The Messianic drive of the liberals to punish the Hun was pursued to a formal decision by popular acclaim, only to be frustrated and sometimes outrightly sabotaged by recalcitrant conservative elements with the ranks. After World War I German reconstruction was fostered by American private bankers, not by the American government. The Dawes Plan

(1923–1929) and the Young Plan (1929–1932) were supported
to some extent by the government and coordinated with the phasing
out of the occupation and reparations programs. But the initiative
and the sustaining interest was that of private business—more
particularly and significantly, of American big business—necessarily, because both plans were conceived against the background
and within the context of the reparations problems, specifically
as pump priming to enable Germany to pay her reparations.
The reparations problem was once removed in the sense that Germany was a debtor to nations who in turn were debtors to the
United States, in the apparently insoluble problem of Allied war
debts. By the end of 1933 Britain, France, and Italy had defaulted
on their war debts to the United States (in fact, the only country
to continue payments was Finland), a development prompting
Henry L. Stimson, then Secretary of State, to reflect later that
"the original and fatal error . . . was the notion that huge, interest-
bearing loans made in emergency conditions for emergency purposes could ever be repaid by one government to another. . . .
Debts incurred in a common struggle will never be repaid to a
country which hates imports."

Stimson's conclusion points up the principle and also the broadest continuing dilemma in American foreign policy since the First
World War: the attempt to sustain, implement, or otherwise exploit the high morale and emotional quality of wartime, and its
immediate results, during peace time (the liberal trait) coupled
with the attempt to restore the "normalcy" of the *status quo ante*
(the conservative trend) to the businessman's refrain of "boys
will be boys and bygones bygones."

Stimson was Secretary of State under Herbert Hoover and he
saw the American conservative's dream smashed to bits on the
rocks of 1929. He witnessed and worked through much of the
Great Depression that closed the *Kreditanstalt* of Vienna and
pulled down the financial roof of Europe along with that of the
United States. In the United States the Crash and the Depression
that followed brought Franklin D. Roosevelt and the New Deal
to power. In Germany the Depression paved the way for Adolf
Hitler and the New Order. The same cause produced simultaneous but exactly opposite effects: America moved to the left,
Germany moved to the right. The two governments were at perfect
odds by nature and from the beginning, the interaction of their
relationship invariably serving to increase the estrangement.

The accession to power of the Nazis, according to Morgenthau's diary, confirmed Roosevelt in his desire to establish diplomatic relations with the Soviet Union: ". . . he felt, in addition, that the continual isolation of Russia might destroy his hopes of preventing war through the collective moral sense of the nations of the world." Morgenthau added that the President "must have perceived that Russia would be the natural ally in any conflict against a resurgent Germany." More significantly, in order to lay the foundation for diplomatic relations with the Soviet Union, and in view of the State Department's "distaste if not hostility" to the idea, Roosevelt turned, portentously, to his crony, Morgenthau (who was then still with the Farm Credit Administration), and entrusted him with the delicate mission of opening negotiations. Morgenthau did so by contacting Amtorg, the Soviet trade organization.

Meanwhile, the anti-Semitism of the Nazis, an article of faith of the movement codified in the Nuremberg laws of 1935 and demonstrated so disgustingly in the Kristalnacht of 1937, dismayed and outraged Jews throughout the world, especially those among the intellectuals and academicians of the New Deal.

But the antithetical and antipathetic relationship of the two countries was also, and perhaps basically, a projection of a controversy, partially hidden but nonetheless bitter, within the body politic of the United States itself. This struggle revolved around the theory and practice of economics. When Roosevelt campaigned for the Presidency in 1932, in full appreciation of the violent public reaction against the laissez-faire capitalism that had brought on the Depression, he took the field against the "economic royalty" of America. But the brunt of the New Deal attack on the economics of the conservative establishment was its antimonopoly sentiment. The main thrust of three Roosevelt Administrations was the creation of precedents and the building of a record for a body of doctrine against "monopoly, conspiracy, and restraint of trade."

This continuing campaign reached its high point when the President gave his message to the Seventy-Fifth Congress "Transmitting Recommendations Relative to the Strengthening and Enforcement of Antitrust Laws." Section I of the President's message bore the caption, "The Growing Concentration of Economic Power." This was taken from the third chapter heading of the famous work by Berle and Means, *The Modern Corporation and Private Property,* a thesis of which was that almost all major production in American industry was carried out by corporations. The book also demonstrated that there was concentration even among corporations, that "nearly half of the corporate wealth of the United States" was in the control of two hundred corporations, the largest of which, American Telephone and Telegraph Company, "controls more wealth than is contained within the borders of twenty-one of the states of the country."

The most avid New Dealers were those who had given their hearts and souls to the new economics, and the new economics was grounded on trust-busting, and its variations and equivalents. "National intervention to stimulate competition," said Harry Hopkins before a Senate committee, "is the democratic method, since purchasing power in the hands of the people must then be won by competition. The form of the industrial pattern, therefore, is determined, not by the judgement or caprice of a few monopolists, but by the whole community."

The quest of a corrective for the economy involved the diagnosis of the cause of its collapse. This, the New Deal determined, was big business run riot, avarice divorced from social conscience and outside government control, monopolies resultant from the systematic suppression of competition and the unbridled urge to expand, both vertically and horizontally, by means of the conspiratorial formation of interlocking directorates—in short, the cartel. And this despite the fact that the Sherman Act, which declared every contract, combination, or conspiracy in restraint of trade to be illegal, had been in force well over forty years. This was the great, well-nigh all-embracing secret evil. In the eyes of the New Deal the great corporations represented a kind of economic Mafia. The most zealous partisans of the New Deal, and those occupied in striking the evil at its root, were the members of the Antitrust Division of the Department of Justice and the Board of Economic Warfare of the Department of the Treasury.

It was this aspect of the New Deal that made the determining contribution to the great syndrome of the New Deal—the passionate rejection of the poison, which was isolated and identified as socially irresponsible big business; the insistence on the antidote, which was government intervention, investigation, regulation, and control of the economic life of the nation. It was this activity, the investigation of international cartels involving American firms (particularly in the case of the *United States v. Standard Oil*), that led the vanguard and elite of the New Deal to the door of the veritable homeland of heavy industrial concentration, the cradle of the international cartel, a nation so imbued with and impounded by private business interests that it poised like an octopus with a tentacular grip on the economy of the world—Nazi Germany, the Third Reich.

Thus Nazi Germany, for New Dealers, became not only the prime example but the main proof of the quintessential modern evil—big business expanded and concentrated through private (that is to say, secret and uncontrolled) combinations. This was the worst of all evils because it was firmly believed to be the chief cause of war.

A passage in the first chapter of Henry Morgenthau's *Germany Is Our Problem* states:

> Almost immediately, as a consequence of this unholy alliance between Hitler and the cartelists, Germany's plans for economic warfare, aimed at ultimate world domination, were expanded. The German government became the silent partner in the multitude of agreements among German, American, British, French, and other concerns with which German industry has established cartel relations.
>
> Under cover of cartel agreements, Germany penetrated the economy of other nations, including the United States. Using their cartel affiliates or subsidiaries, German industrialists built up a network which impaired the production of other nations, obtained sources of foreign exchange for Germany, gathered economic intelligence, and spread Nazi propaganda.

Chapter 4

GERMANY: PART TWO

THE most dangerous thing about an extreme position is that it is likely to beget an abrupt and violent reaction in the direction of the opposite extreme. A prime example was British diplomatic conduct toward Germany between the wars. The progression in the extreme anti-German attitude of the Allies had led to a disruption of the balance of power in favor of France (in league with the Soviet Union and the small East European states of the "little *entente*" against Germany). The British believed themselves obliged and justified in signing the naval pact of June 18, 1935, with Germany, an act which violated the Treaty of Versailles, nullified its restrictions on Germany, and destroyed the common front of the Allies against Germany.

The British-German naval pact was the second biggest diplomatic blunder of the interwar period, particularly since it served as a factual basis for Hitler's belief that he had an understanding with England (that the greatest land power and the greatest sea power should hold together), which would prevent that nation from going to war with Germany simply because she was party to a defensive pact with Poland.

In strict accordance with Britain's policy of appeasement, begun with the naval pact and continued through acceptance of the Anschluss, Chamberlain went to Munich to underwrite the cession of the Sudetenland in Czechoslovakia to Hitler Germany. He even sought at first to mollify the British public over the German occupation and conversion of the Czech lands into the Reich's "protectorate." Less than two weeks later he made a sudden and violent about-face. He announced the British government's guarantee to Poland. In the words of Robert Coulondre, who was then French ambassador in Berlin: "Without any kind of transition, and with a rashness pointing to his genuine anger,

Chamberlain turned a complete somersault. He went from one extreme to the other, and diplomacy, which is the daughter of wisdom and caution, does not like such extravagant behaviour. Having been bamboozled by Hitler, Chamberlain was now going to be bamboozled by Colonel Beck (the Polish strong man), and was going to ruin the game the outcome of which was of the most vital importance to the cause of peace."

In another fortnight Chamberlain extended the guarantee to Poland, to include Romania and Greece. About this Coulondre commented: "The British government was now crashing ahead so fast that it even rushed past the situation at which it should have stopped. It was enough to look at the map of Europe to see what a serious diplomatic situation it had created. Rumania and Poland practically form a continuous front from the Black Sea to the Baltic, a front separating Germany from the U.S.S.R. Germany cannot attack Russia without going through Poland and Rumania, i.e., without bringing into play the Western guarantee, and without going to war against Britain and France. Thus, without having to commit himself, Stalin secured a Western guarantee on the East which he had sought in vain for ten years. . . . It must now have been clear to Hitler that only by coming to an agreement with the U.S.S.R. could he dodge that double front the day he decided to attack Poland."

Undoubtedly the most fateful, emotion-propelled "rush past the position at which it should have stopped" was Franklin Delano Roosevelt's proclamation of unconditional surrender at Casablanca in 1942. The propagation of the doctrine of unconditional surrender robbed the German underground resistance of virtually every prospect of success. At once it incalculably strengthened the dictatorship of Hitler because it forced the complete identification of the German people with the Nazi regime, since it was made expressly clear that the only chance of national survival lay in the final victory of Germany. The doctrine of unconditional surrender affixed the penalty of the "general and formal submission of the national will" as the only price for peace at the virtual beginning of the American prosecution of the war—long before the outcome could be assured or even seriously surmised. It removed the buffer state between the converging Allies, forcing them to deal with each other directly over the fate of an inert Germany. The doctrine of unconditional surrender also sealed the division of Germany and on terms relatively unfavorable for Western democracy.

The obsession on the part of Roosevelt and most of the members of his staff with the idea of the total destruction of the German state tended to preclude serious, coordinated study of how Germany was to be administrated after the cessation of hostilities, except insofar as punitive and preventive measures were concerned. It is virtually impossible to explain plausibly in any other way the lack of necessary determination to make at least basic provision for the inevitable and, in its general outline at any rate, clearly foreseeable immediate postwar situation. How else is the sustained squabbling, among the very junior officers who staffed the Working Security Committee, on the question of jurisdiction over occupation policy to be explained?

Proof that the entire complex of zoning and administration problems was secondary to the imposition on Germany of crushing peace terms was provided at Quebec, when Roosevelt willingly relinquished his insistence on the northern zone of occupation for the United States in exchange for Churchill's acceptance of the Morgenthau plan. Despite public outcry even before the war ended, the Morgenthau plan was largely incorporated in *JCS/1067,* the Joint Chiefs of Staff directive on occupation policy which was issued on May 14, 1945, and classified as top secret. *JCS/1067* was not made public until October, 1945, leaving General Clay, the American military governor, in the position of "carrying out a policy whose existence we could not even admit."

It was the trust-busters' conviction that heavy industrial concentration in private hands was the underlying cause of war that constituted the motivational source of that most astonishing piece of American foreign policy expertise—the Morgenthau plan.

The Morgenthau plan proposed the complete demilitarization of Germany, the total destruction of the German armament industry, and the removal or destruction of other key industries basic to military strength. It also encompassed the cession of East Prussia (or that part of it not destined for the U.S.S.R.) and the southern portion of Silesia to Poland, the cession to France of the Saar and the adjacent territories bounded by the Rhine and the Moselle Rivers (*i.e.,* the whole of the Rhineland), the internationalization of the Ruhr and surrounding industrial areas (*i.e.,* the Kiel canal and all German territory north of the Kiel canal). The remaining part of Germany was to be divided into two "autonomous, independent states," one comprising Bavaria, Wurttemberg, and Baden, the other comprising Prussia, Saxony, and Thuringia. In the Ruhr area, the heart of German industrial power, "all industrial plants and equipment not destroyed by military action shall be completely dismantled and transported to Allied nations as restitution. All equipment shall be removed from the mines and the mines closed." Finally, in order to feed the people of Germany and ensure its perpetually peaceful disposition, the entire country was to be "pastoralized" into a predominantly agricultural area.

The German use of economic warfare was a New Deal discovery. Morgenthau was at great pains to point out how insidious economic power can be when turned to a warlike purpose, and above all, how difficult it is to root out—even with the most Draconian measures—when it is so deeply entrenched in the very structure of life, as it was in Germany. For this reason he warned against reparations: "Advocates of a heavy German schedule of recurring reparations are asking us to build up German industry at the direct expense of our own" (because reparations would necessitate restoring or expanding German industrial capacity in order for them to make payment). Again, "industrial reparations would tend to tie the chemical industries of the world once more to a German-dominated cartel"; and finally, "the quarrel (among the United Nations) would develop inevitably because receipt of reparations would create certain vested interests which would resent any stoppage.

"Even more dangerous to peace and Allied unity would be the fact that these vested interests would become pro-German interests, too." There is also emphasis on the contradictory nature and paradoxical outcome of economic warfare: "Five years of totalitarian control over most of the Continent, added to years of economic warfare against other European industry, have left the Reich even stronger in defeat, compared to her neighbors, than she was in victory."

But the conviction that the cartel was the root of all evil does not explain the still more Catoesque aspects of the Morgenthau plan, particularly as they are revealed in the book *Germany Is Our Problem.* "If Germany makes a serious attempt to feed herself, she can do so," proclaims Morgenthau. "But we can expect her to make the effort only if she is forced to it by refusal of the United Nations to take over the responsibility from the German people. If we feed them ourselves—and it would have to be from stores of food which hungry millions of our Allies need—the Germans will not undertake the necessary agricultural reform. They will . . . prefer to intrigue for a return of heavy industry and war." There are more than a few passages which are frankly vindictive: "If peace is to be secure, Germans will be deprived of the luxuries of life for quite a long time. They will have fewer writers, lawyers, teachers, and engineers. There will be a very big decrease in the number of waiters, taxi cab drivers, barbers and clerks. Maybe the personal servant, beautician, clothing model, and fashionable furrier will virtually disappear. Certainly the Germans will see a marked decline in places of entertainment, florists, cafes, and retail shops of all kinds."

The State Department cablegram numbered 482, from Bern, Switzerland, arrived in January, 1943, on the desk of Undersecretary of State Sumner Welles. This was the first official report on the mass programmatic execution of Jews in the Third Reich. Welles forwarded the Bern message to the Jewish organizations in America, and a mass meeting was held to recommend measures for the rescue and relief of the Jews of Europe.

But a year went by before the United States government made a move to relieve European Jewry. Members of the Department of the Treasury were struck by the ensuing strange silence from Bern on the subject. When they asked to see the cable traffic between Bern and the Department of State, all but a paraphrase of the pertinent message was refused. Morgenthau then went to Hull and discovered that Washington had replied to Bern asking the Minister, Harrison, to stop sending reports to "private persons" in the United States, except under extraordinary circumstances. This was a reference to the private Jewish agencies for which the report was mainly but not solely intended.

The Morgenthau team was furious. "For two months," as one of them later wrote, "death had lain on State Department desks. Roughly 200,000 more refugees—political and 'Eastern peoples' as well as Jews—had been killed." The reason given by the State Department for requesting that Harrison desist from sending such messages was that they circumvented the censorship of neutral countries and these neutral countries might respond by closing their lines to confidential, official matter.

This the Treasury Department found to be "fantastic." "It was a matter of record," wrote Josiah E. Dubois, at that time Chief Counsel of the Treasury's Foreign Fund Control, "that for some time, through our legation in Switzerland, State Department wires were sending reports to private United States and British firms giving the status of their property holdings in Europe." Here it was again, the private interests of the captains of commerce and industry took precedence. In attempting to set up the machinery to deal with the refugee problem, particularly the purchase of Jews from the Nazi mass execution program, the Departments of State and Treasury encountered unexpected resistance from the British, first on the grounds that such purchase would provide the enemy with badly needed foreign exchange, and then because of the "difficulties of disposing of any considerable number of Jews."

Roosevelt was so shocked by the entire episode that he ordered the establishment of the War Refugee Board to be headed by Morgenthau, Hull, and Stimson. The frustrations, and they must have been excruciating, did not end there. There followed the offer engineered by Adolf Eichmann for the ransom of upwards of a million Jews through Hungary, which despite a variety of efforts on various sides, came to nothing except the execution of an untellable additional number of Jews and other "racially inferior" peoples of East Europe.

It was against this background of almost apocalyptic human suffering—itself another important contributing factor to the New Deal syndrome—that the Morgenthau plan was worked out and presented. Moreover, the War Refugee Board's efforts chiefly concerned the principal Nazi liquidation camp at Auschwitz. It was here that the final, confirmatory horror awaited Morgenthau's staff. Auschwitz, the most notorious of the death camps—alone responsible for the gassing and cremation of perhaps three million people—was the site of a synthetic rubber factory of Germany's largest cartel, I.G. Farben. The factory, housed within a separate I.G. Farben camp called Monowitz, was largely dependent on slave labor from the nearby death camp.

With his assistant Harry Dexter White, Morgenthau made a trip in the summer of 1944 to England, where he talked to Winston Churchill, Anthony Eden, General Eisenhower, and the Western members of the European Advisory Commission (Lord Strang and Ambassador John G. Winant). During these talks Morgenthau elicited a statement from Eden that it was "vital that the United States and Britain pursue a policy toward Germany as nearly in accord with the Russian policy toward Germany as possible."

Morgenthau: "Say that again."

Eden did.

During these exchanges, Harry Dexter White crossed swords with Lord Strang, the commission member, who resisted the idea of partitioning Germany, pointing out that it would be easier to deal with a unified nation than with three or four parts of a dismembered body politic. White countered that he could not imagine writing a "useful and coherent memorandum" predicating a united Germany, when the original instructions calling for the memorandum, as formulated at the Teheran Conference, explicitly demanded the partition of Germany. According to Eisenhower, in his book *Crusade in Europe,* Morgenthau met with a direct rebuff when, during his visit in England, he asked the supreme commander if it would be possible to put the Ruhr coal mines under water the moment the territory came under Allied control. Eisenhower replied that such an act would be "senseless and criminal."

Not daunted, Morgenthau returned to Washington and presented his plan at the State Department on September 2. Cordell Hull, Secretary for War Stimson, and Assistant Secretary for War John J. McCloy were appalled. In the first session with Roosevelt on September 6, Stimson made very strong representations against the plan and seemed to carry the day with the President. However, three days later Morgenthau arranged for a second session with the President, in which the same arguments pro and con were repeated. But even though the cast of characters was the same—Hull, Stimson, and McCloy in the majority—this time Roosevelt inclined toward the plan.

There were, in fact, a number of other forces at work. Among them, Bernard Baruch, one of the President's closest advisers, was a fervent advocate of the plan. The upshot was that Morgenthau was the only Cabinet Minister to accompany Roosevelt to the Quebec Conference with the British on September 11. The presence of Morgenthau as Secretary of the Treasury is explained by the fact that the chief item of business at Quebec was the negotiation of a very large loan to the British within the scope and framework of Lend-Lease: Morgenthau was chairman of the Lend-Lease Committee.

It was, in fact, the loan to the British that won the day for Morgenthau. Churchill, at first shocked by the plan, was persuaded to accept it by his financial adviser, Lord Cherwell (formerly Professor Frederick Lindemann of Berlin), who contended that the plan "would save Britain from bankruptcy" by eliminating Germany as a postwar competitor. Actually Cherwell himself did not believe this, as he admitted shortly afterward. He was interested exclusively in the loan—and the securing of the loan depended on the good graces of Morgenthau.

When Morgenthau returned to Washington with a redraft of the plan in the form of a memorandum dictated to his secretary by Churchill (who was dissatisfied with Morgenthau's several efforts to produce a précis of the plan), he presented the memorandum, which had been initialed by the President and the Prime Minister, to Hull and Stimson.

Both Hull and Stimson, although thunderstruck by the turn of events, set about undoing the damage as best they could, Stimson going directly to Roosevelt. According to Stimson, the President was already having second thoughts. Soon Roosevelt began wondering what had possessed him to consider the plan seriously in the first place—especially when the document was leaked to the press (it appeared on September 23 in *The Wall Street Journal*) and brought down an avalanche of condemnation. Nevertheless, Morgenthau continued to make the fight and he was by no means alone. He published the book *Germany Is Our Problem,* which enlarged on the plan and insisted on its implementation. *The New York Times* Book Review commented that only by translating the ideas of the book into political realities would America "be able to prevent the third world war for which we know preparations have already begun."

There was a great deal more to the Morgenthau plan than met the eye. In fact, the Morgenthau plan was anticipated and, as it were, conceptually inherent in the doctrine of unconditional surrender proclaimed by Roosevelt at the press conference in Casablanca on January 24, 1943—a year and a half before the plan, as such, ostensibly began to take form.

By definition the concept of unconditional surrender leaves the abrogation of the sovereignty or even the *de jure* existence of a conquered country to the whim, or at best the discretion, of the conquerors—a fact that was appreciated by General Alfred Jodl in his brief statement after the surrender of the German armed forces to the Allies at Rheims in May, 1945: "With this signature the German people and the German Armed Forces are for better of for worse delivered into the victors' hands. . . . In this hour I can only express the hope that the victor will treat them with generosity."

The famous and controversial directive of the Joint Chiefs of Staff, issued as a top secret document on April 28, 1945, bluntly stated that the principal Allied objective was to prevent Germany from ever again becoming a threat to the peace of the world. The special steps in the accomplishment of this objective were the elimination of Nazism and militarism in all their forms, and preparation for the eventual reconstruction of German political life on a democratic basis.

Similarly, the directive issued for Japan in August, 1945, required that "persons who have been active exponents of militarism and militant nationalism will be removed and excluded from public office and from any other position of public or substantial private responsibility."

A directive issued in September went a good deal further, declaring as it did the assumption "that any persons who have held key positions of high responsibility since 1937 in industry, finance, commerce, or agriculture have been active exponents of militant nationalism and aggression." These and the instructions and regulations that shored them up provided the guidelines for nothing less than the removal, punishment, and replacement of virtually the entire leaderships of both Germany and Japan. Moreover, the *leitmotiv* of the official literature of guidance for the occupation was a more or less comprehensive program for the imposition of democracy—the radical re-education of the German and Japanese populations along democratic lines.

"The authority of the legitimate power," reads the Hague Convention, "having in fact passed into the hands of the occupant, the latter shall take all measures in his power to restore, and ensure, as far as possible, public order and safety, while respecting, unless absolutely prevented, the laws in force in the country." This passage is generally regarded as the Convention's proscription of tampering with the political machinery of a defeated country.

Ironically, the War Department's "Handbook" on the coming occupation of Germany, which so angered the President in August of 1944, giving F.D.R. the impression that Germany would be restored to the estate of countries she had conquered in the west, was nothing more or less than an attempt to abide by the Hague Convention. The President's strong reaction to the "Handbook" paved the way for the sponsorship of the Morgenthau plan. The first objective of American occupation policy in Germany was the abolition of all Nazi laws, practices, and institutions.

The language of the Yalta and Potsdam declarations overrode the Hague Convention by calling for a crusade against the outlaw-usurper: the "inflexible purpose" of the Yalta declaration was "to destroy German militarism and Nazism and ensure that Germany will never again be able to disturb the peace of the world."

The Potsdam declaration, made scarcely six months later, stated that "There must be eliminated for all times the authority and influence of those who have misled the people of Japan into embarking on world conquest, for we insist that a new order of peace, security and justice will be impossible until irresponsible militarism is driven from the world." This was the language of the apocalypse, heralding measures unwittingly calculated to emasculate the psyche of both nations.

Thus, for the coming struggle in both Europe and the Far East the battle lines between liberals and conservatives in the American government were drawn well before the end of the war. Stimson and the War Department, and Hull and at least half of the State Department were firmly aligned against Morgenthau and his followers in the Treasury Department and elsewhere. But Morgenthau had the President's ear, his sympathy, and his moral support. Moreover, the Morgenthau plan (which meanwhile had been re-substituted for the Quebec memorandum) was in the works to the exclusion of any alternate or rival plan or concept. If the partition of Germany was no longer in vogue as a result of the publication of the plan in September, 1944, it was only because partition had already become a *fait accompli.*

By insisting on maintaining a free hand until the final negotiations on zoning at Yalta, Roosevelt merely insured that the rough draft for demarcation lines, which gradually emerged from the EAC sessions in London as the lowest common denominator, would ultimately stand as the accepted finality.

It has seldom been remarked, but the fact is that the Morgenthau plan for the partition of Germany and the zonal demarcation lines worked out by the EAC and accepted at Yalta are identical. Morgenthau's south German state became the American zone, his north German state became the Soviet zone, and his Ruhr and Rhine regions (to be separated from Germany and internationalized or given to France) became the British zone (out of the Western regions of the American and British zones a French zone was subsequently created).

Territorially, the only substantive departure from the Morgenthau plan in the zoning of the country among the Allies was in the partitioning of Berlin into sectors (without formally agreed access routes) to accommodate American, British, and French contingents. This the Soviets agreed to as a temporary concession in return for the incorporation of Saxony and Thuringia into the Soviet zone. The Soviets did not expect the Americans to remain in Europe for very long—perhaps a year, at most two years.

Morgenthau and his group devote a full chapter to the necessity of an American withdrawal (Bring the Men Home). In this section of the tract—for it is first and foremost a tract—a good deal of foresight is brought to bear on how the coming struggle between the opposing forces is likely to develop. Morgenthau warns against "the tremendous machinery of government that is necessary to effect emergency economic controls—rationing, price ceilings, and the rest . . . in Germany the Allies began by taking too much responsibility for them, and their only hope of escaping a real dangerous threat to their policy is the dropping of that responsibility."

In exercising too much responsibility, Morgenthau asserted, "failure would be a lesser evil than success. For success would mean a German recovery more rapid than anything that can be achieved by the nations attempting to prevent her from becoming a menace again." As a result, Allied military governments must not be allowed to consider themselves responsible for Germany's industrial and commercial system, for "once they have been given or take this responsibility, the Allied officers quite naturally want to do a good job. They will urge more help for the German civilian, and they will be listened to with more sympathy and respect than German officials could command."

This consideration, in fact, forms the main reason for the demand that American troops quit Germany and leave the business of occupation to Germany's neighbors. "No men in the armies of the

United Nations," writes Morgenthau, "are likely to be susceptible as Americans to the danger of this people's bid for compassion. The misery of hunger and cold is bound to be extreme in Germany this winter. Until the workers in her heavy industry and her demo- bilized soldiers have begun to raise food crops and rebuild houses, there will be malnutrition and exposure for their people. The only possible way to avoid it would be to divert food and materials and labour from other European nations even more in need of them. . . . Soon he [the American soldier] will become, if he is not already now, a ready victim to a campaign for more lenient treatment of Germany."

Even so, the leniency was some time in coming. The experts, in solemn and steady drumbeat fashion, were already deciding the fate of Germany in particular, and Europe in general.

Chapter 5

THE CULT OF THE UNIVERSAL EXPERT

As a writer, professed public philosopher, and psychoanalyst of America's political tribal habits, Walter Lippmann is the embodiment of the cult of the universal expert. No great issue or personality at home or abroad is beyond his examination. His declamations and omniscience are wrapped around a simple, rather lucid writing style. It is easily understandable, most decisive—and usually wrong.

Lippmann's career as a commentator and columnist, heard 'round the world for fifty years, has attracted a vast and inchoate gaggle of imitators. Some—especially the younger breed—think in the comfortably ambitious terms of succeeding to Lippmann's unparalleled pinnacle. A Lippmannesque compliment, in a pleasant word here or an affectionate remark there, encourages hopeful successors that the world-extolled public philosopher regards them benevolently.

In the closed community of the universal expert such a form of benign paternalism is the gateway to the future. Universalists in this category have eagerly associated themselves with Lippmann's concept of that distorted and illusory word *Liberalism*. To his imitators, Lippmann's inquiry into domestic complexities and his evaluation of foreign affairs, especially as the United States conducts them, is the apogee of what many like to call the new journalism.

With Lippmann's stature as a universal expert, he can, of course, dine with kings in name or in power. Men of state he can reach with almost an exquisite facility. Politicians, of all stripes and persuasions, frequently drop everything for the privilege of an appointment with him. This is a peculiar and unique power, hungrily desired by other experts.

True, some of the imitators have become disillusioned with

Lippmann-type assessments. A few have even taken the trouble to delve into his past and present, which leaves them either indignant or baffled. Many, finding the path to acceptance as great universalists pitted with booby-traps, trim their ambitions and become regionalists.

Nevertheless, Lippmann remains to most, in the assorted crafts of journalism, politics, and diplomacy, a sort of sun-king. His has been the unfettered authority of divination. Nobody else, even among the handful of precariously established universal experts, has ever slugged it out in public with so many American Presidents, heads of state, and policies, and been taken so seriously.

For the last few years Lippmann's principal foreign policy views have been intertwined with the war in Vietnam. He is probably the most consistent, needle-sharp critic of President Johnson and governmental attitudes towards Vietnam. The Lippmann thesis is circulated in more than four hundred newspapers at home and abroad. The number keeps growing. Why? His views are regarded as the most authoritative that can be provided in the United States. Yet his record, which can easily be examined in books and clippings, adds up to a disastrous sequence of estimates at home and abroad. On foreign affairs, for example, a staggering start can be made on Lippmann with the rise of Hitler.

A nationally syndicated article Lippmann wrote about a major Hitler declaration of intent—willingness to submit all German military power to international inspection—appeared on May 19, 1933. Lippmann said that it deserved "a very high degree of general approval." He briefly mentioned Nazi injustices and ruthlessness. This particular statement of Hitler's, he noted, was real statemanship.

> There will be some who say that this address is merely a shrewd maneuver and that it must be rejected as insincere. I do not take this view. The truer explanation, I believe, is that we have heard once more, through the fog and the din, the hysteria and the animal passions of a great revolution, the authentic voice of a genuinely civilized people. I am not only willing to believe that, but it seems to me that all historical experience compels one to believe it.

A notable number of dissenting voices didn't. One was Winston Churchill's. Strange as it sounds, Lippmann's views at the time attracted more of an audience than did Churchill's. That was the same year, after the first inaugural of Franklin D. Roosevelt as

President of the United States, that Lippmann observed that Roosevelt was pretty much of a third rater even as a politician. He struck hard at that theme, even in 1936, when he appealed to the electorate to turn F.D.R. out, which he felt confident the American people would do.

Lippmann's egregious misjudgment of Hitlerism extended into all his pronouncements on the evils of totalitarianism. He has never to this day come to any acknowledgment that the Soviet system is aggressive and destructive. Negotiation is his favorite word in troubled times. In Lippmann's lexicon, however, negotiation becomes synonymous with either withdrawal or abandonment.

It is not simply a matter of being beastly to whoever might be running the Kremlin or calling the tune in Peking. Lippmann, whose insistence on a correct reading of history is part of his armory, interprets past and contemporary events as they best suit him. He is a well-traveled gentleman, who worked at an early age with the American delegation at Versailles. From his first-hand experience in treaty affairs, he came to the conclusion that Hitler was trying assiduously to right a grave mistake visited upon vanquished Germany.

Some years went by, during which Lippmann strove with his own brand of cold logic to turn back the revealed horrors of Nazism. When Hitler triggered World War II, Lippmann set his views forward—to the future. He became more obsessed with this idea after Pearl Harbor made us active combatants. When it appeared rather likely that the defeat of the Axis powers was inevitable, in 1944, Lippmann wrote a book, *U.S. War Aims.* The compilation of his insight into the future was indeed curious for Lippmann. He permitted himself, instead of analysis, flat predictions.

"The conclusive defeat of Japan," he declared, "will make the United States and the whole Atlantic Community invulnerably secure in the Pacific; the conclusive defeat of Germany will make Western Europe and the Americas secure."

A short time after the appearance of the book, a Lippmann column contained this pronouncement: "It is easy to say but it is not true, that the Allies of today may be the enemies of the future. . . . Our present alliance against Germany is no temporary contraption. It is an alignment of nations, which despite many disputes, much suspicion and even short and local wars, like the Crimean, have for more than a century been natural allies."

Then, he added in a piece of pure Lippmannesque history: "It is not a coincidence that Britain and Russia have found themselves allies ever since the rise of German imperial aggression, and that the United States and Russia, under the Tsars and the Soviets, have always in vital matters been on the same side."

Simply to set this special sidelight of history straight, it is worth noting that Britain and Imperial Russia were at loggerheads for generations on far-flung geographical areas. After the Bolsheviks took over, Britain and the Soviet regime had no formal diplomatic relations for years. This was true, too, of course between the United States and the Soviet government. With czarist regimes, the United States clashed regularly over Manchuria. President Theodore Roosevelt and Secretary of State John Hay berated the Russians for "imperialism" and hegemonistic plans for much of Asia. Their separate views, from firsthand discussions and negotiations, are available in state documents and papers.

Soon after World War II, when the United States became alarmed at Soviet encroachment under Stalin, the policy of containment was founded. It had been drafted by a brilliant, egocentric, and erratic American diplomatist, George F. Kennan. He was one of our early specialists in Soviet affairs, a talented linguist who was very reluctant to see America get enmeshed in most foreign affairs. Kennan, later one of our ambassadors to the U.S.S.R. and subsequently to Tito's Yugoslavia, concedes that he is a "neo-isolationist." In his own way, he is infinitely more an internationalist than is Lippmann. The very idea of containment, to Lippmann, was an unpardonable thought.

So, Lippmann in 1947 rushed into print with a slender volume entitled *The Cold War: A Study in U.S. Foreign Policy.* There had already been criticism of the Kennan concept, principally on the grounds that it was too negative and defensive. Nearly a year before Lippmann's study appeared between covers—hailed as a most reflective work by cultists of universal expertise—Churchill had delivered his Fulton, Missouri, speech. Historians at least remember clearly what he said about how the Iron Curtain had been rung down in East Europe and all the dangers that lay immediately ahead.

Lippmann, however, was indignant. He forecast containment as a provocation of the U.S.S.R. Along with containment, the Truman Doctrine to protect Greece, Turkey, and peripherally, Iran, was to Lippmann the height of rash folly. We would, he wrote, lose all our allies. Even worse, he saw the Soviet Union's reaction as one of unbounded expansion. He wrote in *The Cold War*: "Either Russia will burst through the barriers which are supposed to contain her, and all Europe will be at her mercy, or at some point and at some time the diplomatic war will become a full-scale shooting war. In either event *Europe is lost* [authors' italics]. Either Europe falls under the domination of Russia or Europe becomes the battlefield of a Russian-American war."

The fact that Greece was torn up by a Soviet-sponsored civil war so akin to the plight of Vietnam was ignored by Lippmann. He also suggested that simultaneous Soviet demands on Turkey for border territory were of no consequence to us. Rather than face up to the simple realities of a situation created by Soviet expansion, Lippmann preferred the line of retreat. He has been absolutely consistent in this respect: Disentangle or disengage by giving up people and places that don't belong to you. The fact of life and living in the world today—that self-interest and morality must preclude such arrogant abandonment—means nothing to the cultists of the universal expert.

He was similarly hostile to the creation of NATO, establishment of West Germany as an armed partner in the Alliance, United States air installations in the United Kingdom, and assorted units that took up fighting roles alongside Americans and South Koreans in the Korean War.

In a column on December 1, 1955, which had international circulation, Lippmann looked back at what he said, disparagingly, were gross errors of United States policy. They were, he wrote:

> The premature attempt to rearm Germany in 1950.
> The irreparable mistake of crossing the 38th parallel in Korea.
> The overmilitarization of the containment policy which has jeopardized our relations with India and several other uncommitted nations.

In 1950 Stalin was actively nibbling on the edges of Germany in general and Western Europe in particular. This is the reason NATO was created as an alliance of collective defense. Without a meaningful German contribution, the defense of Western Europe was strategic hot air. Crossing the 38th parallel will be indefinitely a controversial issue, but not the way Lippmann called it. How it was undertaken—by spreading forces too lightly and splitting them at that—remains the lay topic of debate.

Then, of course, his criticism of "overmilitarization of the containment policy" is basically a mid-fifties cry of the late Jawaharlal Nehru. The Indian Prime Minister lived to rue his own objections when Red Chinese forces came down from the northern frontiers and made mincemeat of the Indian defense units. It was when speaking to American and British military groups, rushed to India to find out how their governments could assist, that Nehru indulged in some privately expressed extraordinary flight of self-criticism.

In the autumn of 1958 Lippmann began to turn more frequently than was his normal wont to the Far East. For decades, his disdain of Asia was conveyed through concentration on Europe and European maneuvers in Asia and, rarely, in Africa. The Far East became a relatively regular target for his examination rather late in his career. His impartiality for yielding one place or another, as he advocated in Europe, was easily transferred across the world with his ambulatory punditry.

When the Chinese Communists began intensive shelling of the off-shore islands of Matsu and Quemoy, Lippmann urged us to get out and turn the areas over to the regime of Mao Tse-tung. The timing of his written appeal was ironic. Only a few months before, Marshal Tito, at a Yugoslavia Communist party congress in the dappled foothills of Slovenia, warned the world about Mao. It was Tito, to the demonstrative Soviet-led walkout of other Communist representatives, who first revealed that Red China thought in terms of a nuclear war. Tito charged flatly that Mao said Communists should be unafraid of an atomic holocaust. There would be more Chinese left alive afterward, Tito quoted Mao, than anyone else. And world power would naturally fall into their hands.

Lippmann's interpretation of contemporary history ignored what had been a historical accusation. His unilateralism—in welshing on an alliance and conceding to an opposing side without a return—he called honorable statesmanship.

"A withdrawal from Quemoy to Formosa" said the Lippmann column, "will liquidate a dangerous liability and will consolidate the strategic position of Formosa. . . .

"Were we disengaged from Quemoy and disentangled from Chiang's ambitions, there would be time to consider calmly what in the long run is truly important to us in Formosa. We know that in the long run our interest in Formosa cannot be tied up with Chiang's government. For that government is manifestly living on borrowed time.

"Our true interest in Formosa, having done our duty to see that Chiang's people have a safe asylum somewhere, is that the island should not be militarized for an advanced Chinese base against the Philippines. . . .

"So, we should disengage in Quemoy. We should stand at Formosa for the purpose of negotiation. We should prepare for the passing of Chiang's regime."

Nearly ten years have ensued since Lippmann urged this plan. In that time, the economy of Formosa (Taiwan) has burst almost at the take-off point in gross national productivity. Neither Matsu nor Quemoy have been abandoned, and they are less threatened today than when Lippmann wrote of the dreadful trials ahead. The Chiang regime is far less vicious than many of the power-motivated governments Lippmann has called entrenched, or even safe. Certainly its economic development is proportionately superior.

Lippmann has traveled very little in the Far East. His background on Asian affairs and ambitions is porous. Thus, if his supporters excuse him for that uneven experience, as they fervently do, it is much harder for them to offer apologia for Lippmann's European sorties. Take, for example, his column of October 10, 1961.

The burden of the article contended that when the regime of goat-bearded, despised (even by East European comrades) Walter Ulbricht raised the Wall, physically dividing Berlin, conditions altered. The status quo for the already split city, asserted Lippmann, was radically redressed by the infamous Wall.

"The truth is that West Berlin today is a stricken city without a future and to negotiate is not to surrender what we have, but to bargain for much that is necessary and that we do not have. What we do not have is a visible future for West Berlin."

Intense, ever-busy Willy Brandt, then lord mayor of West Berlin, would thoroughly disagree with the Lippmann thesis. Now vice-chancellor and foreign minister, he obviously has political axes of his own to grind that go all the way to maybe becoming chancellor of the Federal Republic. But Brandt has seen the establishment of the Wall for what it is; namely, a defensive sealing operation by a propped-up regime. He is essentially interested in reunification of the two halves of the old capital and East and West Germany. That may not occur in his lifetime. Lippmann suggests, again, withdrawal and negotiation of a settlement, which has been more or less the Khrushchev proposal for a "neutral" West Berlin.

Lippmann's assessments of Khrushchev have been even more bewildering than most. His wife and he were given the real red carpet treatment at the Black Sea villa Khrushchev used summertimes, when he held power. Lippmann and Khrushchev, through interpreters, made long examinations of the world scene. Lippmann was delighted, as he subsequently wrote, with Khrushchev's alertness and his grasp of political problems. Lippmann has always been pleased with authoritarian rule, when it received him—as did General de Gaulle, in another instance—and measured up to his own views. The pay-off of this trip to the U.S.S.R. was Lippmann's published findings that the "peasants of Eastern Europe" see hope ahead.

The point is that Lippmann probably never encountered a real-life peasant except when they were pointed out to him. Moreover, the longest strike in recorded history is the slowdown of the Russian peasants against the collectivization imposed on them. An attempt to encourage more agricultural productivity, for example, has recently been to exercise the temptation of a little profit incentive. Lippmann's pleasure with his discovery of the Khrushchevian talents—and trumpeted proposals for co-existence with the United States—blinkered his reading of present-day Soviet history.

In the first place, Khrushchev as the reformer was an idea Lippmann bought without question. He never regarded him as an international adventurer and a rather dangerous one. The introduction of missiles into Cuba was an outstanding example of that fact. He was also transitional and rather mediocre as a man of state. Yet he was described by Lippmann and his adherents as "A Man of Peace."

Robert Conquest, a gifted poet and a renowned Slavic studies scholar, wrote an article toward the end of 1965, which he called "Russia: the Great Illusion." He examined, on the basis of his own unemotional research and experience, Khrushchev and what the demoted number one Soviet leader did in his time. Some of the "reforms," as in the economic field, got Conquest's surgical treatment, which they certainly did not from Lippmann.

"Back in 1957, we were told that the U.S. was about to be

caught up with in milk and meat production," wrote Conquest. "The abandonment of these promises passed unnoticed, covered by the spectacular proposals of the Seven Year Plan. That Plan, in turn, was overtaken by the dynamic long-term Plan of 1961.

"The plans evaporated but the air of immense economic perspectives remained. Similarly, each new reorganization is greeted as showing a fresh, uninhibited outlook that will solve all problems. The de-centralization of 1957, the re-centralization of 1960, the de-centralization of 1965—each, in its turn has been the radical hard-thinking sign of a new era."

The latest new spirit, by the mediocre directorate that runs the Soviet Union today, elicits fresh cries of wonderment. Its on-again, off-again vague gestures to the West are invariably greeted as signs of a desire for accommodation with the West in general and the Americans in particular. Lippmann seizes on it as often as he can, within the framework of his demand that we leave Vietnam as soon as possible.

In his historical asides, Lippmann may have missed what was said recently by Pietro Nenni. Almost as old in years as Lippmann, but having spent all his adulthood in the rough-and-tumble of Italian politics, Nenni today is one of the leaders of the coalition government in Rome. For years his left-wing Socialists cooperated with the Communist party. Nenni was on active working terms with the late Italian veteran Communist leader Palmiro Togliatti. For some years he chafed under the arrangement. His associations with Italian Communist leadership and, most of all, with Russians brought a total change of mind.

Roly-poly Nenni, his outsized black-rimmed spectacles falling down the bridge of his nose, had this to say about present-day Russia: "Despotism and abuse became systems of government, and one cannot but fear that despotism and abuse will rear their heads again tomorrow as they did yesterday if the denunciation of the 'shameful facts' of the Stalin era is not followed by full and complete restoration of democracy and liberty."

Nenni speaks out as a life-long Socialist, and one who tried for years to maintain a working coexistence with Communists. He is profoundly attached to the workers and peasants, about whom Lippmann has written so loftily with no experience of them whatever. Most recently Lippmann has absorbed himself, his supporters, and the reading public with his views on Vietnam. We doubt that Lippmann has even set foot in Vietnam let alone nearly all of Southeast Asia. Nevertheless, the universal expert does not hesitate to pore over far-flung upheavals and examine them as he might a badly prepared soufflé.

Lippmann has been probably the foremost critic of President Johnson's policies in Vietnam. He has shown an active personal dislike of L.B.J. after an initial warm glow when he could talk to the President. In those early days, after the shock of the Kennedy assassination, Lippmann saw L.B.J. as "a great healer" of the nation. Today, as Lippmann sees him, Johnson is an undereducated divider.

Lippmann has capsulized his own vanities, half-century of experience, and demonology to diagnose our ills in Vietnam. Interestingly, all his past errors of judgment—including the one on Hitler—have been magnanimously forgiven by anti-Johnson intellectuals and unswerving admirers of the cult of the universal expert.

On *The New York Times*—a newspaper that boasts of its public record, but has shown a distinct anti-American role in Vietnam both as news and in editorial treatment—one columnist stands out. He is Cyrus L. Sulzberger, a regional expert with background to support the claim. In a column published in the *Times* on February 25, 1966, Sulzberger took off on Lippmann and, incidentally, George Kennan. As often occurs, Lippmann and Kennan today hold, for the most part, the same views on Vietnam. In this, Lippmann disregards his anticontainment views and their variance from those of Kennan.

Sulzberger prefaced remarks about Lippmann and Kennan's attitude with: "The Great Debate on Vietnam policy has been featured by mis-information, passion, political opportunism, and hints of a smarmy dislike for President Johnson. Both Peking and Hanoi must have gained fresh encouragement by the joining of our Know-Nothings with our Know-it-Alls.

"As a nation, we venerate pundits who make occult pronouncements on strategy. Public opinion and those who aspire to guide it are indeed vital factors in war and revolution."

Sulzberger refers briefly to Lippmann's examination of Hitler in 1933. With quiet scorn he adds: "Lippmann already knew Europe and Germany well so there was a basis for such lucid and reassuring prescience. He knows Asia little and Vietnam not at all. His Jungle Stories parable comparing Chinese and American power to a whale is pleasant nonsense. Were the southeast Asian peninsula to fall under Chinese suzerainty, as Lippmann seems almost to recommend, island Indonesia would patently go along. Australia and the Philippines would be directly menaced.

"One must only hope the counsel President Johnson receives in private is superior to that he gets in public."

Sulzberger's voice, admittedly, is a strong and active one. His opinions are shared by the newspaper's military analyst, Hanson Baldwin. But Baldwin belongs to a part of the apparatus in the still-medieval chain of command at *The New York Times*. He is one of the editorial board, presided over by John B. Oakes, a pleasant, little chap who is determined to prove the "liberal" side of issues—whatever that means today. The editorials are above reproach inside the newspaper. With its collective head above the clouds, the editorial board has permitted Robert Kleiman to chart its Vietnam course.

Kleiman, as most others on the heavily manned board, is fascinated by Lippmann's universal expertise, on Vietnam in particular. For years he worked for David Lawrence's *U.S. News & World Report,* scarcely fertile ground for instant *New York Times* views. He was for a while in Bonn and then for many years in Paris. Briefly, he transferred to CBS. His talents were not for electronic journalism. He impressed Oakes and went to work for the *Times* in 1963. His views on Vietnam, and why we should never have become involved there, prevailed above those offered by more experienced editorialists. Kleiman, at this time, had never been near Vietnam.

Tillman Durdin's transfer from the editorial board provided an open sesame for Kleiman. He was staunchly, and fruitlessly, opposed in the field by an able *Times* correspondent, Seymour Topping, now foreign editor. The editorial board, remember, is inviolate and a law unto itself in the paper's hierarchy. Kleiman, a man in his late forties, specialized as a multiregionalist. He swings from France and the Common Market to Vietnam. The French attitude toward Vietnam, as envisaged so grandly by General de Gaulle, corresponds closely to Kleiman's. When he went briefly to Vietnam, Kleiman wrote an editorial a few hours after arrival. Even for magic carpet journalism, this is quite a feat. It hewed precisely to what he had been writing before and was hailed at one of those grandiose Washington dinner parties. By whom? Walter Lippmann. But the *Times* has its own universal expert. He is James "Scotty" Reston, a pipe-smoking, hard-working reporter. On the small side physically, Reston is all quiet charm as a person. He had been a sports writer, articulate in that specialty. Interested in widening his fields of interest, Reston did some foreign reporting, then worked in Washington as a diplomatic correspondent, and rose to chief of bureau. He divested himself of the boring administration that goes with the post and stuck to a three-a-week column and the title Associate Editor.

It hasn't taken long for the column and the universality of his scope to bring Reston access to the great, near-great, and imitators. For a long time he was needled pleasantly by Joseph Alsop—the third of the triumvirate of universalists—to go East, the Far East. Alsop, a sophisticated man of abstract erudition, thought that if Reston saw things for himself, his views about Vietnam would alter. Alsop's own insights stay unchanged. He despises signs of weakness, real or imagined. Because he flies out to Vietnam frequently to update himself, Alsop also goads Lippmann.

Reston finally went out, twice in succession. He was a little Hamletlike, melancholy over what he assessed the first time. The second go-round, he was decisive. The United States, in Reston's eyes and mind, should get out as cold-bloodedly and as swiftly as possible. That has been the distillation of his opinion on Vietnam, often written with the sports writer's tinge of bitter humor. In much the same manner, with calculated detachment, he views other parts of the world and the American scene. To most professional and trained journalists, the deferral to Lippmann is clear. They are both held up as shining lights—Lippmann first, of course—by supporters of the collective anti-Vietnam, anti-L.B.J. thesis.

Careful reports from other observers on the spot do not attract even transitory notice from down-the-line Lippmann-Reston adherents. As late as the November 3, 1966, issue of *The Reporter* magazine, a serious and substantively liberal-minded periodical, a fresh evaluation of Vietnam appeared. It was written by veteran CBS correspondent Richard C. Hottelet.

> The tide is turning politically and militarily in Vietnam, with power the central factor. Military success—seizing and exploiting the initiative, harrying and punishing the enemy—is an indispensable condition of political success. A change in the climate is evident—

resistance to Communist influence grows with the confidence that the Communists will not prevail. Election of the Constituent Assembly marks a new phase in a trend toward political stability that coincides with and may be largely due to military successes.

On its own, before and after the Hottelet article, the highly respected and thoughtful *Economist* of London presented its own assessments. In the last few years, the *Economist* has never wavered from the idea that on balance American policies in Vietnam were correct. Late in the summer of 1966 the magazine examined Red China's maneuvers and internal aberrations.

"And every time," it noted, "that Mao Tse-tung does something to justify everybody's worst fears, the critics' job gets that much tougher."

Then it waded into Lippmann, whose own eccentric pronouncements the magazine often pinpoints with a bit of deliberate understatement. "Mr. Lippmann, for his part, has walked into a couple of traps," the lead article observed.

He tried to argue on July 26th that there is no connection between the guerrilla war in Vietnam ("one small corner of the world") and other guerrilla wars that might follow it elsewhere. But Marshal Lin Piao (Mao's chosen No. 2) saw the connection all right for China's purposes in the article on "people's war" that the Peking central committee has just commended: "The people in other parts of the world will see . . . that what the Vietnamese people can do, they can do, too."

That was one trap and Mr. Lippmann dropped into it. The other is bigger and deeper, and goes right down to the fundamental question about the whole war: How can you defend the non-Communist parts of Asia unless you are ready to fight a war in Asia? . . . The blunt truth is that this is now an academic argument. China has nominated Vietnam as a test case for what it claims to be a new kind of war.

Two months later, during the Manila conference and President Johnson's grueling tour of Southeast Asia, the *Economist* had this headline on its front cover: "It's Starting to Pay Off." The editors described it as the "Johnson Doctrine for Asia." A generation earlier, the paper noted, President Truman committed the United States to the defense of Greece and Turkey, so violently opposed by Lippmann. With his commitment, Truman provided non-Communist forces in the area a center of power around which to rally.

Besides he exploded fierce argument in the Communist camp between those who wanted to recoil in the face of the United States commitment and those who wanted to fight the Greek civil war to a finish.

"It took two and a half years from the declaration of the Truman Doctrine in 1947 for the Greek Communists to accept that they could not take over power in Athens by armed force," said the *Economist,* but accept it in the end they did.

> A similar process is now visible in Asia's crisis. On the non-Communist side Mr. Johnson is building up a Pacific consensus. On the Communist side the gap between China and Russia is getting wider by the minute, and Mr. Kosygin [Soviet Prime Minister] is finding it remarkably hard to get even his smaller Communist allies to agree to a common position.

Imperturbably, Lippmann ignores these grave assaults on his own logic and presentation. Emulating the Lippmann stance as a legislative universal expert is Senator J. William Fulbright. The lean senator from Arkansas is chairman of the Senate Foreign Relations Committee. He has been a Rhodes scholar and is the architect of scholarships known to the world as "Fulbrights." A little examination of Senator Fulbright's claim to expertise is revealing. That will be handled later at some length.

His lectures and papers on what he called "Old Myths and New Realities"—the changing scene in East Europe—have been shocking studies in superficiality. During a few mealtime encounters, we discovered through persistent questioning that he hardly knew prominent Communist names, let alone the profound issues. Since he scarcely realized the name of the game, how could he be expected to provide Americans with inquests on policy?

But Lippmann deemed it necessary to give Fulbright a special tribute during his race for re-election in 1962. "The nation is greatly in his debt," wrote Lippmann. "The role he plays in Washington is an indispensable role. There is no one else who is so powerful and also wise, and if there were any question of removing him from public life, it would be a national calamity."

A strong plea, certainly. It totally overlooked Fulbright's survival tactics on issues like Little Rock or over-all integration. He is, on the record, opposed to civil rights as advocated by several administrations, Democrat and Republican. Through his committee chairmanship, TV inquiries, and trips abroad, Fulbright acquired the patina of full expertise. He has supported Lippmann on Vietnam. His prudence, as in civil rights, took priority when L.B.J. talked in midsummer, 1966, of Asian policies, which took form in Manila. Fulbright complained that the President should have consulted Congress first. His argument might have been more logical had he done a little homework. Truman didn't consult Congress before deciding that we must defend Greece and Turkey in 1947—the Truman Doctrine. The senator, for background counsel, consulted elder statesman Lippmann.

Lippmann was opposed to the earlier doctrine as he is opposed to the newer one, on the other side of the world. Somehow, his is a special brand of history—his own creation. If he was not taken so seriously as a supreme expert, Lippmann might be agreeably amusing. Perhaps it will now turn out like that, since he has announced semiretirement. Only occasional, if lengthier, evaluations of the world are promised by Lippmann. The fewer Lippmann contributes, the fewer mistakes he makes. This is bearable.

Chapter 6

THE INTELLIGENCE PROBLEM

THE cult of the spy has become an extraordinary phenomenon with the Western public. Picaresque tales of the agent who survives the most ghastly experiences and outwits the enemy are also transmitted to the screen and hold vast audiences in the grip of near-total fascination.

So James Bond, nimble creation of the late Ian Fleming, has become bigger than real life. More morbid, sharply sensitive composites, like *The Spy Who Came in from the Cold,* drawn by John Le Carré, are truer portrayals, but nevertheless fictional. Both Fleming and Le Carré had actual service in the twilight land of intelligence, which has today become amorphously labeled "espionage."

Yet these two contemporary architects of the "spy novel," have been most painstaking in employing the fictional form around which to weave their stories. In the United States, with the over-riding passion for expertise in vogue, fact-fiction is presented as plain fact. It has added another dimension to complex facets of government, its techniques, and direction. Most recently, the tragic assassination of President John F. Kennedy has provoked self-appointed inquests that point solemn accusations at the government with indignant claims of conspiracy and cover-ups.

These inquiries, published to the accompaniment of publicity and tantalizing printed queries, have joined the so-called fact-finders in the tortured paths of intelligence operations. Probably the most interesting so far—and the most destructive—examination of intelligence in the United States has been the work of David Wise and Thomas B. Ross, in their book *The Invisible Government.*

Promotion for the authors hails the work as the "first full, authentic account of America's intelligence and espionage apparatus

—an invisible government with the CIA (Central Intelligence Agency) at its center . . ." It may have been the first book of its kind. Authentic, it is not. To make so grave a charge against these two serious and diligent writers requires profound substantiation.

An examination of them and their background is essential before assessing their *Invisible Government* in some detail. They are both fairly young—thirty-six at this writing—and have been working newspapermen since college graduation. Wise had been White House correspondent for the New York *Herald Tribune,* and for about three years, until its demise, chief of its Washington bureau.

In 1958 Ross became a member of the Chicago *Sun-Times.* He had been in the Navy during the Korean War. His collaborator and he plunged into the maelstrom of American intelligence activities with their first joint work, *The U-2 Affair,* an account of the special spy plane that didn't come to public notice until Captain Francis Gary Powers was brought down alive in the Soviet Union.

Experience in compiling that first book, as Wise has told it, made the authors feel there was a lot more to be sifted in the field of intelligence and espionage. Thus, they spent a year or so in research that provided the ingredients for *The Invisible Government.* When the book was published, in 1964, it provoked a furor, at home and abroad. The CIA accused the authors of multifarious mistakes and gross misrepresentation. In foreign fields the book has been translated (in Communist-run countries without permission, naturally) and held as a reference work to refute claims of American emissaries and official representatives that accusations similar to those contained in the book aren't necessarily so.

Aside from being sober-minded, hard-working newspapermen, what talents and qualities do these authors have to qualify them as experts in this strange field? Neither of them has ever worked abroad as a foreign correspondent. Indeed, aside from the experience he gained on a fast trip with the late President Kennedy and a couple of holidays, Wise would have difficulty assessing the composition of most foreign governments. The same is essentially true of Ross, whose trips abroad have been limited to some holidays and rather hasty research jaunts.

Neither of them, to our knowledge, speaks any foreign language with any fluency. Yet their book is mainly about CIA-inspired foreign upheavals. They have written sententiously, for example, of intelligence and espionage operations in Germany. Before they drafted the book, they had spent only a little time in Germany. Because of its saturnine quality, they refer to CIA chiefs of station abroad, as "spies." Any reporter, working in a specific foreign capital, knows much better. A chief of station is a *staff officer*. He is usually known to the community at large. A spy, by definition, works in the shadows.

Anyone who doesn't know the difference between a spy and a staff officer has no business writing about intelligence within a fact format. But Wise and Ross believe themselves—with the success, fustian, and treacle engendered by their book—to be "acknowledged experts in the field of intelligence." So Wise has put it in his solemn, humorless manner. Their success set them off to wider horizons. Wise declared they were engaged in putting together a book on "International Intelligence."

Since the subject is infinite, they both took short trips to West Europe and its eastern approaches, including the U.S.S.R. Wise was rebuffed in a correct manner by the British. Among other things, which Fleming, le Carre, and other British innovators of the spy novel recognize, Britain has an official secrets act. You just can't walk in and interview chiefs of MI-5 or MI-6 and get direct answers to direct questions. That didn't apparently faze Wise, convinced of his expertise. He began his research into British intelligence work by perusing the clippings of a popular English journalistic writer. This writer's contribution to knowledge of the intelligence community draws gales of laughter from his colleagues as "fact-fiction," with emphasis on the second word.

The new evaluation of the world's intelligence networks, as seen by Wise and Ross, recently appeared entitled *The Intelligence Establishment*. It caused little fuss. Therefore it is judicious to examine their "authentic" account that bears the title *The Invisible Government*. Early in the book, and repeated in a later section, the authors note that United States ambassadors' authority, as evaluated by a Senate subcommittee, is "a polite fiction." That is to say, the CIA supersedes the Ambassador everywhere abroad.

We know of at least two dozen ambassadors in key posts who can, and would, contest that view. It is, as a former ambassador and a highly talented and respected editor (since returned to his own career) remarked to one of the authors: "No ambassador with any wit, or worth a damn, would permit this to happen. Any CIA chief of station knows it, and there always is a meeting of the minds. Wise and Ross have taken an isolated case, or two, and built on it. From my own personal knowledge, I know that their charges are unfounded."

Fortunately for American policy and national attentiveness a fairly sizable number of diplomats and economists-turned-diplomat have served—still do in many cases—with intelligence and distinction. Among the most notable, who have never puffed themselves into pillars of unassailable expertise, are David Bruce, Ellsworth Bunker, Mike Blumenfeld, Bert Elbrick, Walter (Red) Dowling, and James Riddleberger. The list hardly ends with them. But they are among the best we have to represent us, with dedication, throughout the world.

The authors of *The Invisible Government*—which they made visible by their own lights—slightly rephrase their evaluation in the middle of the book, as noted by a Senate subcommittee: "To a degree, the primacy of the ambassador is a polite fiction." The writers might have come to a more rounded conclusion had they spoken to not just the ex-diplomat quoted above but a whole group of career ambassadors. Some are retired and would be accessible in Washington, for instance, where the authors work.

Needless to say, any huge intelligence community commits errors of judgment and action. To extract episodes of CIA mishaps and link them with associated agencies into a government-within-a-government makes of successive Presidents of the United States and their chief executors either willing robots, stooges, or feckless fools. No matter how one feels about the peculiar talents of any postwar President, they do not fall into any of these categories. But in their expert round-up, this is the stark accusation made by the authors.

Wise and Ross observe that their book is not an exposé, although much of the material has "never been printed elsewhere." There is sound reason for much of it never before having seen the light of day. In our opinion the contents of this book are patently distorted or the figment of lively imagination. Just take the sweeping statement that "CIA men and women lead a cloistered life." Maybe they do—for Wise and Ross.

Any correspondent abroad, with the most normal sense of curiosity, knows most of the table of organization of the CIA in the city where he has his assignment. Around the world, the authors have known and are acquainted with perhaps one hundred. Visiting correspondents from Washington are on personal terms of friendship with many. They visit them, never to extract secret information, but to exchange views, anecdotes, and restoke old acquaintanceship. A great number of CIA people are worldly, highly educated, and interesting. Frequently they are much more interesting than the career diplomat. Perhaps this talent has led Wise and Ross to assume that the agency abroad transcends the office of the ambassador.

These authors also pinpoint names. A debate has sprung up ever since the publication about whether this was the correct thing to do, even in the name of a quest for truth. We don't happen to believe it was correct or even served a purpose. All it did was publicize people already known to their enemies and opposition. Wise and Ross obviously believed the revelations—known for years to foreign correspondents—gave a sliver of additional reality to their "authentic account."

They go somewhat further than just mentioning names, in identifying Henry Pleasants, former CIA chief of station in Bonn, as the agent who moved in with General Reinhard Gehlen and lived with him for several months. Gehlen, wartime intelligence chief for the Germans on the eastern front, is an enigmatic personality who has never been interviewed, and whose physical identity often alters. His intelligence organization cooperates with the Americans and was, in the beginning, subsidized by the United States.

A rebuttal by the CIA and other American governmental agencies has been that there are scores of questionable statements in *The Invisible Government.* Challenged to show how and where, official critics of the book demurred into official silence. They are not supposed to talk about such matters. That is a matter of opinion. But beholden to nobody official or otherwise, we want to expose some of the mistakes made, which, by the way, could be picked out by any knowledgeable and experienced foreign correspondent.

Toward the end of the book, in a section headed "Black Radio," Wise and Ross strongly imply that broadcasts of Radio Free Europe kept stirring up Hungarian Revolutionaries, even after their cause was lost. Both of us have been in Hungary many times, before, during, and after the rebellion. We have been personally acquainted, through the years, with many of the Hungarians who had a direct role in the uprising. Moreover, one of us speaks fluent Hungarian.

Wise and Ross inflated an accusation, made emotionally after the United States failed to come to the young revolutionaries' aid, by understandably bereft Hungarians. This charge also was picked up by outsiders, including Americans, who wanted disassociation from the rising and its aftermath as quickly as possible and saw in RFE broadcasts a convenient explanatory scapegoat.

The point is that had Wise and Ross sought assiduously to get to the heart of this matter, they would have learned that RFE—which broadcasts to East Europe, except Yugoslavia, the U.S.S.R., and East Germany—had nothing whatever to do with the uprising. It was caught drowsing, as were East and West, when the revolt nearly blew the Soviet Union out of East Europe. In quoting Freedom Fighters' frantic appeals to Munich, site of RFE, Wise and Ross conveniently ignored a few factual conditions.

The revolutionaries had, alas, no contact with the West or Western sources. For years—even when it was jammed at great cost to Communist regimes—people tuned in to RFE. They listened to news accounts, stories of refugees, music, and homely sketches they could not hear on their controlled radiocasts. So, when they made their last-ditch, fruitless appeals, they beamed them on RFE.

Going to a far-flung corner of the world, Indonesia, the authors are horrified over what they say they discovered the CIA was up to in spinning a spy plot against the now-deflated President Sukarno. They mention a pilot in the employ of the CIA who bombed a town as part of a conspiracy to overthrow Sukarno. Never once do they mention that a Moslem-led underground opposed Sukarno for years and waged guerrilla war against him.

In a rather tragicomic comment, the authors write that General Eisenhower feared Sukarno would fall completely under Communist domination. Wise and Ross might have done a little more research, even in 1963, and obtained a more balanced picture of Sukarno's ever-increasing attachment to Red China. They scoff at anti-Communist Indonesian maneuvers, as exemplified by Chief of Staff General Haris Nasution. Not once is there any mention of General Suharto, present strongman who really directed the gradual isolation of Sukarno. Had the writers ever been in Indonesia, even for a couple of days, they might have learned about Suharto and the oncoming clash between Sukarno cadres, including the Communists, and the army, abetted by those same Moslem groups in constant revolt against Sukarno.

With their sad smattering of ignorance about Asia, they never get into an unprecedented diplomatic situation which has been reported. When our then-Ambassador Howard P. Jones was about to be rotated for reassignment, Sukarno personally asked President Kennedy to keep him on as our emissary. Jones, whose efforts to cultivate Sukarno were honestly motivated, was regarded as a patsy by correspondents and many fellow diplomats. Kennedy agreed to Sukarno's request. The CIA, in this case, is studiously ignored by Wise and Ross.

Since the scattered archipelago that comprises Indonesia happens to be one of the key countries of the world, the sponsors of *The Invisible Government,* might have attempted to learn a little more about the disparate islands. At the end of their book they ask questions. One on Indonesia goes: "Was it worth running the risk of permanently alienating Sukarno by supporting his enemies?" The answer is self-evident and contained in what Indonesians themselves did. It underlines the lack of political knowledge the writers labor under despite their self-aggrandizement.

As these experts wander around the world, within the confines of their book covers, they drop an occasional sneer for the deficiencies of certain unquiet Americans. One of them is the late John Peurifoy, mentioned by the authors in connection with his ambassadorship to Guatemala, when a United States-supported revolt was launched against a Communist-tinged regime. Among other inadequacies they relate of Peurifoy was that he never learned languages. When did they?

Because they are the "foremost experts" in intelligence, as Wise concedes, much time and space must be devoted to their work of the past, and what may be expected to be in a similar genre, their work of the future. *The Invisible Government,* as Wise also said, has been published in Russian. He was told so by a Soviet journalist in Washington. He must also know by now that it is, in French, a handbook for North Vietnamese party cadres. English-language editions are carried by those Asians and Africans who use it as proof that their opposition to American policies is correct.

Their emphasis on the emasculation of the American ambassador by the CIA persists right up to their philosophical conclusions. They insist that the ambassador be in charge of all activities in a foreign country, lest he be hamstrung by covert affairs. Many ambassadors we personally know have gloomily observed that they have been handicapped by the expertise of Wise and Ross.

In its own heavy-handed, grandiloquent manner, *The New York*

Times repeatedly calls for some type of Congressional watchdog supervision over the CIA. The editorial page, under the direction of chunky John B. Oakes—a member of the owning Sulzberger-Ochs family—keeps reminding the public of an overpowering need to set up a system of checks and balances over the agency. In an epoch of overweening security consciousness some form of additional inspection of the CIA is bound, in the long run, to evolve. The manner in which the *Times* conducts its campaign is ever-reminiscent of Cato the Elder, demanding the destruction of Carthage at the conclusion of most of his speeches.

To pursue its theme, firmly accepted by Oakes, the newspaper, with its smug slogan about all the news fit to print, set about on a special *Times* inquiry. Correspondents around the world, especially those in areas under Communist control, were asked to provide answers to specific questions. These included queries about CIA personnel in a given capital, what they performed, and how they tackled certain East-West problems. In an effort to prevent the questionnaires falling into, say the hands of Communist or unfriendly governments, they were posted through the American diplomatic pouch!

A team of writers, drafted from the huge staff of the paper's Washington bureau, was assigned to cull the material and write the series. The writers, because of their Washington connections, presumably could contact informed opinion about the information they received from the field. In effect this was a private attempt to discover what inimical regimes spend inexhaustible time and vast sums to learn. The argument has been made that the public has a right to know.

Public knowledge and responsibility have been thrust forward as a burnished shield of protection whenever controversy becomes inflamed. The argument, as was kept within the top offices of the *Times* in this particular investigation, was resolved in favor of the ineffable right of the public domain. Thus a series was hammered together to prove the *Times'* contention that there was a necessity for wider and closer scrutiny of the CIA. Ironically, a substantial slice of the published reporting came almost directly from the pages of *The Invisible Government*. David Wise was the first outsider to point with pride to this "confirmation."

But the biggest furor since the Bay of Pigs fiasco swept through the country with the student-scholar revelations. It snowballed into uncovering CIA ties, via funds, with trade union operations abroad and a host of tax-free foundations. The tendency of Americans to indulge in an emotional kick, when they feel outraged, takes them out of the realm of reality, however unpalatable the excursion.

Symptomatic of this sanctimonious indignation was a wrenching episode some years ago in Austria. A hard-working American journalist heard of an "escape route" used by Czechoslovakians to filter across the border. He asked a CIA man if the facts he had were essentially correct. They were, he was told, but he was urged not to divulge them.

"The American people have the right to know," was the self-righteous response of the journalist. He sent the story, which was published. In the following week seven known would-be escapees, including a child, were seized by Czech security. Two were shot and killed. By the writer's standards, the "American people" got the information. Victims of the exposed route paid dearly for the revelation.

The right to know, as we demand in mid-twentieth century, imposes restraints and disciplines. Great Britain, as the prototype for all parliamentary society, indeed imposes these restraints.

It is exercised by an Official Secrets Act and so-called "D" notices. The notices are circulated to all public media, as letters of advice and request. They warn editors of items that may be protected by the Official Secrets Act promulgated in 1920. These are regarded by defense authorities as important. Their publication would be contrary to the national interest. At the height of our own orgy of self-criticism over the CIA and student foundations, Prime Minister Wilson bitterly attacked a mass-circulation newspaper. He told the House of Commons the journal sensationalized security checks on private cables dispatched from Britain out of the Post Office. In effect, charged Wilson, the paper violated the D-notice advice.

This was a restraint Britain lived with comfortably, *New York Times* columnist Scotty Reston noted. He pointed out that the financial association of the CIA with the United States National Student Association (NSA) was established in the most frozen epoch of the cold war. If Communist-led and financed students would not have a walkover in world student meetings, we had to see they could go places and confront the others. Money was the requirement. And, as Reston observed, the students did a splendid job in debate. The authors of this book attended many of these meetings as reporters. It is singularly doubtful whether any of the participating American students and scholars believed themselves to be agents.

Walter Lippmann, from his own approach, saw in the proliferation of revelations, more corruption of American society. If the United States government had set up an institution as did Britain long ago in the British Council, with branches around the world, there would still have been the fuss about government sponsorship. All West European governments of any consequence finance such institutions. The U.S.S.R. and East European régimes have for years organized, selected, and financed student delegations as an arm of the state and party. The CIA was handed the job of financing the NSA trade union affiliates and assorted educational projects abroad by the mandarins of the State Department. They wanted no part of it. But the job had to be done. So, as in matters where policy goes sour, the problem is passed to the CIA. That was how the agency originally became involved in operations that culminated in the Bay of Pigs.

There is among Americans a glaring lack of sophistication about clandestine work in conjunction with policy. This shortcoming provokes all types of revelations, expertise, and lecturing-hectoring on vest pocket projects. The thunder of smugness accompanies any exposure with the cry of "the right to know." It is nearly always accompanied by reflections that maybe we should have the safety devices of the acts as they exist in Britain.

Given the American temperament, it is not the answer. What any secrets act serves, through tradition and usage, is self-discipline. In this context, the way we go about exposing activities raises a most sensitive point: Perhaps we have a better intelligence service than America deserves. It remains a pretty well-regulated arm of American government despite cries of corruption. There have been four United States Presidents, in twenty years of the existence of the agency, who can attest to that.

But the unflagging war of the shadows and the spread of the spies and their undercover operations have lately been cast into one of America's most neuralgic episodes—the assassination of President Kennedy in Dallas on November 22, 1963. Conspiracies and plots are implied in a spate of the latest books on the tragedy. Although the special commission headed by Chief Justice Earl

Warren concluded that twenty-four-year-old Lee Harvey Oswald was solely responsible, "new material" was supposedly uncovered and hastily published. The commission had the assistance of a full-time staff of twenty-six (mostly legal experts). It published an 888-page report from twenty-six volumes covering 17,815 pages of testimony and exhibits assembled over a ten-month period.

Despite the probity of Chief Justice Warren and six other distinguished public members assigned to the Commission, books began to tumble off the presses beginning in 1966 contesting the conclusions. In the United States, at first, there had been little critical reaction. Abroad, where plots and coups have for centuries riddled political life, the general assessment was one of cynicism or belief that the Warren Commission was covering up for the Johnson Administration.

One of the august group assigned to the Commission, Allen Dulles, had for years been involved in the craft of intelligence. He was, for a long time, director of the CIA. Foreign writers and self-appointed analysts and investigators seized particularly on his role with the commission to ridicule its objectivity.

Unrevealed until now, as well, was the outburst of the late President's brother, Senator Robert F. Kennedy. Grief-stricken at the sudden calamity that cut the President down, Bobby Kennedy telephoned a ranking official of the CIA, who, dumbfounded, heard him demand with commingled anger and emotion: "Did your outfit have anything to do with this horror?" Bobby Kennedy, subsequently regaining his composure, never mentioned the call again. But he has often encountered the man he phoned, who, as it happened, had been a dedicated pro-Kennedy supporter.

If Bobby Kennedy, in an initial seizure of grief-ridden suspicion, thought of the CIA as a collective culprit, foreigners looked immediately at a whole spectrum: It went from the far left to the extreme right; the Dallas police, the FBI, and of course, the CIA and its covert network of all types and mentalities. Abroad, especially in Europe, the great tragedy became a universal whodunit. Interest has steadily risen in the possibilities of plots and counterplots that might have been directly involved in the murder of the President. The spread of macabre interest and the inclination to believe that all types of dark forces were involved has lately been matched by many books, inquiries, and opinions at home. Even an "authorized version," written by William Manchester, has appeared. He was the writer chosen by the Kennedy family and spent many hours tape-recording Mrs. Jacqueline Kennedy.

The Manchester book had tremendous advance publicity. To make certain that its impact would not be deflected, Mrs. Kennedy even wrote to Jim Bishop requesting that he refrain from writing his own version. Manchester, Mrs. Kennedy wrote, was the duly selected man with exclusive interview rights. These interviews have been profoundly bitter and even shocking to the succession in the White House. What this "authorized" book managed was to whet the appetite for more detail—fact or fancy doesn't seem to make much difference.

But the world still boggles at the squalid spectacle of Jackie Kennedy, Bobby, and the Kennedy entourage slugging out rights and wrongs with Manchester. Thousands of words, supposedly inside comment, titillated and baffled the public, either in the serialized version appearing in *Look* or in the book itself, published by Harper and Row. The furor demeaned the principal protagonists. It also uncovered a political killer instinct, rather fearful to hear and see, in New York's junior senator and his advisers, waiting for their moment to ascend to the corridors of power.

Some previous supporters, if not admirers, of Bobby got an unhappy overnight education. Jimmy Breslin, brass-bound and talented chronicler of people, had his arm twisted hard. In the end, after an acrimonious telephone conversation with R.F.K., Breslin blasted the Kennedys for seeking censorship prerogatives and exercising strong-arm pressures. He told the authors of this book that "I never was on the receiving end of so many implied threats from guys with college educations and big-time degrees. They tried to get me to angle my column in their favor. First, it was with nice, long words. Then, it was like pointing a loaded gun at me."

Murray Kempton, a veteran column writer of moods, mores, and behavior patterns, was the target of similar pressures. But the man who got the biggest shock treatment was William Attwood, recent ambassador to Kenya and Guinea, a seasoned journalist and editor, who became editor-in-chief of Cowles Magazines and Broadcasting, Inc. Four articles extracted from Manchester's book were serialized in *Look* magazine, owned by Gardner (Mike) Cowles. Attwood, close to the late Adlai Stevenson and one of the earliest New Frontiersmen of the 1960 Kennedy campaign and Administration, was bombarded with demands by Bobby's outriders and troubleshooters. The leading mandarin of the senator's team, historian Arthur Schlesinger, Jr., was enraged at Attwood's dissent to requests that *Look* omit specific passages from the serialization. Schlesinger's direct exchanges with Attwood on this subject were neither scholarly nor gentlemanly.

In day-to-day confrontation, Attwood dealt with Richard N. Goodwin, a friend of the Kennedy family and once a White House adviser. They are no longer on speaking terms. Attwood resisted imperious demands, as he saw them, to "play the court jester." Any hitch, any piece of trivia, was reported immediately by Goodwin to Senator Bobby. Attwood recalled: "I learned a lot the hardest way possible that forced me to shed lots of old dreams."

Midway in the searing squabble, John Kenneth Galbraith weighed in as a defender of the Kennedys and their special rights. A Kennedy-appointed ambassador to India, he acquired expert standing with his book, called *The Affluent Society*. It was an articulate and nimble effort. Although few academicians ever agree with their colleagues, Galbraith has minor support from fellow-economists. Through envy or critical superficiality, ascribed to Galbraith, he is to his own critics something of a pop economist. It doesn't ruffle him.

A towering man physically and possessed of an acerbic intellect, he has entered the national-international political jungle. Accepted as an expert by a devoted following, Galbraith became chairman of Americans for Democratic Action. He is sharply critical of the American role in Vietnam. When the Middle East explosion blew other Vietnam critics into all-out support for Israel, Galbraith demurred. He ignored the Middle East, even when Ho Chi-minh reiterated a pledge to support the Arabs in their quest to exterminate Israel.

This is most unusual for a personality of pronounced controversial views, particularly in the cause of "liberal" persuasions and politics. Galbraith, a self-avowed champion of the oppressed and pressured, chooses to remain mum on the Middle East. He feels it vital, however, to offer his opinions and specialist knowledge on most other issues. He didn't hesitate, for example, to air ideas about Vietnam or the bitter book episode of the Kennedys. Writing as a presumed insider, he declared in the *Saturday Review* that the ground rules for the authorized book would have been accepted by hundreds of writers. Galbraith ignored the fact that the first two writers approached said *no*. Manchester was the third.

But Galbraith also is very much a factor in what is known as the

"Kennedy government-in-exile." Its apparatus encompasses a selected group of Kennedy men, once in the White House, who have hitched their stars of power to the Bobby wagon. One of its main centers today is Harvard's new Institute of Politics, supported by the John F. Kennedy Library Corporation. Ironically, it took the investigative tenacity of a British writer, Henry Fairlie, working in the United States, to spotlight the meaning of the institute. His article, appearing also in the Washington *Post,* charged that the Kennedy family intended to "move in on Harvard" and husband brainpower for future political staffs.

Fellows of the institute, a branch of the Graduate School of Public Administration which changed its name to Kennedy, earn up to $15,000 annually. They happen to all have served under the late President, and they associate these days with Bobby. Their pursuits are scholarly, for which they receive no academic credits. Twice a month they assemble for political dinners with selected guests. An eleven-member advisory committee includes Jacqueline Kennedy. The institute has an endowment of ten million dollars and the former graduate school, 3.5 million dollars. As Fairlie pointed out, this is a glaring difference in priorities. He was indignantly rebutted by Dean Don K. Price, of the Kennedy School of Government. Indignation was insufficient for Fairlie, who stated: ". . . Harvard, in fact, degraded itself by accepting this condition. . . . [The John F. Kennedy School of Government] provides the most convenient opportunity for attracting under the name of the Kennedys men who are at present serving in the Johnson Administration, who are hoping to be employed by, and would be useful to, another Kennedy Administration, and who, as influential political journalists, have valuable services to offer in the future. . . . By means which are entirely legal and respectable and discreet, the Kennedys have established, with funds collected in memory of John F. Kennedy, a recruiting college. That valuable work may be done there is beside the point."

A staunch defender of the institute is Galbraith. It is consonant with the conviction that the "right to do" bears no examination if a power elite deems a project appropriate for any community or state. Galbraith's prickly defense of the Kennedys for veto authority over *Death of a President* shows indifference to other moods and personalities. In his advocacy, published in the *Saturday Review,* Galbraith summarily thrust into the background and ignored

Oswald's most recent past. The phase he overlooked was the penultimate one of Oswald's life before he was gunned to death by Jack Ruby while a national TV audience sat in frozen horror.

Oswald, an ex-Marine, defected to the Soviet Union. There he married a Russian girl. He didn't do well at any job and decided to become a repatriate. Returning, he drifted to Texas and Louisiana. Oswald became associated with some pro-Communist groups. Then ensued a mysterious episode in Oswald's movements. He paid a few visits to the Soviet Consulate in Mexico City. The last one dragged on a few hours. Nobody in authority can—or will—shed light on the visits.

In the Warren Commission Report some guarded attention is devoted to Oswald's strange visits to the Soviet Consulate. Virtually all the critical judgments heaped on the commission ignore those mysterious occurrences. They prefer, instead, to perform autopsies on the commission report and hector the American public-at-large with their own "expert" assessments and recommendations.

Before the Kennedy family authorized a version of the assassination, two books were produced whose provocative attacks on the Warren Commission elicited immediate attention. They were so designed. One is a meager volume, 151-pages strong, by a young, post-graduate student. His name is Edward Jay Epstein. The book, *Inquest,* started as Epstein's thesis for a master's degree in government. It becomes quite swiftly an indictment of the Warren Commission for unseemly haste in presenting a "version of the truth."

In common with a book that became a best-seller, *Rush to Judgment* by New York lawyer Mark Lane, a peremptory demand is made for a commission to examine the Warren Commission. The documentation for both volumes, taken interestingly from the original report, contends distortion from the real facts. The writers have claimed, by some super, unrevealed ratiocination, to possess detail supposedly concealed by the Warren Commission.

Because of the sustained suspicion current abroad of the "real plot" behind the Kennedy killing this self-acclaimed expertise threads its way into interstate affairs on high and low levels. Lane tried some years ago to bulldoze his way into a place of influence in New York State politics. He was chopped up as more or less a loner.

Then he devoted himself to his law practice and to causes that had combustible possibilities. He was retained for a time as counsel for Oswald's mother. In his book Lane dwells deeply on how his advocacy of Oswald would have unfolded had there ever been a trial. The Lane findings can be summed up by the lawyer-author in a phrase near the conclusion: "The commission covered itself with shame." To float his views and thereby simultaneously promote his book, Lane went to Europe to have himself shown and heard. His appearances and charges restoked the embers of ever-smouldering European wonderment about the entire episode.

Manchester, given infinitely more access to witnesses, information, and collected evidence, contends flatly that Oswald was the assassin. Lane, today the self-made gadfly of the Warren Commission, insists that isn't so, by any means. The owl-eyed advocate of underdog causes, who keeps up an unremitting campaign to win headlines, also got into the movie business. He put together a four-hour film on the assassination. The BBC, in Britain, paid $50,000 for it. To our knowledge it has never been shown on any major American network.

Lane's theme was demolished in a critique by Richard Warren Lewis that appeared in *New Yorker* magazine, January 22, 1967. Entitled "The Scavengers," most of Lewis's article was devoted to Lane, among others he examined from a series of critics of the Warren Report. The Lewis article was adapted from the Capitol Records album, "The Controversy," produced by Lawrence Schiller. "The significance of the scavengers' myriad theories is the unsettling sway they have had on public opinion," declared Lewis. "Lane likes to take credit for stirring most of the ashes. . . ."

Modestly, Lane has said that six weeks after his book was published "a poll taken by Lou Harris showed that only one out of three Americans believed and accepted the conclusions of the Warren Commission."

Lane, in his flamboyant style, wasn't content to have his book—also published abroad—make out his case. He declared that by telling it to sophisticated Europeans, his message would get back to the people at home, because, he hinted darkly, forces were at work to keep him and his championship of Oswald mute. His personalized presentations caused many of the skeptics of the Warren Report to recoil. Nevertheless, his challenges to the Commission and deliberate suggestions that he had a specialized well of intelligence brought a devastating and learned rebuttal. Lane's extracurricular credentials are peculiar. His style is that of a reformer-muckraker. He is also a director of the Bertrand Russell Peace Foundation, which backed the Russell tribunal intent on indicting the Johnson Administration for war crimes in Vietnam.

The dissection by Lane—and to a lesser extent that by Epstein, because he is so junior—came from Professor A. L. Goodhart, a Queen's Counsel (Q.C.) in Britain.

Professor Goodhart's knowledge of the law on both sides of the Atlantic has earned him immense academic prestige. In a lengthy examination of the Lane book and later the Epstein book, Professor Goodhart wastes little time in decorticating the American lawyer's legal references. Lane was refused an application by the Warren Commission to represent the dead Oswald. Hence, Lane and his supporters stressed the absolute need for the book.

Denial of counsel to the late Oswald, Lane insisted, was unprecedented and unfair, citing English law to bolster his claim. Lane, in his book, writes: "In England the rule of law is perhaps better understood and the role of counsel better appreciated. A Royal Commission engaged in hearings to determine the innocence or guilt of one deceased as a matter of course provides that counsel for the family may participate fully and without reservation, and such counsel would not be heard to disclaim his function as an advocate."

Goodhart dryly states: "This statement is both utter nonsense and completely false. There never has been such a trial and there never has been such an appointment."

A few paragraphs later, he examines the introduction for the Lane book by Oxford Professor Hugh Trevor-Roper. The university don had written: "If the Warren Commission had allowed Mr. Lane to contest the evidence there would have been no need of this book."

Goodhart, partly agreeing—that there is no need for such a book —sets out painstakingly to show why there should be a crisis of confidence in the Lane advocacy. He points out that Lane refused to provide to the Commission the name of an important and anonymous informant on which he based a large portion of his criticism. He promised to try and obtain a release from his source. It never happened.

When he appeared before the Commission months later, Chief Justice Warren, as quoted by the meticulous Professor Goodhart, told Lane: "We have every reason to doubt the truthfulness of what you have heretofore told us. . . . If you can tell us . . . who gave you that information, so that we may test their veracity, then you have performed a service to this Commission. But until you do, you have done nothing but handicap us."

In reply, Lane declared he was prepared to supply information but not his sources.

Then Goodhart notes: "This must be the first time in history that a Chief Justice of the United States has deliberately accused a lawyer of telling an untruth." In England, added the professor, "Mr. Lane would have been sent to prison if he had refused the Commission's demand for an answer."

Running through a welter of detail, given verbally and in writing by Lane, Goodhart takes up a point chewed over by Ruby, the unsavory slayer of Oswald. Mindful as are few others of the tight British strictures on libel and slander, Goodhart does not hesitate to observe that Ruby's own explanations of the mixed-up mosaic in Dallas were more logical and succinct than Lane's.

"Ruby," writes the professor, "seemed to have been a better lawyer than Lane."

Epstein's thesis, although differing from Lane's, is pitilessly destroyed by Professor Goodhart. The premise Epstein holds out, that the Warren Commission sought to protect the national interest and save the nation a shock, is invalid. Goodhart writes that "this is psychology run mad."

The introduction to the Epstein book, written by the normally astute Washington correspondent for *The New Yorker* Richard H. Rovere, draws Goodhart's scorn, too. Rovere declared that most of the published attacks on the Warren Report were blithely errant or cavalier. "There seems to be no reason why the present books [i.e., Lane's and Epstein's] should not be included in the same category," concludes Goodhart. His comments, made in a lengthy review for London's Sunday *Telegraph,* hardly got the sensational treatment accorded the books he analyzed.

The new Kennedy-family-authorized book obviously has special claims all its own. Busy Bill Manchester, a former newspaperman with an attenuated opinion for his inherent talents, has even called the Warren Report a limited work.

"The Commission," he has said, "concentrated on identification of the assassin and the question of conspiracy. It met its mandate superbly. But it did not answer all the questions. Actually, Oswald is a minor figure in the story."

That point is highly debatable. Not only have books and supposed "inside" stories spilled from the presses, but television has dispatched teams to track down the assassin theories. One of the latest, and most exhaustive in detail, was a four-part presentation by CBS. It sought "convincing evidence of a conspiracy." None was found.

"Lee Harvey Oswald, alone, and for reasons all his own, shot and killed President Kennedy," was the CBS conclusion.

Investigative reports like the one by CBS won't terminate other inquiries like that launched by New Orleans District Attorney Jim Garrison. His is wound up like a post-Manchester coil of conspiracy, ready to spring on a public, confused, horrified, but fascinated.

Long before publication Manchester predicted his book would cause a major sensation. It did, having maximum exposure in world-serialization rights, sold at fancy figures with all the attendant publicity. The reading world, which for generations to come will be unable to genuinely satisfy its curiosity about the assassination of the President, got a transfusion of perplexity and expanded interest from Manchester.

He covered a wider context of events than other authors could manage with their own ideas and inquests. After all, nobody before or since has had authorized access to inside interviews. Anyway, Manchester, now one of our newer experts by fiat of the Kennedy family authorization, evidently agrees with the Warren Commission that Oswald was the true assassin. The conspiratorial aspects of the black episode are, however, given additional currency by specialist Manchester. Plenty of cloak-and-dagger, homegrown and foreign, are interwoven in this book. About all these exposés and "real stories," intelligence in the end may necessarily stem from a combination of common sense, logic, and healthy skepticism. We have been given the shadows of particular prejudice, not the substance of the truth. The expert has adroitly managed the trend.

Chapter 7

THE TRUST-BUSTING EXPERTS:
PART ONE

🙴

IN mid-February, 1945, a team of experts—from the Economic Warfare Section of the Department of Justice and the Foreign Funds Control Division of the Treasury Department—was sent to Western Europe and Germany to find and examine records and interrogate German industrialists, "the masterminds who had laid their plans for turning military defeat into economic victory." The general purpose of this task force of investigators was to unmask, by means of documentary and testimonial evidence, the German big businessman, the Ruhr captain of industry as the *spiritus rector,* promoter, and helpmate to aggressive militarism.

There was also the intention—a product of unavoidable necessity —to prove complicity between German cartelists and foreign businessmen, principally British and American industrialists, and specifically, the existence of large vested American and British interests in the restoration and recovery of Germany. The experts of the Treasury and Justice Departments pointed out, about a billion and a half dollars was loaned to Germany by private American investors between 1924 and 1929.

They contended that two American investment banking houses were chiefly concerned with this continuing transaction: Dillon, Read and Company, and the J. Henry Schroder Banking Corporation, both of New York. The latter, in its German dealings, and particularly with the General Aniline firm (a part of the German supercartel I. G. Farben), was represented in America by the law firm of Sullivan and Cromwell. Allen W. Dulles, chief of the European Mission of the Office of Strategic Services, was a director of the Schroder Bank until 1944, while V. Lada-Mocarski, United States consul in Switzerland during the war, was vice president of the Schroder Bank.

A senior partner of Sullivan and Cromwell, was Allen Dulles's brother, John Foster. Dillon, Read and Company, which had floated the German United Steel Works bonds in the United States in the twenties, produced Clarence Dillon, James V. Forrestal, and General William H. Draper, Jr., (who became the head of the Economics Division of America's military government in Germany). This was the nucleus of the "permanent foreign policy establishment," "the New York foreign policy syndicate," which coupled the divine right of wealth with the divine right of foreign policy making, a communion that included Henry L. Stimson. Even assuming that the facts concerning these changes are true, which we do not know, the conclusions drawn by these experts don't seem to us to necessarily follow.

One of the first ports of call of the Treasury Department's *T* Force was the "bank of the cartel kings," the Bankhaus J. H. Stein, of Cologne, whose director general was Baron Kurt von Schröder, a scion of the Hamburg banking family. A cousin of Kurt's, Baron Bruno von Schröder, had moved before 1900 to London, where he later became the director of the banking firms J. Henry Schroder and Company of London and the J. Henry Schroder Banking Corporation of New York, founded by an earlier emigrant in the von Schröder family, who had anglicized his name.

While there was no community of ownership between the Stein bank in Cologne and the Schroder banks in London and New York, the two groups did act as correspondents for one another and so maintained a community of interests. Since the Schröders who went to England became British subjects, the banks in London and New York were not closed down as German firms during the First World War. By the Second World War, the British-American group had become a prestigious house in its own right. The J. H. Stein bank of Cologne was completely destroyed by Allied bombs, but in the villa of Baron Kurt von Schröder in Bonn the Treasury investigators found the files documenting the contributions of "well-known directors of the biggest German industrial firms" to a special account (S-Konto) set up for the personal use of Heinrich Himmler, and from which the Reichsführer SS made frequent and regular withdrawals.

The *T* Force early noted the special concern of the "international brotherhood," that is the representatives of American and British big business, to protect their own kind in Germany. While touching base in the finance division of General Wickersham's headquarters at Bushy Park in England en route to Germany, *T* Force officers encountered Captain Norbert A. Bogdan, in civilian life vice president of the P. Henry Schroder Banking Corporation of New York. The following day the investigators discovered that two members of Captain Bogdan's staff had requested travel orders to Cologne to investigate the Stein bank. This was before Cologne had fallen and so amounted to a request to join the *T* Force traveling just behind the combat units. The request was denied.

This was only one of innumerable examples of the conservative conspiracy already operative in the field, attempting to foil the investigations of the *T* Force by anticipating the evidence. Indeed, as James Stewart Martin, one of the chroniclers of the Treasury's campaign, described it, it was not long before the investigators had to show cause why they should be "permitted to prowl about" among the business papers of reputable German concerns. By 1947, investigations the Germans considered troublesome would appear "doubly objectionable" to "American businessmen acting as military government officials in Bizonia" (as the economic fusion of the American and British zones was called).

In the end the investigators were caught between business-men representing private interests and others of the same persuasion holding official positions in military government, "where they had the power to change the orders under which we operated."

For a brief period in 1945 matters were not so well under control. Even so, wrote Martin, "we found a number of members of the international brotherhood, commissioned as colonels and brigadier generals in the army, moving about rather freely in the field on matters of their own concern; but by the same token it was also possible for representatives of the government to get around freely as all did in the Standard Oil case."

This was a *leitmotiv* of the reports filed by the *T* Force. There were many arrangements between particular American companies and particular German companies which were the basis of "the many conspiracies between German business leaders and their counterparts in the United States and Great Britain to help in keeping alive bridgeheads for future 'economic warfare.' " At the time we discovered them it would have been hard to forget the other side of the coin: that these same German organizations—I. G. Farben, Krupp, Flick, Mannesmann, Siemans & Halske, and a few dozen more—had shown their less gentlemanly and more brutal side in the slave camps and murder factories, and in the looting of occupied Europe, all by "legal" means under Nazi laws.

But the heart of the conspiracy was at the top. As Josiah E. DuBois, Jr., the chief prosecutor at the I. G. Farben trial in Nuremberg, put it: "That [Potsdam] was the program the world heard. But there was secretly circulated among the top leaders of the British and American delegations a memorandum prepared by certain top officials in the American government saying in effect that the whole approach was wrong and our real interest lay in rebuilding Germany as quickly as possible 'as a bulwark against Communism.' As early as September 1944, while American boys were still being killed by Nazi soldiers, this same group of officials had circulated a similar memorandum within the United States government, contending that as soon as the war was over we should rebuild Germany as quickly as possible. These men were later placed in charge of carrying out America's obligations under the Potsdam agreement."

For the *T* Force, the topographical location of the central source of all evil in Europe was the German Rhineland (specifically, the Ruhr Valley). Martin wrote: "We were finding that the very existence of the Rhineland Group had depended on their determination to build and maintain a concentration of heavy industry in a place where by economic and technological standards it did not belong. They had built so much steel capacity that the rest of Germany could not use it. As Hitler said, 'Germany must export or die.'

"One definition of 'Rhineland industrialists,' we decided, is that they are those who combine together to carry out a program of heavy industrial expansion, regardless of economic consequences, and then try to counteract these consequences by looking for a man on horseback."

The investigators were convinced that the excessive concentration of heavy industry at the expense of all else caused a thirst among the German people for consumer goods that the home country could not and would not satisfy from its own production. This thirst in itself constituted an additional incentive for war—for the sake of loot. Martin writes: "So this organized looting would go on through city after city and country after country. The Wehrmacht did more than just sack and loot individually, as armies have always done. They were dipping systematically into a large reservoir of consumer goods as the only way to supply needs of the German population while they continued the production of heavy goods for war."

Indeed, this was the main reason for the trust-busters jubilation over the Potsdam Agreement's provision: "At the earliest practicable date, the German economy shall be decentralized for the purpose of eliminating the present excessive concentration of economic power as exemplified in particular by cartels, syndicates, trusts and other monopolistic arrangements."

By bringing about a more balanced German economy, the Potsdam Agreement could end the consumer goods shortage "which had been an incitement to looting other countries, and make it impossible for any clique of elite guardsmen in striped pants to mobilize the German population for such a purpose." "The elite guardsmen in striped pants," the Rhine-Ruhr industrialists, were the true culprits; for, as Martin concludes, "the Nazis were only a surface phenomenon compared with the deep-seated and persistent mania of the Germans for centralizing authority and concentrating power." In September 1926 iron and steel producers of France, Germany, Belgium, and Luxembourg signed their first international agreement. The sponsors of the cartel had declared that this was the first step toward an "economic United States of Europe." For Martin, this was tantamount to government by cabal in the making.

By the same token, Morgenthau's Treasury group and the questing members of the Antitrust Division of the Department of Justice regarded themselves as the true experts, who saw clearly what the trouble was with Germany, whence it came, and whither it needs must lead. Martin concludes: "Except for its military outcome the Nazi experiment appears to have been a success in the eyes of its original sponsors. The unity of German business and finance in backing the Nazis was matched only by the precision with which the Nazi government moved in to support the aims and interests of the dominant financiers and industrialists. They, in turn, have been waging a hard postwar fight to keep the economic lines of the Nazi system intact."

This characteristically flat equation of fascist government with unbridled, uninhibited industrialists (by no means only German industrialists) dated back in the minds of the experts to the dawn of antitrust legislation in the United States and the sheerest form of antitrust fervor and big combination dread as expressed by Woodrow Wilson (to be sure, for election campaign purposes): ". . . there is a power somewhere so organized, so subtle, so watchful, so interlocked, so complete, so pervasive, that they had better not speak above their breath when they speak in condemnation of it."

The trust-busters' bugaboo, said Wilson, had in fact already triumphed: "The masters of the government of the United States are the combined capitalists and manufacturers of the United States . . . the government of the United States at present is a foster-child of the special interests." Martin bemoans the new postwar era that "has become one of 'co-operation,' amounting almost to identification, between business and government." As a consequence, "we cannot hope to end the concentration of economic power in Germany until we are able to deal with the concentration of economic power in the United States." This is the crux of the matter: "The moral of this is not that Germany is an inevitable menace, but that there are forces in our own country which can make Germany a menace."

The real danger, then, was a kind of fascist international. It was in this light that Martin and his codisciples regarded the Düsseldorf Agreement of 1939 between British and German industrial groups, which was drawn up—as the use of cartels is—to eliminate competition and arrange markets among themselves and, if necessary, to enlist the aid of their governments in the pursuit of these objectives. The antitrust legislation in the United States, writes Martin, was a particular enemy, "which stood in the way of this new form of private world government."

Here, by way of perfect contrast, is the criticism of Lucius DuBignon Clay, writing at about the same time as Martin (1950), with regard to the European Recovery Program: "It is now the economist in a government office who with sharpened pencil and an over-all trade agreement determines what goods can be sold and to whom they can be sold. Frequently the price is related neither to the production cost nor to the world market price. No longer is there incentive for the manufacturer to develop new processes to reduce expenses, to watch production costs closely so that his product may sell in the free competition of the open market. Certainly some degree of economic planning is desirable. However it can easily be carried into programming, which makes free enterprise

difficult if not impossible. That to me is the danger which we face
in the present work of the Organization for European Economic
Co-operation."

The subject of both complaints is the same: the suppression of
competition and the arrangement of markets; the standpoints from
which they are made are diametrically opposed.

When the knights of the Antitrust Division and the Treasury Department took the field to save Germany from herself and her
friends, they found themselves confronted with the Old Guard of
the international conservative conspiracy. It was a highly representative confrontation, in which the knights were not only out-
numbered (as was to be expected of an elite) but also badly
outranked.

The American military governor was the three-star and later
four-star general, Lucius DuBignon Clay. Clay was a professional
soldier, not an investment banker, but he had been Director of
Materiel and hence on the Executive Committee of the War Production Board. The War Production Board had annihilated the
Antitrust Division's transport program in the United States. At the
head of the powerful Economic Division of Clay's command was
Brigadier General William Draper, Jr., who had been a combat
officer in World War I but in civilian life was an investment banker
of the noted Dillon, Read and Company, of New York. The deputy
director of operations of the Economics Division was Frederick L.
Devereux, a retired vice president of an American Telephone and
Telegraph subsidiary. The chief of the steel section of the industry
branch of the division was Rufus Wyssore, a former president of
the Republic Steel Corporation. Moreover, the Director of Economic Affairs of British military government was Sir Percy Mills, in
civilian life a leading industrialist.

And so it went. The patent explanation for the presence of the
"international brotherhood" in such force on Clay's staff and generally was that they were all experts in their fields and hence the
best qualified men for the job of running the German economy.
Thus the confrontation in the American zone and sector of occupied Germany was a confrontation of experts of the old and new
style and persuasion.

The Treasury and Antitrust Division men, for their part, were
field grade officers or, more often, civilians with assimilated rank
and were concentrated in the Cartels Division, later (actually as

early as December 1945) subordinated to the Economics Division as the Decartelization Branch. Occupational attrition in both division and branch was high: Colonel Bernard Bernstein lasted barely three months, resigning in October, 1945; his successor, Russel Nixon, resigned two months later; Martin, as chief of the new Decartelization Branch, lasted until mid-1947; Martin's successor became General Draper's son-in-law.

To their advantage the knights had pretty much the entire corpus of official policy on Germany, specifically the modified Morgenthau plan as set down in JCS/1067, which provided for mass dismantling and deportation of German industrial plants, and prohibited the taking of any steps to rehabilitate or maintain the German economy "except to maximize agricultural production."

The support provided by the nature and content of "1067 and all that," however, was a mixed blessing. The directive also provided for "a just, firm and aloof administration which would discourage any fraternization." Nonfraternization was, of course, the *opéra bouffe* fiasco of the occupation; it was repealed abruptly in September, 1945. Indeed, it soon became axiomatic that the most effective way to sabotage 1067 was to lend it unqualified support.

But there were also draconian orders and regulations so severe that they have never been made public, such as the order coordinated between Washington and London in the summer of 1945, which stipulated that Ruhr mines were to be returned to full production within three months, and that all but 10 per cent of the full production of the Ruhr coal mines was to be shipped out of Germany to other countries in dire need. These shipments were to be denied the German population regardless of the consequences . . . "using bayonets if necessary."

Here, apparently, was a head-on collision between a directive from Washington and the pragmatic (and increasingly autonomous) policy of military government under Clay's command. Restoring the Ruhr mines to full capacity in three months was a pipe dream: it took four years. As for supplying foreign nations with 90 per cent of the Ruhr's coal production (such as it was and presumably would be in the foreseeable future), a memorandum dated October, 1945, and circulated by Dr. Don Murphy of the Economics Division in effect countermanded this portion of the order: "It is recognized that the claims of the nations importing coal are persuasive, and that, for the moment, we are operating under a directive. Nevertheless, the point must be driven home that this decision is tantamount to subsidizing the coal-importing nations from the German economy, thereby forcing us, the Americans, to subsidize the German economy."

It quickly became apparent that Ruhr coal was the key to economic stability, "the factor limiting production." It therefore had to be used, as the only means of stabilizing the economy, for the production of those exports deemed most likely to balance Germany's foreign trade.

By the spring of 1945 it also became apparent that the United States and Great Britain were pouring food into their zones of Germany, while the Soviet Union, whose zone included the agrarian area of Germany, had its troops live off the land and withdrew huge quantities of raw materials and finished products for which she steadfastly refused to render any accounting whatever.

The Anglo-Americans soon began to suspect they were making up the difference and in effect subsidizing reparations to the Soviet Union as well as supporting the Soviet occupation. There was also the mysterious episode of the printing plates for the Allied occupation marks, two sets of which the United States government had somehow seen fit to deliver to the Soviet authorities in return for their promise to render a strict accounting for the marks they put in circulation. The Soviets flooded the market with such marks, especially in Berlin, where Soviet and American troops were thrown together. In fact, Red Army Finance made up from several months to as much as two years back-pay to their combat troops in this fashion. Since this currency was valid only in transactions with Allied troops, Soviet abuse of the arrangement acted as a powerful infusion in an already flourishing black market in the American Army. The Soviets repeatedly promised to render an accounting to the Americans on their use of the plates. An accounting was finally and solemnly set in prospect for the foreign ministers' conference in Moscow in March, 1947. It was never rendered. Until military scrip was introduced in September, 1946, the Soviet occupation marks had to be redeemed by the United States Treasury—in the amount of approximately one quarter of a billion dollars.

Clay realized that the Soviet Union was mainly concerned with preserving the appearance of unity among the four occupying powers as a means of securing maximum reparations from Germany as a whole. Hence she accepted the form of unification, while carefully rejecting the content. From the first, and throughout the occupation period, the Soviet Union never relaxed her rigid hold and control of East Germany, denying all substantive access to her zone, even to the highest Allied military authorities.

It was this policy that effectively prevented the free movement of goods between East and West Germany and spelled the doom of quadrapartite control for Germany. This—the Iron Curtain—was in direct violation of the article of the Potsdam Agreement stipulating that "during the period of occupation Germany shall be treated as an economic unit." The Soviets and their supporters maintained that economic unity could not be established until reparations had been made in full. Reparations were of course provided for in the Potsdam Agreement but with no sequence stipulated and no sum totals agreed upon (the Soviets demanded the equivalent of ten billion dollars). This was the central dilemma, for if Soviet demands were to be met, it would necessitate stripping the American and British zones of the great bulk of their plant instead of building up the economy so as to take reparations out of current production. This, in turn, would have meant the destruction of the German economy at its base—which was precisely and avowedly what the Morgenthau group was after—and this at a time when famine and pestilence were always an imminent danger.

Clay's perception of this fact moved him to place an embargo on all reparations deliveries until the Soviets agreed to the economic unification of Germany. His understanding that the Russians would probably not be able to bring themselves to agree to effective unification moved him at the same time to propose the merger of the American with the British zones into "Bizonia," an economic unit that formed the nucleus of the Federal Republic.

It was Soviet insistence on separate occupation zones of authority, on any terms short of economic chaos, that dictated both their insistence in early 1948—when the necessity of a general currency reform became obvious—on having their own plates for printing new currency in Leipzig and their consequent refusal to have the new presses set up in an international sector in Berlin (to be created for the purpose and kept under quadripartite control). This refusal brought the separate currency reforms that led to the blockade of Berlin and effectuated the division of Germany. General Clay wrote: "In the preamble (of the Declaration Regarding the Defeat of Germany) the four governments assumed supreme authority in

Germany by virtue of its unconditional surrender and the absence of competent authority which resulted. . . . Thus . . . the four occupying governments eliminated the last vestige of national government in Germany [the Doenitz government] and replaced it with four commanders in chief. It was a fateful decision which can be judged fairly in its effects only by time and history."

Twenty-one years later Konrad Adenauer commented on the "fateful decision" in his memoirs: "The unconditional surrender of the German armed forces in May 1945 was interpreted by the Allies to mean a complete transfer of government authority into their hands. This interpretation was wrong from the point of view of international law. By it the Allies in practice assumed a task which it was impossible for them to fulfill. . . . Their attempt to govern this large disorganized country from outside, often guided by extraneous political and economic criteria of their own, was bound to fail. It brought about a rapid economic, physical, and psychological disintegration of the Germans which might have been avoided."

In theory it is possible for the commandants of four major sovereign powers to agree on an occupation policy for a conquered country. In practice, in the case of Germany, it was not. "The ability of the Control Council to reach such decisions (the development of agreed recommendations in December 1946 for the Council of Foreign Ministers) had deteriorated so much that it was almost impossible to agree in the face of our instructions to the submission of a report summarizing largely our disagreements." The members of the Control Council could not even agree to disagree.

When Harry Truman refused to allow Morgenthau (whose plan he did not hold in high esteem) to accompany him to the Potsdam Conference, Morgenthau felt constrained to submit his resignation. It was readily accepted. Nevertheless, Morgenthau continued to advocate his plan, and a "hard policy" toward Germany in general, by taking public potshots at the conduct of American and British military governments. In a press conference on October 6, 1945, Morgenthau aired his conviction that "the inability of the Anglo-American occupation forces to carry out the resolutions of the Potsdam Conference with regard to the liquidation of German heavy industry has had an unfavorable effect on the working sessions of the foreign ministers' conference in London."

He added that the Soviet Union "had reason to be disturbed" over the way in which relations of the United States and Britain to Germany were taking shape. Morgenthau also emphasized again: "Lasting peace in the whole world can be achieved only by way of dismantling German industry." He directed this warning to "certain representatives of big business and representatives of American Military Government, who advocate the creation of an industrially powerful Germany as a support against Communism. I think," Morgenthau concluded, "that certain industrialists—military men as well as civilians—who had financial interests in prewar Germany, are still concerned to protect those interests and are planning to make agreements with postwar Germany."

In a statement in early May, 1946, Morgenthau announced his concern over the "unclear" goals of Secretary of State James Byrnes. He explained: "Ever since the Quebec Conference in 1944 he had nurtured the suspicion that influential American and English circles were desirous of sabotaging the true goal which later found its expression in the Berlin Accords (the Potsdam Agreement). To date we have still not prepared the final list of plant and equipment which must be transported out of Germany for reparations. I can therefore understand why the Soviet Union is so energetically protesting against such violations of the Berlin Agreement."

Inevitably, these and like statements by Morgenthau were picked up by Tass and featured as front-page, headline news to bolster the Soviet position in the continuing dispute within the Allied Control Council. Thus on April 2, 1946, the East Berlin *Berliner Zeitung* front-paged Morgenthau's protest against the appointment of Lewis Douglas as director of the World Bank: "A selection of this sort," declared Morgenthau, "would nullify the efforts of the Roosevelt administration to give the American people the power to control financial problems which concern the United States."

In the late forties Morgenthau was still a public figure of considerable interest, and his comments continued to attract attention in the West as well as in the East, particularly in publications left if not far left of center. In October of 1947, the West Berlin *Telegraf* brought out a summary of a Morgenthau magazine article in which he had charged that the Truman Administration foiled the original plans for the reconstruction of Great Britain through its sudden termination of Lend-Lease in August, 1945. According to Morgenthau, who had been the chairman of the Lend-Lease Committee, the committee had determined that Great Britain was to receive—in the first year after the end of the war—an American loan in the amount of five and one half billion dollars.

A *leitmotiv* of Morgenthau's book, *Germany Is Our Problem,* is the enduring, unbreakable nature of Nazi hard-core resistance:

> Millions of Germans have been raised as fanatic Nazis. Most of the men and women who are and will become parents have been pretty thoroughly debased and brutalized by Nazi education. The potential fathers of Germany, the returning soldiers, have participated in atrocities, have helped to loot foreign people and will remember with nostalgia the days of their supremacy.

It is this finding that serves as a basis for the contention that a postwar Nazi underground is inevitable:

> It would be unthinkable that these self-same fanatics who must have already recognized the inevitability of defeat *this time* have not been making intensive and extensive preparations to maintain a hard core and nucleus of organizational activity to facilitate their resurgence next time. With all the resources of a rich and powerful state at their disposal, and with their previous experience, it will be a comparatively simple matter for them to establish an underground apparatus both at home and abroad in order to function as effectively as possible in the disturbed period which lies ahead for Germany.

This was written in August of 1944 as an early draft of the Morgenthau book. The wartime popularity of this thesis engendered a genre of journalism and political analysis that was carried over into the postwar period. An article entitled "But the Hitler Legend Isn't Dead!" by Stefan Heym in the January 20, 1946, Sunday *New York Times Magazine* is an essay on the Nazi underground. Heym, who is described in a subhead as "a former officer of the Psychological Warfare Detachment of the United States Army," wrote:

> The Allies thought that a crushing military defeat in accordance with the doctrine of unconditional surrender would knock the doctrine of Hitlerism out of the Germans. But we forgot that any experience can terminate in a variety of reactions—and not necessarily the right one. . . .
>
> Once the Hitler period becomes "the good old times" to the majority of Germans, they will make an effort to achieve their

previous national status and power. Germans who already think along these lines know that open action or large-scale sabotage will not get them very far. And because the Germans are realists, there is no widespread underground movement as there was in France or Poland or Yugoslavia. Those classic underground movements were backed by England, the United States and the Soviet Union, which served as bases of operations and propaganda. Nevertheless, there exists, without a national government and probably without a large apparatus, something very similar to an underground.

In the practice of daily life this movement expresses itself in elusive but annoying ways. The same Germans who had so little sympathy for the minorities persecuted by the Nazis, are sorry for the poor Nazis if and when they are finally removed from administrative office or are put behind bars on a high caloric diet. In fact, many a removed Nazi official finds a comfortable job in what remains of industry and trade; and it is in German homes that the Nazi leaders still not rounded up are hiding.

Another phenomenon which makes one suspect that there is planning behind the German attitude is the wave of rumors which never cease. In general these rumors are patterned in such a way that it is most difficult to disprove them. In the American area rumors are constantly springing up that the rations are better in the Russian Zone. In the Russian Zone, meanwhile, identical rumors are spread about the American area. Often rumors penetrate into our own forces.

The most frequent rumors deal with a possible clash between the Western Allies and the Soviet Union. Any time we move troops East or North, one can be sure to get this news hot from the local Germans plus the information that the outbreak of war can be expected any day—that pitched battles have already taken place in the vicinity of any town which strikes the fancy of the German spreading the tale.

Unfortunately these rumors appear to the German mind to be substantiated by reports in the American press and radio—both eagerly devoured by the Germans. A glint of hope comes into the eye of many a German when he learns of a difficulty between the Allies and he is very conscious of the fact that in many parts of the globe we have not been able to settle post-war problems in a reasonable manner.

Benighted soul, he hopes that if ever there should be such a conflict between the Allies, one or both of the parties to the struggle would call on the Germans to furnish mercenary troops, that Germany once more would be armed and equipped for war and that in the course of events it would again emerge as a major power ready and able to suppress other people, to take revenge and to reap the spoils of war.

It is not too late to remedy the situation. Not yet have all the Germans been reconverted to Hitlerism. We still have the support of quite a few of them although their number is dwindling.

A solution can be found together with our Allies and within the framework of the settlement of all post-war problems. . . . We Americans must adopt and act on long-range educational, political and economic policies.

Chapter 8

THE TRUST-BUSTING EXPERTS:
PART TWO

THE most sophisticated exposé of German hard-core resistance and the Nazi underground is made by James Stewart Martin in his autobiographical account *All Honorable Men*. The United States, Martin points out, took no action during the war to stop American participation in the Bank for International Settlements at Basel, Switzerland.

This was a private bank set up by Hjalmar Schacht—or so Martin tells us—when he was president of the Reichsbank, in connection with the Dawes and Young plans, in order to facilitate foreign exchange transactions among the countries that were to receive reparations from Germany. When reparations were abandoned, the bank acted as a clearing house for foreign investments in Germany. The president of the bank during World War II was an American, Thomas H. McKittrick, although the Germans continued to hold the controlling interest.

One of the resolutions adopted by the International Monetary Conference at Bretton Woods in July, 1944, barred from the International Monetary Fund and the International Bank for Reconstruction and Development any nation that had not broken all relations with the Bank for International Settlements. Despite this ban, the Bank for International Settlements remained in business. As its president, McKittrick, said shortly before D-Day: "We keep the machine ticking because when the armistice comes, the formerly hostile powers will need an efficient instrument such as the B.I.S."

In 1948 the BIS became an agency for clearing foreign exchange for countries participating in the European Recovery Program. McKittrick, who had meanwhile advanced to a vice presidency of the Chase National Bank, became a financial adviser to W. Averell

Harriman, roving ambassador for the Economic Cooperation Administration.

Martin charges that the Bank for International Settlements arranged to receive from the Nazis, during and after the war, large quantities of gold looted from occupied Europe. No accounting has ever been made of these transactions (Switzerland has a bank secrecy law) Martin sums it up: "What we do know definitely is that over four hundred million dollars in German assets, spirited out of Germany before the end of the war, never have been traced. These funds are now being used somewhere in the world by ex-Nazi Germans and their friends. They can finance propaganda and German national 'recovery' programs at will. . . . No one knows whether any of the 'spontaneous' sympathy in the United States for a resurgent Germany is the product of a well-paid public relations program." Again, even assuming that Martin's charges are based on facts, which we do not know and (as Martin himself suggests) cannot know given the Swiss bank secrecy law—the implication that the bank did not scruple to help Nazis is patently wayward. The Bank for International Settlements, in fact, was created in Baden-Baden, Germany, in 1929, not by Hjalmar Schacht but by a committee made up of the central bank representatives of seven nations and chaired by an American, Jackson E. Reynolds. The original purpose of the bank was to handle reparation transactions in connection with the Young Plan. Germany never controlled the bank. On the contrary, Germany was the debtor nation for the servicing of whose debts (reparations) the bank was founded. In 1948 the bank became the agent of the Organization for European Economic Cooperation (OEEC) in connection with the European Recovery Program.

For Clay and his command the military government of Germany was a battle on two fronts—a confrontation within a confrontation. Within the wider context of the East-West struggle—particularly as the machinery of quadrapartite control gradually broke down—there was the ceaseless, bitter struggle within his own government and within his own command. Clay set himself quietly but firmly against his decartelization branch and against the "public" policy of Washington, many aspects of which he could neither in conscience nor in character take seriously, except to contravene. Regarding JCS/1067 he wrote: "We were shocked—not at its punitive provisions— but at its failure to grasp the realities of the financial and economic conditions which confronted us." The realities were staggering.

For Germany the Second World War was a catastrophe without precedent or parallel. It was the greatest bloodletting in the nation's history. The losses in dead and missing in the Wehrmacht alone amounted to three and a half million. Another six million German soldiers were captured or abducted. Half a million German civilians were killed and another three million died in flight or are still missing (railway stations, airports, post offices, and other public buildings display long lists of photographs and personalia of those who were lost during and immediately after the war and are still missing). In sum, thirteen million Germans were either killed during the war or are still missing twenty-one years after its close. Some twelve million Germans lost their homes and property as a result of the war. An additional two million left their homes and property in areas overrun and occupied by the Red army for the comparative security and freedom of West Germany.

The administrative structure of the state was in ruins. The all-powerful, efficiently organized police force was found to be non-existent. It had simply disintegrated. In the beginning there were upwards of six million displaced persons—the majority of them slave laborers brought to Germany by the Nazis—some of whom roamed the country in bands, robbing and pillaging. Here was by far the most important meaning of the doctrine of unconditional surrender: it was coterminous with total collapse.

In this regard the performance of the economy of the American Zone from August 1, 1945, to June 30, 1946—as it were, the first fiscal year of the occupation—is instructive. During the period exports amounted to $7,277,000, while imports totaled $242,285,000. In short, imports exceeded exports by more than 3,000 per cent. Of the imports, well over $200,000,000 went for food; of the exports, only slightly more than 10 per cent represented fabricated and semifabricated products of industry. One of the principal reasons for this disastrous showing was the absence of natural resources and raw material stocks in the American zone.

As the American military government's annual report stated: "Thus the newly erected zonal boundaries of segmented Germany have been one of the major factors in the almost complete stagnation of internal trade." Accordingly, after repeated admonitions, in the spring of 1946 Clay placed an embargo on all reparations deliveries until the Soviets agreed to the economic unification of Germany. When, despite this, as in July, 1946, a team of investigators from Washington arrived in Berlin "to find out whether the dismantling of certain German war plants for delivery to European countries was proceeding on schedule," Clay simply refused to accept their credentials. Further, Clay questioned whether Ambassador Edwin Pauley, who was in charge of the investigatory mission, had any authority to make the investigation. When Pauley thereupon remonstrated with Clay during the foreign ministers' conference in Paris, Clay threatened to resign. As a result, the investigation came to nothing.

"For three years," wrote Clay, "the problem of food was to color every administrative action, and to keep the German people alive and able to work was our main concern." Articles 53 and 54 of the Hague Convention Decree for Land Warfare of 1907 stipulate that occupation forces are responsible for the prevention of famine, pestilence, and internal disturbances. To prevent famine the American military government in Germany fixed the daily per capita consumption of calories in its zone and sector in Berlin at 1550. A military government declaration in December, 1945, stated that "the United States is importing wheat (into Germany) in order to achieve this calory quota. This is not sufficient to maintain the population in health over a longer period of time, but as a basis for the normal consumer it should suffice to prevent mass starvation during this winter."

American authorities who did not understand the implications of JCS/1067 actually expected that within a year or two German production of industrial goods would reach a level that enabled the Germans to import the necessary food stuffs to feed themselves. Nothing of the sort happened. On the contrary: by 1947 the situation had deteriorated to such an alarming extent that the Allies found themselves unable to satisfy the minimum needs of the population in their zones of Germany. In April, 1947, the Americans were forced to reduce the daily per capita calory quota from 1550 to 1275, and one month later to 1180.

These were the rations of starvation. There is no complete statistical record of the effect of these three years immediately following the war and the merciless winter of 1946–1947 on the German mortality rate, let alone the physical suffering and sociological disorder that were the inevitable by-products of this "time of troubles." But the deaths in the prime of life of children and adults who were felled by some common disease and whose resistance had been weakened by prolonged undernourishment were the order of the day.

In the first volume of his memoirs Konrad Adenauer recalls that the worst blow in the food situation fell in the spring of 1946, when the fat ration (400 grams per person per four-week period) was cut in half. This led to an enormous increase in tuberculosis and hunger edema. By November, 1946, health authorities estimated the number of edema cases at several hundred thousand. At the same time forty-six thousand cases of open and infectious tuberculosis were registered in the British zone. The mortality rate per thousand inhabitants had been 11.8 in 1938. By June, 1946, it had risen to 18, an increase of more than a third. But the result of this situation on the performance of the individual worker was utterly disastrous. The average production total of the individual miner per shift in 1938 was 1,547 kilograms. By March, 1946, the corresponding production figure was 711 kilograms, a decrease of more than half.

Adenauer points out that this decline was by no means exclusively due to malnutrition. It was also due to the lack of a will to work, which resulted from extremely adverse and worsening social conditions, cuts in pension claims, and the reduction of workers' rights in the factories, circumstances or measures that were either the consequence or essential elements of the occupation policy embodied in JCS/1067. In addition the systematic dismantling of factories for shipment outside Germany acted as an enormous and continuing psychological depressant not least because it threw a great many Germans out of work.

In the spring of 1947 former President Herbert Hoover submitted his field report on the food situation in Germany. The report was definitive: By its territorial losses (to Poland, the Soviet Union, and the French—the Saar), said Hoover, Germany had lost 25 per cent of its food production, 30 per cent of its coal production, and 25 per cent of its consumer goods production, as compared with 1936. Meanwhile the population of Germany had increased from sixty-eight million in 1936 to a projected seventy-one million in 1949. The notion of agrarianizing Germany, Hoover reported, was illusory: "such a step would require twenty-five million Germans to be either exterminated or resettled."

For the Treasury and Economic Warfare alumni there could be
no definitive answer in favor of the private interests and free
enterprise of the German *status quo ante*. But the members of the
Decartelization Branch were puzzled by Clay's conduct. He gave
solemn expression to the well-known deconcentration stipulations
of American policy and then just as solemnly circumvented them.
Delbert Clark, *The New York Times* correspondent in Berlin, whose
daily reportage on military government lent strong support to the
Decartelization Branch, attributed to Clay the quality of "frank
guile" in his condemnatory book on the occupation, which had the
portentous title *Again the Goose Step*.

Martin, the Decartelization Branch chief, scored Clay for rein-
troducing the old leaders of the combines into the management of
the economic revival and insisted that a "complete overhaul" of the
still existing "German ecopolitical forces" had been and should still
be the first and foremost task of military government. "Will American public policy recognize its public aims?" he asked. "Or will it go
back to serving the interests of a limited group under the aegis of
temporary expedients like saving the taxpayers' money or protecting American private interests abroad?"

In fact, the policy itself was in question. The split personality
of military government was merely the prolongation of the split
that began at the heart of American government. American policy
on Germany, having always been ambivalent in effect, had now
become so officially. In November, 1946, the Republican party had
won a congressional majority, a fact which necessitated a bipartisan
foreign policy—in order to avoid having the acts of a Democratic
administration repudiated by a Republican Congress. In Germany's
case this meant the inclusion of widely disparate if not contradictory points of view in policy formulations.

Clay paid frequent tribute to the sheer unfeasibility of the
occupation within the terms the Allies had set themselves and
with the means at their disposal. He wrote: "By the end of 1945
there were in our zone alone more than 100,000 Nazis, classified
as dangerous under our definitions, in internment camps under
guard. There was no law to govern their trials and it was against
our tradition to hold them indefinitely without trial. It was clear
that American tribunals could not be established, since we had been
able to secure competent personnel for the smaller Nuremberg and
Dachau trials only with great difficulty. Our Public Safety Officers

had received and examined more than 1,650,000 *Fragebogen* (questionnaires) and had refused employment to more than 300,000 persons in other than common labor. These persons had been excluded by administrative decision without benefit of trial."

Of the "Four D's" (Demilitarization, Denazification, Democratization, Deconcentration) of the Allied military occupation of Germany, the denazification program—which was implemented to a greater or lesser extent in the American, British, and French zones—was by far the most ambitious. The Soviets practiced a different form of denazification: in all but the most extreme cases, a former Nazi had merely to enter the German Communist party in order to assure himself of complete amnesty.

The American denazification program was based on a questionnaire, "an intimate autobiographical statement" consisting of 131 searching questions, immortalized by Ernst von Solomon in his best-selling novel (the first best seller in postwar Germany) *Der Fragebogen*. This "intimate autobiographical statement" (von Solomon was one of the Freikorps assassins of Walter von Rathenau, the Weimar government's foreign minister) followed the format of the military government's questionnaire, each chapter being the detailed answer to one or more questions. The filling out and submitting of the questionnaire was enforced by making the issuance of ration cards and other necessary documents dependent on compliance. These questionnaires were issued to every German adult in the American zone of Germany, a total of over thirteen million persons.

The denazification program lasted exactly four years. Over twenty-two thousand Germans were employed to examine the questionnaires. Several hundred "public prosecutors" were appointed by the military government to make their presentation before 545 tribunals. What bothered Clay and many others was that these proceedings were not trials in the conventional Western sense of the term. There was neither prosecution nor defense (the proceedings being *ex parte*). There were no public hearings and no rules of evidence governing the submission of testimony.

All those found guilty were divided into four categories: "Major Offenders" were sentenced to from two to ten years at hard labor and were subjected to property confiscation, permanent loss of civil and pension rights, residence restriction, etc.; "Offenders" received sentences of up to five years at hard labor; "Lesser Offenders" were subjected to combinations of lesser strictures; while the last and catch-all category of "Incriminated" or "Followers" were given fines and sometimes short sentences at hard labor (such as cleaning up rubble).

Clay illustrated the confusion caused by these and other such arbitrary definitions with the story of two former Berlin bank officials who had become street cleaners in the fall of 1945, "one employed within the Military Government grounds in Berlin and the other by the borough of Zehlendorf in which these grounds were located. One day they met while pursuing their street-cleaning activities and recognized each other. Their mutual question was 'What are you doing here?'

"The Military Government employee spoke up proudly: 'I was able to get work and a hot noon meal here as a street cleaner because of my clean record in never having associated with the Nazis.'

"The other replied: 'Under the law I am required to work too, so I applied to the borough office where I was told that since I had belonged to the party the only job open to me was to be a street cleaner, so here I am.' "

The statistics regarding the carrying out of the denazification program speak for themselves: only 38.6 per cent of the registered cases were screened by the time the program was discontinued in mid-1949. Of those screened, 25 per cent were found guilty and 8.66 per cent were removed and excluded from office. As the program progressed it became increasingly unpopular; its haphazard execution created the impression that only the little fellow was made to suffer the consequences.

Early in 1948 the Case subcommittee of the House Select Committee on Foreign Aid submitted a unanimous report to Congress recommending that denazification proceedings be terminated on May 8, 1948, with full amnesty for lesser offenders and followers. Clay objected strongly. In a cable to the Department of the Army he stated that "each month of trials and release leaves a constantly smaller backlog, which, however, contains increasingly the really bad actors. A general amnesty would free these bad actors and would really discredit the entire program."

This is precisely what happened. In 1947, 60 per cent of the population considered denazification "justified" but only 32 per cent were satisfied with the way the program was carried out in the

American zone. (This represented a decline from 57 per cent in March, 1946.) By 1949 only 17 per cent expressed support for the program (only 12 per cent thought that the cases before the tribunals involved "big Nazis"). In 1953 only 17 per cent of the population of the whole of West Germany considered that the denazification program had in any sense fulfilled its purposes, 23 per cent considered it wrongly executed, and 40 per cent opposed it as "harmful or undesirable."

Perhaps the most astonishing thing about this performance is the fact that the Allied "planners," while "not actually expecting public gratitude as a response to the denazification of the national leadership," were quite unprepared for anything like the determined resistance they encountered as the program floundered on.

In the end, denazification generated resentment against the Allies and sympathy for the Nazis as a group. (After all, as a result of the doctrine of unconditional surrender, the population had generally had to suffer along with the Nazis.) In a cabaret skit in 1950 a German enters a military government office and informs the Allied officer that he wishes to be denazified.

"But the denazification program was discontinued more than a year ago," expostulates the officer. "Why didn't you come before the program ended?"

"I wasn't a Nazi then," answers the German.

Worst of all, however, the denazification program was a boomerang even within the confines of its narrowest purpose: the removal and exclusion of Nazis from public office. In 1948 Bavaria reported that 40 per cent of its civil servants were former Nazi party members (three-quarters of these had been removed by denazification tribunals). The incidence in the judiciary was especially high—60 per cent of the judges and more than 75 per cent of the prosecutors had been Nazi party members. In the Bavarian schools eleven thousand of the twelve thousand teachers dismissed by reason of party membership were reinstated by 1949. In 1949 another state reported that 46.2 per cent of its judicial officers had been Nazi party members, 46.2 per cent of tax and customs officers, 53.4 per cent of primary and secondary school teachers, etc., etc.

A comparison of statistics revealed that in 1948 there were more former Nazi party members in the postal service administration of the combined British and American zones than there had been during the Nazi regime. In 1952, 35 per cent of the employees in the Foreign Office were former party members (31 per cent had served under Ribbentrop). Among senior Foreign Service officers 65 per cent were former Nazi party members.

In March of 1948 the trust-busters mounted their last major offensive in Germany. This was the war crimes trial against twenty members of the board of directors and four managers of the I. G. Farben concern on five counts, including preparing and waging aggressive war, participating in a conspiracy to wage aggressive war, using slave labor, and plundering. In more than one sense the I. G. Farben trial at Nuremberg was far more important than the Nuremberg trial for war crimes of the Nazi government and military leaders before an international tribunal. This was the classic and wholly unprecedented trial of industrialists as the arch-conspirators and prime movers of aggressive war, a trial in which the very essence of the antitrust thesis would be put to the test.

The trial was not held before an international tribunal: three of the Allies had lost interest; the four judges were American and they had let it be known that they expected the prosecution (also American) "to delineate this crime of preparing and waging an aggressive war so clearly that any industrialist in the future would know what course of conduct was legal and what was to be regarded as illegal."

In virtually every respect, I. G. Farben was made to order for the antitrust enthusiasts to sharpen their teeth. It was a cartel in the fullest sense of the word; almost alone—through research, development, and strategic expansion—it had all but made the German economy independent of raw material imports from abroad. It had, for example, reduced German rubber imports from 95 per cent of the amount used to only 7 per cent.

The prosecution contended that I. G. Farben, in order to perform this prodigious feat, had received two-thirds of the entire amount allocated to German industry under the four-year plan in eight months; that after 1939 four-fifths of the entire allocation went to Farben; that Farben had engineered this immense investment by a program of expansion so precipitous (using the threat of military invasion to realize outrageous take-over bids of foreign firms, as in Austria, Czechoslovakia, Poland, and France) that it virtually, if not literally, forced the Wehrmacht and the Nazi leadership to make good the threat.

This was the recurring theme of chronic and increasing overproduction as a result of a *perpetuum mobile* of deliberate expansion—"not separate crimes but a country to country chain of robberies . . . a chain of events in which each link was precision-made." The surpluses resultant from programmatic overproduction then forced the government to resort to radical measures, *i.e.,* military conquest, in order to acquire the necessary disposal areas for their surpluses, usually in the form of reinvestment and construction for further expansion.

Accordingly, the prosecution tried to show that I. G. Farben exploited the German war production effort as an excuse for overproduction, this time of armaments and munitions, in order to make war inevitable. Thus it was contended that the government rubber quota had been set up four years before the war by Karl Krauch, Farben's liaison officer and plenipotentiary with the Armed Forces Procurement Office, "in excess even of Reich requests . . . and was continually increased over the opposition of Army Ordinance." As the foremost munitions makers of the Reich, I. G. Farben had constructed a dynamite factory "within every fifteen square miles in Germany" so that the country resembled a gigantic munitions depot in keeping with "the giant economic plan," which "was about to ignite" as the fall of 1939 approached.

The accused, states Josiah E. DuBois, the chief prosecutor, in his book on the trial, *The Devil's Chemist,* "not only put the dynamite combine behind the government's growing lust for war, but wilfully drove the machine to the very edge of war, knowing it carried a power even greater than the government knew!"

The prosecution was so impressed with the construction of the I. G. Farben rubber factory at Auschwitz and the combine's use of slave labor during the war—especially at the Auschwitz site—they tried to show that the Farben management was directly responsible for the inhuman conditions obtaining at the Farben factory in Auschwitz in defiance of the intercession of the SS, which was in charge of the neighboring concentration camp. "The Monowitz hospital [of the Farben compound]" writes DuBois, "had only three wards with about three hundred beds. The bedsheets were dirty sources of infection. The SS urged Farben to install more and cleaner beds. But the technical committee turned down the request."

The trial of twenty-four conspirators of the I. G. Farben Cartel at Nuremberg lasted eleven months, ending on May 28, 1948—less than a month before the beginning of the Berlin blockade. The prosecution failed in its attempt to show the defendants guilty as charged in counts one and five. They were therefore acquitted of preparing or conspiring to wage an aggressive war. Ten of the defendants were found not guilty on all counts, thirteen (one was excused because of ill health) were found guilty of slave labor or plundering counts or both and given sentences ranging from one and one half to eight years, the average sentence amounting to slightly less than four and a half years.

No one was satisfied with the verdict: The trust-busters were outraged at the acquittal on the charges concerning aggressive war and at the leniency demonstrated in sentencing those found guilty; the conservatives were indignant that the trial had been held at all.

DuBois was "reliably informed" that "even before the trial started, one of the judges had expressed the view that he didn't believe it was ever intended that industrialists be brought to account for preparing and waging an aggressive war." As it was, the four American judges were fairly split down the middle on virtually all findings, with the presiding judge usually finding for the defendants.

A telling piece of evidence was produced by the defense in support of the contention that the general impression of a "threat from the East" had served as a justification for the German armament program. This was the declaration, on March 18, 1938, by Cardinal Innitzer and the Bishop of Austria, that "we are also convinced that through the National Socialist Movement, the danger of all-destroying, godless bolshevism was averted."

The fact that I. G. Farben was decentralized into five separate concerns was no great consolation, for this was the trust-busters' only major success, and it was offset by the fiasco with Krupp, a failure all the less excusable because it appeared to be the continuation of an Allied tradition of fiascoes with Krupp.

In their breakneck haste to disarm Germany after the First World War, the Allies demanded the extradition of greater amounts of German arms than there were extant in German arsenals. The result was that German "disarmament" began with a contract for Krupp to produce additional arms in order to meet treaty obligations. Krupp rushed arms deliveries to the Allies, who promptly destroyed them.

In their drive to liquidate German heavy industry (as the means of production of armament) after the Second World War, the Allies decided to dismantle Krupp, the most famous of the German industrial giants, first. Who was designated to dismantle Krupp? Krupp.

The cost of dismantling the Borbeck works alone amounted to twenty-seven million marks (the original construction cost was 120 million marks) which went to Krupp. The dismantled works, which during the war had produced Germany's largest and most effective tank, the Tiger, went to the Soviet Union as reparations. This sort of transaction was fairly typical of the early stage of the occupation. A few months of Allied Control Council experience sufficed to show that while the Western Allies were busy dismantling trusts and combines in their zones, the Soviets were busy building bigger trusts and combines in the Soviet zone—in many cases with the plant and material supplied by the Allies as a result of their dismantling activity. The game of Allied "give" and Soviet "take" reached its zenith when the American tribunal at Nuremberg invited the Soviets to Essen to participate in negotiations on the Krupp combine, after the Soviets had begun their blockade of West Berlin.

The most curious legal action brought by the Allies against a German legal person was almost certainly "the case of *The United States vs. Alfried Felix Alwyn Krupp von Bohlen und Halbach, et al.*" in which the accused, who had had little or nothing to do with the conduct of the firm at that point, was tried, found guilty, and sentenced *in loco parentis*. It was done because Alfried's father, the pipsqueak German-American martinet, Gustaf von Bohlen und Halbach, whom the Allies regarded as the real culprit, was on his deathbed.

Krupp was sentenced to twelve years' imprisonment and the forfeiture of all his property, both personal and real (*i.e.*, the firm). Krupp heard the sentence, as an American trial interpreter describes it, "as if the whole circus didn't concern him." Indeed, it scarcely did. His firm, like Alice at the trial of the Knave of Hearts, was actually growing apace during the trial. The sale of a few Krupp properties under Allied deconcentration rules supplied the firm with almost three million dollars in much needed capital. Just two and a half years later John J. McCloy, the first American commissioner for Germany, granted an amnesty to all Krupp convicts. McCloy also declared the confiscation order of Krupp's fortune null and void and "generally repugnant to American concepts of Justice."

Then came a last-gasp attempt to curb Krupp by treaty. The

Allies insisted that he sign away his right to buy new steel mills after he had sold his old ones as required by Allied deconcentration laws. Krupp finally signed a treaty but let it be known he considered it merely a scrap of paper. "We attribute to it," he said, "only a declamatory meaning, for instance for publicity in American newspapers." One would do well to pause and consider the significance of this statement. In Alice's Wonderland, this might have been said by the Gryphon about the written evidence against the Knave of Hearts.

Norbert Muhlen, author of the book *The Incredible Krupps,* relates how Colonel E. L. Douglas Fowles, the first British army "controller" of Krupp, called Krupp's directors into the general meeting room of the firm four months after the war: "He pointed to the window through which could be seen the dim outlines of ruin-plants, fallen smokestacks, and broken walls. . . 'Out there, gentlemen,' he said coolly and matter-of-factly, 'no chimney shall ever smoke again. Where once stood the cast-steel factory, there will be greenery and parks and meadows. The British Military Government has decided to put an end to Krupp forever. That's all, gentlemen.' " "Thirteen years later," comments Muhlen, "everyone then present would still recite the colonel's words on the slightest provocation—verbatim."

Nothing availed. Most of the restraints and prohibitions imposed on Krupp by the Allies turned out to be blessings in disguise for Krupp. When Krupp dismantled Krupp he was paid handsomely for doing so and bought new machines to replace the old ones. (The sacred tenet of Western democratic free enterprise—"no confiscation without compensation"—puts the confiscator in a peculiar position and renders the act of confiscation highly questionable if not nonsensical.) As often as not foreign competitors, the putative benefactors of the transaction, were stuck with Krupp's old machines.

Allied policy, especially British policy, forced Krupp to compete successfully against the Allies in their very oldest markets, such as India and South America—an interesting boomerang effect of the original pastoralization plan. Krupp became stronger than ever as did the antipathy of its management toward the Anglo-Saxons, particularly the Americans. Alfried Krupp von Bohlen und Halbach, although amnestied by the Americans, could not visit the United States unless he agreed to appear regularly before a parole officer while in the country. Convicted and sentenced by an American court, Krupp had the status of a permanent parolee. Every attempt by the Krupps—and there were several—to have this condition abrogated by the State Department proved futile.

In March of 1948 Clay issued an order which rejected a number of test cases under the decartelization Law No. 56, reinterpreted the meaning of the anticartel policy, and required a considerable reduction in the size of the Decartelization Branch. In retaliation, as it were, and on the heels of the Democratic Presidential election victory of November 1948, the Ferguson commission, made up largely of members of the Federal Trade Commission and the Antitrust Division, was sent to Germany to investigate the progress of decartelization.

The Ferguson commission found that the policy of eliminating the cartels and big combines was sound, and "this policy should have been, and should now be, energetically enforced." During its investigation of the reasons for the signal failure of the decartelization program the commission took a deposition from Alexander Sacks, a member of the Decartelization Branch. Sacks wrote: "The men charged with the highest responsibility by the Commander-in-Chief have failed to carry out the explicit orders of the July 15, 1947, Directive of the Commanding General and Military Governor in Germany [Sacks could not make out Clay's role]. The policies of the Roosevelt and Truman Administrations have been flagrantly disregarded by the very individuals who were charged with the highest responsibility for carrying them out."

For making this deposition Sacks was dismissed on a charge of "making statements attacking the integrity and good faith of the Undersecretary of the Army (General Draper's position at the time) and of key United States military government officials charged with the implementation of the decartelization program. . ." At the insistence of a former head of the Antitrust Division, Sacks was reinstated pending the completion of the Ferguson commission's report. As expected, the commission's report tended to substantiate Sacks' accusations. Nevertheless, on May 14, 1949, the day before he retired from the Army, Lucius D. Clay ordered the suspension of Sacks and a resumption of the proceedings against him. Sacks was finally cleared by a three-man review board in Berlin and again reinstated—but not in the Decartelization Branch.

Martin, chronicling these events, remarks that the Department of the Army did nothing to carry out the recommendations of the Ferguson report. The Department of the Army, like its sister services in national defense, has always been a bulwark of the conservative establishment. Moreover, the Ferguson report was compiled and submitted in the winter and spring of the blockade of Berlin. "In Germany," summed up Lucius Clay, "the conflict between a controlled economy and an economy of free enterprise cannot be avoided and it may prove to be the most difficult problem to be faced by West German government."

The point is that the issue was to be left to West German government. During the occupation the pattern had been reset—in the form of the *status quo ante,* that is, unmistakeably in favor of free enterprise. This was the main import of Clay's *Decision in Germany.*

Chapter 9

THE CONSERVATIVE COUNTERATTACK

T<small>HE</small> application of free enterprise, of course, meant introduction and acceptance of what are called conservative concepts. The ideas and the men behind them inevitably provoked a showdown.

On their side of the confrontation, the conservatives (many of whom did not know they were conservatives until the confrontation took place) were shocked to discover that the ranks of the American Army and military government in Germany had been infiltrated by Communists. During the "honeymoon" of the anti-fascist crusade, immediately after the war, foreign Communists were necessarily accepted, since a major ally was the Soviet Union.

At the outset, editorial staffs in the American zone and sector were required to have at least one Communist member. These were of course subsequently dismissed, most of them authentically, on grounds of professional incompetence. Domestic Communists were unexpected, however, if only because the Communist party of America had always been minute and insignificant politically.

But within the first year of American military government a number of employees had to be dismissed because of their Communist activity.

The danger of infiltrators in key positions of American military government was all the greater since the Communists had done their work rapidly and well in the initial stages of the occupation. This was particularly true in the labor and trade unions. Seven of the eleven members of the Ruhr Labor Board in late 1945 were Communists. Their number was gradually reduced only with the greatest difficulty and due to the outstanding ability of Irving Brown of the AFL/CIO, who happened to be on the spot as a trade union representative. As for the American Communist infiltrators, "some of these fellows," as Clay has remarked, "were commissioned."

In December 1946, Stephan Heym, author of the best-selling

novel *The Hostages,* lieutenant in the psychological Warfare Branch of the American Army, and co-founder of the military government sponsored daily newspaper *Die Neue Zeitung,* was demobilized because of his Communist affiliations and sent back to the Zone of the Interior. As Heym recounts the provenance of his *New York Times* article—"But the Hitler Legend Isn't Dead!"—on the eve of his departure Brigadier General Anthony Powell of the Psychological Warfare Branch asked Heym to convey his (Powell's) great apprehension of an "imminent Nazi takeover of American Military Government" to Powell's friend, General Julius Ochs Adler of *The New York Times.* Heym, who fully shared Powell's apprehension, saw General Adler in his *New York Times* office the day after his return. He delivered a disquisition in support of General Powell's message to the company there assembled. The company included Lester Markel, Scotty Reston, and Shepard Stone. Heym's report had such an effect that, as he recalls, it was decided then and there to assign a correspondent full time to the Nazi underground. The correspondent chosen for the assignment was Drew Middleton, who had already distinguished himself in this vein in a magazine piece titled "The Great German Alibi," published more than six months before the war ended.

It was also decided during this meeting that Heym would write a series of four articles on the Nazi underground. The first was published, as cited, the second was written and submitted but never published. Heym never wrote a third. In 1950, after publishing the war novel *The Crusaders,* Heym renounced his American citizenship and moved to East Germany in protest against American involvement in the Korean war.

In the spring of 1947 Captain George Wheeler of the Labor Branch, Economic Division, was recommended for demobilization by the Officers' Review Board because of his background of Communist affiliation. Wheeler pleaded with Clay to overrule the Review Board. He had recognized the error of his youthful ways, he said, he had been a good soldier and was proud of it. "Well," said Clay, "if that's the way you feel about it, all right." Two weeks later Wheeler returned to Clay's office with his wife and two children, saying that he had wanted Clay to meet his family and his family to meet their benefactor. He added that he had decided to resign, now that the Review Board had been overruled in his favor, and said goodbye. Not long thereafter Clay was informed by telephone from the American embassy in Prague that Wheeler had requested and received political asylum in Czechoslovakia and was teaching a course in communism at a Prague high school.

In 1948 Representative George Dondero of Michigan took Secretary of War Patterson to task for his failure to weed out "Communist sympathizers" who had infiltrated "key army posts." Among the ten sympathizers Dondero named on this occasion was Josiah E. DuBois, Jr., the chief prosecutor in the Nuremberg trial of I. G. Farben, then in progress. Dondero described DuBois as a "known left-winger from the Treasury Department who had been a close student of the Communist party line."

"Was it more than a coincidence," asked DuBois in reference to Dondero's charge, "that Dow Chemical was located in Dondero's district?" Major Heinz Norden was also on Dondero's list. Although cleared by the Loyalty Board, his contract as editor of the American licensed magazine *Heute* was not renewed.

In 1949 Delbert Clark, *The New York Times* chief of bureau for Germany and author of the book on the Nazi underground and the general resurgence of German imperialism *Again the Goose Step,* was exposed as a registered member of the Communist party of America by no less an authority than the late Kurt Schumacher, long-term concentration camp inmate and chairman of the Social Democratic party of Germany. Clark was recalled to New York forthwith, where he died a year later.

According to Clay, the Communists had two positions of strength in American occupied Germany: decartelization, over which they had total control, and labor unions, over which they came close to achieving total control. James Stewart Martin, the most noteworthy of the decartelization chiefs in Germany, is described by Clay in *Decision in Germany* as "the very liberal Wallace supporter."

General Draper considers that Martin was nothing more nor less than "unbalanced."

Martin himself recounts his impression that Attorney General Biddle considered the trust-busting bent of the Economic Warfare section to be "the product of a somewhat amusing mental aberration."

The trust-busters dread of a government takeover by a combine of mammoth corporations is by no means "the product of a somewhat amusing mental aberration."

It is an essential element of the class warfare doctrine and enshrined as such in the *Manifesto of the Communist Party* written by Karl Marx and Friedrich Engels: "Government is a commission made up of the business managers of capitalists." In the Communist credo the takeover of government by big business has long since been effected: Indeed, it is the essence of capitalism. For Lenin, who considered the United States the archcapitalist country and the home of the trust and the combine, Theodore Roosevelt's trust-busting activity was the exact opposite of what it was given out to be. It was merely a shift to secure control over government by private interests. There is a very considerable Marxist literature on the development of cartels in Germany between the wars, their takeover of the Weimar government during Brünning's chancellorship, their systematic construction of the ramp for Hitler's accession to power, and the crucial role of American capitalism in the entire process.

Indeed, according to the Communists, America served as a model for the German process. A recent study out of East Berlin quotes a passage from the speech of Carl Duisberg, chairman of the Reichs Association of German Industry in 1926, on the occasion of his founding the "State Political Union": "In the treatment of important economic questions a change must be made. We can see what must be done by looking at the example America has set. There all policy is made by a group of economists. When it is necessary to decide larger questions, this group convenes, discusses these questions thoroughly, sets guide-lines and then work proceeds accordingly. But how should we accomplish this in Germany? All these things are decided in parliament."

Communists credit American capital investment in Germany and the general "support of the most influential American firms" between the wars with the salvaging and stabilizing of German "monopoly capital."

The Brünning government program for the stabilization of the economy was apostrophized by the Communist leader, Ernst Thälmann, in a speech in the Reichstag in February, 1930, as the "internal Young Plan. . . . a general offensive of the German bourgeoisie against wages and bread, against the life and limb of the German proletariat. . ."

The fact that the trauma of a big business *Putsch* (achieved or imminent, international or local) is a Marxist-Leninist patent does not of course mean that a fervent trust-buster is necessarily a

Communist. It does mean that he is almost certain to be especially susceptible to Communist propaganda, "disinformation," and operational influence. It does mean that he qualifies preeminently as a target for Communist-mounted (specifically Soviet) disinformation and influence operations. Here some definitions are in order. The term *agent of influence* is used by the KGB to describe a highly placed foreign contact who is in a position (or gives promise of reaching such a position) to influence his country's policies to the benefit of the Soviet Union. Normally he is not an agent in a technical sense; that is, formally recruited, working for a salary, etc. However, the KGB is very flexible in this regard and judges cases on the basis of production and results rather than formalities.

Contacts with agents of influence is maintained by senior Soviet officers (usually KGB staff officers but at times officers of Soviet military intelligence or GRU) often masquerading as Foreign Office or consular or Ministry of Foreign Trade officials. In such operations every effort is made to pander to the ego of the agent of influence and to his sense of propriety. The chief criterion, however, that distinguishes the agent of influence from the "friend of the Soviet Union" (a member of the National Council of American-Soviet Friendship) is that the agent of influence is directly responsive to instructions or "suggestions" put to him by his Soviet contact. Typically, the Soviets will assist the agent of influence in the furtherance of his political and other professional ambitions.

The KGB term *dezinformatsiya* (disinformation) describes the use of false or misleading information for deceptive purpose, in a variety of ways designed to confuse and confound the enemy. As used by the KGB, the abbreviation *deza* covers the gamut from narrow, classical counterintelligence operations to broad political action programs. From the counterintelligence point of view the uses of *deza* are to build up spurious sources of information that have been fed to the opposition, to cast doubt on information that has been received from genuine sources (and to discredit the sources themselves), to confirm false information in possession of the opposition, to relieve opposition intelligence pressures against sensitive Soviet targets, and to lure them on against other targets, where the KGB is well equipped to detect and control them, etc.

On a broader, political action scale, *deza* operations include forgeries (particularly of incriminating documents), rumor campaigns, defamation. Such operations can become both massive and complex. The objectives of such operations can be widely varied, encompassing the dismissal or removal of some anti-Soviet states-man, misleading foreign governments and publics as to Soviet military strength, etc. There is a Department *D* (Dezinformatsiya) in the Foreign Intelligence Directorate of the KGB, which is responsible for keeping track of information known to be held by the opposition, for providing disinformation for various KGB operations as needed, and for planning and coordinating all disinformation operations generally.

How these operations were mounted against the American government is explained in the book *I was Stalin's Agent* by General Walter Krivitsky, a division chief of the KGB—then the OGPU—who defected in 1939 (he was assassinated the same year in his Washington apartment by Soviet agents). Here is a key passage:

> In the United States the Communist party, as such, never played any serious role and was always regarded by Moscow with supreme contempt. For all its long years of activity up to 1935, the American Communist party had almost nothing to show. Organized labour did not respond to its slogans and the mass of American people were barely aware of its existence. Even in those years, however, the party was important to us because it was more closely connected than any other Communist party with our OGPU and Intelligence Service. During the mechanization and motorization of the Red Army, we had members of the American Communist party as our agents in aircraft and automobile factories and in munition plants.
>
> In Moscow several years ago, I told the Chief of our Military Intelligence in the United States that I thought he was going too far in mobilizing such a large percentage of American party function-aries for espionage. His reply was typical:
>
> "Why not? They receive good Soviet money. They'll never make a revolution, so they might as well earn their pay."
>
> With the thousands of recruits enlisted under the banner of democracy, the Communist party OGPU espionage ring in the United States grew much larger and penetrated previously untouched territory. By carefully concealing their identity, Communists found their way into hundreds of key positions. It became possible for Moscow to influence the conduct of officials who would not knowingly approach a Comintern or OGPU agent with a ten-foot pole.
>
> More challenging, perhaps, than this success in espionage and pressure politics, is the Comintern's penetration into labor unions, publishing houses, magazines and newspapers—a manoeuvre accomplished by simply erasing the Comintern's label and stamping anti-Hitlerism in its place.

Thus it was generally within the context of the New Deal liberal syndrome and specifically against the background of what came to be the chief element of the syndrome—the gathering antifascist crusade—that the Soviet Union, working through its intelligence and espionage agencies and the Comintern, mounted and successfully completed the greatest political action operation in history. The antifascist campaign of the thirties and early and mid-forties, precisely because it debouched into the greatest and most destructive war in history, inevitably became a far greater boon to the left than the subsequent anti-Communist crusade could ever become to the right. Soviet espionage officers and their American agents—those regularly recruited, as well as "agents of influence"— were not only able to influence American policy, particularly foreign policy, to the benefit of the Soviet Union, they actually managed to achieve the status and function of co-conceptors of American wartime and immedate postwar policy.

In the case of Germany they achieved the status and function of chief conceptors of American policy. This was the most spectacular —as well as the most unsung—espionage *coup* of all time. "American policy on Germany" said a ranking American security officer, "was conceived and formulated in Derzhinsky Square in Moscow (KGB Headquarters)." This is a craftsman's exaggeration: American policy on Germany was conceived and formulated in the Kremlin; it was prepared for transmission in Derzhinsky Square.

It is true that the Soviet project could not have thrived had it not been for the kind of atmospheric predisposition to the left that was the ambiance of the New Deal (a natural enough ambiance considering the inane excesses of American capitalism during "normalcy" and Silent Calvinism). Krivitsky's point that the Communist party of America was politically impotent is well taken, but within the New Deal syndrome the CPA did receive a kind of seedy, eccentric respectability, to which it reacted by plumping slogans calculated to convey its autochthony, such as "Communism is Twentieth Century Americanism!" and "The Quiet Man from Kansas—Earl Browder."

A section chief in the Treasury Department could maintain publicly and with impunity that being a member of the Communist party was just like being a member of the Democratic or Republican party. Moreover, there was the steady development of a pro-Soviet attitude throughout the thirties, interrupted but not reversed when the Soviet Union attacked Finland. In 1937 George

Kennan, who had painstakingly put together a small reference library in the State Department on the Soviet Union, returned from a trip to discover it gone. When he made inquiries he was told that Eleanor Roosevelt had inspected the library, found it to be anti-Soviet, and said that it ought to be dispersed. Dispersed it was.

Clay has made the point that the leftist liberals could do nothing at the OMGUS level ("nobody ever tried to bring any influence to bear on me") but always took recourse to their friends in Washington, who would then attempt to bring influence to bear administratively—from the policy-making level—by directives, instructions, regulations, and the like. In dealing with Washington, Clay reckoned with the Communist infiltration of the Treasury Department and what he has called "the Economics Section of the State Department." In dealing with the State Department, Clay enjoyed the protection and cooperation of his sponsor, James F. Byrnes, who was Secretary of State until early 1947.

Clay, well aware of the existence of a subversive apparatus within the State Department, usually managed to keep his lines of communication to Byrnes clear. The existence of the apparatus was detected at least as early as the beginning of 1946 and in all probability much earlier.

Clay's special adviser for major problems, Joseph A. Panuch, had been instrumental in exposing the Hiss group and had been sacked by Acheson. In early March, 1947, Panuch, then Deputy to the Assistant Secretary for Administration in the State Department, had submitted a memorandum to his superior concerning the Alger Hiss plan for the reorganization of the Department.

"If Dr. Hiss," wrote Panuch, "should succeed in causing Dr. Appleby to be designated as the UNO Assistant Secretary General for Administration, the Hiss group will have achieved infiltration in, or control of, four critically strategic points, i.e. (a) UNO itself (Feller, Appleby), (b) the United States delegation (Stettinius and Rothwell), (c) State Department (Hiss, Ross, UONOA), and (d) Bureau of the Budget (Harold Smith, Schwarzwalder)."

In order to insure that the leftist liberals could accomplish nothing at the OMGUS level, Clay insisted that all instructions, whether emanating directly from the State Department or relayed via the War Department (the approved channel), be directed to his office. In his cable to the State Department on November 17, 1945, Clay stresses that the authorization enabling his political advisers to communicate directly with the State Department in the latter's code will result "in the frequent reporting of views of subordinates which may not be my views, and instructions based on such views may have to be reopened by me."

His meaning is clear. Clay was not satisfied with the existence of a separate communications channel between Washington and the State Department personnel in his command (in Japan MacArthur had simply ordered the State Department's separate communications channel out of existence), and he thus brought one half of the channel under his control. In *Decision in Germany* Clay cites this cable at length "because an early impression, never entirely erased, was created that Military Government was unwilling to work for the State Department." In Japan MacArthur made it perfectly clear that military government was not working for the State Department.

There was an almost amusing attempt on the part of the State Department's "economic section" to implement a major aspect of the Morgenthau plan. In attempts of the Anglo-Americans to secure treatment of Germany as an economic whole in accordance with the Potsdam Protocol, it was necessary to fix the nation's productive capacity while limiting industrial requirements so as to provide a standard of living not greater than the average of the European countries, excluding Russia and the United Kingdom.

The obvious key to any agreed level of industry for Germany was the level of steel production. In early fall, 1945, Clay's economic experts brought over the economist Dr. Calvin Hoover to assess German economic needs. Dr. Hoover arrived at a steel capacity of 7,800,000 tons annually as the minimum necessary to sustain the German economy. This figure outraged the trust-busters in Clay's command and elsewhere (the Soviets proposed 4,900,000 tons; the French 7,000,000 tons; the British 9,000,000 tons). Clay then received, to his amazement, a "suggestion" from the State Department that 3,500,000 tons would be adequate. This "suggestion," which considerably undercut the Soviets, was disregarded by Clay, although he admits that it influenced his bargaining position. The compromise figure eventually reached was 7,500,000 tons allowed capacity, but an annual production restricted to 5,800,000 tons unless increased by the Allied Control Council. Even the compromise figure "drew some rebuke from the State Department."

Clay perceived that he was in a better position than most to discern the direction and speed of developments. The ring was closing around the "economic section" of the State Department, which in any case had without luck set itself against the exigencies of the German situation. Morgenthau had resigned, and his assistant, Harry Dexter White, left the Treasury at the beginning of 1946 to accept the position of American representative on the executive board of the World Bank. He retired on grounds of poor health a year later.

In 1948 there began, with the sworn denunciation of Alger Hiss by Whitaker Chambers, a process of investigation and prosecution in the House and Senate that lasted seven years and unearthed the greatest espionage complex in American history. The findings of these investigations were compiled and summarized in a series of government papers published by the Senate's Committee on the Judiciary, under the title "Interlocking Subversion in Government Departments," an interesting counterpart, both as a term and a phenomenon, of the conspiracy of interlocking directorates in big business.

Unfortunately, this process of investigation and prosecution acquired a partisan aspect from the beginning, partly because President Truman rightly or wrongly decided that the fortunes of his administration could not bear the onus of an unprecedented government scandal in 1946 (an evaluation that tended to be borne out when the Republicans won a Congressional majority in November 1946).

Congress, specifically the House Committee on Un-American Activities, finally moved to launch the investigation only in the national election year of 1948. Quite apart from Senator McCarthy's demagogy the timing was bound to brand the investigation not only as a product of partisan prejudice but also as a singularly disreputable piece of election campaign strategy. Before he was forced, by the gravity of the charges and the weight of evidence, to establish a government board of loyalty investigation, Truman quite understandably called the Hiss case "a red herring." It was election campaign considerations that also caused the Democratic administration to conceal the fact that Harry Dexter White, two days after perjuring himself before the House Committee in August, 1946, committed suicide by jumping from a fourteenth-story window in Washington. Because of the initial partisan campaign atmosphere and the political witch hunt that characterized the McCarthy era, the nature, extent, and significance of the Communist conspiracy that flourished during the late thirties and early forties was largely obscured and has remained so.

Harry Dexter White was the most important because he was the most effective American agent of the Soviet Union. He was recruited by the KGB (then the OGPU) in the early twenties, while an undergraduate at Leland Stanford University. White was not an agent of influence, therefore, but a regularly recruited, trained Soviet agent who was groomed and managed by his Soviet case officers for his career. Specifically and technically, White was a KGB staff career agent.

When he entered the Treasury Department in 1937 he soon contrived to bring in his fellow Communists in such numbers and into such positions as to make the Treasury Department and most of its branches a Communist stronghold in American government.

According to the Senate report White's appointment book and guest lists revealed that he arranged meetings of "a number of selected, high-ranking, policy making officials from various departments of the Government." Such meetings were arranged "for the purpose of exchanging opinions and influencing policy. . . . With White as initiator and activist, such meetings could (and did) result in far-reaching changes in our government."

Others at meetings called by White were agents of influence. They were assortedly witting or plain gullible, eager to assist an ally in the war. One of those accused of being an agent of influence brought into the Treasury Department by Harry Dexter White was Nathan G. Silvermaster. He headed a section of the Board of Economic Warfare, which controlled the Economic Warfare Section set up by the Justice Department. (The latter was James Stewart Martin's parent organization.) Silvermaster was saved from possible expulsion from government in the summer of 1942 (when a report from Army Intelligence charged him with being a Communist in the early 1920's) through the intercession of White with Undersecretary of War Patterson. At that time Silvermaster made an unsworn statement denying the charge. In 1953, when under oath before the Senate Internal Security Subcommittee, Silvermaster claimed the privilege of silence provided by the fifth amendment in answer to all questions concerning his Communist espionage associations and activities.

Mr. MORRIS. Were you a member at that time of the Communist Party, at the time of your naturalization?

Mr. SILVERMASTER. I claim the privilege of refusing to answer this question under the fifth amendment.

The CHAIRMAN. At that time you had to take an oath of allegiance to this country, when you became a citizen of the United States, so how could you take refuge behind the fifth amendment?

Mr. SILVERMASTER. I refuse to answer this question.

The CHAIRMAN. You are under two oaths. You are under an oath there and you are under an oath here today. When you took that oath of allegiance to this country were you a Communist?

Mr. SILVERMASTER. I refuse to answer the question under the privilege of the fifth amendment.

The CHAIRMAN. You understand that if you are not a Communist there is no need for you to invoke the fifth amendment?

Mr. SILVERMASTER. I refuse to answer the question.

The CHAIRMAN. You understand, do you not, that if you were not a Communist at that time there is no need for you to invoke the fifth amendment? Do you understand that?

Mr. SILVERMASTER. Is this a question?

The CHAIRMAN. Yes. Do you not know that if you were a loyal American citizen at the time you took the oath, if you were not a Communist, there is no need for you to take refuge behind the fifth amendment?

Mr. SILVERMASTER. I refuse to answer the question under the privilege of the fifth amendment.

Mr. MORRIS. Mr. Silvermaster, are you presently active in a Communist espionage ring?

Mr. SILVERMASTER. I claim the privilege of refusing to answer this question under the fifth amendment.

The CHAIRMAN. Going back again, Mr. Silvermaster, to your statement, I will ask you this question. First, would you read the question, please, Mr. Reporter, that was just asked the witness?

(The record was then read by the reporter.)

The CHAIRMAN. What is your answer to that question?

Mr. SILVERMASTER. I refuse to answer it under the privilege of the fifth amendment.

The CHAIRMAN. Under oath you have just made this statement to the committee: "I am not a security risk." Now, which is correct, Mr. Silvermaster?

Mr. SILVERMASTER. I see no contradiction.

Mr. MORRIS. Where did you obtain your doctor's degree?

Mr. SILVERMASTER. At the University of California.

Mr. MORRIS. What was your doctor's thesis at that time, Mr. Silvermaster?

Mr. SILVERMASTER. I claim the privilege of refusing to answer this question.

Mr. MORRIS. You mean you won't tell us what the subject of your doctor's thesis was?

Mr. SILVERMASTER. I so claim the privilege of refusing to answer this question under the privilege.

Mr. MORRIS. Is the subject of your doctor's thesis Contribution of Economic Thought Prior to the Bolshevik Revolution? That is, Lenin's Contribution of Economic Thought Prior to the Bolshevik Revolution?

Mr. SILVERMAN. I refuse to answer this question under the privilege.

The CHAIRMAN. You refuse to answer the question whether or not that was your doctor's thesis?

Mr. SILVERMAN. I do, sir.

Silverman was never tried in connection with these charges, possibly because of the statute of limitations.

Harry Dexter White, Silvermaster's sponsor, was Assistant Secretary of the Treasury from 1941 to the end of 1945. Here is a list of the governmental bodies on which he served as representative of the Treasury Department during his tenure:

The Interdepartmental Lend-Lease Committee
The Canadian-American Joint Economic Committee
The Executive Committee on Commercial Policy
The Executive Committee and Board of Trustees of the Export-Import Bank
The Interdepartmental Committee on Inter-American Affairs
The National Resources Committee
The Price Administration Committee
The Committee on Foreign Commerce Regulations
The Interdepartmental Committee on Post-War Economic Problems
The Committee on Trade Agreements
The National Munitions Control Board
The Acheson Committee on International Relief
The Board of Economic Warfare

The Executive Committee on Economic Foreign Policy
The Liberated Areas Committee
The O.S.S. Advisory Committee
The U.S. Commercial Corporation
The Interdepartmental Committee on Planning for Co-ordinating the
    Economic Activities of U.S. Civilian Agencies in Liberated Areas

This list provides a survey of the possibilities, afforded by White's position, to influence the making (and breaking) of foreign policy in its conception, formulation, and implementation. The position of the Department of the Treasury in American government and White's position within the department were so crucial that he was afforded operative access to literally every area (major and minor) of American foreign policy.

White, who was reputedly indefatigable, made full use of his opportunities. He performed prodigies of policy making, and the catalogue of his achievements is Homeric. At the outbreak of the war White managed to have the old Trading with the Enemy Act discarded as "insufficient." He then drafted a new one, which no longer provided for a trusteeship over German property sequestered in the United States during the war but actually constituted confiscation and liquidation. It was a procedure Everett Dirksen, a leader of the Senate Investigating Committee, described fourteen years later as "fully in accordance with the destructive fanaticism directed against Germany by the Morgenthau plan, which the same author was able to draft a few years later." Dirksen also revealed that the American Bar Association, the American Chamber of Commerce, and the State Department all protested against the new legislation but were unable to prevent its passage. The stipulations of White's act are so stringent that it may well be fifty years before any legal steps can be taken to return the property to rightful owners (who in some cases were victims of Nazi persecution).

At the Bretton Woods International Monetary Fund Conference in 1944 White was the chief American delegate and dominated the proceedings (despite the presence of Lord Keynes, who after all, was representing a bankrupt Great Britain). Bretton Woods, among other things, created an international instrument for the control of currency exchange rates. Some of the constabulary features of the agreement, such as the resolution barring any nation from membership which had not broken with the Bank for International Settlements, proved to be unenforceable as well as impracticable. These were simply ignored by most, if not all, members.

These and like deviations from the plan were not White's fault. After his retirement from the bank it was expected that the conspiracy would manage to appoint his successor, just as it had managed to effect the appointment of White. Morgenthau was most upset when Clay's old friend and financial adviser Lewis Douglas was appointed.

There is something akin to poetic justice in the takeover of the Treasury Department, the nerve center of American financial and economic policy, by agents and tools of the Communist conspiracy. The Treasury Department was the ideal spot from which to carry the fight against private industry. This was especially useful against private industry in enemy countries or foreign countries occupied by the enemy during the course of a world war fought in the name of an antifascist, anti-imperialist crusade.

The great Communist specialty is the use of wars for long-term, if not lasting, political purposes—domestic as well as foreign. What better way of dealing crippling but inconspicuous blows to big business at home than by annihilating their partners abroad. This was the beauty of the approach: Every blow against the enemy without was also a blow against the enemy within. During the war the Board of Economic Warfare froze enemy assets and imposed financial blockades virtually at will: Robert Murphy recounts in his memoirs how the invasion of North Africa was hindered for months by the Board's refusal to lift the absolute embargo against Vichy France—and this despite an order handwritten and signed by the President. This is the sense of Martin's otherwise incomprehensible remark that "when we get into the discussion of postwar reconstruction plans, we run into the diplomatic fiction that sovereign nations are sovereign nations."

The expression of frustration was apropos of Martin's *T* Force having been refused access to an Amsterdam bank where they wished to ascertain whether Dutch firms were cloaking, *i.e.,* fronting for Germans. The *T* Force moved in just behind, but not *with,* the fighting troops. It was too late because after liberation sovereignty, like *rigor mortis,* had already set in. This is also the sense of Martin's remark: "We cannot hope to end the concentration of economic power in Germany until we are able to deal with the concentration of economic power in the United States."

During and immediately after the war this order of priority was reversed; for this was the ultimate object of the entire exercise and the cause for the frantic, almost neurotic, attempts to sustain the antifascist crusade at its highest moral pitch after the war was over and the enemy crushed. These attempts were perfectly complemented by the Communist party directive "to create maximum emotional opposition to German reconstruction." In this sense Martin's statement is an admission of defeat.

By the end of 1953, when the long series of Congressional investigations had been boosted to new intensity by the accession of a Republican administration and had merged with the McCarthy era, it was established that White had been responsible for the enormously costly transfer of the two plates for the printing of German occupation marks to the Soviets.

Before the series of investigations ended, Harry Dexter White had been credited with certainly the neatest technical coup of all —the engineering of runaway inflation of the Chinese yen. It was a development that contributed decisively to the economic chaos characterizing the final stages of Chiang Kai-shek's China in its war against the Communists. Even so, White's greatest feat was his role in foisting the Morgenthau plan on the Roosevelt Administration. In its way, it was deft and expert.

Chapter 10

THE CONSEQUENCES OF EXPERTISE:
BERLIN

ᵠ

WHAT came to be known as the Morgenthau plan was actually a complex of considerations and guidelines embodying the Soviet Union's postwar aims for Europe. Sumner Welles has recorded that in 1941 Stalin proposed "the detachment of the Rhineland from Prussia as an independent state or protectorate, and possibly the constitution of an independent state of Bavaria." This was the Russian plan for the partition of Germany. It is identical with the Morgenthau plan. The partitioning of Germany (to which Roosevelt secretly agreed at Teheran) obviously presupposed unconditional surrender. Indeed, the two concepts—as foreign policy measures to be imposed on a combatant enemy by a grand alliance—are mutually inclusive: "What could have been more absurd," asked a high ranking Soviet officer after the Berlin blockade was over, "than the idea of two countries with diametrically opposed political systems embarking on a joint effort to re-educate a conquered enemy country?!" Unconditional surrender—as the conceptual complement of partition—was not Roosevelt's original idea, although he was undoubtedly painstakingly led to believe it was, but Stalin's.

Similarly, Roosevelt (and his closest advisers when they were not themselves Soviet agents or agents of influence) were kept under continual suggestive bombardment with the aim that they concentrate on military considerations to the exclusion of eventual and even inevitable postwar problems. The British, who were wise in the ways of Continental wars and their aftermaths, saw the danger. They clearly did their level and devious best to persuade Roosevelt to invade "the soft underbelly" of the Continent as the best means of intercepting the Soviets in East Europe. There was simply too much going against them.

There was Roosevelt's dislike of the State Department as a foreign policy making institution and his penchant for "the great game," for making full use of his prerogatives to conduct foreign policy off the cuff and under the board. He ran "a very loose shop" as Robert Murphy, one of the President's many special representatives with a direct line to the oval office in the White House, has characterized it. He certainly ran rough-shod over, across, and between command channels. His Secretary of State was frequently and deliberately kept in the dark on major foreign policy decisions.

There was, moreover, the purely military obsession of the Joint Chiefs of Staff to end the war by "an invasion of the mainland by the shortest possible route at the earliest possible date," meaning a cross-channel invasion from the staging area of Great Britain.

Field Marshal Alanbrooke's reply to this insistence was that it would indeed finish the war quickly "but not the way we hope to finish it."

In his memoirs General Mark Clark writes that Roosevelt had expressed interest in the idea of an invasion from the Adriatic, but that he had been dissuaded by Harry Hopkins (on whom the Soviets did a superb job of bringing influence to bear—directly, as in his last mission to Moscow from which he returned as a fountain of disinformation, and indirectly, through their agents in the White House).

As Hanson Baldwin notes in his book *Great Mistakes of the War,* the Intelligence Division of the War Department submitted a memorandum forewarning of the dangers of Soviet predominance in the Balkans. Nothing availed. The main object of the wartime phase of the Morgenthau plan was to bring the Red army into the heart of Germany (*i.e.,* the heart of Europe) and secure for Russia a zone of occupation.

The Harry Dexter White papers, found in White's summer home in Concord, New Hampshire, include the working draft of the book *Germany Is Our Problem,* published under the signature of Henry Morgenthau, Jr. The draft was initialed by J.E.D.— assumed by the investigating subcommittee to be Josiah E. DuBois, the chief prosecutor at the I. G. Farben trial in Nürnberg and the author of the book *The Devil's Chemists, 24 Conspirators of the International Farben Cartel Who Manufacture Wars* whose preface carries the initials "J.E.D."—I.S.F.—assumed to be Irving S. Friedman of the Treasury Department—and others.

Immediately preceding J.E.D.'s draft in these papers is a "Table of Contents" which, as the subcommittee's report notes, "is primarily an outline of the substantive points in the book." In fact, the "Table of Contents" is a KGB disinformation brief. Some of the chapter headings as given in the "Table of Contents," are highly significant, such as "III The Problem Is How to Deal with Germany, Not How to Make an Enemy of Russia" (in the published version the title of the third chapter is "A Strong Europe Is Better than a Strong Germany"), "X Deindustrialization of Germany Is Only True Solution" (in the final, published version Chapter Ten reads "Germany and Democracy"), and "XV Withdrawal of Troops" (in the published version "Bring the Men Home"). The bald "Conclusion" of the draft becomes "Partners in Peace" in the published version.

According to the White papers five or more men worked on the various drafts of *Germany Is Our Problem*. The most prominent of these was Josiah E. DuBois (or "I.G. Joe" as Ambassador Edwin Pauley called him because of his obsession with I. G. Farben), a legal adviser in the Treasury Department, chief counsel of the Treasury's Foreign Fund Control, etc. He was also, according to the appointment records, one of the most frequent participants in the interdepartmental conferences and meetings conducted by White.

In a letter written by Henry A. Wallace in July, 1945, and cited by the Senate subcommittee, the then Secretary of Commerce thanks White for his "helpfulness and interest in the early stages of the preparation of my forthcoming book, *Sixty Million Jobs*." Wallace also asks that White convey his "very sincere appreciation" to DuBois, Silvermaster, Coe, Kaplan, Friedman, and others "for their wholehearted interest, suggestions, and contributions."

"It would seem," comments the subcommittee report, "that this group wrote the document to appear under Mr. Wallace's name." Much the same group wrote the document to appear under Mr. Morgenthau's name.

Not the least of the policy–making achievements attributable to Harry Dexter White was the Italian Peace Treaty. It granted $360,-000,000 in reparations to the Soviet Union, Yugoslavia, Greece, Ethiopia, and Albania (all of it billed to the American taxpayers since the war had left Italy destitute). The treaty also delivered almost half the Italian merchant marine and more than half of the Italian navy to the Soviet Union (three of Italy's five battle-ships, five of her nine cruisers, seven of eleven destroyers, six of sixteen torpedo boats, all eight of her submarines, etc.).

White's great achievement, of course, was his complete psycho-logical subjugation of Henry Morgenthau, Jr. Observers who knew both men have reported that White held Morgenthau "in a kind of thrall." Morgenthau was indeed the unwitting agent of influence par excellence (as was Henry Wallace), the consummate tool. He was at once vain—and hence susceptible to flattery—and syco-phantic. Above all he was one of the oldest cronies and closest intimates of the fountainhead of foreign policy, the President of the United States. Morgenthau wielded enormous influence with Franklin Roosevelt and with Eleanor Roosevelt as well. Moreover, in the last year of his life, which was the crucial year for American postwar policy, the President was moribund. His friends, aides, and immediate subordinates were aware of this. Some at least, includ-ing Edward Stettinius, resolved to plead with him not to seek a fourth term, but none could bring himself to do so in the event. Others, the White group in particular, exploited the President's incapacity to the maximum.

Thus it was that hardly a month after the Quebec conference the President could not even remember having initialed the Mor-genthau plan and could not imagine what had moved him to do so. It was on this occasion that he quipped wanly to Stimson that "Henry [Morgenthau] has pulled a boner." Morgenthau had indeed, but White hadn't. Even more important than prompting the initialing of such a document was the molding and reinforcing of opinions and attitudes of the President and his key advisers. Here the greatest achievement was moving and holding the President to the resolve not to consider postwar problems until after the war was over. This attitude, through careful cultivation by the White group, became almost a fetish with Roosevelt. It dovetailed with his belief that the most important policy was to persuade the Rus-sians to trust Americans.

This was especially true of negotiations at all levels on the occu-pation zoning of Germany and sectoring of Berlin. It led to an incredible episode. George Kennan, one of the original members of the European Advisory Commission set up at the Teheran con-ference, to zone Germany for the occupation, came upon a *National Geographic* map of Germany. It had been marked by the President showing half of Berlin included in the northern occupation zone, which was designated for the United States.

Intrigued, Kennan returned to Washington from London to find out the status of the negotiations on the subject. "Why don't we do what this map indicates—take the Northern zone with all the industry in it, and see what we can do?" he asked James Dunn, Assistant Secretary of State.

Dunn replied that only the President could decide such matters.

Kennan went to the President, who also put him off. "May I take it," asked Kennan finally, "that the United States does not have a position on postwar zoning?"

The President answered, "Yes!"

Shortly before Kennan was to return to the Advisory Commission in London he was transferred to another post.

The most preposterous and fateful aspect of the zoning negotiations concerned the problem of Allied access to Berlin. When the ECA agreed upon a draft of the occupation zones in Germany in September, 1944, a number of State Department officials and military officers noticed that no access routes had been provided for Berlin, although the German capital had been agreed upon as the administrative center for the occupying powers.

Robert Murphy recounts in his memoirs how he pressed Ambassador John Winant, who was the chief of the American delegation in the EAC to insist on the definition of the right of access from the American and British zones to Berlin. Winant exploded: "You have no right to come along at this late date and make such a proposal just after we have agreed upon a draft!"

Winant then related that the agreement had been achieved "only because he had established a close personal relationship with Ambassador Gusev, after months of patient effort, and had gained the Soviet envoy's confidence."

In other words, Ambassador Winant, an incredibly vain eccentric, whom Kennan later described as the most hopeless man he'd ever met, was thoroughly "had" by his Soviet counterpart. It is true that in no other profession do ends and means become so quickly and easily confused as in liaison work—but this is the nature of the game.

The object of the exercise is to establish rapport in order to secure concessions—not to make concessions in order to establish rapport.

The various Allied officials responsible, through negligence, pusilanimity, and self-indulgence, for the scandal of the access routes that never were can thank their stars they were the servants of a democracy and not a dictatorship, where their lives would have been forfeit for the commission of such a colossal gaffe. But then, of course, servants of a dictatorship realize this and conduct themselves accordingly. In a democracy it is the country and its people that pay for such nonsenses.

If the Western Allies had taken the trouble to insist on agreed access routes to Berlin (as they might easily have done, since they traded well over one third of the territory that became the Soviet zone but was originally held by American troops for the privilege of entrapment in Berlin), the history of Germany and Europe would have been very considerably different. For one thing, there could not have been a Soviet blockade of Berlin.

As a gloss for the neglect to secure access routes to Berlin, the Allies used the formula that their very presence in Berlin carried with it the right of access to Berlin. If this is so, then the Soviet blockade of Berlin was an act of war.

Had Clay attempted to force his way through to Berlin with a tank column, as he originally intended to do, the Soviets would almost certainly have backed down. In 1948 the United States enjoyed monopoly of the atomic bomb. But Clay was warned by his government that if the Soviets resisted, he would have to withdraw because the necessary reinforcements could not be brought up in time.

In this sense, another major aspect—and perhaps the most disastrous one—of the Morgenthau plan had virtually found fulfillment. Within hardly more than a year the point system of discharge ("the only fair way of doing it," according to General Draper) had melted down and transformed a superb fighting machine of three and a half million men, most of them veterans—certainly the best equipped and probably the most effective fighting force the world had ever seen—into a conglomeration of raw recruits.

"By the end of 1945," said Clay, "there were only three hundred thousand American soldiers left in Europe. By the end of 1946 there were only one hundred and fifty thousand high school boys in uniform."

The whole disastrous development came under the heading of "Henry Morgenthau's" fifteenth chapter. The striking incongruity between title and final chapter of the White group's book (*Germany Is Our Problem,* Chapter Fifteen, "Bring the Men Home") reveals the true import of the operation. The men were brought home.

"We should not forget the losses after World War Two as a result of the demobilization of Allied forces," said Dean Rusk at the final NATO meeting in France in December, 1966. "We've been picking up the pieces ever since."

Clay makes the point about the Berlin blockade that the Russians reckoned that the Americans would withdraw from Germany and Europe "within a year or two" and leave the field to them. The Russians had good reason to so consider. "Bring the Men Home"—and leave the occupation of Germany to her neighbors! They had watched the decimation and redecimation of the American Army by the demobilization stampede and were assured by their American and British agents that the Anglo-Saxons would soon tire of the game. The blockade was an attempt to force the issue, an attempt that came within a hair of success.

Nine out of eleven American ambassadors consulted by the President when the blockade had been imposed voted that the Allies withdraw from Berlin (as did the British commandant of Berlin and the government he represented). To a large extent Clay was personally responsible for President Truman's compromise decision to stay. Truman's decision was a compromise because the President postulated successful recourse to the airlift, the one means of access for which the Allies possessed a written Soviet agreement. But the very success of the airlift exercised a diversionary and ultimately deceptive influence on all parties concerned except the Soviets. The sustained exhibition of consummate technological expertise that was the airlift was so spectacular that it diverted official as well as public attention from the issue itself: guaranteed, agreed access to Berlin from the West.

When they came, the negotiations on the lifting of the blockade unaccountably fell into the hands of a shambling professor of international law with no experience whatever in dealing with Soviets, Phillip C. Jessup. As a result, the *status quo ante* blockade was simply restored with no agreement on the modalities of access. The airlift had broken the blockade, but it had also demonstrated to what lengths the Americans would go to avoid a showdown in Europe. The Soviet reaction to this course of instruction on the anatomy of Allied pusilanimity was the unleashing of the North Korean invasion of South Korea a year later. They leapfrogged the containment intent of the Truman Doctrine for Greece and Turkey.

Instead of forcing America out of Europe or the Asian continent, the Soviets performed the function of prompting and promoting the evolvement of the United States from its tradition of isolationism into a world governing power. Clay is of the opinion that without the airlift the Marshall Plan would never have been ratified by Congress. Most American military leaders, and certainly Clay, realized that the blockade spelled the rearmament of Germany if the United States government were resolved to stay on the Continent. Here we have an unbroken view of the causal chain, from the failure of the Allies to zone postwar Germany properly for the occupation to the utter necessity for rearming Germany as a member of a Western alliance.

The glint of hope that Stephan Heym describes as coming into the eye of the benighted German soul when he learned of difficulty between the Allies was a piece of prophecy based on two and a half decades of experience with Soviet, East European, and above all, German Communists. In the three years before the Nazi takeover, the German Communist party was the second largest political party in the Weimar Republic, polling over six million votes in the 1931 elections and receiving an even one hundred seats in the Reichstag in the 1932 elections. Moreover, the one unshakable belief of the Nazi rank and file, which they never failed to propagate as the last, best hope of the German cause, was the conviction that the Western Allies would never succeed in coming to terms with the Soviets.

Indeed, Hitler and Goebbels converted this conviction, which was also widely held by the German populace, into the dictum that the essential differences between the capitalist and Communist systems would even preclude their effective cooperation in the prosecution of a war against Germany. Almost certainly, this belief was responsible for the carelessness of the Nazis in allowing the evolvement of a two-front war (Hitler repeatedly swore that he would never make that particular, deadly mistake of Imperial Germany), a risk that was explicit in the decision to attack the Soviet Union without having defeated the enemy to the west, Great Britain. The same conviction was the principal consideration in the final Wagnerian plan of the Nazis to take refuge in a specially prepared "Alpine Redoubt," whence they would issue forth to join the anti-Communist crusade against the Russians after East and West had fallen out (as they were presumably bound to do, as soon as they had met in the middle of Germany).

In his strangely prophetic article in *The New York Times,* Stephan Heym rightly credits the Germans with a good deal of schooling in *Realpolitik.* The basic *Realpolitikal* consideration of the twentieth century is the postulation of the immiscibility of Communist and capitalist powers. This postulation led the Nazis to a false conclusion in the Second World War because they failed to reckon with the New Deal. The same postulation provided the forces of German classical conservatism, led by Konrad Adenauer, with prophetic insight because Adenauer and his colleagues reckoned with the parallel resurgence of conservatism (that is, anti-Communism) in America—especially in the face of fanatic Soviet intransigence in the quadrapartite control of Germany. In George Kennan's words:

> The most helpful thing to understand about this recent war is the extent to which it was prejudiced, as a military encounter, before it was begun—the extent to which, you might say, it was not fully winnable. . . . Before the war began the overwhelming portion of the world's armed strength in land forces and air forces had accumulated in the hands of three political entities—Nazi Germany, Soviet Russia, and Imperial Japan. All these entities were deeply and dangerously hostile to the Western democracies. As things stood in the late thirties, if these three powers were to combine their efforts and stick together in a military enterprise, the remaining Western nations plainly had no hope of defeating them on the land mass of Europe and Asia, with the armaments at hand or even those in prospect. In Europe and Asia, Western democracy had become militarily outclassed. The world balance of power had turned decisively against it.
>
> I am not claiming that this was perceived, or would have been easy to perceive, by Western statesmen. But I believe it was a reality. And, as such, it plainly limited the actual prospects for the West, if war were to come. Of the three totalitarian powers, Japan was the only one which could conceivably be defeated by the democracies without invoking for this purpose the aid of one of the other totalitarian powers. In the case of Germany and Russia, circumstances were bitter. Together, they could not be defeated at all.

Individually, either of them could be defeated only if the democracies
had the collaboration of the other.

But such collaboration, if permitted to proceed to the point of
complete victory, would mean the relative strengthening of the col-
laborating power and its eventual appearance as a greedy and
implacable claimant at the peace table.

It is in this context that the folly of insisting on unconditional
surrender emerges in something like its true dimensions.

Heym's characterization of the Germans in their hope of a war
between the Allies was equally applicable to the Eastern Europeans
at large. Poles, Czechs, Hungarians, Romanians, and even Yugoslavs (the Bulgarians were possibly an exception) had their hopes
and fears of war based on the same conviction that the Western
Allies could never collaborate with the Soviets for any appreciable
length of time. According to this view—which was borne out for
all Europeans, not just Germans, with each passing day's frustration in the Four Power Allied Control Council in Berlin—a clash
between the Allies and a subsequent turning of fronts was ultimately
inevitable.

This conviction was daily reinforced by Communist propaganda,
which, emanating from Soviet control points throughout Eastern
and Middle Europe, proclaimed the tenets of Marxist doctrine
and the equation of capitalists with fascists. It is a curious fact
that the doctrine, reinforced as it was by both military and party
discipline, simply proved to be too strong, despite the best of goodwill on the Allied side and the most cogent tactical considerations
on the Soviet side. A combination of doctrine and discipline was
so strong that it could not be bent, but only broken.

The thousands of Soviet defectors of all ranks only heightened
the distaste of the Allies for the Soviet system and hastened Western acceptance of the challenge on terms requiring that each side
strive to enlist the support of a recently conquered (and prose-
cuted) people. Also, the combination of Russian primitiveness, the
brutality and intransigence born of an age-old inferiority complex,
plus the proletarian atheism of Marx and the fact that Soviet
troops were obliged to live at free quarters quickly estranged and
embittered the populations of Eastern and Central Europe almost
to a man.

To this very considerable extent the turning of the front in
Europe against the East was inevitable. Likewise the very nature

of the situation both created the need and laid the foundation for a continuation of the crusade in Europe. It was entirely in keeping that Dwight D. Eisenhower, former Commander-in-Chief of SHAEF (whose instinctive desire was to preserve the administrative apparatus of SHAEF after the war as a nucleus for the occupation adminisration) should be the first Supreme Commander of SHAPE (Supreme Headquarters Allied Powers Europe), the executive and administrative organ of NATO.

It was precisely this course of events—stretching over at least two decades—that provided the historical accommodation for Konrad Adenauer, ostensibly one of Heym's "elderly gentlemen with good intentions" who survived the Nazi era only because "even the Nazis considered them too inconsequential for liquidation."

When Adenauer was arrested again at the end of the war and sent to a Gestapo prison, the warder asked him please not to commit suicide. Adenauer asked him what prompted his suspicion. The warder replied that since Adenauer was almost seventy years old and "had nothing more to expect from life" it seemed reasonable to suppose that he would put an end to it. It was anything but coincidence or an old man's whimsy that the moment the war was over Adenauer went to work on the creation of his conceptual and organizational masterpiece.

Instead of a reconstitution of the old strictly confessional Center party he created a political organization with the broadest possible base—a catch-all for the adherents of the cultural heritage of the Christian West. In short, this was the raising of a bulwark against the only remaining threat to the cultural heritage of the Christian West after the defeat and destruction of Nazism.

In this sense Adenauer both anticipated and made a determining contribution to the anti-Communist crusade that began at the end of the forties and lasted a full ten years. In the course of the crusade he brought Germany back once more, "armed and equipped for war" and emergent as a major power clearly recognized as the centerpiece of a united Europe. Or did he?

The blockade of Berlin by the Soviets and all that it signified— the necessity for rearming Germany and leaguing with her against the Soviet Union, the permanent exposure of Berlin as a lever of power-political blackmail to be applied against the West at will by the Soviets—is demonstrated proof of the colossal folly of unconditional surrender. Committing this folly, the West mortgaged the future of Europe, and the world, to the Soviets for generations. More ominously, it resulted in the compromising of American foreign policy, as it were, at its conceptual source. In effect it split the American national will and turned it against itself, since the American political attitude toward Germany inevitably became ambivalent (in some respects, of course, it had always been ambivalent).

Thus the original concept of NATO not only deliberately excluded Germany, but was meant to prevent reunification rather than foster it—since reunification was widely regarded as the first step toward German resurgence. When the three Western Allies set about forming the North Atlantic Treaty Organization, their main purpose was to achieve a tolerable if makeshift balance of power within the framework and an interplay of East-West tensions.

As Paul F. Nitze, who took part in laying the foundations for NATO put it:

> We did not see how the reunification of Germany in a form acceptable to the Bonn government could be *prevented* if Russian military forces were not directly present in support of the Eastern regime. Far from wishing Germany or any other part of Central Europe to become part of NATO, it was thought that the influence of the NATO powers would be directed to keeping Central Europe a buffer area, incapable of disturbing the security of the West or of challenging the East.

In short, in a peculiar, roundabout, and tortuous way, the creation of NATO was meant to provide a means of shoring up the *status quo minus* left by the Soviet blockade of Berlin. One of the principal but well-hidden functions of NATO throughout the postwar period was to act as a prop for the Four Power Statute of Germany, which had all but collapsed.

When the necessity for a German defense contribution forced the inclusion of West Germany in NATO, the organization became an alliance of partners whose aspirations were not only at odds but potentially in direct conflict. The source of the deception was the anti-Communist crusade. It was the anti-Communist crusade that caused the Adenauer government, like its allies, to regard and treat Germany as though it were not divided at all, but rather engaged in the front line of a holy war against the heathen East.

The fact that the front line happened to run through the middle of Germany was neatly concealed by the sense and direction of the crusade. The perfect compatibility of German national goals with the crusade (as originally exemplified in the "rollback" policy of John Foster Dulles, and later set forth and practiced in the NATO strategic concept of "forward defense") made a collective security treaty look like a reunification policy. Thus the double purpose of NATO—crusade *with* the Germans against communism, but security *from* the Germans by incorporating them in a broader role—doubly complicated the German problem. It sowed the seeds of a series of confrontations between the Federal Republic of Germany and Communist states and concluded with the confrontation of Germany and her postwar allies.

Chapter 11

THE CONSEQUENCES OF EXPERTISE:
GERMANY

I N September, 1957, the Soviet Union launched its first Sputnik. The psychological effect of this "first" can hardly be exaggerated. It struck dismay in the hearts of Germans. A high-ranking American diplomat went on a two-day drunk out of despair over the event. This was especially true in Berlin. Berlin had drawn its *esprit de corps* and its will to live as a bulwark deep in Communist territory nine years earlier from a somewhat similar event— America's spectacular demonstration of technological superiority— the airlift.

Indeed, it was their very acute sense of America's technological superiority that had buoyed the Germans and enabled them to face the unremitting threat of the Soviet Union from the first. America's clear lead in the development of atomic and hydrogen bombs had taken the edge off the ominous presence of the Red army poised on the demarcation line and surrounding Berlin. It made the blockade of Berlin a kind of exercise in power politics, in which the ground rules were laid by the United States' exclusive possession of the atom bomb.

All the more dismaying therefore was the Soviet Union's spectacular move into the lead in space technology, ostensibly the most modern and advanced branch of science. As such it signaled a strategic advance that boded ill for the West generally, and particularly of course for the West's most exposed outpost—Berlin. The average German was convinced that the newly won Soviet superiority over the West would not go unexploited politically for long. He was, therefore, not surprised when hardly more than a year later, Nikita Khrushchev presented the Western Allies with an ultimatum on Berlin, demanding the conversion of the Western sectors into a "demilitarized free city" of West Berlin. Indeed, the first sputnik was virtually the *sine qua non* for the ultimatum. Only two years had passed since an outraged crowd of tens of thousands of West Berliners had almost invaded East Berlin during the Soviet crushing of the Hungarian Revolution. In Germany the tide affecting the position of the Allies in Berlin was beginning to turn, but the actual turning was still to come. There was some apprehension in Berlin to be sure, but the suspense concerned *how* the Allies would meet the crisis rather than *whether* they would meet it. Adenauer, though deeply worried, felt that Germany was secure enough within the NATO Alliance to announce that he would resign from the chancellorship and run for president.

But it was then—shortly before the six-month limit of the ultimatum ran out—that the first great blow against the Federal Republic itself fell: Instead of meeting the Berlin crisis with NATO, the Western Allies relapsed into their old ways, set NATO aside and reactivated the Four Power Agreement, arranging to meet with the Soviets in Geneva. Not only that, they agreed to allow the East German delegation to participate in the conference on the same basis as the Federal Republic. This slighting of NATO and the consequent reduction of Germany from its status as a full and equal partner in a grand alliance to that of a mere object—a conquered country that had surrendered unconditionally and had no rights or even existence as a sovereign state—upset Adenauer so much that he abruptly renounced his intention to retire, explaining that the situation was much too critical for such an action.

The foreign ministers' conference itself, which lasted from May to mid-August, 1959, was uneventful, providing little more than a ramp for the "summit conference" at Camp David between Khrushchev and Eisenhower. It did, however, reveal some disquieting aspects of Allied policy with regard to Berlin. At Geneva, in their proposal for an interim Berlin solution, the Western Allies agreed to a ceiling or limit on Allied troops in West Berlin to include a "symbolic reduction of troops." The Allies had theretofore argued that the size of their troop contingents in Berlin was already merely symbolic—to restrain subversive activity and "outright propaganda" in West Berlin in return for a Soviet agreement to do the same in East Berlin. They wanted the Russians to cooperate in the establishment of an advisory committee for West Berlin, made up of representatives of the Four Powers plus representatives from East and West Berlin.

These concessions were offered in the hope of receiving formal confirmation by the Soviets of Allied rights and privileges in Berlin—especially the right of access to the city—until reunification. Fortunately the Soviets refused the proposal for an interim solution, just as they had earlier refused the so-called Herter plan for the reunification of Germany in four stages with a "Mixed Commission" composed of twenty-five West Germans and ten East Germans and requiring a three-fourths majority for decisions, thus conceding East Germany (which has considerably less than one-third of the population of West Germany) the power of veto.

The West German government and, more particularly, the West Berlin Senate were so alarmed by the compulsion of the Allies to make concessions that they beleaguered the Western delegations in Geneva with special envoys and memoranda pleading for a return to the Four Power Commission formula rather than an all-German committee. The Foreign Ministers' Conference at Geneva was adjourned *sine die* in mid-August and forgotten in the political sensationalism of the Camp David meeting.

But the Geneva Conference of 1959 did serve to make it clear that the Soviets were not at all interested in the reunification of Germany—not even on Communist terms. In politics, as Count Sforza once said, appearances are sometimes more important than realities. If the Soviets had accepted the Herter plan—even with the protection of the built-in Communist veto—it would have created the impression that reunification was in progress, or at least that the process of reunification had begun. Soviet acceptance would have projected an *arc en ciel* of expectation for the German populace East and West. Great expectations in the mass are often dangerous and always dynamic. In Germany such expectations might well have forced the hand of the Communists.

Nevertheless the momentum of the crusade was still such that Adenauer could content himself with efforts and announcements to "politicize" NATO. He could still believe, however wistfully, that something might be done to salvage the Alliance as an instrument of the crusade, by the judicious use of which Germany's vital interests could at least be protected, if not actively promoted.

In 1959, also, the "eternal opposition" in Germany, the Social Democratic party (SPD), with a weather eye out for a change of American administration, jettisoned its notorious Germany plan, proposing the creation of an all-German conference from which an all-German parliamentary council was to be elected—both on the basis of parity between East and West Germany. Instead it adopted the Godesberg Program, which stripped the party of most of its ideological ballast and streamlined it along the lines of the vote-catching Christian Democratic Union. But the main object of the exercise was to make the party "Alliance-worthy" vis-à-vis the chief Ally. As die-hard opponent of all forms of integration into Western Europe and the Atlantic Community, the party could hardly expect to be favored in any way by the Allies—including even a British Labour party.

The development was all the more important because it marked the beginning of a bipolarity in postwar German politics to match the bipolarity in American political life. Until then the Christian Democrats were rather closely identified with the Republican party—as the conservative parties of the Weimar Republic had been. But the Social Democratic party had steadfastly refused for ten years to identify with anything American. In effect, indeed, the Social Democratic party had placed the United States on a par with the Soviet Union as being equally obstructive of reunification. Thus for the first time, the American government was provided with an alternative in Germany: the possibilty of supporting or promoting, by whatever means, the opposition rather than the incumbents in the forthcoming national elections, scheduled to take place less than a year (ten months) after American Presidential elections.

Meanwhile the cold war was working to the advantage of the Western Allies in a way that went all but unnoticed. The familiarity of the phenomenon obscured its significance, but by 1961 it loomed so great by sheer accumulation that it commanded attention. The number of East Germans who had fled the Soviet zone for West Germany had passed four million. This was more than a fourth of the present population of East Germany.

This was the greatest voluntary mass migration in recorded European history. More significantly the refugee flow had entered its seventeenth year virtually undiminished, the average annual total since the founding of the so-called German Democratic Republic in 1949 being about 230,000. But the really striking aspect of the refugee flow was its uniformity. For sixteen years and more, 50 per cent of the annual total were under twenty-five years of age, 74 per cent under forty-five, and over 90 per cent under sixty-five.

The effect of these numbers on the population structure of East Germany was devastating. The East German statistical yearbook for 1960 showed a loss, over a nine-year period, of almost a million (or 32 per cent) in the age group from six to fifteen years. In the age group from twenty-five to fifty a loss of more than a million and a quarter (or 25 per cent) was recorded. Conversely, the segment of the population over fifty years of age had increased by well over half a million (or 10 per cent). Hence the mass of the East German population was either retired or rapidly approaching retirement. In January, 1960, the East German State Planning Commission predicted that the country's labor force would decrease by 600,000 workers before 1966 because of the faulty population structure. This calculation did not reckon with a further loss of population. By January, 1961, another quarter of a million had gone West.

The most frequent reason for the refugee flow, given by the refugees themselves in reception centers, was the "unsatisfactory or insufficient education of children" (i.e., a Communist education). The second reason given was the "lack of opportunity to travel abroad"—in most cases meaning West Germany. The third most frequent reason given was "political pressure."

Over the years the Communist authorities tried desperately to stop the flow, but as often as not their efforts backfired. When they increased restrictions, more people left (restrictions imposed to prevent flight became of themselves additional reasons for flight). When they relaxed restrictions more people left (access invited flight). Moreover, the regime's attempts to mollify certain segments of the population, particularly the industrial elite and the professional classes, tended to disaffect the unprivileged masses still further.

The rampant labor shortage caused by the refugee flow was chiefly responsible for the extreme lack of equilibrium in the East German economy. This chronic and increasing disequilibrium in turn made it impossible for East Germany to do without imports from West Germany, particularly in specialized steel parts. Economic dependency on West Germany was institutionalized in 1951 in the form of the Interzonal Trade Agreement. By 1960 over half of East Germany's exports to and imports from the West (i.e., hard currency areas) were made within the framework of the Interzonal Trade Agreement. In May, 1960, in answer to continued harrassment along the canals and highways between West Germany and Berlin, the Federal Republic cancelled the Interzonal Trade Agreement and suspended deliveries. When the agreement was renegotiated a few weeks later, sobered East German officials (who had thus been forced to appraise the true nature and extent of their dependence on the West German economy) were forced to accept a "Berlin clause," a stipulation that the agreement would remain valid only so long as passenger traffic between West Germany and West Berlin was not disturbed or interrupted.

Worst of all, however, was the fact that nothing could be done to alleviate shortages in critical specialist and professional categories. From 1954 through 1960, 3,100 doctors of medicine fled East Germany—this was 20 per cent of the total number of doctors resident in East Germany when the so-called Democratic Republic was formed in 1949. The result was that there were several areas in East Germany where no doctor was available within a radius of forty miles.

On the contrary, the West Germans mounted a concerted campaign to recruit specialists, technicians, and professional men of every sort for West German industry, where the boom of the economic miracle had created an unprecedented labor shortage. This was in spite of the continuing infusion of East German labor into West Germany via the refugee flow. There were upwards of a million foreign laborers—principally Italians and Yugoslavs—in the Federal Republic as early as 1960. West Berlin newspapers and the Berlin editions of West German newspapers were full to bursting with help wanted ads for every branch of West German industry, but particularly for construction workers and electrical and chemical engineers.

The East German and Soviet Communists loudly protested West German recruitment of East German workers, branding the action *Abwerbung,* or the weaning and winning away, specifically recruitment by means of inducing disaffection. Before August 13, 1961, Berlin was, as Willy Brandt once described it "the clamp that holds the two parts of Germany together."

A German journalist, during then Vice President Johnson's visit to Berlin, said: "Before they built that terrible wall, a mother from Frankfurt an der Oder could visit with her son from Frankfurt am Main in Berlin. Last year nine million theater, concert, and cinema tickets were sold in West Berlin to East Germans.

Berlin was the clearing house of East and West Germany, the only place where the twain could and did meet. Now it is finished." The Four Power Statute was the guarantee that the German problem had not yet been decided; the abrogation of the Four Power Statute, accomplished by sealing off West Berlin, was the signal that the Communists had decided the German problem unilaterally.

As early as July, 1958, Otto Grotewohl, the Prime Minister of the East German regime, stated that "the continuing flight from the Republic is problem Number One, a problem to which we have in every case taken a frivolous and formal attitude. This cannot go on." But he concluded the statement by admitting that the East German regime was "today still not in a position to draw the necessary, definitive conclusions."

By 1961 everyone had drawn the "necessary definitive conclusions" about the refugee flow. Indeed, the West Germans and the Allies had drawn their conclusions much earlier. Ever since 1951 West Germany had made regular and frequent appeals to the East Germans to stay put. But whenever the refugee flow diminished, there was an undercurrent of alarm in the official expression of satisfaction, and whenever the refugee flow increased there was an undercurrent of satisfaction in the official expression of alarm. The "rollback" policy of John Foster Dulles was a thing of the past. A new administration was in office and its leaders were fervently seeking new answers to old questions.

The passive "hedgehog" policy of the Western Allies in regard to East Germany was apparently based on the expectation that the East German Communist regime would never be able to stabilize itself because of the refugee flow. The refugee flow was expected to continue undiminished until such time as the Russians saw themselves forced to come to terms. The calculation began to prove correct as early as 1958. Khrushchev's precipitation of the Berlin crisis of November, 1958, was the first Soviet response to the realization that the East German situation was rapidly becoming untenable. The Soviet six months' ultimatum on West Berlin was in reality a defensive reaction disguised as a political power threat. As such it was a fairly desperate bluff. The bluff produced the ten weeks' mummery of the foreign ministers' conference at Geneva and finally the "Spirit of Camp David."

While miming insistence of their maximum demands, the Russians achieved their minimum objective—gaining time to do anything possible to stop the refugee flow. By various administrative and control measures they actually succeeded in diminishing the total of refugees for 1959 by better than one-quarter of the 1958 total. During this period a trickle of returnees from West to East Germany increased to produce some semblance of a "refugee" flow in reverse. But the cause of both was not what the Communists assumed. Whenever negotiations on Berlin were in process, or an atmosphere conducive to negotiations existed, the East Germans would watch and wait—and the refugee flow slacken accordingly. 1959 was the year of the foreign ministers' conference in Geneva. While it lasted there was hope that something might come of it. But when Khrushchev torpedoed the summit conference in Paris in the spring of 1960, the flow increased abruptly to more than twenty thousand for the month of May alone. 1960 was also the year of the total collectivization of agriculture in East Germany —in a campaign lasting just six weeks. Farmers fled by the thousands. From then on it increased steadily, rising to a flood in the summer of 1961, when the construction of the wall stemmed the tide and reduced the flow to the merest trickle.

In February, 1961, six months before the wall was built, one of the co-authors of this book wrote an article on East Germany, which appeared in *The Reporter* magazine under the title, "The Disappearing Satellite":

> There are some indications that the Soviet Union and its East German minions have finally drawn the ultimate conclusion: the only way to stop the refugee flow is to seal off both East Berlin and the Soviet Zone by total physical security measures. The regime has already alerted specialized Communist formations to man the East Berlin sector boundary sometime this spring. . . . They are transferring tough and experienced customs officers from zonal border duty to check points in the city. Berliners are reckoning with the distinct possibility that Khrushchev will make good his threat of a separate peace treaty and ring down the Iron Curtain in front of East Berlin—with searchlight and machine gun towers, barbed wire and police-dog patrols. Technically this is feasible. But the very feasibility of the measure poses two questions: Why was it not taken long ago? Can it be taken now?

The substance of Bailey's answers to these two questions was that neither the East German populace nor the Western Allies (including the West Germans) would accept the sealing off of East Berlin. The East Germans would rebel and the Western Allies retaliate with severe economic sanctions, beginning with the automatic cancelation of the Interzonal Trade Agreement. So matters seemed to stand in the first two months of 1961. But 1961 was a very eventful year and especially for Germany. A great deal happened in the spring and early summer of 1961 to change the climate and even the context of the German problem before the onset of high summer 1961. At the Vienna summit in early June —hastily improvised by the Kennedy Administration to convince Khrushchev of American determination to stand firm in Berlin— Khrushchev presented Kennedy with an *aide-memoire* in which Soviet demands on Berlin were couched in terms more intransigent than ever before. Khrushchev backed up this "reminder" with his usual bully-boy hectoring.

Kennedy was visibly shaken by Khrushchev's belligerence. He later described the effect of the summit meeting as "sobering." In fact, it was disastrous. On June 10 Tass released the text of the *aide-memoire* and the tidal wave of refugees that was to engulf Berlin in July and August began to gather. On June 14 Senate Majority Leader Mike Mansfield once again regaled the Senate with his plan for the conversion of West Berlin into a "demilitarized free city."

A week later, Mansfield again criticized his government's determination to remain in Berlin. Thus, instead of countering the concerted Soviet propaganda offensive against West Berlin, the American government—or various of its representatives—seemed more concerned to aid and abet the Soviet move. This impression, which registered on the Germans more than all other interested parties, was not erased by President Kennedy's speech of July 25. This speech, while it emphasized the firmness of the American stand, was the first Presidential utterance on the subject in seven weeks after the Vienna summit.

It was also noted—especially by the Germans—that the President seemed careful to allude to "West Berlin" as distinct from Berlin as a whole, indicating to the Germans that the United States was concerned to maintain its rights only within the Western sectors of the city. But for the Germans the most damaging statement came from Senator Fulbright on July 30 during a nationwide television interview. Senator Fulbright was asked whether he "would be willing to accept any concessions on the part of the West" which would have the effect of closing the escape hatch for refugees in Berlin. Fulbright answered:

"I think that that might certainly be a negotiable point. The truth of the matter is, I think, the Russians have the power to close it in any case. I mean you are not giving up very much because I believe that next week if they chose to close their borders they could, without violating any treaty.

"I don't understand why the East Germans don't close their border because I think they have a right to close it. So why is this a great concession?"

Two weeks later the East Germans did so. Fulbright's statement is not only inconsistent within itself (the Russians have the right, the East Germans have the right); it reveals an ignorance of, or was made despite, the stipulation for freedom of movement within Greater Berlin that is contained in the Four Power Statute; it reveals an ignorance of Soviet and Communist foreign policy procedure that is bewildering in the chairman of the Senate Foreign Relations Committee.

Beginning on July 1, the flow of East German refugees into West Berlin suddenly doubled and then tripled. By the middle of July East Germany was losing an average of one thousand citizens a day. By the end of July the flood became a tidal wave, averaging two thousand refugees a day. On Saturday, August 12, the day before the boundary was closed, somewhere between five and ten thousand refugees entered West Berlin. Because the refugee camps in West Berlin were already hopelessly overcrowded, a great many refugees postponed entering the camps or even registering for as long as two weeks after the border was closed, living in hotels or staying with friends or relatives.

On the afternoon of August 13, 1961, Chancellor Konrad Adenauer issued a declaration to the German people in answer to the construction of the Berlin Wall, which had begun early that morning. After branding the action an open breach of the four power agreements, and acknowledging the seriousness of the situation, Adenauer came to the heart of his message: "In concert with our allies," ran the declaration, "necessary countermeasures will be taken. The Federal government asks all Germans to put their trust in these measures."

What Adenauer himself had in mind when he used the term "countermeasures," he made clear in an election speech the following day in Regensburg. Employment of the economic weapon, he said, according to press reports, was the most promising weapon the West could take against the East bloc. Great unanimity existed among NATO partners to proceed against the Soviet zone "with very severe measures." He added that Secretary of State Dean Rusk had "gladly" seized upon suggestions that countermeasures be taken in the economic field.

It is a matter of record that no such countermeasures were ever taken. Instead, Allied reaction, when it finally came, called for negotiations on a four power level. This in itself clearly ruled out the prospect of any "countermeasures" whatsoever.

Adenauer announced the imminence of countermeasures out of sheer desperation. What else could one say to Berliners during the sixty-hour period when the American commandant was waiting for instructions? In spring and summer of 1961, talk of economic countermeasures in answer to unilateral Soviet action was much in vogue in NATO circles and, indeed, was hailed by many as clearly preferable to any sort of military measures.

One of the few measures—as distinct from "countermeasures" —taken in direct response to the Wall was the spectacular trip of then Vice President Lyndon Johnson to West Berlin. The fact that Adenauer himself did not appear in West Berlin until two weeks after construction of the Wall—more specifically, the fact that Adenauer did not accompany Johnson to Berlin on August 19— angered and dismayed countless Germans and probably cost Adenauer an absolute majority in the national elections of September, 1961. This necessitated formation of the coalition government, which, in turn, presaged the end of the "Adenauer era."

Shortly before "the Old Man" became an old man on October 16, 1962, Adenauer was asked the cardinal question of his career during a German television interview: "Why did you not go to Berlin with Vice President Johnson?"

Answered Adenauer: "Because Vice President Johnson asked me not to go."

In point of fact Adenauer instinctively reacted to the Wall like the loyal Ally he had always been. His first move—apart from the declaration to the German people on August 16—was to consult with Allied ambassadors in Bonn. He conferred with American Ambassador Walter Dowling on Monday, August 16. Then, or shortly thereafter, Dowling gave Adenauer to understand that the American government did not consider it advisable for him to go to Berlin at that time.

By Tuesday it was patently in Adenauer's interest, both as a statesman and a politician, to go to Berlin as quickly as possible. An apparent consideration militating against the trip was a vague Allied fear that the appearance of the West German Chancellor in Berlin at that time would spark revolt in East Germany.

Another consideration was an article of protocol stipulating that the West German Chancellor, like the president of the republic, fly to Berlin in an American or Allied military aircraft, specifically, in the personal plane of the commanding general of the USAFE. This was and still is the undeviating practice, not merely a courtesy extended by the Americans. The point here is that only aircraft of the three wartime Allies are permitted to fly the air corridors to Berlin. A head of state is also the nation's *erster Geheimnistraeger,* its chief bearer of official secrets. It is not in the interest of the Allies to have the German Chancellor forced down in the Soviet zone by interception. Hence the military protection.

Of course Adenauer could have ignored protocol and chartered a flight on one of the three Allied civilian airlines. It was just this that the young men of the CDU implored him to do in defiance of American desires. Adenauer refused, maintaining that he would not act counter to the expressed interest of the Allies.

When it became known that Vice President Lyndon Johnson would fly to Berlin, Adenauer immediately requested American permission to accompany him and even released a statement to that effect to the press. Dowling was obliged to inform Adenauer that his presence in Berlin with Johnson was not desired. When Johnson arrived in Bonn on his way to Berlin, Adenauer repeated his request. He was again refused. At this point the young Turks begged him to fly to Berlin in a Pan American plane chartered by Foreign Minister von Brentano, who was to meet Johnson in Berlin. Adenauer again refused, saying that the Americans had made it sufficiently clear that they did not want him to go. The old man's pride and his sense of acceptance had been hard hit.

In November, 1963—one week before President Kennedy was assassinated—Bailey interviewed Adenauer, who was still furious over this aspect of Johnson's trip to Berlin. Here is a pertinent passage from the interview:

> At that time Vice President Johnson twice refused my request that he take me to Berlin with him. At such a moment that was really an affront. I was deliberately kept away from Berlin. Why?

I can't understand it either. I could not go there by any other means than in an American (Allied) aircraft. And it was a bitter pill that Johnson, who had entertained me in Texas in such a frank and friendly way a year before, refused to take me with him to Berlin. Just imagine, if you please, what an impression it would have made in Berlin if Johnson had been there and I at his side—with him—I, the representative of the Federal Republic to emphasize in this way the unity of our views.

I will tell you something: If I had gone to Berlin with Johnson at that time in August, 1961, we would have had the absolute majority in the Bundestag (through the national elections). By virtue of the fact that I was not there, we lost the absolute majority. In whose interest was it to keep me away from Berlin? You answer me that question now. Well, you asked me just now, and I didn't want to put it in that way. I merely make the point that you can look at the polls and see how high the percentage of our majority was before the construction of the Wall, and how far we fell afterwards. Is that quite clear? We would have had the absolute majority. In whose interest was it? It was not in my interest that we should lose the majority.

The young men who had heretofore been Adenauer's strongest support in the party never forgave him. At that moment they transferred their allegiance to Ludwig Erhard. It is in the nature of a historical irony that the one quality above all others that assured Konrad Adenauer's unparalleled success as a German statesman and politician was the same quality that ultimately encompassed his political ruin; namely, his unswerving loyalty to the Alliance.

Adenauer's personal reputation and his stature as the German political leader rested mainly on his excellent relations with the Allies. His successful cultivation of such relations was universally regarded as his signal achievement. Also he had made unashamed use of his relations in his political campaigns. Hence, in addition to underlining the solidarity of the Federal Republic with its chief Ally in time of crisis, his appearance with Johnson in Berlin would have worked as an enormous campaign boost. By the same token, his failure to appear with Johnson in Berlin was all the more damaging; it gave the impression that Adenauer either was in some sort of stubborn opposition to the Allies or had lost Allied support —as in fact he had. There was also a much broader effect: Many of the placards that were held up to Johnson while he was in Berlin bore the slogan, "Washington is closer than Bonn." It was this effect that Johnson's solo visit to Berlin was primarily designed to produce.

The decision to make and keep Johnson's visit to Berlin exclusively an American show was not the result of plotting but policy. The Kennedy Administration's determination to find new solutions for old problems resulted in what later became known as a "policy of relaxation." The focal point of this policy was necessarily Berlin. Its first purpose was to demonstrate the feasibility of peaceful coexistence on the basis of the *status quo*. In Berlin this meant a kind of disengagement—in lieu of returning toward four power status of the city (a proposal Khrushchev rejected in Vienna). A unilateral disengagement in Berlin, as a demonstration of goodwill, mainly involved de-emphasis of the Federal Republic in Berlin in the interests of an inoffensive status in limbo. This policy reached its pinnacle after the Wall in a drive to make West Berlin a cultural center, a sort of "world capital of medieval woodwind instruments," as one Berliner put it. The policy was backed by broad, concerted effort to find and exploit "areas of agreement" with the Soviet Union, particularly disarmament and more particularly atomic disarmament. Necessarily, as basic postulate, the policy discounted the German drive for reunification. On the face of it, American architects of policy could afford to do so, for the German drive for reunification is not readily visible.

On the face of it, West Germans under Konrad Adenauer occupied themselves exclusively with the arduous business of establishing their bona fides as well-behaved, peaceful, prosperous, and above all stable citizens eminently worthy of acceptance as equal partners in the grand alliance with traditional democracies of the West. They have fulfilled all the requirements of the model and paid the price of appearing complacent. The resultant picture is paradoxical: It is both true and deceptive.

Faced with the apparently perfect dilemma of pursuing reunification actively but also inconspicuously, the Germans took the only way out: They harnessed their claim in the articles and official trappings of statehood. The West German reunification policy is the Federal Republic. The preamble of basic law (constitution) of the Republic explicitly states, and a formidable body of internationally legal agreements (*Das Vertragswerk*) enshrines, the political and territorial claims of the German state. Every major diplomatic instrument signed by the Federal Republic stipulates that the Republic is the only legitimate German state, the only German state legally entitled to represent Germany as a whole. Every member of the Bundestag must take a solemn oath to uphold basic law and hence pursue the goal of reunification. The Federal Republic does not rest on territory but on a legal definition: the definition is territorial claim. Willy Brandt wrote in 1957: "According to the word and spirit of the basic law, the Federal Republic is nothing other than the manifestation of our state—political life (Staatsleben) in those parts of Germany in which external power relations have made it possible to inaugurate the reorganization of state—political life as a whole. The legal committee of Parliament has even prevailed upon the officials of the Ministry of Justice to speak of 'area of validity' of the constitution rather than the territory of the Federal Republic. The territory of the Federal Republic is therefore identical with the German state within its borders of 1937."

The Germans are pursuing their claim for reunification, as it were, by due process of international law.

Chapter 12

THE CONSEQUENCES OF EXPERTISE: NATO

༄

THE growth of the German Federal Republic, stimulated by a mammoth economic recovery, excited envy, suspicion and above all, Western determination to incorporate the vast potential into its own organization. The Germans were pleased at being courted. They were generally eager to become members in good standing of Western society—and prepared, too, to pay a big price. Pariahs no longer, was the enthusiastic cry of West German politicians to the courtship.

Western Allies blithely and even gratefully signed various instruments binding the Federal Republic to Western democracies—collectively and individually—and most significant, securing West German defense contribution. They were apparently unaware or unconcerned that the same instruments also bound Western Allies to the Federal Republic. "The point is," said Willy Brandt in 1960, "that two areas of authority—that of the Western Allies and that of the Germans—interconnect." In practice during the last several years the Allies have left the decision of what should happen in Germany to the discretion of the federal government and the Berlin Senate.

As a matter of fact, the complimentary responsibility of the Western Allies and the West Germans is documented specifically in the *Deutschland Vertrag* (Paris agreements) of 1955. In the main body of that contract the Western allies specify those areas of responsibility in Germany which they reserve to themselves. But there is a codicil to the contract in which the Federal Republic accepts the responsibility for the financial status of West Berlin—primarily the monetary system—and also for economic development of West Berlin." It should be noted here that the acceptance of the responsibility is tantamount to the assumption of authority.

The authority of the Federal Republic in Berlin, as accepted by allies in formal agreements, is immense. It includes the right to extend federal legislation to West Berlin matters of currency, credit and foreign exchange, nationality, passes, immigration and emigration, extradition, unification of the customs and trade area, treaties on trade and navigation agreements, free movement of commodities, agreements on foreign trade and payments, and ensuring of the representation of Berlin and the Berlin population abroad. In short, with major exceptions of security and air access, the federal authority in West Berlin is virtually total. The one significant reservation is the Enabling Act, which specifies that all federal laws must be reviewed and accepted by the Berlin House of Representatives—and simultaneously approved by three Western Allied military commandants before they become valid for West Berlin.

The Kennedy Administration ran afoul of the *Vertragswerk* at almost every conceivable turn in attempting to implement its policy of *detente*. This was the issue behind the Grewe incident. As the representative of the Federal Republic in Washington, and particularly as a member of the Allied planning group on Berlin, Grewe tried to impress upon the Allies that they were legally bound to support the Federal Republic in its claims and interests in Berlin. The concerned American officials very sharply denied this, citing the Enabling Act. Grewe is a professor of International Law. It was for this reason he was selected as ambassador to Washington. He made his case thoroughly and persistently. For his pains he was accused of "legalistic hair-splitting" by the Americans.

In pursuing the policy of *detente,* the Kennedy Administration was forced to slight the *Vertragswerk*. In order to skirt the objections of the Germans to a plan for an international authority controlling access routes to Berlin (the authority included and hence recognized the East Germans), the Americans submitted detailed proposals of the plan to Bonn for approval within twenty-four hours. The short time limit angered every German official involved. The Germans leaked it to the press. This killed the plan, whose realization in any case depended on the willing suspension of disbelief. But it also infuriated the Americans, who branded the leak a "breach of trust" and held Grewe responsible. Shortly thereafter the Americans engineered Grewe's recall.

The Germans, however, had long since accused the Americans of "breach of contract," pointing to the bilateral summit meeting in Vienna and Allied acceptance of the Wall. In the eyes of most Germans the fact that the allies countenanced the Soviet breach of the four power agreements in erecting the Wall made the Allies party to the breach. The Germans were again given one day's notice in advance of the initialing of the atomic test ban agreement in Moscow. In this case the notice was so short that it was considered nil, constituting denial of right of consultation. To a man, the members of the Federal Republic were incensed, swearing that they had been hoodwinked and vowing that they would not be hoodwinked again.

The principal complicating factor in the German situation is that there are actually two alliances involved. The Western Alliance and the Federal Republic as an integral part of it were formed in answer to the breakdown but not the destruction of the wartime Alliance (the four power agreements).

The Soviets have been careful to keep the four power agreements just enough alive to prevent burial. As a result, the resurgence of the four power agreements would destroy the Western Alliance. Contrariwise, an effective consolidation of the Western Alliance would necessarily obliterate the residual four power agreements.

There has always been this magnetic field between two opposite poles. In times of crisis one pole increases its power to such a point that it inevitably activates the other pole. During such crises the Anglo-Americans have always tended to revert to four power posture. It has proved impossible to break out of this magnetic field. Every time the Federal Republic has suffered down-grading as a result of reactivation of the four power agreements, it has kicked back and paralyzed the Western Alliance.

There is evidence that the Franco-German treaty of cooperation had its inception in the conclusions Adenauer drew from the treatment of Germany within the framework of the policy of *detente*— particularly as that policy was continued in face of the Wall. There is also reason to believe that Adenauer's siding with de Gaulle against British entry into the Common Market was prompted by the same situation.

The four power status of Berlin was a reflection in microcosm of the original (theoretically) four power status of Germany. Conversely, the Western Alliance in its basic form (the three Western Allies plus West Germany) is a reflection in microcosm of the *de facto* three power status, plus the Berliners, that made up the original entity of West Berlin. The connection between the two complexes is direct and essential. Berlin is at once the *raison d'etre* and the *raison de nier* of the Federal Republic. As a divided city it is the *raison d'etre,* as the great Berlin of four power status it is the *raison de nier.* Hence, the Federal Republic's attempt to strengthen its ties with West Berlin immediately, once the Wall had effectively destroyed the four power status of the city, was entirely in keeping with that development as was Adenauer's announcement of economic countermeasures. However, the Anglo-American reaction to the Wall was a complete reversal of this trend. The call for negotiations from Washington and London was, by definition, an attempt to deal with the situation on a four power basis and hence a negation of the Western Alliance. Instead of being a new answer to the old problem, such insistence on negotiating in the face of the Wall was in reality an old answer to a new problem.

The duality inherent in the German situation has plagued West Germany from the start, for it has necessitated a diplomatic struggle on two fronts. Within the Western Alliance the overriding influence of the United States in West Germany tended to make the head of the Federal Republic an honorary member of the political party in the White House. It is significant that a close personal relationship between John Foster Dulles and Adenauer was replaced by a personal relationship between John F. Kennedy and Willy Brandt, the mayor of West Berlin and the Social Democratic party's candidate for Chancellor.

The point of maximum American leverage in influencing German affairs is, of course, Berlin. The security of Berlin is totally dependent on American power and American willingness to use its power. It was Konrad Adenauer's immediate recognition of this fact and his use of his close relationship with the American leadership that assured his unparalleled tenure in office. It was the Social Democratic party's blind refusal to accept this fact that doomed the party to "eternal opposition."

Early in 1960, however, the SPD made an historic about-face, accepted the Western Alliance and the complex of treaty obligations that went with it. The purpose of this radical change in both the foreign and domestic policies of the party (the change was formulated in the Godesberg Program) was to render the party *buendnisfaehig* (alliance-worthy). In so doing the party had a weather eye out for a change in the American administration in the Presidential elections of 1960, and a change in American foreign policy, particularly as applied to Germany, which the accession of a Democratic administration was likely to bring. It was equally clear that any basic change in American policy in Germany would be opposed by Konrad Adenauer and, probably, by the CDU-CSU coalition at large.

In this context it should have been clear to the American administration in August 1961, in the midst of the West German election campaign, that Johnson's arrival in Berlin without Adenauer would inevitably help Brandt, who awaited him there, as much as it would hurt Adenauer. But the SPD's obstructionist past was still fresh in the minds of the electorate. Brandt was obliged to split the electoral take with Erich Mende and the Free Democratic party. As a result, neither opposition party became "alliance-worthy" but both became coalition-worthy. In the long and tortuous negotiations to form a coalition the American ambassador, Walter Dowling, often expressed his earnest hope for a grand coalition of the CDU, CSU, and SPD. In the peculiar open-end structure of the Federal Republic, only a grand coalition would be immune to massive outside influence in favor of one major party against the other. The attempt to form a grand coalition failed at the last minute because of the refusal of certain key SPD members to participate in a government under Adenauer's chancellorship. The minor coalition with the Free Democrats that finally emerged could be formed only on the proviso numbering Konrad Adenauer's days of leadership and heralding the accession of Ludwig Erhard.

Successive American administrations since the Second World War have had to think of Berlin as a separate entity somehow lifted out of the German context. In this attitude the Americans have the support of their British Allies: According to the British postal directory Berlin is nowhere, simply existing in and of itself, being a part of neither West nor East Germany.

This attitude was not so fanciful as it may now seem. Before the construction of the Wall, West Berlin was an ideological suburb of Washington, D.C. It was apparently in a forlorn attempt to re-establish the Berlin *status quo ante murum* that President

Kennedy appointed General Lucius D. Clay—the "political general" par excellence, who had made his name in the Berlin of the Four Power Statute and blockade period—as his personal representative in Berlin.

When Clay arrived in Berlin in September, 1961, he began by making a helicopter flight over a half mile of East German territory to the West Berlin exclave of Steinstuecken and visiting with the virtually marooned inhabitants. The East German regime reacted violently to this "infringement of sovereignty," publicly threatening to shoot down the helicopter if the flight were repeated. The flight was repeated. The helicopter was even used to ferry out East German refugees, who, frustrated by the Wall surrounding West Berlin proper, had sought sanctuary in the exclave. The flights to Steinstuecken were continued in the face of the direst Communist threats and became routine. The threats of violence ceased, and there were no incidents.

Even so, the British objected strenuously to the Steinstuecken action. They affirmed their support of the United States in all major issues, but questioned the wisdom of risking an incident over such a trifling matter.

Clay contended that it was precisely the small issues that constituted the weakest points in the Soviet position. He argued that the Soviets would not allow a minor issue to become an international incident through mishandling by their East German puppets.

Most of Clay's actions in Berlin were designed to demonstrate Soviet responsibility as set down in the Four Power Statute for Berlin. When he reintroduced military police patrols on the Autobahn, the Soviets soon stopped them, asserting that the maintenance and security of the Autobahn was a Soviet responsibility. Having gained his point, Clay went on to circumvent the ban on patrols by directing that American convoys between Berlin and West Germany be broken up into patrol-sized columns passing back and forth with the frequency of patrols. In effect, he replaced convoy patrols with patrolling convoys. This put the Soviets in an awkward position. The military convoys are an essential part of the Allies' right of access to Berlin; the patrols strictly speaking were not. Once again a minor issue was deftly converted into a major issue and so a point was proved.

The same reasoning was operative in the Friedrichstrasse incident. Clay seized upon and forcefully defied an East German decree that all civilians, not excepting Allied officials, would be required to show identification to East German officers at the crossing point. After four days of concentrated humiliation produced by American military police forays into East Berlin, backed by tanks poised on the sector line, the East German military seemed on the point of panic. In a television broadcast the East German deputy defense minister announced that the "People's Army" was ready to crush the American provocateurs in Berlin. Instead the Soviets were constrained to put in an appearance with their own tanks.

The confrontation of Soviet and American forces drove a wedge between the Soviets and their East German "allies," revealing the latter as mere Soviet proxies. The wedge demolished an essential element of Soviet strategy in Berlin, namely the assertion that East Germany was a legitimate, sovereign state acting in its own interests. Moreover, the sudden American pressure in the Friedrichstrasse powerfully brought home the point that the East German Communists could not be trusted with the issue of war and peace in Berlin.

To the Soviets the reminder was painful. It pointed to the main reason why, after three and a half years of threats, announcements, and promises, the Soviets had still not signed a separate peace treaty with East Germany. A separate peace treaty would create an extraordinarily tense situation between the Western Allies and the East German regime. In the Friedrichstrasse, Clay demonstrated that the Soviets could not trust the East German Communists to carry out what would have been at best an extremely difficult mission. Before transferring a package of highly explosive issues—such as the control and administration of access routes—to the East Germans, the Soviets needed some form of agreement stipulated, perferably in the peace treaty itself.

Clay's triumph in demonstrating Soviet responsibility at the Friedrichstrasse brought a storm of protest and condemnation from all sides of the Alliance. Washington ordered the tanks withdrawn one day later, thus spoiling the second and almost equally important purpose of the exercise—the demonstration of America's determination to fight, if necessary, to maintain Western rights in Berlin.

The day after the American tanks were withdrawn, the deputy chief of the British mission visited the Soviet commandant and assured him that Clay would be recalled. Americans as well as

Allied authorities charged that Clay had gone to the brink of war over the minor issue of identity controls. In reality Clay had gone just far enough to demonstrate the essential point of Soviet responsibility for East Berlin and an all-important corollary—that a major war cannot be started in Europe by accident. There is little doubt that it was Clay's expert counterpunching that caused the Soviets to throw away their highly publicized timetable ("a peace treaty before the end of the year") and abandon their plan to use the East German Communist regime as a stalking horse in the Berlin crisis.

And yet Clay's very successes also demonstrated that the sweeping American commitment to defend Berlin would ring hollow if not implemented from day to day with determination. The question in Berlin is not *whether* the United States will resist Soviet encroachment by force, but *when* and *where*. Moreover, a boxer cannot coordinate his counterpunches with his manager, his seconds, the referee, the promoter, and occasionally with his opponent, unless he means to take a dive.

From the first the Soviets attempted to use the formal entrapment of the Allies in Berlin as a lever to force acceptance of their policies for Germany as a whole. When the Allies announced their decision to carry out a currency reform in their zones of Germany in 1948, the Soviet Union charged that they were "prejudicing their right to remain in Berlin," contending even then that Berlin was part of the Soviet zone. The Soviets have always had an obvious tactical advantage in Berlin, which they have tried to turn to a political purpose. The Allies have had a political advantage—including their popularity and the legality of their position in Berlin—which, in their confrontation with the Soviets, they have attempted to convert to tactical use.

If Berlin were primarily a military situation, the loss of the city by the Allies would be a foregone conclusion. When the Soviets imposed their blockade in 1948, the British commandant could see no alternative but to withdraw from Berlin. But Berlin is primarily a political situation, and political considerations determine tactical moves. By the same token, tactical moves have enormous political implications. For this reason the commandant in each of the Western sectors, usually a major general with little more than a division commander's experience, has been seconded by a deputy chief of a diplomatic mission. The titular chief of each sector's diplomatic mission is that particular nation's ambassador in Bonn. Formally, therefore a diplomat of subambassadorial rank is buried in the machinery of an army command post.

Actually, the deputy chief of each sector mission pretty much runs the show, primarily because he is a trained diplomat in a predominantly political situation, but also because his line of communication and command is much more direct than that of his military counterpart. The American deputy chief has a direct line to the State Department, while the commandant's line runs to Army headquarters in Heidelberg, thence to Headquarters United States Forces Europe in Paris, and thence, finally, to the Pentagon.

Despite the fact that Clay was not given a formal command function, it was inevitable and surely intended that local authorities, Allied and German should turn to Clay for advice. One result of this situation was that Clay advised the President at the top of the command channel as well as the American commandant and the deputy chief of mission at the Berlin end. In part, therefore, his appointment had the effect of short-circuiting the American command structure as it affected Berlin and—insofar as America leads the Alliance—the Allied command structure as well. Friction was thus inevitable. But the friction produced enough light to reveal the structural defects of the inverted pyramid that forms the Berlin command, and a good deal more.

Article Six of the NATO Charter commits that organization's armed forces to assist in repelling an attack on the occupation forces of any member nation. This is the letter of the NATO commitment to Berlin, and through it the Berlin command ramifies into the executive councils of fifteen nations. The NATO high command is a collegium, and a command decision of the fifteen nation alliance must be unanimous. Collegial reaction is almost by definition too little and too late. Instead of strengthening the Allied position in Berlin by bringing to bear the combined power of the Alliance, the involvement of NATO in many ways actually weakens the Western position by hamstringing it with the necessity of coming to a combined command decision. The Allied position is not fortified by the weight of additional numbers but dissipated by the variety of interests the additional numbers represent. A local command trumpets alarm to NATO headquarters, only to hear—after a long silence—the voice of Denmark pleading caution.

This situation is further complicated by the fact that the Supreme

Allied Commander Europe (NATO) and the commander-in-chief of the United States Forces in Europe are one and the same man. If he in his capactiy as American commander in Europe makes a strong proposal to the NATO high command, he must then turn to preside over the discussion of his own proposal and various Allied counterproposals in his capacity as Supreme Commander of NATO. The two functions, exercised by the same man, frequently compromise each other.

An all-out armed attack on Berlin obviously means war. But there is often great difficulty about the interpretation of lesser incursions. If the full significance of the Wall could have been forseen or fully appreciated the moment construction began, it is at least questionable whether the action would have gone entirely uncontested by the Allies. But the difficulty of interpretation also lends itself as an excuse to weasel out of any specific fulfillment of the Allied commitment in Berlin. When a Soviet fighter plane attempted to force down an American military transport in February 1962, for example, Allied spokesmen in Berlin protested to reporters that they could not be certain that a grounding was actually intended. To be sure, the Soviet pilot had flown just six feet from the American plane's wing tip and had lowered his landing gear, the standard command signal to land. Still, inadvertence could not be ruled out. Because of the news blackout, it was not ruled out until nearly a month later, when it was revealed in Washington that the Soviet pilot had radioed his commander for permission to fire a burst from his machine guns, the aeronautic equivalent of a shot across the bow, because the American pilot did not respond to his signal to land. The fact that permission to fire was refused was then adduced to show that the Allies were right not to take any counteraction.

But by March matters had gone far enough. The Allies sent up French, British, and American fighter planes to circle at the mouth of the corridor and to patrol the length of the corridor from time to time. The Soviet attempts to obstruct or intimidate air traffic between the West and Berlin abruptly ceased. On April 11 it was announced that Clay had "accomplished his mission" and would be leaving Berlin in the near future. Willy Brandt, speaking before the Foreign Press Association, explained that Clay would remain at President Kennedy's disposal and would return to Berlin "in a few hours at any new sharpening of the situation." Brandt felt constrained to add that there could be "no question that General Clay has been relieved." There could indeed be no such question. Rather it was a question whether Clay did not resign out of frustration. To those who knew Clay that question was rhetorical.

The fundamental safeguard against rampant militarism in the new army was the replacement of the old German general staff by the civil service apparatus. The Bundeswehr is the only army in Europe that does not possess its own national command. This is because it was created expressly for integration in an Allied defense force under international command. The concept of integration was itself the great external safeguard designed to provide the Germans with a feeling of equality, and their Allies—and their potential enemies—with a feeling of security against the emergence of a national German army. In short, the West German army is directly dependent on integration in an international force, not only structurally but also psychologically: it draws its morale, its *esprit de corps,* its very justification for being, from the political philosophy of the Atlantic Alliance.

Although a statement of this fact is beginning to sound quaintly declamatory, it is no joke in Germany. The German insistence on codetermination in nuclear planning and targeting and copossession of tactical atomic weapons was always based on the premise of nondiscrimination, at least within the European community.

The two-key arrangements under which German units were equipped with tactical atomic delivery systems while the United States retained the warheads were more than merely token recognition of the unattainable yet valid egalitarian ideal in a military alliance of atomic and nonatomic powers. This was the basis of the forlorn fascination of the Multilateral Force for the Atlanticist wing of the Christian Democratic Union. When the choice was forced between France and the United States, those Germans who clung single-mindedly to integration as the only practicable formula for Germany seized upon the additional degree of atomic pooling provided by the MLF proposal as a substantial step toward meaningful collective security, or, to the same purpose, a valuable pawn to be surrendered only in return for meaningful political concessions from the Soviet Union. As Konrad Adenauer never tired of emphasizing, "The disarmament problem can not be divorced from the German problem." For the Germans, nuclearization became coterminous with integration.

The Starfighter crisis reflects almost every aspect of the German national dilemma. The F-104 was designed and developed primarily for assignment to a tactical nuclear role. This was the principal if not the only reason why Bonn purchased at enormous and continuing expense some seven hundred of the aircraft—as an investment in nuclear integration. The Federal Republic's enforced and extraordinary dependence on its Allies, particularly the chief Ally, for weaponry, instruments, and equipment, was formalized in November, 1964, when Defense Minister von Hassel signed an agreement to purchase some 700 million dollars worth of arms and equipment annually from the United States to offset the outflow of dollars for the maintenance of United States troops in Germany. Long before this, von Hassel's predecessor, Franz Josef Strauss, used to quip that German generals were no longer militarists but industrial buyers, since their chief activity was arms procurement by long-term purchase contracts in the United States, and to a far smaller extent, elsewhere in the West.

The German version of the Starfighter is designed to carry atomic bombs and has been burdened with 320 pounds of extra electronic equipment. In addition to increasing the volume of procurement purchases from the United States, this specialization made the Starfighter probably the heaviest and most complicated single-seat aircraft in operation. But as maintenance and operation of the aircraft became more difficult, the number of qualified technicians available to the German armed forces—particularly the number of noncommissioned officer pilots and maintenance personnel in the Luftwaffe—sharply decreased. In one air-transport squadron, for example, 40 per cent of the noncommissioned officer pilots failed to re-enlist in the eighteen-month period from January 1, 1965, to mid-1966.

More than twice as many short-term draftees as originally planned are now being used in Starfighter maintenance crews, a fact that is both a direct and an indirect cause of the steady increase in crashes, since the decrease in the quality and quantity of maintenance crews curtailed the number of flying hours needed by trained pilots to maintain proficiency. The over-all problem is even greater. According to statements by von Hassel, there is a shortage of some forty thousand noncommissioned officers in all three branches of the service. They have a combined strength of about 430,000. For the last two years, approximately half of all draftees for the Bundeswehr have requested deferment, and more than two-thirds of the requests have been granted, the majority to students in technical and scientific disciplines.

The towering indifference toward the Bundeswehr has thus kept pace with the increasing disillusionment of the youth of Germany with the Atlantic Alliance and its goals. In this sense the crisis in the German armed forces and government is a local manifestation of the NATO crisis and much more.

Every aspect of the German postwar situation has conspired to make maximum integration with Germany's Allies the overriding domestic political passion. For it is only from the evidence they give to themselves and to the world of having outgrown nationalism that the Germans can draw the strength they need to achieve the national aim. The federation of Europe was, and somewhat wistfully still is, regarded as the first step toward reunification. What the Common Market most urgently needs, as far as the Germans are concerned, is a common foreign-trade policy, specifically "a real and generally acceptable concept for the coordination of East-West trade."

For NATO, the German's chief concern was the achievement of unanimously accepted strategic doctrine. As the Christian Democrats' foreign-policy troubleshooter, Kurt Birrenbach, summed it up in the Bundestag NATO debate in March, 1966, "Integration is the life principle of German foreign and defense policy."

Conversely, the Germans have an obsessive fear of isolation. Their preoccupation with avoidance of discrimination is part of this fear. They are determined, as Helmut Schmidt, the Social Democratic party's chief defense spokesman, put it, "to allow no regulation which *de jure* or *de facto* would bring us still more into a special situation vis-à-vis our contractual partners, because every special position of the Federal Republic aggravates the danger— in the event of crisis or conflict—that the Federal Republic will become isolated."

This complex of considerations and factors accounts for the almost pathological dread of the Germans that they may be sold short or betrayed; that their Allies, and particularly the United States, may come to an agreement with the Communist enemy at their expense. This is the basis for the Germans' unceasing quest of assurances. De Gaulle's eviction notice to NATO was seen as a deliberate act of disintegration, and it has given the Federal Republic pause for the most agonizing reappraisal of its brief history. The Süddeutsche Zeitung wrote:

> The consequences [of this act] could make themselves felt very soon on three levels: first in a disruption of the world political balance between East and West, second in a disruption of the inner European balance in the West, and third in a disruption of the internal political balance in the Federal Republic. Between these three levels there is a fatal connection. . . . The platform of German policy remains the incorporation (of West Germany) into a system in which legitimate and unrenounceable goals should be made the common cause to be realized jointly and by peaceful means.

If making "legitimate and unrenounceable" national goals the common cause of an international community seems quixotic today, it must be remembered that the necessity for banding together to form a solid front against the Communist threat provided a gigantic diversion from the German moral dilemma proper. The anti-Communist crusade of the 1950's provided, or seemed to provide, a legitimate path toward national rehabilitation as well as territorial restoration.

But with the policy of coexistence and its United States counterpart of relaxation, the basis of the great diversion was withdrawn, the high road of rehabilitation and restoration by crusade was closed. The Germans suddenly found themselves overextended abroad, divided at home, and in danger of ultimate abandonment by their Western friends (never by their Eastern enemies). When the great mantle of the crusade was withdrawn, it left the nation in danger of being reduced to its original pariahdom. The corollary of that pariahdom is this: The moment the common cause becomes merely the German cause, it is doomed.

What the Germans fear most—and the Communists most desire —is the isolation of the cause. The Germans have tried to bind the Allies contractually to active support of the German national cause. They have failed. They have been unable to fix the commitments and pledges of the Allies in terms that were juridically binding. The language of the undertakings of the Allies in the various instruments and treaties of the Atlantic community remained eloquent expressions of sympathy or more or less sincere emotion inspired by the crusade.

It was hardly coincidental that a crisis in the German military should have brought down the Erhard government in the fall of

1966 and thus put an end to seventeen years of uninterrupted Christian Democratic tenure in the Federal Republic. Nowhere has Germany's position been so grotesque and yet so tragic as in the armed forces. A German army joke recounts the return of a German general from a prisoner of war camp in the Soviet Union in the mid-fifties. He asks after his former colleagues, beginning with the Commander-in-Chief and Chancellor at the end of the war, Admiral Doenitz.

"Doenitz," answers his friend, "is in Spandau" (a suburb of Berlin).

"But what is an admiral doing in Spandau?" asks the general.

"He's in prison, naturally."

"Ah yes, naturally. And what is Rommel's former chief of staff, General Speidel, doing now?"

"He is in Paris."

"In prison?"

"No, at NATO headquarters, naturally."

"Ah yes, naturally. And what is the famous general, 'Panzer Meyer' doing?"

"He's in Canada."

"With NATO?"

"No, no, in prison, naturally."

"Naturally. And what is our former chief of the general staff, General Heusinger, doing?"

"He's in Bonn."

"In prison?"

"No, no, in the Ministry of Defense, naturally."

At this point the general rises and prepares to leave.

"Where are you going?" asks the colonel.

"To a mental institution," answers the general, "for if all that you have told me is 'natural' then I am stark raving mad!"

German opinion—indeed, Allied and world opinion—was soon to be rocked by American tribal habits that tore violently at the Presidency and the Presidential image. The shock had enduring and unfortunate repercussions which no expert can blithely explain away.

Chapter 13

CROSSED COMMUNICATIONS AND
COMMUNICATORS

Ŷ

FOR most of the outside world the real Chinese puzzle these days is in the United States and its prominent personalities. Foreigners boggled—still do—at the spectacle raised by the storm around an "authorized" book by William Manchester. There it was, a Kennedy family-sponsored compilation, *Death of a President,* which the very world-favored widow of the President challenged. Foreigners, by tradition, are accustomed to noted people and families of the past offering through heirs or protégés the assessments of famous men and women.

Never, not even in medieval times, had such a furor been raised about a book. Instant communications gave the world a ringside seat at the rather squalid spectacle of recrimination and legal sparring. Mrs. Jacqueline Kennedy, with her special place on a pedestal, elicited mass sympathy and voluminous perplexity. Her brother-in-law, junior Senator Robert F. Kennedy of New York, interestingly, lost stature. His role in having the book commissioned and the subsequent titillating drama became intertwined with accusations that he had been responsible for a great deal of "bugging" as Attorney General.

Around the world, but particularly in Europe, the last-minute Kennedy family effort to stop serialization in magazines and exercise special editing prerogatives went down badly. Censorship, however subtle, is too enmeshed with European remembrances of recently past restrictions. Mrs. Kennedy, the widow, has gotten off far better in the minds of foreigners than Robert Kennedy. Rightly or wrongly, with millions of words in publications and on TV purporting to provide an insight, Bobby is held responsible. Why? Having been convinced, especially under the Johnson Administration, that politics are an invidious American tribal habit, Bobby is singled out for seeking to deflate anti-Johnson excerpts in the book. He never managed the golden youth appeal of his late brother. Actually, his high-handed treatment of European officials and his interest in striking a fast deal on diplomatic levels always upset foreign authority. They plainly don't care for his methods and his personality.

Therefore, it was with easy sarcasm that they sympathized profoundly with Jacqueline Kennedy and observed that they expected nothing more than authoritarianism from Bobby. The whole episode left a trail of global distaste, bound to linger for a long time. Similarly, the wire-tapping controversy intruded itself on the fiasco of the book arrangements. Foreigners, for the last twenty-odd years, have felt themselves very bound up in American political upheavals. They remain so entranced, despite General de Gaulle. Alliances through war and peace, American generosity, and what many regard as callousness or naïveté in power, all impinge on other lives.

So the vast bulk of foreigners believe, whether they say they care for our behavior and interest or not. When J. Edgar Hoover, director of the Federal Bureau of Investigation, charged that Robert Kennedy knew about a good deal of wire-tapping, interest abroad grew. Again, as with censorship, bugging is something many know about personally with genuine aggrievement. The director of the FBI has never been, to outsiders abroad, a very pleasant personality. Their reasoning is based on how their own police systems —past and present—use wire-tapping.

Shocked befuddlement was the general reaction to Hoover's charges. A fortnight after he divulged that wire-tapping and electronic eavesdropping increased during Robert Kennedy's tenure as Attorney General, confirmation came from a former top aide, Edwyn Silberling, now in private legal practice. Silberling had for two years been chief of the Justice Department's crime and racketeering section. He remembered distinctly Bobby putting pressure on the FBI to use more "technical equipment." It was, recalled Silberling, to combat organized crime.

It went, unfortunately, far afield from Silberling's province. Surveillance through bugging, at Bobby's recommendations, extended to hitherto undisclosed places and people. Emmet John Hughes, writing in *Newsweek* magazine of February 6, 1967, on "Trials of

Government-in-Exile" (about the Kennedy political entourage)
skirted the edges: "And all merchants of political gossip have
found rich, new fare to market—above all, the haunting question:
precisely how—according to Mrs. Kennedy's taped interviews—
did the late President and his Attorney General show distrust and
practice vigilance over Vice President Lyndon Johnson?"

The "haunting question" of Emmet Hughes's article has provoked a welter of comment, direct accusation, and recrimination.
None of the people behind the tantalizing comment, however, will
permit themselves to be quoted by name. There is only the suggestion that the bizarre account may well be placed before the
electorate in the campaign of 1968. A conviction is growing that
J. Edgar Hoover will turn on the tap of revelation through documentation. One of the most controversial personalities in high
American official position, his enemies are numerous and vocal. At
the same time, Hoover is something of a national monument. A
highly experienced political infighter, he would never have made
his anti-Bobby disclosures unless he had facts, figures, and times
on record.

That Hoover's accusations involved Robert Kennedy rapidly
became a topic of prime interest to foreigners. Bobby's denials
seemed very lame, indeed, when heard abroad. The political habits
of Americans, in this field of electronic eavesdropping, were held
up to pitiless examination. Even the Russians cynically published
reports about how American society was permeated with suspicion.
Theirs was probably the most lopsided version offered in the gamy
episode.

Yet such experts as Lippmann, Senator Fulbright, Harrison
Salisbury, and Henry Shapiro have never condescended to speak
or write of bugging in Communist-run communities. In the
U.S.S.R., for example, most of us used to try to detect microphones
in obvious places in walls, telephones, and elaborately decorated
chandeliers. On a Sunday afternoon, four of us went around a hotel
apartment. We dug out with penknives and screwdrivers fourteen
listening devices. Granted, they were primitive. Every Western
government, however, employs special technicians assigned to
"debug" embassies in Communist capitals. Our newly built embassy in Warsaw produced a harvest of bugs, many equipped with
special infrared devices.

Communist regimes, nevertheless, played the Hoover-Kennedy

wire-tapping fracas as part of the "credibility gap." This phrase has been applied by critics of the L.B.J. Administration against what they contend is half-truth, secretiveness, and suspicion. All the experts in Washington tirelessly search for examples of the "credibility gap." Scotty Reston, in one of his regular columns in *The New York Times,* wrote of Bill Moyers' resignation as press secretary that Moyers had been badly wounded at "Credibility Gap." Unpleasant affairs at home and bungling, when it occurs, are shown as proof of the remark. The major effort is launched against United States policy in Vietnam. In this field the experts single out the top advisers to President Johnson, when they are not after the President himself. Lippmann, as foremost expert, in an article actually gave L.B.J. to the end of 1967 to settle the war—or else.

For unmitigated ˙arrogance, Lippmann's ultimatum was unexceeded even by his challenges to F.D.R. and Harry Truman.

Toward the end of 1966, he assumed: "Our people do not think that, measured by our official objectives, we can win the war." The flat declaration was utterly contrary to all the polls, as far as polls are valued, which stated that the majority of Americans wanted to win the war and as swiftly as possible. Lippmann never once, since his criticism began by talking only to like-minded experts, gave Johnson marks for striving to contain the objectives of conflict in Vietnam. Yet it is useful to remember that when L.B.J. followed Kennedy, after the assassination, Lippmann often called him "the great healer."

Less high and mighty, almost to the point of humility, Scotty Reston stared at the "credibility gap." There has been plenty of guff from the Administration to toss back at, say Defense Secretary McNamara. He has asserted all too confidently, all too often, that the war in Vietnam would be over in six months. His calibrated mind, so much respected, seems to have lost a few decimal points here and there. Reston, the reserved expert, believed that the top administration personnel were stale and tired. Fresher minds and voices were required, he wrote, to find a solution to Vietnam and to the war in the American cities.

Reston's melancholia did not—all experts feel themselves invulnerable—undertake any subjective search. Isn't it possible for a Reston, even a Lippmann, to be tired or stale or both? An expert may feel free to preach his own gospel, whether it be out-of-date or avant-garde. The suppleness of his cerebral creations may also be far below his fluent gift of gab or word imagery. Reston, always fond of drawing baseball analogies, could provide an interesting diagram for an infield on the top foreign policy levels of his own newspaper. The Tinker-to-Evers-to-Chance combination of old runs this way on the *Times*: Herbert L. Matthews-to-Robert Kleiman-to-Harrison Salisbury. It's a completely offensive operation, because its members obviously feel no need for any defense. No other public medium in America can field such a double-play combination, which is so oblivious to reality—and often to simple matters of fact. Now Matthews has retired.

Salisbury's eminence on the *Times* has been watched by his own colleagues, mainly those who once worked abroad with him, with commingled distrust and outright hostility. He became number one assistant managing editor. How did he join the *Times*? After years with the United Press, he talked to the late Edwin L. (Jimmy) James, then managing editor of the *Times*. Nothing was available, James said, unless Salisbury got a visa to Moscow. The *Times* bureau had been closed down by order of the Soviet regime under Stalin. James considered his interview with Salisbury a closed chapter. In a short time, however, Salisbury returned. He could get the visa if the *Times* job was open, he said. Salisbury went to Moscow for the *Times* in 1949, the height of Stalin's rule, and stayed five years. He has been a special expert on Communist affairs ever since, including his return to editorial promotion.

To our knowledge Salisbury never dwelt upon Stalin's cruelty; only his "benign" qualities.

A gangling man, with a storklike posture and earnestness etched into an expression made a little avuncular with silver-rimmed spectacles and a toothbrush mustache, Salisbury had staff pets. Animosity in upper, working echelons toward his ideas, newspaper and personnel, created a neo-Byzantine atmosphere. An attempt was made early in 1966 to reshuffle the high command, where Salisbury was number one assistant to E. Clifton Daniel. Salisbury fought back. After all, at fifty-eight he knew how to deflect intrigues. Let him rove abroad, was one solution. He did—ten weeks around the periphery of China. He concluded that the mainland had become an implacable enemy of the Soviet Union. Salisbury's dispatches were as if he had never left the U.S.S.R., consistently emphasizing the positive. Returning to New York, he was offered an appointment to head the books division of *The New York Times,* and he rejected it.

The tug of war within the august hierarchy of the newspaper about where to install Salisbury terminated with an indecisive compromise. He would divide the chore of being first assistant managing editor with Abe Rosenthal, who made a remarkable record in a short time as metropolitan, or city, editor. Salisbury also would be available for special assignments in the field. He had applied, as did dozens of other American correspondents, including some from the *Times,* for a visa to North Vietnam. In six months, at a time when the Communist world was in full cry denouncing United States air raids over Hanoi as all-out attacks on civilians, the visa came through.

"Salisbury getting the visa was predictable," a ranking *New York Times* editor, obviously in the anti-Salisbury faction, remarked to us. "So the controversy over his pieces will revive his lease on life in a top job on the paper and its policies."

Salisbury obtained approval from the State Department to make the trip. Normally, United States passports are invalid for travel to Hanoi. He flew to the Cambodian capital, Pnompenh, and took a plane to Hanoi. It didn't take long for him to begin cabling eyewitness reports back home. As his colleagues wryly observed before he landed, Salisbury's dispatches were, indeed, predictable. Salisbury said: "All casualty estimates and statistics in these dispatches are provided by Vietnamese officials, but the bomb damage descriptions are based wholly on visual observation. So far as I am aware, there has been no censorship of my dispatches; but they are read by North Vietnamese officials before being transmitted."

His explanations of transmission conditions hardly differed from those he offered when correspondents were compelled to submit to censorship in the Soviet Union. To a few they sounded plausible and reasonable, as in the times Salisbury wrote of Stalin as a benign grandfather.

By writing of visual impression, Salisbury conveyed the idea that he was keenly aware of bomb damage from the air. This is in the nature of instant expertise. There was a bare suggestion that maybe the bombing was launched against places where military stores had been hidden among civilians. It was a very thin suggestion. Professor Honey, for instance, as a former resident of Hanoi, can cite chapter and verse where military hardware is dispersed among civilians. From the time the United States undertook to bomb targets in North Vietnam, its precision has been remarkable. Consider the surface-to-air missiles thrown up against oncoming planes, as well as late-model Soviet-made antiaircraft batteries in rapid fire at the fighters. The North Vietnam regime, pledging endless resistance, must have been hurt badly—and not by civilian casualties.

In Washington, the administration clearly led itself into a snare when it repeatedly insisted that civilians could not be targets. Thus the "credibility gap" was pried wider by the experts in a reinvigorated clamor for termination of the war on terms largely suitable to the Communists. Only at the last minute did the government reveal the code name of an operation, "Big Eye," used for the bombing attacks. This involves sending a bomb control officer in a military version of a super-constellation airliner. The plane is packed with electronic equipment. The officer can plot the tracks of enemy and American planes on a radar screen. He calls back those United States planes that stray from their targets. American pilots over North Vietnam have standing instructions not to release bombs unless they are absolutely sure they are over their assigned target. The authors have been at pilots' briefings in widely assorted areas and heard those directives repeated.

The uproar, over civilians being caught in the raids and houses being demolished, once more ignored depredations by the Viet Cong and regular North Vietnamese units against southern civilians. During the height of the clamor, Viet Cong guerrillas smashed into a village of refugees from bitter combat zones. They gunned down workers putting together a makeshift Buddhist temple. Then they herded off 170 other men, women, and children. In the spring of 1966, we came on the twisted wreckage of vehicles and broken bodies of thirty-four people of all ages. The ambush occurred on a road not far north of Saigon a couple of hours before our arrival.

In 1965 alone, there were 15,200 recorded incidents of this type in South Vietnam. None of them involved military action— only terror. They somehow never make headlines or attract expert sympathy. On the propaganda side, the United States is and must remain at a disadvantage. We are left to infer that the regime of Ho Chi-minh does not dispose of a large and vociferous minority eager to believe the worst of its rulers. Salisbury's articles prompted our legislative expert on foreign affairs, Senator Fulbright, to say he expected to extend hearings to encompass the raids. The ranking Republican member of the Fulbright committee, Senator Bourke Hickenlooper, of Iowa, wondered about that point. Far from being even a regional specialist, Hickenlooper simply questioned the objectivity of Salisbury as a reporter.

Far more concerned with foreign issues on a daily basis is the Washington *Post*. It has often been critical of American policy in Vietnam, and squabbles among its own set of doves and hawks occur regularly. Salisbury's dispatches from Hanoi, however, brought a meeting of the minds to the *Post*. Keenly aware of his "visa-writing" habits from Moscow, the newspaper cast doubt on the reliability of Salisbury. In his first report, the *Post* noted, Salisbury wrote of civilian damages and casualties. Its own story compared the Salisbury presentation with a pamphlet published in Hanoi in November, 1966.

The two versions were identical in the number of civilian casualties, number of raids, number of people made homeless, types of bombs employed, and types of aircraft used. Salisbury's first account gave no source for his information—a requirement dinned into every reporter during his training. That omission also speaks loudly about the quality of editing on *The New York Times*. Thus, the first Salisbury piece gave the general impression that it was the result of his own research. Two days later he reported casually that he obtained statistics from the North Vietnamese. His offhand reference was buried deep in the article.

In the ensuing uproar, Hanson Baldwin wrote an article which the *Times* published on page one, obviously in an attempt to show that it provides two sides of a picture. The Baldwin piece contradicted Salisbury, without mentioning his name, in every major detail. It was an extraordinary presentation of newspaper ambivalence. The most bizarre behavior of the paper appeared about a week after the first Salisbury reports from Hanoi. In a lead editorial, headed "The Tragedy of Vietnam," *The New York Times* came as close to disavowing its correspondent Salisbury and his articles, which it had published, as any publication in modern history.

While contending it remained critical of United States policies in Vietnam and wanted a unilateral end to American bombing of the North, the *Times* wrote: "Yet, while posing the bombing, we reject the sweeping deductions and false conclusions many Americans seem to have drawn from the statistics of civilian deaths and the pictures of destruction reported from Hanoi last week by this newspaper's correspondent, Harrison Salisbury."

In further isolation of Salisbury, a top editor as well as correspondent, the newspaper denounced the mish-mash of evasiveness and administration bumbling on handling the information side of the raids. But, it went on: "That is quite different, however, from saying that there is even a shred of evidence to lend credence to the Communist propaganda that the U.S. is deliberately bombing civilian targets and that the campaign in the North has been one of terror, aimed at urban and residential areas and non-military targets. Such assertions bear no relationship to the truth. The targeting restrictions in the North have been precise and definite—so precise and definite that the military feel some American pilots have given their lives because of them. . . ."

It was not exactly a famous victory that Salisbury, the expert, scored.

We learned from editors at *The New York Times* that an "avalanche" of messages had been cabled to Salisbury in Hanoi. The queries were rushed after he failed to mention his sources—the North Vietnamese—in the first few dispatches mentioning civilian casualties. Called to testify before Senator Fulbright's Foreign Relations Committee, Salisbury conceded: "This was an error on my part, a simple journalistic error."

Simple, indeed! Any newspaperman, reporting from the field, is under obligation to source statistics. Salisbury's explanation, in light of the anguish it caused many of his own colleagues and editors as well as governments around the world, is too easily ingenuous. Further, much of his testimony to the committee didn't square with what he wrote from North Vietnam. Some samples are perplexing, if not contradictory. He said that he opposed a unilateral halt in United States bombing raids on North Vietnam.

When asked if the bombing in the North should be halted without a reciprocal move by Hanoi, Salisbury said: "If the question is, do we stop bombing them right out of the blue with nothing from them, I'd say *no.*"

Senator Stuart Symington asked Salisbury if American pilots had a right to jettison bombs to save their lives.

They did have that right, was Salisbury's answer.

Nevertheless, Salisbury's impressionistic and interpretative assessments of the Communist scene over the years always accentuated the "positive." On the spot in the U.S.S.R. he ignored Stalin's reign of terror, as noted earlier. A sampling of Salisbury's reporting is thus worthy of some attention.

Take the period, about a week, when Stalin had his stroke early in 1953 and Salisbury's comments published in *The New York Times* during the dictator's last illness and events immediately following his death. He wrote: "It may be difficult for persons in other lands to grasp it but it is true that to the ordinary Russian the phrases bestowed upon Premier Stalin—genius, architect, great leader, great teacher—have had genuine meaning. Premier Stalin has been to ordinary Russians a person apart from other humans, a figure of legendary qualities come to life."

After Stalin's death, when the old tyrant's first aide, Georgi Malenkov, took over with the dread secret police chief, Lavrenty Beria, at his side, Salisbury had this to say in the March 9, 1953, issue of *The New York Times*: "Mr. Malenkov's words were those of a man who sounded as if he were prepared to negotiate frankly and honorably with other nations in the interests of peace. . . . Good to Soviet ears were Malenkov's words and Mr. Beria's pledge of security and constitutional rights."

Beria, as chief executioner for Stalin, had jailed and liquidated millions. He was hated and mistrusted by every Russian family with a relative who had been a victim of the regime. From Soviet defectors and escapees from labor camps, the outside world had already for some years been given a realistic and macabre picture of the terror and the permanent purge. In a few months, Beria himself was liquidated when his comrades ganged up on him to preserve themselves.

In that same article, Salisbury indulged in prophecy. "Foreign suggestions," he wrote, "of a rift between China and Russia seemed far-fetched at least to some observers who watched Malenkov mount the podium of Red Square with Chou En-lai." Quite a flat prediction, in the light of what has since occurred between Russia and Red China.

Salisbury's predilection for visa writing from a difficult spot—in this case North Vietnam—got a big assist from the administration in Washington and some of its chief components in the Pentagon. Their eagerness to present an image of rosy optimism led to attempts to manage news breaks and offer for years the impression that the war was virtually over.

The bombing of North Vietnam, however precise, must have hit some civilians and civilian installations. Only when examples were shown that these casualties did indeed occur, was there any effort to lay some of the hard facts on the line. This has been true too of the predictions of victory. General Paul Harkins, ex-commander in Vietnam, was most prolific with optimism. Thus, the country-at-large paid scant attention to the danger of an ever-encroaching Viet Cong triumph, abetted by the North.

Secretary McNamara, too, with rapid and frequent trips to Vietnam, underrated the state of affairs. When the necessities of fighting the war compelled an expensive build-up of men and material, he foresaw the operation as a limited one bound swiftly to produce victory, once in 1965, and then in 1966. The neglect until a late date, even in a public affairs manner, of the vital pacification program is perhaps one of the most tragic omissions of the government's role in Vietnam. Robert Shaplen, an author and long one of the most experienced and astute observers of Vietnam, urged a little preoccupation with the civilian programs on both the Kennedy and L.B.J. Administrations. Very late in the game his pleas have been heard—and heeded.

Then, the cost in blood and treasure for the United States was belatedly presented to the public. It had been hinted at for some time, but never held up with something of a brutal frankness, as it was by President Johnson in a State of the Union message. After he disclosed the melancholy statistics, other ranking members of government seemed to have got the message and said what they thought the war costs really were. The spate of fresh frankness also moved the administration to admit a huge error in aircraft losses. The Defense Department said that we had lost 1,815 planes since 1961—at the start of 1967—which was nearly 1,000 more than have before been acknowledged.

That announcement, combined with sober estimates by L.B.J., immediately provoked critics into accusations of calculated misstatement on the part of the government. It also had the affect of refreshing the vigor of all opponents of American policy in Vietnam and Southeast Asia into redoubled complaints and demands that we withdraw entirely. In short, it has too often not been management of news or deliberate deceits but mismanagement in holding back the essentials. The end results are grief for the government and fast-and-loose play by critics, who either ignore or don't understand the stakes involved.

It becomes downright dangerous when Allies, would-be intermediaries, and self-seeking men of state propel themselves into the act. Part of their plight can be ascribed to the spiral of what is today known to the diplomatic trade as "peace probes," or smoke signals from Hanoi. The remainder of the dilemma is comprised of subjective interpretations relayed as the real thing—interpretations that conflict with declarations from men at the top of American government.

In this way a sand castle of hope was built quickly, early in 1967, when craggy and taciturn Soviet Premier Kosygin came to Britain on a state visit of a week's duration. Harold Wilson, the British Prime Minister, as slick a showman as there is on the modern political scene, let all sorts of hints drop. They added up to the same tune, reverberating around the world: Kosygin and he were coming closer to negotiations. They were frightfully busy, Wilson suggested strongly, and he had L.B.J.'s ear on a direct line. Two specialists—their presence carefully concealed—were rushed from Washington to stand vigil at our embassy.

Then, there came the dramatic 2 A.M. visit by Wilson and Foreign Secretary Brown to Kosygin's posh suite at Claridge's. Ho Chi-minh, in effect, said *nyet* to the proposals, which included a gesture of de-escalation in response to America's termination of bombing raids over North Vietnam. The *no* was relayed to Washington, which waited for Kosygin to get home before bombing again, after extending the bombing pause beyond a lunar New Year truce in Vietnam. Wilson, on TV and to the House of Commons, kept saying that Kosygin and he came a finger's span away from agreement—on negotiations.

There is no evidence available that this is so. The only proof we have is of confusion coursing through Soviet, British, and American policy-making echelons. In Washington, for example, Defense Secretary McNamara told a Congressional committee that bombing would not pay off militarily. But, he added, he didn't believe it should end. We modified our position somewhat; we'll talk with the Viet Cong in the South as well as Ho Chi-minh. The northern regime will not—perhaps cannot—say how negotiations might progress if we permanently end the bombing.

In what may have been their first overt concern about possible governmental and political stability in South Vietnam, the North decried the South's new constitution. It was drafted by a Constituent Assembly, put in office by elections the Communist guerrillas couldn't control, or make farcical. The concept of elections is pooh-poohed by critics outside the Communist world, who never take into account that they somehow can work under harrassing conditions. Elections in authoritarian communities, especially those in Eastern Europe, have usually been 95 per cent-plus for the regime. It was more equitable in South Vietnam, where parliamentary society has never really been known. Yet so aggravated, confused, and diffused has feeling become about how and what to do in Vietnam that a start on the road to political stability gets critical short shrift.

The intensity of the fighting in Vietnam, matched by expanding passion and compassion, also provoked a controversial spiritual note. Pope Paul VI urged extensions of Christmas and New Year forty-eight-hour-truces. To forces in Vietnam, the late Francis Cardinal Spellman of New York said anything less than United States victory in Vietnam was inconceivable. That was on Christmas Eve, 1966. The Vatican was faced with the disappointment of a resumption in hostilities and by the tone of Cardinal Spellman's address. Within the Vatican clerics who are authorized to make anonymous comments contended that there was a complete contradiction between the Pope's declared aspirations and the Cardinal's remarks.

To emphasize the Pope's attitude, the Vatican newspaper, *Osservatore Romano*, called for unconditional loyalty to the Pope's quest for peace in Vietnam. Using this pointed difference, Soviet commentators cynically plunged into the act. They accused the seventy-seven-year-old Cardinal of contradicting the words of the Pope. It would seem that clerics of assorted faiths have become intertwined in temporal affairs from which the practice of modern statecraft had excluded them.

The problem of peace on earth can be hammered out with reality today only by men of political authority and power—with all their ambitions and frailties. This fact of life, however morbid, has been overlooked by some other religious leaders. They are out to end the war in Vietnam—a worthy purpose—but deplore the American role. Among them are the ex-World War I U-boat commander, German pastor Dr. Martin Niemoeller; Dr. Ambrose Reeves, former bishop of Johannesburg; A. J. Muste, Presbyterian minister and veteran of left-wing movements; and Abraham Feinberg, American rabbi of Holy Blossom Temple, Toronto. They form part of an international movement, "Volunteers for Peace in Vietnam." Feinberg and Muste were more outspokenly critical of the United States than Niemoeller or Reeves. A search of their declarations on many issues throughout a fifteen-year period did not reveal any consequential protest against Soviet repression of workers' demonstrations in East Berlin or on behalf of Hungarians who rose in revolt in 1956.

Theirs is clearly infatuation with the premise that anything calling itself "left" or "socialist" must have inherent good. Dr. Benjamin Spock, the child-care expert using his knowledge for peace and disarmament, carefully skirts ideological confrontations. He endorsed in the January, 1967, issue of *Ramparts* the statement that 250,000 Vietnamese children have been killed accidentally since 1961. The article, by William Pepper, charged that 750,000 youngsters were wounded or burned by napalm. The magazine, once reputed to have a "liberal" Roman Catholic outlook with a shock treatment editorial needle, is a consistent critic of Americans in Vietnam. Pepper conceded in his piece, however, that no accurate figures are available on the number of child casualties. His estimate is based on what he regards as a "conservative" interpretation of semiofficial figures for the early years of the war.

Dr. Spock, as a baby expert, attaches himself to foreign affairs experts by applying his child guidance views to Vietnam. The grim article about children in *Ramparts* seems oblivious to Viet Cong and North Vietnamese harassment of children.

Dr. Spock, in his attack on American government "crocodile tears," has a similar attitude.

His therapy does seem rather selective. Never has Dr. Spock shown, for example, any concern about German children who suffer from a "Wall neurosis." It could be that they escaped his expert notice because isolation may not seem so dramatic as a grievous injury. Yet Spock is supposed to concern himself with all ailments in children.

It took the foresight of an Englishman, J. E. Finch, to see that twenty-five German youngsters from Berlin have a respite. They were brought to a holiday home of International Help for Children, to which Dr. Spock has easy accessibility. The majority stayed for six weeks at Little Pond House, the holiday home of the International. Others were lodged with private families, none of them expert in any way except compassion. Finch, who is warden of Little Pond, had this to say: "This Wall neurosis shows itself in a greater nervousness than you get in a normal child. Also there is a feeling of claustrophobia in West Berlin. It is a sealed-off city, and families cannot get out into the open country. The only open spaces they have are the parks."

The death toll of those who have sought to escape to the West since the Communists built the Wall came to 144 by mid-December, 1966. The Wall was built on August 13, 1961, but has in its grim appearance come to be accepted—with degrees of piety, sanctimony, and some mortification—by the experts. They have agreed to illuminate a beacon of approval for President Johnson's avowed interest in building bridges between Eastern Europe and the West. The Berlin Wall, they declare, is something for East and West Germans to resolve.

Coming to grips with a changing Eastern Europe, these opinions hold to be of prime importance once the Vietnam war is terminated. Salisbury, who thought that in Hanoi the behavior was quite like that of the defenders of the Alamo, is a leading expert in this field, too. The much-vaunted "credibility gap" is evidently as applicable to our experts as to the administration at which they launch their guided missives.

It is most useful to simply tick off a few things committed by East European regimes, particularly the Soviet, since L.B.J.'s declaration of October 7, 1966. His was a classier call to coexistence, which has been hailed as "*detente.*" It had become so popular that the last time NATO saw Paris—the December meeting of 1966; next time it's Brussels—many Allies figured it was time to get on a bandwagon. General de Gaulle began the procedure with his abandonment of the Alliance and unilateral *grande strategie* to the East. By aspiration and tradition, the compulsion persists in the West to try and find a way in which to live tranquilly. A tendency to become fed up with defense obligations or to run scared from the plangent overtones of war, such as the one in Vietnam, courses through the Western consciousness. It leads to uneasiness and uncertainty.

That it evokes only a cyclical response from the other side is normally overlooked. There was a time, back in 1959, when ex-Soviet leader Nikita S. Khrushchev, visited the United States. His trip, which transcended a foreign ministers' conference on Germany, was greeted with a huge sigh of hope. Gaullist-administered France joined in the fervor. The Eisenhower Administration decided on the Khrushchev visit as a tactical ploy to circumvent another possible crunch on Berlin. All the prominent experts, from Lippmann down, approved Khrushchev's tour. It was, they wrote benignly in the searing summer of 1959, "the end of the Cold War."

All warnings to go slow and examine each step of cooperation prudently and calmly were rejected by experts. Their rejoinder in a euphoric welcome to "The Thaw" was to call critics *cold warriors* and pay no heed to them. Well, events proved in dreary sequence that the Cold War was put for a time in cold storage. Today the popular word is *detente*. It is rolled over the tongue as a finished melody. In the few months to the end of the year, following President Johnson's October 7 declaration, sour notes from Eastern Europe made the sweet song sound like a cacophony from Dingbat the Singing Cat.

Consider briefly the conflict between the Polish regime run by party leader Gomulka and the country's leading intellectuals. Professor Leszek Kolakowski, one of Poland's foremost philosophers, was expelled from the party. He asserted that the party failed miserably to keep its promises made in the autumn of 1956, when the nation trembled on the verge of revolt. Kolakowski also declared there was no rule of law in present-day Poland. A letter protesting his expulsion was signed by twenty-two leading Polish writers. Offstage, in backroom maneuvers, they stand their ground. Gomulka has warned them to toe the line or face the consequences.

In the Soviet Union itself, sixty-three writers offered to stand as personal guarantors for the release of Andrei Sinyavsky and Yuri Daniel. They had been jailed for their satirical commentaries on the Soviet system. This, in the view of a former classmate of Sinyavsky, was the "first reflection of genuine public opinion since the revolution." Real names were signed to the petition. What happened since? The dreaded Soviet security service—held up by experts as rather meaningless today—has been pressuring the petitioners. Sinyavsky and Daniel remain in the roughest possible prison conditions.

Soviet justice, "liberalized" in expert eyes, also has been ruthlessly applied to some young Americans in calculated and political ways. There was the tragedy some months before the "bridge-building" speech by L.B.J. A young American, Newcomb Mott, was jailed for eighteen months. He strayed across the Norwegian-Soviet border. When transferred to another prison, Mott met death—by accident.

Then, came the spiraling ruthlessness against tourists.

Two other young Americans felt the lash of Soviet justice. They were charged with black-marketing a small sum of dollars for rubles. In the West the sum involved is petty larceny at worst. One of the young men also was accused of having stolen the small statue of a bear from a Leningrad hotel. One defendant was fined and released; the other imprisoned. The Russians were within their legal rights, just as they were when millions were summarily shot in purges. Being humane doesn't count. Once the late Andrei Vyshinsky, in a heated argument in Bucharest, shouted at the authors: "What matters is the letter of the law; not the spirit."

In this spirit the Russians, also diverted an Aeroflot plane to Prague to unload an unsuspecting ex-Czechoslovak, now an American citizen. He is Vladimir Kazan-Komarek, in the tourist business. He had been invited to Moscow by Intourist. His flight home was scheduled directly for Paris. Instead, the Russians landed in Prague to turn the hapless man over to Czech authority, which accused him of treason eighteen years earlier. In the future, let the tourist beware.

On wider issues that presumably do not affect human dignity, the Russians pressed ahead with an antimissile-missile defense against all American entreaties. This is the springboard for another arms race. Simultaneously, the U.S.S.R. increased its military budget. Reason? American "escalation" in Vietnam.

To make the Soviet policy plan clear, Kosygin spoke of Germany before departing from a state visit sponsored in France by de Gaulle. Germany, declared Kosygin, must remain divided. It was flatly irreconcilable to the experts, who urged the new German coalition government in Bonn to compose quietly their Eastern approaches. If Germany tried to reunify, observed Kosygin, there could be no peace in Europe. Pay no attention, interpreted such assessors as Lippmann. Kosygin, in effect, was bargaining. For what? The Soviet leaders never trim their power aspirations to suit times and climates. Only policy planners and experts in the West do that. The myth they wave today is that Russia is our ally against Red China.

A more realistic view is that the Russians maneuver and work hard at isolating separately the United States and China. To seek the cooperation of the United States would be self-defeating for the Russians. This was the considered judgment of Dev Murarka, Moscow correspondent of the *Indian Express* and *The Spectator* of London. Murarka's perception of Russian *Realpolitik* has been shrewd and hard-headed in recent years. Of course, he is not regarded as an expert. It only requires a little judiciousness to comprehend that if there is tension in Asia, there is certain to be tension in Europe.

In this respect, de Gaulle has ignored the international power tremor within the world. He is, with limited sights leveled essentially on a French-led Europe, an isolationist. Hence his appeal and "style," which so many of our own neo-isolationists find so absorbing and grand, particularly the Gaullist view of the "Detestable War" on Vietnam.

A more down-to-earth assessment was provided by a writer along in years who went to Vietnam. He was John Steinbeck, whose invitation to the young Russian poet Yevgeny Yevtushenko to join him was rejected. Steinbeck went to "go up the rivers and into the mountains to listen and see the war by myself." He wrote of a little village put together by refugees driven from their homes by the "liberating" activities of the Viet Cong.

"I don't know whether communications are open to Fulbright or Wayne Morse country," wondered Steinbeck, "but wouldn't it be nice if one or two of their constituent towns would revolt and be *for* something for a change."

Later in the same article, Steinbeck observed: ". . . I've never had much sympathy for the innocent bystander. I want to be a guilty bystander if necessary. Peaceful though I am, there's a great difference between a dove and a pigeon."

This is quite a different view of human behavior and understanding from that of such a universal expert as Lippmann, who declared that modern man is "isolationist." Lippmann, who "retired," transferred from Washington to New York. His plans include four months a year in France, where he is certain to obtain a special view of Vietnam, war's end or no. In France he can be perfectly at home with the blinkered Gaullist concept of the world. It is a varnished view far at variance from that of Dev Murarka, who sees the entanglements not only as an Asian but as an observer in Moscow. He wrote: "The antagonism between Peking and Washington may be sharp at the moment, but it is of recent origin. The antagonism between Moscow and Washington, however, is older, on a greater scale and very deep-rooted. It also takes the form of an open and direct competition for influence, besides which Washington's obsession with China may only be temporary. . . . A wary suspicion is all that can be expected of mutual relations between Moscow and Washington in the immediate future, and even after."

Our experts put it precisely the other way around. They even peer daringly into the future and see the vision of a Soviet-American alliance—a grand design—to contain China. When Mao Tse-tung's scientists detonated a hydrogen bomb device at the height of the last Middle East war, they saw it only as added impetus toward an arrangement with the U.S.S.R. For them, it seems, people and their unpredictable ways are a nuisance. This is the biggest, most dangerous credibility gap of all.

Chapter 14

AFRICA: PART ONE

🜊

AT THE high resort grounds of Bandung a siren song wafted to the outside world from an international gathering of African and Asian political personalities. It was in the spring of 1955, and President Sukarno, as host for Indonesia, strutted happily for the benefit of photographers and delegates in multiribboned, fresh uniforms. In the stuffy conference hall, where droopy delegates fanned themselves whenever the erratic air-conditioning wheezed to a stop, the catchword *nonalignment* was created.

It became a drumbeat theme. Before the conference was even over, nonalignment was seized upon as something special to cultivate, as a biologist might experiment with an interesting bacillus. The researchers were the two super powers, the United States and the Soviet Union. In nonalignment they each saw equally the seeds of accommodation and possible exploitation. The Russians had a head start, though. The handmaiden of nonalignment was the unstinted praise of "socialism." The countries represented and the potential governments also thrust aside *underdeveloped* as an unworthy description of their conditions. Instead, *developing* was happily discovered and came into vogue.

Five points of coexistence were agreed upon, and accepted even by blandly smiling Red Chinese Premier Chou En-lai. It was a time for African and Asian self-determination, although the Asians sought to take pride of place and experience. They turned the conference name around from Afro-Asian to Asia-African. In public speeches and private caucuses, the most prominent of the personalities had an afterthought. Latin-America, too, was in a developing stage but in the grip of colonialist-minded America despite United States interest in extending a helping hand to the nonaligned.

Latin America would, so promised the architects of the Bandung conference, be accorded every sympathy and moral assistance. Unmentioned publicly, but emphasized, was the coming of age of Asia and Africa in a tumultuous world. Sukarno feted his principal guests in regal style, replete with a new wife at his side. Prominent were India's late Prime Minister Nehru, mournful of mien but highly articulate of speech. The golden boy was Colonel Gamel Abdel Nasser, so recently risen by *coup d'etat* to the Presidency of Egypt. He was the principal spokesman for Africa, as the Bandung sponsors saw him. Then, there was gay and gentle U Nu, ex-Prime Minister of Burma. He was the least militantly ambitious of the group.

The vast assemblage, housed in Dutch-built hotels and villas, were heavily protected. A few miles down the road from Bandung, anti-Sukarno Moslem rebels still ambushed government vehicles. They might, so suggested Indonesian officials, try to invade Bandung itself during the conference as a show of strength. All sorts of special pleaders for anticolonialist causes appeared. Some were the most curious lobbyists imaginable. The Mufti of Jerusalem, once Hitler's pet Moslem, appeared in turban and flowing robes. He was once installed as a delegate of the Yemen. Harlem Congressman Adam Clayton Powell, impeccable in light summer grays and blues, showed too. He held a press conference, saying his grandfather had been a slave, and look what he, Adam, amounted to these days in the world!

The brew of nonalignment, socialism, and developing trends was headier than the drinks Sukarno secretly supplied guests not supposed to quaff a cocktail. Before the conference was over, some overtly suspicious delegates—notably those from Turkey, the Philippines, and Ceylon—urged fellow-conferees to be practical and refrain from being drawn into competition for the most unassailable nonaligned record. They were disdained as neo-colonialist stooges. The first conference at Bandung decamped with triumphant declarations that the nations that participated would shortly make their impact on the world. Quite a superclaim for a conference that pointed proudly to "nonalignment." As it turned out, Bandung was also the last conference of its kind that made any impression.

What happened sooner than later was the rise to eminence among nonaligned nations of Marshal Josip Broz Tito, Yugoslavia's maverick Communist leader. His break with Stalin and his long-established heterodoxy gave him instant admission to the club. He could not pretend to be African or Asian, but was first honorary citizen. His policies led him to espouse African and Asian causes. They went from President Sekou Toure of Guinea, Kwame Nkrumah of Ghana, Nasser, above all, to Nehru of India, and Ho Chi-minh of North Vietnam. Yugoslavia, a debtor nation, frequently loaned borrowed funds and credits to people and causes that it espoused in Africa and Asia. It still does, in a drastically reduced manner. Domestic demands and sweeping economic reforms simply mean it's more important to keep the money at home.

The African nations, soon to emerge as independent entities of their own, were rather swift to look askance at the condescension of their nonaligned Asian friends. Colonial rule had been dismantled without great bitterness, except in Vietnam, for new Asian countries. African territories ascended into nationhood only some years after those in Asia. The real competition involved Africans and Asians. But the United States, determined to deflect any intrusion by Soviet teams holding "socialism" high as a trail blazer, plunged into the Africa arena with money, projects, technicians, and experts. It may have been that because we felt a guilt complex about Negroes and civil rights at home, we sought to help out in Africa.

The real burst of African states began with momentum in 1960, although Guinea and Ghana became independent somewhat earlier. Because of this timing, Guinea and Ghana believed they should lead, and all others south of the Sahara should meekly follow. Sekou Toure and Nkrumah depicted themselves as "African revolutionaries." Neither of them led any armed rebellions. Power was handed over to them. In Nkrumah's case, a huge cash reserve from the British went with nationhood.

Just as African personalities felt abused by the switch of the Bandung conference title to Asia-African, so did they begin to smart under the arrogant direction Nasser took in all their collective names. The Americans—fortunately for us, the Russians as well—didn't begin for some time to separate conflict, personality clash, and combustible self-interest from varying regions of Africa.

North Africa, as an Arab enclave, generally looks down on what is called, "Black Africa," south of the Sahara. The blacks in power usually remember that Arabs traditionally were slave traders. West Africa, separated by vast jungle and desert from East Africa, feels smugly ahead of the Easterners in development. Where they quite naturally almost all agree is on elimination of those countries still under minority white rule. Otherwise, many conspire to topple each other's regimes, are engulfed in internal upheavals, and are far behind the goals they vowed were modest back in 1960.

With scant assessment of requirements, the United States plunged into the miasma of emerging Africa. We had regional experts, to be sure. They were nearly all Arabists. Of this group, most were fully embroiled with the future of Nasser and his expansionist hopes for a United Arab Republic. On balance, the regional experts— most of them are professional diplomatists—thought nobody but Nasser could hold back Communist takeovers. One of our most persistent pro-Nasser advocates has been Phillips Talbott, a genial chap who once was a newspaperman himself.

Talbott is now our ambassador to Greece, after having been head of the State Department desk for the Middle East. Nasser extended himself and his ambitions throughout Africa, especially where a community was Moslem. His broadcasts, as with anti-Nasser Arab politicians, never hesitated to appeal to the populace for bringing down an African regime that suspected his motives. Talbott, as assorted colleagues contend, managed always to find hidden per- suaders to prove that Nasser deserved all-out support.

To the extent that he managed well, a solid body of thought and planning remains entrenched in the State Department. Nasser preaches "Arab Socialism." An exasperated American businessman, after an extended stay in Cairo, defined it as: "Neither Arab nor socialist, but pure Nasser. It's a combination of unbridled power, protected by maneuvers Americans swallow." Although a charter subscriber to nonalignment, Nasser has come down on the side of the U.S.S.R. in most major external issues. He does not hesitate to denounce any setback as an American conspiracy. To prove that he is nonaligned to whichever side among Africans, Asians, and Latin Americans listen, Nasser points out that he is on cordial terms with Red China and Russia. So, in a strict diplomatic sense, is Switzerland. By tradition Switzerland is a truly nonaligned nation. Its practical associations have never prompted a Swiss government to demand that a hostile regime be toppled or that special people be targeted for assassination. Nasser's regime is on record for ap- pealing for mayhem and destruction of neighbors and fellow-Arab states. Lately he tells the world repeatedly that the United States is totally in the wrong in Vietnam. His argument goes that the North is in the right and the winds of change, as detected by Nasser, blow favorably for North Vietnam.

Whenever members of the American Congress demand to know why we still supply credits or surplus wheat to Nasser, excuses pour from our Arabists—a monopoly once held by the British.

Explanations by regional State Department experts usually run: Nasser is always suspicious of Jewish influences in American policies toward the Middle East. He remembers too poignantly the late Secretary of State John Foster Dulles's refusal to aid his own pyramid, the Aswan High Dam. He was compelled, therefore, to turn to Moscow for assistance as well as for the arms which we denied him.

The expert's defense of Nasser is oversimplified. They never say that he will be picking cotton for the U.S.S.R. for years to help defray the cost of the dam and Soviet armaments. Invariably, his employment of a large group of unrepentant Nazis to work on rocket projects is pooh-poohed as nothing meaningful.

The main thing, the experts contend, is that Nasser kept Communists and their sympathizers well in check. Did he? His propaganda services are riddled with pro-Communist voices. Virtually all proclaim the themes as laid down in Moscow, rather than in Peking. Similarly, Nasser's pilots and military technicians are trained by Russian specialists. They either go abroad to the U.S.S.R. for long spells to learn about weaponry or are taken in hand in Egypt at special sites at the disposal of the Russians. Even after the recent, shattering defeat by Israel, the same training system remains in effect.

His own brand of expansionism, which brought him far afield as a self-appointed liberator of the Yemen, also blurred security concepts of one-time brother Asia-Africans. By installing a puppet republican regime of his own, backed by fifty thousand Egyptian troops and a large air force, Nasser's expedition costs heavily. It would have bogged down without the free wheat our experts urged we provide. The Yemeni royalist regime, to be sure, was medieval by backward Arab standards. But Nasser decided on his own, and through the instrument of violence, to recreate conditions in his own image.

It has backfired in a terrifying manner. Tribal units, loyal to the feudal system, remain a fierce, guerrilla force. In the early flush of Nasser the liberator's remodeling scheme, our regional experts urged that his republican stooges be recognized. Don't do it, was the advice of the oft-maligned Central Intelligence Agency. The CIA said Nasser would not pull back. But our ambassador to the

Yemen, John Badeau, backed the Arabist. The late President Kennedy, acting on his advice, agreed. It proved to be, since recognition, that a unilateral war of liberation won backhanded American approval. Nasser bombs undefended Yemeni villages and burns up tracts of territory with napalm. Calmly, he berates the United States for its military operations in Vietnam, where we have a compact of alliance with the South Vietnamese. Nasser, in the Yemen, had nothing but personal aims of inflated glory.

His ambitions haven't diminished by the fiasco in the Yemen, where he used poison gas supplied by the Russians. Nasser becomes even more reckless, thereby going further into hock to the Russians. Their technicians help keep his big troop transports in a state of repair. Soviet airmen fly copilot on most missions, and Russian gunners are at the elbow of Egyptians. The Soviet military missions to these forces facing Israel expanded. All these extra services are for a price. The figure can only be estimated, and it comes to at least 20 million dollars annually just for added military expertise. Chicken feed for a big power but enough bread for thirty million Egyptians for months.

Besides becoming more deeply involved in Yemen—with almost no effort being made to compel him to get out—Nasser's raiders have taken to bombing Saudi Arabian border communities. In their sweeps they hover close to Ethiopia, to show off Nasser's air command. The United States is committed to helping protect the integrity of Saudi Arabia, with its vast oil wealth, and Ethiopia, which tries to exercise a measure of practical sense in African affairs.

Instead, some of our newest regional experts defend purely localized interests which our people adopt as their own. The American Ambassador to Ethiopia, Edward M. Korry, a tall man of pallid complexion who had been a foreign correspondent, sends off reams of cables regularly to Washington. Most concern the frontier hassles between Ethiopians and Somalis who have invited both Soviet and Red Chinese technical and hardware help.

Korry's wires have become something of a checker game for our diplomatists. They call the messages *Korrygrams*. In them he always refers to Haile Selassie, Emperor of Ethiopia, as HIM, standing of course for His Imperial Majesty. "HIM warns that if we cannot deliver the equipment he needs he will be forced to ask the Russians," is a sample of a *Korrygram*.

Between firing off HIM's demands for immediate United States aid, Korry has feuded with the ambassador to Somalia, whoever he happens to be. This is one of the more thankless—some would say, luckless—diplomatic posts in our service. Apparently Korry has operated on the theory that because he is stationed in Ethiopia, this is the only post of any real consequence to Washington. Advocates for other African regimes, sometimes even the Somalis, Korry cuts up in messages.

Korry, by virtue of stamina, has become an African expert; yet he was assigned as our ambassador to Chile. He never looked just outside or even deeply inside Ethiopia, to catch Nasserite agents smuggling guns to the Somalis so Nasser could keep his hand in that area, too. Actually, since his entry into Yemen, Nasser has put out large cash sums for exiles and places. He gets the money by excising it from the Egyptian economy.

Take a look at some of the people on Nasser's payroll: About $1,500 a month goes to the family of Moroccan Prince Mohammed El Khattaby. The prince's brother Abdel Krim fought the French and Spaniards. The present prince and family are useful for Nasser to have in reserve whenever argument flares between him and Moroccan ruler King Moulay Hassan. Other beneficiaries of Nasser's largesse, all of them opposed to regimes presently in their homelands, include the former chief-of-staff of the Jordanian army, Colonel Abdullah Tell. Nasser and Jordanian King Hussein are usually on the outs.

He hands out around $1,200 a month for the personal use of Abdel Hamid El Serraj. Once the strongman of Syria and still fairly young, El Serraj plots for his return home. A couple of former emirs of South Arabian states, under British protection, are living on Nasser's generosity. He makes no secret of wanting the areas from which the exiles fled under his own benevolent guidance. He also takes care of ex-Premier Abdul Rahman Razzak of Iraq. The widow and family of Patrice Lumumba, former Congolese premier, are generously assisted by Nasser.

His most glamorous beneficiary is Fathia Nkrumah, wife of the deposed "Redeemer," of Ghana. She is Egyptian-born, but her husband supported Nasser on virtually every position. Nasser accepted Nkrumah's claim to pan-Africanism, south of the Sahara belt. They were both revolutionaries, according to Nasser. When Nkrumah grandly gave a partnership to Sekou Toure as a pan-

Africanist, Nasser applauded the gesture. He could, and has, manipulated them both.

Nkrumah had the rug pulled out from under him while on a state visit to Red China in the early winter of 1966. He vowed a quick return and ruthless reprisal. Instead, he had to settle for his wife going to Cairo and his sharing what Sekou Toure offered him —an equal share of rule in Guinea. When the successor regime in Ghana began to reveal what they were discovering about Nkrumah's methods and how his cronies enriched themselves, both Russians and Red Chinese became mum. Nkrumah, overnight, didn't exist. Nor did his roundly applauded "socialism" ever exist, but on paper. That was the surly complaint from *Izvestia*.

An espionage network, linked to East Berlin and Moscow, was uncovered, and details of its operations were exposed. The apparatus was to coordinate all subversive work in Africa. Neither the Russians nor the Chinese seemed to have canceled out each other. They competed to control the system. Neighboring African states were singled out as targets for subversion and subjugation. Russia and Red China, in this instance, cooperated cheerfully with Nkrumah's concept of what he called "Continental Union Government."

Ghana was intended as the base for Nkrumah's export of revolution. An East German, thirty-three-year-old Juergen Kruger, whose real surname was Rogalla, was in charge of the school for spies. Second in command was another East German, Captain Rolf Stollmayer. They had both been trained in the U.S.S.R. by the Soviet KGB (all-inclusive secret service) and GRU, military intelligence. On that blustery day in early winter of 1966, when General Joseph Ankrah set off the coup against Nkrumah, Stollmayer smuggled himself aboard a commercial airliner and escaped. Kruger was arrested, interrogated at length, and expelled. But they had no chance to destroy many of the documents they compiled with Teutonic efficiency.

Pro-*coup* Ghanians, some of whom had been infiltrated into the vast espionage network to take over Black Africa, held caches of notes and books. More than thirty thousand documents remained in their hands. Involved were 1,100 Russians and 430 Chinese. They have all been deported except for the twenty-five Soviets who made up Nkrumah's palace guard: they were shot down, to a man, when they tried to surrender. But the professional proponents of nonalignment and apologists for Nkrumah have tried to laugh away the evidence.

In Nkrumah's own handwriting, for example, there is a set of instructions for espionage work in Nigeria. Included is a protocol between Ghana and China to furnish instructors, for bugging hotels in the sprawling, ramshackle capital of Accra. To compensate for the aid, Nkrumah promised the Chinese his own cooperation for toppling the monarchy in strife-torn Burundi.

All these contrived machinations have gone unnoticed by one of the world's leading Africanists who instead tells rallies in New York that the Americans should stay out of Vietnam. He is Dr. Conor Cruise O'Brien, presently holder of the Dr. Albert Schweitzer chair at New York University.

An active combination of educator-writer-political philosopher, O'Brien first made himself known to the world in the Congo. He came from Eire and made his mark on the United Nations quickly. At Dr. O'Brien's goading and persuasion, the UN made an international intrusion into domestic affairs. Its units forced their way into the copper-rich province of Katanga. The object: To get rid of Moise Tshombe, ambitious and slick governor. The UN achieved O'Brien's purpose—briefly. After a short exile, Tshombe returned as Premier of all the Congo. Then he lost out himself to an army *coup*. That was the eighth military takeover in Africa in a six-month period of 1965–1966.

In the series of *coups* O'Brien remained unmoved. As vice chancellor at the University of Ghana, he was paid by the state. To our knowledge he never mentioned, while in the post, the system Nkrumah used of teachers reporting on one another, of pressures on Ghanian instructors from their own regime, and of the introduction of police agents into the faculties. Before Nkrumah's downfall, whenever an outside or exiled charge was aimed at Nkrumah, O'Brien was among the most vociferous to refute accusations against him.

O'Brien stays steadfast, however, in the belief that a so-called nonaligned state, especially in Africa, must not begin to sympathize with the West. The fetish is not unique with O'Brien except that he is rather well known internationally. Established "liberal" thinkers of the O'Brien persuasion believe it is profoundly sinful for a nonaligned community—when it so designates itself— to ever think in positive, pro-Western terms. He even contends that: "Revolutionary social and economic changes must occur throughout the whole of the under-developed—'non-aligned'—world and . . . such changes are not likely to be carried out except by disciplined, revolutionary, political movements which are likely to be of Communist type. . . . It is not enough to say that an under-developed country has the right to be non-aligned; it is necessary to recognize its right to 'go Communist.'" [authors' italics]

Dr. O'Brien refuses, therefore, to concede that should a country so desire, it can also go pro-West, pro-mixed economy, or even become aligned. He has even, because of preconceived notions, ignored the possibility that nonalignment has diminished to the vanishing point. The last meeting in New Delhi, of Mrs. Ghandi, Tito, and Nasser was a bore and an embarrassment for the Indian Prime Minister. Her press wanted to know whether this meeting was necessary, with India convulsed by riots around the country and prospects of famine. Tito's own entourage, among the original architects of these meetings when Prime Minister Nehru was alive, told us: "It will be better for future meetings to be held by technicians. Then, they might fade away entirely."

Only Nasser remains lukewarm to the conclaves as a frayed symbol to his own global prestige. But O'Brien, in his narrow defense of nonalignment, won't even recognize changes that have swept over states once loud in espousal of nonalignment who shudder today at the terminology. Nkrumah was the embodiment of modern totalitarianism. His leftist slogans and phrases always kept him free of the taint of authoritarianism or even fascism. So long as the totalitarianism was couched in a leftist lexicon, Nkrumah could and did get away with murder.

The classic individual case was his imprisonment of J. B. Danquah, a lawyer in his late sixties. Danquah had been known as the grand old man of Gold Coast (later Ghana) nationalism. When Nkrumah was jailed by the British, Danquah defended him. But Danquah, a tough-minded veteran of nationalist affairs, objected to the rapid Nkrumah construction of a one-party state beholden to him. For this he was hounded by Nkrumah's police and then jailed in wretched conditions for a man of his age.

A lithe and solemn African nationalist of many years experience, the former President of Nigeria Dr. Nnamde "Zik" Azikiwe wrote eloquently of Dr. Danquah. He also exposed the ever-encroaching totalitarianism of Nkrumah. His documented details made no impression on the Africanists who saw the figure of the future in Nkrumah. Its tone, ironically, was held up to scorn when the vast federation of Nigeria nearly disintegrated in a coup. Yet when the coup that removed Nkrumah shook the world a month later, it seemed to have aroused sympathy for the deposed dictator. Again, the magical word "socialist," was invoked in Nkrumah's favor, whereas that label was inapplicable to the dangers that since have beset multitribal Nigeria.

In Africa, though, the case history of Ghana as exemplified by the cult of personality surrounding Nkrumah, is by no means closed. He holds co-office with fellow African "revolutionary," President Sekou Toure of Guinea. Between them, they set their own ground rules. When the post-*coup* regime of General Ankrah detained a delegation of Guineans in an airplane, Sekou Toure also reacted unwisely. Ankrah claimed he was holding the Guinean group bound for an Organization of African Unity (OAU) meeting to prompt return of Ghanians held in Guinea. Most of them are pro-Nkrumah, anyway. Sekou Toure retaliated. How? By putting the American ambassador under house arrest.

Ever since he made the show of putting Nkrumah on a propped-up pedestal, Sekou Toure blames the Americans for anything that goes wrong. It was once different with him. That was when we had a level-headed, determined noncareer ambassador, William H. Attwood, in constant communication with Sekou Toure. The result, in a short while, was that Sekou Toure was able to nip a Soviet-sponsored youth plot to remove him. He booted out the Russian envoy and saw his future—for a time—in pragmatic terms.

Attwood, a highly talented editor and ex-newspaperman, was re-assigned to the other side of Africa, in Kenya. Nkrumah's emissaries and his Western world Africanists kept up a drumfire of dire predictions: That Sekou Toure was going back on his "revolutionary" precepts; that he was becoming a marionette of the Americans. The coup that deposed Nkrumah, "His Messianic Dedication," as well as coups that preceded the one in Ghana changed Sekou Toure's tactics almost overnight. He saw himself beleaguered. Thus, he provided high-level sanctuary to Nkrumah and pledged to restore him to Government House in Accra.

That declaration of intention by one sovereign state against another has never been seriously challenged by the United Nations.

For one thing, Secretary General U Thant seems preoccupied only with issues that matter most to Asia, although he claims impartiality. For another, the Dr. O'Brien thundering thesis of nonalignment strikes a chord of selective prejudice in the UN, where he still has many friends who share his Africanist views.

The United States has, since 1960, sought in policy matters with African states to suffer abuses gladly. For several years we had as our peripatetic envoy Assistant Secretary of State G. Mennen Williams. Williams, six-time governor of Michigan who is known to the electorate and political trade at home as "Soapy" was totally unprepared for the in-fighting among African states. He was well intentioned but was caught in all-African recrimination and enmity every time he went out to shake hands and ask to be friends. One of his closer associates, an ambassador in Africa, lamented: "Soapy's trouble is that he thinks this is like dealing with civil rights in Michigan. He never got hep to the fact that if you are pleasant to the regime in country 'A,' this might be taken as American support against country 'B.' Worse, it didn't take Africans very long to realize that the White House never took old Soapy seriously."

Like Nasser, who paid handsome salaries and living allowances to ex-Nazis, Nkrumah kept some notorious Germans around, too. Most prominent since the coup has been Dr. Horst Schumann. He had been protected by Nkrumah since 1959. Aged about sixty, Schumann ran a health clinic for the Ghanian civil service. The West German government asked for his extradition repeatedly on charges that he must stand trial for murdering thirty thousand lunatics and Jews. Among other accusations, Schumann has been charged with sterilization and castration experiments at Auschwitz. Nkrumah rejected demands for extradition. Why? They were, he said blandly, "of a political nature." The post-Nkrumah regime deported Schumann to face charges in West Germany.

But the image of Nkrumah remains more untarnished than not. The corruption of a regime like his, that in eight years went from a treasury with around 500 million dollars in hard cash to a thumping debt of $1,140,000,000 is an incredible achievement, even among profligates. Along with the resounding deficit went the spoils of power. Kickbacks to greedy officials of 5 to 10 per cent from his National Development Corporation (NADECO) were demanded and paid for handing out contracts. It wasn't just the traditional "dash"—wee bribe—traditional in West Africa. Anyone who was anybody in Nkrumah's Convention People's party believed he or she was entitled to ask and receive big cash settlements.

They became brazen abroad. The wife of one of Nkrumah's chief cronies, Krobo Edusei (known at home as "Crowbar"), bought a golden bed in London. It cost $8,000. She refused to return it. In Accra, "Crowbar" said her station in life entitled her to the gilded couch.

What Nkrumah furthered and his entourage built for him and themselves was essentially a *Fuehrer prinzip*. Nkrumah emulated Hitler's brand of leadership. Fascism had, of course, lost in 1945. Therefore, any similarly guided ideology was enthusiastically received by self-styled liberals when it waved a pennant called "socialism." Except for the use of the slogan, Nkrumah-ism was the most highly developed state of fascism in a developing world. The sociologists and political scientists who saw in Nkrumah's own "socialism" an unimpeded progressive road are responsible today.

George Orwell had a lasting thought for this: "When one sees highly educated men looking on indifferently at oppression and persecution," he wrote, "one wonders which to despise more, their cynicism or their short-sightedness."

Tibor Szamuely, who saw first hand how the Ghanian dictatorship operated, has described it in rather chilling minutiae. Having been born in the Soviet Union of Communist parents exiled from Hungary, Szamuely knows what he writes about. He was educated in the U.S.S.R., lived on collective farms and was returned in World War II with the Red army to Hungary. He remained there and was assigned to missions abroad because of his linguistic gifts.

Long before he defected, Szamuely and his wife decided that they would somehow take their family with them. They managed to do it when he was assigned to a branch of Ghana University. Szamuely also was sent out to be in touch with Communist intelligence agents in the area. When he was airborne with his family to Budapest via Britain, on a home leave in 1964, he stayed in London. He is a university lecturer there today. His experiences with Western Africanists during the time he was in Ghana were a deep shock. "Their unreality is unbelievable," he said. "Even by osmosis,

they had to absorb a little something of what Nkrumah was up to.
"The story of Nkrumah is a highly cautionary tale but its
moral has not yet been learned. The tributes, the applause, which
until quite recently were conferred upon the Osagyefo by an influential segment of Western public opinion, have found new
recipients. Other times, other heroes. Only the double standard
remains unchanged."

Quite an indictment. When we even briefly recall, however,
what a fuss the Osogyefo and Nasser kicked up over Ahmed Ben
Bella, warnings of the double-standard should not be surprising.
Ben Bella, one of the original sponsors of the Algerian revolt
against France, sidetracked or purged virtually all the nationalists
who helped direct the war, during most of which he was a prisoner.
A consumptive army colonel, Houari Boumedienne, deposed Ben
Bella on the eve of the big conference. Ben Bella, who praised
Fidel Castro between visits to the United States, was fiercely defended as an African progressive by latter-day American Africanists. Even when he sneered at black African states for lack of
spunk, his defenders appealed for understanding. When the Algerian army, with Boumedienne, took over, there were even proposals that the UN do something.

Algeria hasn't done better or worse, economically, under the
administration that took over with the coup. Its foreign policy
has not altered. That is, America remains the bogey. And it pursues
a declared policy of helping "revolutionaries." One of the most
glaring episodes occurred in Dar-es-Salaam, the little picture-post-
card capital of East Africa's Tanzania on the Indian Ocean.
Headlights dimmed, a black sedan with diplomatic license plates
inched its way over the airport tarmac to a hangar. So quietly did it
glide, that sentries, lulled by chirping cicadas and nightbirds, continued to doze. Stygian predawn darkness, so common in Africa,
mantled the hangar. Inside was equipment for a big show to be
given by Tanzania's first cadre of Israeli-trained paratroops.

Out stepped the slender driver, dark glasses perched on his nose.
He slid through a narrow door discernible in the dark only to
someone who knew its location. A pencil beam from a tiny flashlight
stabbed the hangar's darkness. It was a few minutes before 3 A.M.
Fifty yards away a sleepy sentry slapped at a big moth. The slap
roused him. The flickering light in the hangar caught his eye.
Shouting for help, he ran for the hangar, stumbling right into the
car. Inside, the light flicked off, but it was too late. Soldiers sur-

rounded the car and hangar. An officer and several men pushed their way inside.

"Hello," was the greeting boomed out heartily to them. "Can you help me out? I've lost my way." Smiling, the man in dark glasses identified himself: "I'm the ambassador of Algeria."

So he was, Noureddine Djoudi. Only a few years ago he was graduated by one of our older New England colleges. Back home he went to urge militant revolution throughout Africa rather than use his university training to mend his country's poor economy. His blatant espionage, the kind of spy who laughed off his capture, was conveniently hushed. President Julius Nyerere, slender and introspective, doesn't want to offend fellow African states. Had a Westerner been caught, there is no question but that a huge uproar would have followed. One of Nyerere's aides told us as much. Ever since revolution in the nearby spice island of Zanzibar and mutiny in his own little army, Nyerere stopped being a moderate. He opted for the "revolutionaries," even those committed to getting rid of Nyerere one day. He was also marked for elimination by Nkrumah. But Nyerere displayed amazing survival qualities, which ran completely contrary to all State Department assessments and expectations. He simply switched totally to the side of anti-Americans and militant African leaders.

Once Nyerere ceased interposing his logic and earlier prestige between challenges of the militants and moderates, he became a wise man in the eyes of African activists. He had been reviled by them as a willing puppet of the Americans and British. Although rescued by Britain, who answered Nyerere's appeal for help against an attempted *coup,* Tanzania's number one man wants to prove today that he is as anti-West as Nasser.

His capital city seethes with intrigue fomented by Red China's embassy. A "liberation committee," bankrolled by the U.S.S.R., operates openly. It claims dedication only to rolling back Portugal from its East and West African possessions. To date its success has been in wrapping up Nyerere. He insists that he look north to Cairo and Nasser for guidance and some material help.

In the spiral, Nasser looks northward too. He remains "uncommitted," in the political jargon of the times, by strict reliance in the U.S.S.R.

In their turn, the Russians sponsor nonalignment, especially Nasser's, to the point of war and political aggrandizement.

Our Middle East experts in the State Department kept insisting that there was nothing to be alarmed about: Nasser was a wily man and would protect his protégés in Africa and the Arab world from falling into any Communist trap. Senator Fulbright concurred, as we heard when he delivered his views to a small group in Washington.

Directed nonalignment is quite a condition—if you buy it. Israel, under reality of the gun that was called nonaligned, ignored expertise and protected herself. The Russians and Nasser denounced defense as "aggression." We stayed actively aloof.

Chapter 15

AFRICA: PART TWO—
THE MIDDLE EAST AND THE WAR

B ACK in the summer of 1966, General Moshe Dayan was in London on his way to the States before heading to Vietnam. It was a mild summer's evening—for Britain, that is—and General Dayan was talking in a flower-bordered garden to a few friends. One of the authors was present. Dayan, whose eye-patch has since become an international trademark, spoke of war and peace, politics and people.

A highly articulate man, he listened intently as someone asked whether the Russians, the Arab world, and perhaps anti-Israelis would regard his trip to Vietnam as a provocation.

"Our existence in Israel is a provocation to those who feel or think it so, anyway," Dayan replied. "You can simply see speeches by Russians and Arabs to show how anti-U.S. they feel about you, generally, and about what you do in Vietnam, particularly."

He was going to Vietnam, said Dayan, to write about the war and to see how our mobile air cavalry operates.

"Air cavalry is of the utmost strategic importance to a little country like Israel," he mused. "Too expensive for us, though."

Did he believe the Arab states, compelled by Nasser, would try again to snuff out Israel?

"That's the line always peddled," replied Dayan. "Through Soviet military equipment and training, they say now that *Der Tag* —meaning our finish, is at hand."

Wasn't he retired? Dayan shrugged with the hint of a smile on his lips. "People like me never retire," he said.

Didn't he think, another question came, that it was high time to negotiate about Palestinian refugees, borders and to seek some permanent form of coexistence?

"Of course, this is a normal and logical objective," said Dayan, over a lemon squash drink. "The Arabs won't think about it. Unfortunately, they are encouraged in this by the Soviet Union. The Russians want to become dominant in the Middle East. They concede they spent a billion dollars on Nasser's forces. All over the Arab-directed Middle East, it's closer to three billion dollars."

Did he believe, then, that war was inevitable?

"Let me say that our defense is inevitable," he answered. "Help? From whom? We do not know how the Americans will react. You are so engrossed in your probes with the Russians that these take priority. When it happens the next time, we'll be alone. There is no alternative. We will fight. You don't know anything about survival."

What would he do if he were summoned again to take charge of a campaign.

"Hit on three fronts, against the Egyptians, Jordanians, and Syrians," was his concise reply. "This is no secret. The Russians certainly know; so does Nasser."

How would it be carried out?

"Why give details?" he answered. "One thing, though: The Egyptian air force must be destroyed."

Glancing back on the notes taken of that private conversation, Dayan's strategy was implemented to the letter less than a year later. When the other author traveled with Israeli combat forces in the lightning, sixty-hour war that stunned the world, he found troops were as aware of the basic strategy as was Dayan, when he discussed probabilities in the handsomely groomed London garden.

Equally aware were strategists in the Pentagon—and the oft-criticized CIA—who were supplied with up-to-date and accurate assessments from our military attachés and liaison officers in the Middle East. Strangely, professional experts in the State Department consistently deflated the menace of the Soviet-supplied military build-up to Colonel Nasser and a feckless Syrian regime that prattled "active Arab socialism." The principal demurrers were certain, in their verbal and written memoranda, that the United States would resist Israeli demands for assurances of security. Many fortified their views with the contribution that UN Secretary General U Thant was personally persuaded that the new Middle East crisis was like a desert sandstorm. It would make things dusty but would blow away.

For years there had been a diffident attitude among many State Department veterans about our association with Israel. Some of it was pure pro-Arabism; some distaste for a Jewish state and Jews, in general. A prominent American diplomat said more than once that religion was certainly a factor in considering personnel for posts. The White House put out a retraction. The diplomat himself did not, and he was discreetly applauded by Middle East specialists in the department. They were dismayed a few years ago by a political appointmeint to Cairo—redirected at the last minute.

Philip Kaiser, a personable veteran of trade union affairs and a confidant of elder statesman W. Averell Harriman, had served as ambassador to Senegal. He came down with tuberculosis and recovery was somewhat difficult. Back in working shape, Kaiser seemed to Harriman and upper-echelon White House consultants a sensible choice to deal with Nasser. He had already served well in an African post. His trade union background was regarded as potentially useful for communicating with the architects of "Arab socialism." One thing about Kaiser was overlooked. He is Jewish, but so is our delegate to the UN, Arthur Goldberg. The big difference is that Goldberg is posted in New York.

Pro-Arabists in the department, as well as the aloof professionals who try assiduously to husband posts for career men, knew all about Kaiser. They waited until Secretary Rusk considered the appointment—he thought it was sound—and then sprang Kaiser's Jewish origin on the Secretary. The argument, along with the revelation, emphasized that a Jew could not be sent to Cairo without risking the snub of a refusal from Nasser.

Kaiser, who spent post-graduate time at Oxford, wound up in an even better spot. He became number two man, minister, at our embassy in London. It's a job that has traditionally been coveted and held by careerists.

Career men and politicians have been dueling over the Middle East for years. The obvious element was the influence that could be wielded by American Jews on politicians. In turn, a sizable bloc of American politicians have always been resentful and suspicious of State Department officers at large, especially in the expert categories.

At a dramatic moment in mid-1948, when the British discarded their mandate for Palestine, and Israel was born amid war with Arab states, the question of recognition arose in the administration of President Harry Truman. A high-level meeting was called in the office of then Secretary of State, the late General George C. Marshall. As far as a man could be, Marshall was neither emotionally nor professionally committed for or against Israel. Some of his career counselors argued persuasively against United States recognition at the time. Theirs, they said, was a diplomatic decision as opposed to a political one. Calmly, Marshall took soundings. Suddenly Clark Clifford, our present Secretary of Defense, who was then, as later with L.B.J., a Presidential adviser, entered the room.

General Marshall said *hello* to him and looked around the room.

"Gentlemen," intoned Marshall with the faint trace of a smile in the direction of Clifford, "it's a political decision we have reached."

Israel was recognized, and in the big power scramble to be among the first, the Soviet Union also granted recognition. At the time Stalin had no particular policy toward the Middle East, beyond casting around for some kind of foothold to exploit. His tactics concentrated on trying to use the Israeli Communist party. But Soviet refusal to permit Jews to emigrate and a violent anti-Semitic policy toward Russian Jews, culminating in a trumped-up "doctors' plot," just about stifled Israeli Communists. *Pogrom,* noted former Israeli Foreign Minister Golda Meir in a moment of bitter despair, is a Russian word.

The Russians, cracking down hard on Jews in the U.S.S.R., repeatedly made it plain to Israeli officials that their appeals for restoration of Jewish cultural life in Russia was interference. "The Russians made it horribly plain," recalled former Ambassador to Moscow Katriel Katz, "that they held a couple of million Jews as hostages."

With this ever-ready blackmail, the Russians rudely deflected all suggestions about providing Jews—at least on paper—with opportunities accorded other minorities. Keeping Israeli and world Jewish organizations' complaints muted, the Russians saw an opportunity in the spring of 1955 to slip onto the Arab stage in the Middle East. It was a time of euphoria elsewhere. An ebullient dualism was presented to the outside world in the personalities of party secretary Nikita S. Khrushchev and goateed Premier Nikolai Bulganin. The U.S.S.R. had just agreed to a state treaty for Austria, ending ten years of four power occupation. It was the first major postwar four power agreement.

That event, which also started American Ambassador Llewellyn E. "Tommy" Thompson on his way to the post of Presidential counselor of Soviet affairs, swiftly paved the route to a summit meeting. Thompson, who had served before in Moscow, was instrumental in making an encounter possible between President Eisenhower, Prime Minister Eden, Premier Edgar Faure and "B & K," as Bulganin and Khrushchev became commonly known. Thompson was given full credit for negotiating the Austrian treaty and envisaging a thaw between East and West.

The summit in Geneva, which one of the authors attended, had a curiously glaring omission. He was hulking Soviet Foreign Minister Dmitri Shepilov, brought into government in the fresh atmosphere induced by the Austrian treaty and the summit. The late Secretary of State John Foster Dulles was instead treated to conversations with his old adversary, V. M. Molotov. Where was Shepilov? In Cairo, talking arms aid to Nasser. Dulles, over the department's advice to be lenient toward Nasser, held off on a new weaponry arrangement.

For the Soviet Union, while pronouncements of *detente* were filling the shores of Lake Leman in Geneva, the Shepilov visit to Nasser was fateful. It committed the U.S.S.R. to the self-appointed leader of Araby and vice-versa. The cost to Nasser? His cotton crop indefinitely. For the U.S.S.R.? Credits and armaments that subsequently came to between two billion and three billion dollars, plus political expansionism in the Middle East.

When a dubious Anthony Eden asked Khrushchev the meaning of the Shepilov visit, the answer was: "A little of what the Americans and you call fact-finding."

That kind of exploration led Khrushchev a few years later to reject appeals from a group of Canadian Jews to go easy on their co-religionists with: "Don't mention this again. Jews are only useful to build synagogues."

Shepilov was dismissed in the power struggle that enabled Khrushchev to stay on top. That struggle also cost Bulganin his job. But Soviet policy toward the Arabs in the Middle East, initiated by Shepilov, assumed costlier, more permanent, and wider commitments. In the State Department, pro-Nasser, pro-Arab arguments held that Nasser was the real anchor in the Middle East. His growing dependence on the Russians was airily excused with the usual contention that he was really "neutralist" and could withstand

Soviet penetration. Just like Indian Prime Minister Jawaharlal Nehru, was their attitude.

When the Israelis smashed Nasser's first Russian-equipped forces in 1956, and France and Britain were involved, the U.S.S.R. threatened to rain rockets on Western Europe unless hostilities ceased. Khrushchev had just brutally crushed a genuine people's uprising in Hungary. We sided with the Russians on the Middle East and wrung our hands about the Soviet repression in Hungary. It was the time of a national election for us. Peace, said Dulles, was paramount. The Israelis had behaved badly, said our Middle East specialists. Dulles told the Russians that we would not succor the revolutionaries in Hungary and deplored the Israeli lightning action against a Soviet-advised and equipped Egyptian combat force sworn to crush Israel as soon as possible.

On a national scale, we said we were embarrassed by the Hungarian revolt. Nasser was irksome but we could retrieve associations with him. Why? There was nobody else, and he was the wave of the Arab future. This was the studied advice of career diplomats like Phillips Talbott, presently our ambassador to Greece and a veteran Middle East specialist. Later Rodger P. Davies, Deputy Assistant Secretary for the Near East and Southeast Asia, appealed constantly to higher-ups to refrain from making concessions to Israel. The Russians pursued their advocacy of the Arabs with material assistance. For our part, we forced the Israelis from the Gulf of Aqaba, the principal motive for their response when Nasser moved in again during May of 1967.

The UN would provide the proper guarantees, declared Dulles and Henry Cabot Lodge, subsequently our ambassador to Vietnam. Interestingly, and for different reasons, neither the Russians nor the Israelis believed these high-flown guarantees could be implemented. The Russians went ahead, at a faster and more expensive pace, retreading Nasser's military establishment. In return, the basic security services of Nasser's United Arab Republic (U.A.R.) became totally Soviet-trained and ran on Soviet time.

To keep apace of the massive Soviet armaments' infusion into Egypt and later Syria, the Israelis dealt with France. General de Gaulle, after winding up the French role in Algeria, didn't begin to adopt a hands-off attitude toward Israel until a few months before Nasser's last debacle. French Mirage fighter planes and parts were sold as regularly as in pre-de Gaulle days. The only hitch:

Prices were often and unexpectedly increased when the Israelis sought spare parts. Higher costs was the only explanation, supplied with a shrug and a grimace.

We strove, in policy maneuvers, to have third parties provide Israel wherewithal for its military requirements. The West German Federal Republic, which had with ex-Premier David Ben Gurion arranged a compensation system, agreed to furnish armor and other weapons to Israel after protracted American pressure. Our Middle East policy advisers in the State Department came up with this plan to show a stance of innocent nonpartisanship. But Nasser led most Arab states in a collective rebuff to West Germany by breaking diplomatic relations.

They simultaneously turned their ire on the United States for our part in the concealed persuasion behind the German decision. Nasser's propaganda against the United States became even more venomous as we slowed down and halted free grain shipments to Egypt. The slowdown started during the latter phase of President Kennedy's Administration and trailed off under Johnson. By that time Soviet involvement in key Egyptian ministries alarmed all but the most resolute—like Davies—pro-Nasser career men. Others, like Tommy Thompson, advocated a no-attention attitude toward Soviet involvement in the Middle East.

Thompson emphasized priority, as he has always seen it since 1955, in a United States-Soviet accommodation. The fact that the Russians supported volatile Middle East politicians and stoked passions through a huge arms build-up didn't especially concern Thompson. He has looked on Soviet excursions in the Middle East as an unpleasant sideshow, which the Russians would not tolerate if it came close to a fresh explosion. Yet distasteful facts piled up indicating direct Soviet participation in a regional adventure of vast consequence.

The Egyptian Intelligence Service, like Russia's KGB, penetrates every part of Nasser's domain. Although Nasser long proclaimed he kept his own Communists under lock and key, he had no qualms about Soviet KGB advisers offering know-how to his service, generally called the "EIS." This work-a-day security cooperation with the Russians was part of the price Nasser knowingly paid for Soviet assistance. Nasser's EIS rapidly became, in the five years from 1962 to 1967, the biggest, most costly network in the world, proportionate to the size of the country.

With technicans who turned up in Egypt to work on the Aswan High Dam came Soviet security agents. They peeled off, by prior arrangement, to EIS departments. These are divided into five specific offices that maintain vigilance throughout all communities in Egypt, the Middle East, Africa, and to a lesser extent further abroad. EIS agents have, since 1962, worked with on-the-spot Soviet counterparts in Nasser's expedition in Yemen. In Cairo, however, the active cooperation between KGB and EIS is of daily, operative form. In toasts, this togetherness has been praised by Premier Aleksei Kosygin and Defense Minister A. A. Gretchko as evidence of Nasser's full understanding of "socialist cooperation."

Think of how it works in these forms:

First, there is the General Intelligence Department. It is headed by General Salah Nasr, no kin of the U.A.R. President, but a close and old comrade. Within General Nasr's office is a division called, simply, Secret Service. It handles conspiracies, organization of *coups,* and assassinations. KGB agents have their own offices next to Nasr's and confer with him daily.

Next is Military Intelligence. This was recast into the image of the Soviet GRU, military intelligence. When GRU became subordinate to the KGB with the appointment of Yuri Andropov to direct Russia's superagency, Egyptian military intelligence became immediately number two to General Nasr's division. The General Security Department is the fourth arm of the U.A.R.'s supervisory control pattern. It deals with internal affairs. This division was going through a purge and face-lifting as President Nasser moved troops close to the Israeli border.

Because the Moslem brotherhood, sworn to dispose of Nasser, came close twice, the Russians proposed overhauling internal security. President Nasser quickly agreed.

Finally, there is the Presidential Intelligence Department. In that office the Russians installed some of their most veteran, knowledgeable KGB operatives. Analyses from all other intelligence units are sent to President Nasser. He reads what this main office judges he should see. The Russians actively help in preparation of reports and assessments.

From air bases and ground installations, where Soviet specialists trained Egyptian forces and reported back to KGB officers, a full orchestration of Russian penetration was accomplished. Moreover,

Soviet agents cooperated fully with old Nazis Nasser kept on his payroll to help develop a rocket program, designed to annihilate Israeli cities. They also worked closely in the huge "Voice of the Arabs" propaganda radio services.

Reports, detailed and frequently updated, on Soviet manipulations of the whole Egyptian regime, attitude, and technique, were supplied to the West by the Israelis. United States experts in the State Department usually tended to disparage them as loaded in favor of taking up an all-out pro-Israel stand. The Israelis, who are conceded by all other Western security services to have the best information-gathering net in the Middle East and East Europe, kept trying. When confirmation of some of their more alarming reports was dispatched by assorted Americans in the area, they were largely discounted. The same spirit rejected British and West German evaluations.

It was the same mood that prevailed as a new socialist regime triggered its way to power in Syria. The coup was the ninth and bloodiest of all that ripped Syria from 1948 to 1965. As President of the new regime in Damascus, a medically certified manic-depressive was installed. He was Nureddin el-Attassi, a bearded, violent xenophobe, especially about West Europeans and Americans. His regime, predicated on army support, went directly to the U.S.S.R. for immediate transfer of arms and military advisers. To this request, favored enthusiastically by the Syrian army, both Kosygin and Brezhnev readily agreed.

They dispatched a team headed by General N. E. Grishin, a staff officer who had been in operations from Finland to North Vietnam. Grishin's record was well known to every outside, interested government. Our experts in diplomacy disdained his team's appearance and the subsequent Soviet military build-up in Syria as rather inconsequential, giving the Russians just a little extra nuisance value. They also ignored the sudden, accepted trips by old-line Syrian international Communist, Khaled Biqdash. His headquarters are in Prague.

Although there is only one legal Communist party in the Middle East—ironically, the Israeli—both the Egyptians and Syrians permitted pro-Russian Communists and other extremists to hold high governmental and propaganda offices. This has suited the U.S.S.R. as compliance with "progressive" advances in developing areas. The Syrian regime of el-Attassi rapidly became an especially favored pawn of Soviet policy. Not only had he asked—and received—arms aid, but he began demanding that all Arab oil-producers withdraw hard cash earnings from the United States and Britain. Total nationalization of all oil resources was his accompanying behest. The U.S.S.R. was highly pleased.

At the same time, the Syrian regime's rallying cry was the final and complete extermination of Israel. El-Attassi and his entourage needled President Nasser for his do-nothing policies. Syria quite blatantly trained Arab terrorist gangs for marauding expeditions into Israel. They had gaudy names: *El Fatah,* or Conquest; and *El Asefa,* or Storm. The saboteurs were drawn from the army of the Palestine Liberation Organization, or PLO, which President Nasser forged in 1964. It was created as a face-saving operation after the Arabs failed to react when Israel tapped the Jordan headwaters.

Like most Nasserite schemes it sounded, as it was intended to, more belligerent than it was. Nasser miscalculated, as he so often has, and got away with it. This time it was in his choice of a PLO leader: uncontrollable Ahmed Shukairy, dismissed from his job as Saudi Arabian delegate to the UN. He was fired because he devised his own foreign policy as it occurred to him. Shukairy was big on terrorism against Israel, which suited the militant Syrian regime perfectly. His gangs launched, from Syria and Jordan after training near the Gaza strip, 113 sabotage forays. They killed seventy-three Israelis and maintained a border state of turbulence.

The attacks invited an escalating response from the Israelis. General Grishin's mission, busily outfitting and training Syrians on the ground and in the air, ignored sudden, unexplained appearances of terrorists at special centers where they operated. These PLO marauders obtained specialized training from the Russians just as if they were regulars assigned by Syria. The raids accelerated, with the U.S.S.R. in full knowledge of what happened.

In September, 1966, many of the Syrians in government fell out with each other. There was an attempted coup, frustrated by units rushed up from Soviet-sponsored training centers. If there had been an Israeli reprisal at that time, it would certainly have brought down el-Attassi and his group. To deter Israel, Nasser—with Soviet recommendations and the pressure of urgency from Russian trouble-shooters sent from Moscow by Kosygin—contrived a hasty "defense pact" with Syria. Information about the role of the Russians, in this instance, was again passed by the Israelis and some benevolent Asian neutrals to the United States. It was ignored, as were the other reports of growing Soviet direction over Arabs in the Middle East.

A fortnight after Nasser's pact with Syria, Israel launched her biggest offensive since Suez against Jordan. It was on November 13, 1966, as a reprisal on a Jordanian village that harbored Syrian terrorists. The Israelis smashed forty houses and killed nineteen Jordanians. Promptly, Jordan's harrassed little King Hussein pointedly demanded to know why he received no support from Nasser. For their part, the Syrians boasted how invulnerable they were to Israeli reprisals.

Syrian self-satisfaction burned deeply into the coalition Israeli government of Prime Minister Levi Eshkol. He faced, in the opposition, the strong personality of David Ben Gurion, so long a Prime Minister himself and a tough-minded one, as well as Ben Gurion's protégé, General Dayan. Israel simmered, and her politicians stewed, until April 7, 1967. A minor border incident provided Israel with an opportunity to humiliate Syria. Artillery, tanks, and mortars dueled in the demilitarized zone, southeast of the Sea of Galilee. Into the air went Israeli French-built Mirage fighters. They shot down seven of Syria's most modern Soviet Migs, as Russian advisers watched in frustrated rage.

Despite the pact with Syria, Nasser didn't budge to help. Thereupon, the Syrian regime—with approval from Soviet helpmates— stepped up their hit-and-run raids into Israel. Their options, they told East European comrades who passed the word along, compelled them to make up for being discredited in battle and patently abandoned in a fire-fight by big brother Nasser. Israel, holding back a collective temper with amazing national discipline, endured the terrorist onslaughts and tried to blunt them.

Repeatedly, warnings about Israeli patience wearing thin— "understand our obsession with survival," said Dayan—circulated to the United States. They made their way to Cairo and Syria as well. For months, until just before the last storm blew over the Middle East, our embassy in Egypt had no ambassador. This was our indignant snub at Nasser and his anti-Americanism. He inflamed feeling further, in the early spring of 1967, by an emotional outburst in favor of the Viet Cong. That poured out in a face-to-face meeting with one of our most experienced Middle East career diplomats, Raymond Hare. About a year before Nasser had pro-

vided even more house room in Cairo for a National Liberation
Front embassy (Viet Cong) than a similar mission obtained in
Moscow.

Our chargé in Cairo, David G. Nes, pleaded for a Number One
to be assigned. The Nasser regime regarded him as an errand boy
and hardly deigned to receive him. Junior as he is in the career
service, Nes proved in reports to be acutely perceptive. He warned
constantly that the lid could easily blow off the Middle East very
quickly. To help maintain an American position of persuasion,
however small, he urged the State Department to send out a top
man. Nes's pleas became controversial. A junior doesn't goad if he
envisages career promotions. Finally we sent an ambassador, Richard Nolte, as the Middle East gyrated in mid-crisis. Lightly regarded by his own colleagues, Nolte's appearance was too little
and too late.

The pernicious pattern for the great crisis began to unfold shortly
after 7 P.M. of May 14. Egyptian Chief of Staff Mohammed Fawzi
boarded a plane from a military airdrome outside Cairo. In fifty
minutes he touched down in Damascus. He had news that silenced
even babbling President el-Attassi. The Israelis were planning a
parade the next day, May 15, in their half of Jerusalem to com-
memorate independence. It could be easily witnessed by Jordanians
holding the other half of the city.

Acting on Soviet intelligence information, the Egyptians calculated that Israeli units were veering *away* from Jerusalem—one
of the most monumental misinterpretations and miscalculations.
Soviet intelligence reported that detachments were bound for the
forty-seven-mile, tortuous Israeli-Syrian border that winds around
either end of the Sea of Galilee. Russian information was apparently confirmed when the Israeli parade turned out to be rather thin
in weaponry. It reported that fourteen Israeli brigades were a few
miles from the Syrian frontier. The gist of this information was circulated among Asian and African nations to arouse anti-Israeli
feeling.

In truth, there was no particular build-up on the Syrian frontier.
When Israelis regrouped after mobilization, they were massed on
the other side, against Egypt, once Nasser's forces were at the
border. The Syrian sector was reinforced only after the war began
and following the speedy destruction of the Egyptian units. But the
Soviet intelligence assessment sent a shock wave of fright among

Arab leaders. It quickly reached such a state of panic—far from the menace and intransigence of propaganda declarations to wipe out Israel—that Soviet advisers sought desperately to shore up morale. They urged Moscow to invite top officials from Cairo and Damascus for talks as a Soviet show of solidarity. This was acted upon swiftly.

It will be a long time before a coherent explanation will emerge as to why the Russians miscalculated in such an egregious way. They compounded their tremendous mistake by reiterating what was generally known: Israeli chief of staff Yitzhak Rabin calculated that his striking forces could be inside Damascus within twelve hours of hostilities. American and other Western military attachés in Israel knew first-hand that there was no special Israeli build-up on the Syrian border. State Department's airy Middle East assessment was that the Soviet report suggested the Israelis were trying to scare the Arabs. As for the Russians, they were only trying hard to protect their clients. So went the strange, rather smug State Department conclusion.

Our Ambassador Tommy Thompson, striving hard to maintain his theme of accommodation with the U.S.S.R., urged a neutralist role on the United States, lest we become embroiled with the Russians. That the Russians, for their part, miscalculated and kept egging on their Arab protégés, Thompson ignored. As a longtime Presidential adviser on Soviet affairs, Thompson's recommendation prevailed. Nasser, consulting with Russians assigned to Cairo, now felt he had to show active leadership of the Arab world. He drafted a fuzzy message that went to the Indian commander of the UN Emergency Force (UNEF) in Egypt, Major General Rikhye. On May 17, Rikhye received a confusing message from Egypt. He was asked to move his frontier forces—there since 1957 —into the narrow area of the Gaza strip.

There was, at this point, no demand by Nasser for a withdrawal of UNEF forces posted at Sharm el Sheik. They had the vital responsibility of keeping the Gulf of Aqaba and the Straits of Tiran open for vessels using Israel's oil port of Elath. Yet when news hit the UN in New York of Nasser's demand for UNEF units to be regrouped in the Gaza strip, total confusion riddled the Secretariat. Secretary General U Thant appealed to Egyptian representative Mohammed el-Kony. Get clarification, he begged.

After a series of telephone calls, Kony conceded he was no wiser. Frantically, U Thant buttonholed representatives of the seven countries that contributed soldiers to the peace-keeping force. From the start of his conversations, India and Yugoslavia were absolutely clear on one point: Whatever Nasser was up to or wanted, his request must be accepted unquestionably.

By May 18 the situation was even more confused. Nasser moved troops next to a UN detachment in the Gaza strip. The move prompted a declaration from the Israeli Foreign Ministry that it could not allow "a second Pearl Harbor." Right after lunch, New York time, el-Kony got "clarification" from Cairo. Nasser escalated his demand. He wanted all UN forces in Egypt, including troops at Sharm el Sheik, to be withdrawn.

Our official Middle East analysts—concurred with by the British —regarded the demand as a calculated phase of Nasserist bravado. They felt he never expected his demand to be met, at least not all at once. Both governments were fully aware of a 1957 secret memorandum drawn up on agreement between the late UN Secretary General Dag Hammarskjöld and Nasser. The memo contended that Nasser agreed to limit the use of his sovereign right to expel UN peace-keeping forces from Egypt. The Israelis had never allowed the UN to station such units on their side. What the memo meant, essentially, was that UN forces would not be withdrawn until Cairo and the UN agreed they had completed their task.

It has been charged that U Thant was aware of the agreement, left in the Hammarskjöld files. Before he was killed in a plane crash in Africa, Hammarskjöld gave a copy of the memo to a close friend, Ernest A. Gross. A former United States representative at the UN, Gross agreed to publication of the memorandum to the American Society of International Law. The agreement provided the Secretary General with a mandate to stall in a crisis, which is essential for him in any crisis and was something Hammarskjöld exploited with consummate skill in his term of office. In a lame explanation U Thant dismissed the memo as transitory suggestion open to all types of interpretation and thus invalid.

But U Thant, in twenty-four hours, capitulated to Nasser's demands. He didn't try to stall, claiming the legality of a sovereign nation to clear guests from its territory. The U Thant decision, in the light of the memorandum and past maneuvers of predecessors, stunned the Western powers and seems, from the absence of immediate Soviet-Egyptian reaction, to have taken them, too, totally by surprise. The chance to turn the crisis into a typical UN talkathon vanished. Nasser, once the astonishment of U Thant's acquiescence trailed off, became more aggressive. The Russians helped by asking for even more prominent Egyptians to come to Moscow and consult.

Off to Moscow flew Nasser's first vice president, Marshal Abdel Hakem Amer. To provide the Syrians pride of place as well, the Czechoslovak regime exchanged military delegations for the purpose of discussing additional arms transfers. The Russians manipulated the Syrian-Czech exchanges, as el-Attassi boasted, in the "interests of fraternal socialism." At the same time, as dangers progressed geometrically in the Middle East, the Russians for the first time formed a Mediterranean task group. The flotilla disposed of guided missile destroyers of the Kynda class, 4,800 tons, and the Kashin class, 4,300 tons. Submarines and escort vessel were attached.

Making this known to Marshal Amer, Soviet Defense Minister Gretchko declared the Soviet purpose was evident to the Arab peoples as a show of solidarity and support "against hostile elements of imperialism." Nasser and the Syrians were elated. They figured the Russians intended to bail them out of any possible problem with Israel. Wildly encouraged by Soviet statements of support, Syria clamored for a blockade by Arab forces—meaning Egyptian—from Sharm el Sheik. Nasser sent in Egyptian troops after demanding that the UN vacate the area. Then, on the evening of May 22, a blockade was declared of the Gulf of Aqaba, to "ships flying the Israeli flag and ships carrying strategic goods to Israel."

That made the third stage in the Egyptian escalation: First, there had been the demand for UN withdrawal, then the occupation of sensitive Sharm el Sheik, and finally, blockade. Soviet advice and consent was paramount in every phase. Their policy in the Middle East was predicated on the concept that the Americans, despite earlier pledges of integrity to Israel, would recoil from a confrontation with the U.S.S.R. There was, so their diplomats told Asians and Africans around the world, American preoccupation with Vietnam. And there was, they observed indulgently, United States persistence in probing ways and means with the Russians for workable coexistence. Israel, trumpeted a ranking Soviet analyst of foreign affairs, was an extension of crumbling imperialism. Its disappearance, he asserted, would help the cause of peace. His name? Viktor Mayevsky, foreign editor of *Pravda*. (Mayevsky proved his loyalty to the line by testifying against a brother in the notoriously anti-Semitic doctors' trials of 1953. His brother was executed.)

Through all the Arab escalation, the Israelis sat tight. But the prospect of losing access to Elath and Egyptian-Syrian utterances of triumph induced profound restiveness. A declaration by President Johnson, sternly demanding the right of free passage through the Straits of Tiran, didn't mitigate Israeli concern. Our Middle East division, with some success, persuaded the President to vitiate anything that sounded like an offensive ultimatum to Nasser. Thompson, long the President's special Sovietologist, urged consideration of priorities. His was, as always, mediation and accommodation with the U.S.S.R. The fact that the Soviet Union had buoyed Arab aspirations to eliminate Israel didn't distract Thompson from his ideas.

Internal pressures compelled the Israeli government to start mobilizing—a smooth and speedy process. The first stage was achieved on May 20. A few days later came a midnight alert. All taxis and private cars were taken over to expedite mobilization of the last reservists. In the tensest of times, U Thant took off for Egypt to confer with Nasser. He was greeted by demonstrators waving banners that chimed with their chants to crush Israel forever. It was hardly a peaceful backdrop. U Thant could do nothing to change Nasser's mind or to alter his position regarding the three steps taken in escalation. He had already assented to every Nasserist demand. Cutting his visit short by twenty-four hours, U Thant returned to the UN, filled with foreboding and strident Arab claims of superiority over Israel.

The confrontation of Arab and Israeli forces lurched toward reality. Debate and intemperate accusations reverberated around the chamber where the Security Council aired the crisis. It was a macabre talkathon in which Israeli Foreign Minister Abba Eban smeared his accusers, whose regimes kicked off the crisis, with brilliant English acquired at Cambridge. The Arab insistence on a final solution for Israel reawakened dimmed remembrances of the recent, grisly past, when Nazis attempted to carry out "the final solution."

A violent reaction was provoked by the Arabs' clamor to destroy Israel and the Soviet's unflinching, public support of their cause. Most of the American intellectual community, which had been bitterly critical of the United States role in Vietnam, demanded active governmental support of Israel. A wave of pro-Israeli emotionalism washed over the country at large. It was by no means confined to Jews, who contributed vast treasure and services when the appeal was issued. Israel, anti-Vietnam sponsors of aid to Israel asserted, had commitments from America which South Vietnam had never obtained. The role of the U.S.S.R. in the Arab world was assailed by many who tacitly favored patient coexistence with the Russians. Three prominent anti-Vietnam personalities declined to endorse a call for American aid to Israel.

They were Arthur Schlesinger, Jr., John Kenneth Galbraith, and poet Robert Lowell. Invoking aid to Israel, they contended, was incompatible with their stand on demanding an end to our role in Vietnam. Actually, their passive view on Vietnam drove a deep division between them and a vast majority of Vietnam critics, who displayed feverish militancy on behalf of Israel. A new term in political ornithological language arose: *Dawk,* a combination of dove and hawk. So impassioned did the intellectual champions of Israel became that they even flung back at Schlesinger, Galbraith, and Lowell declarations like these: From Ho Chi-minh's North Vietnam regime: A pledge to all Arab states to support them to a "victorious" conclusion against Israel. From the National Liberation Front, or Viet Cong: A pledge of "eternal" support for Arab aspirations over Israel. From Red China: Mao Tse-tung's all-out pledge of assistance to the Arabs. This was coupled with a warning that the Russians would sell out the Arabs, a line China pumped for several years, which proved accurate when Nasser and cohorts pleaded for Soviet intervention.

While the intellectuals traded mutual recriminations, our government dispatched units of the Sixth Fleet to the troubled waters. They were stalked by Soviet ships all the way. The new American Ambassador Nolte waited in his air-conditioned office for a call from Nasser. It never came. Nolte, accomplished in Arabic studies, had never been regarded as a political heavyweight by his department. Journalists were amused by his appointment because they reckoned he'd never be taken seriously. He is an earnest man, though. "Look at it from Nasser's situation," Nolte liked to say.

When U Thant returned from his fruitless mission to Cairo, on May 24, adroit and sophisticated Israeli Foreign Minister Eban was under pitiless criticism at home. The defense force insisted that diplomatic niceties brought no copper-riveted assurances from the

States. Dayan's point, sharpened by this time, penetrated cabinet meetings with the thunderous word: *Survival*. The Arabs, headed by Nasser's propaganda agencies, gloated that they had already faced down the Israelis. The finish, they chortled, would come soon. Russian diplomats told Indian colleagues—as they later recounted —that Nasser had won a momentous, bloodless coup.

Hemmed in and seemingly trussed in UN inadequacy and American forebearance, Israel acted to unite the nation. Dayan, hero of the 1956 campaign, was appointed Minister of Defense. That was June 1. His strategy, sketched to us the summer before, was known in detail to General Rabin. Israel's tactics are dictated, of course, by her situation as much as by her mood. The army hardly bothers to prepare defensive positions. Their real estate resources, militarily, are so meager that Israel's forces must fight on enemy territory. This is precisely what happened as Israel exploded by going it alone in the dawn of Monday, June 5.

It will be a long time, if ever, before historians can rightly pinpoint that Jordanian, Syrian, and Egyptian fire came first. What the world does know is that the Israelis annihilated Soviet-supplied Arab air forces, armor, and ground units. For practical purposes, the war was won in sixty hours, an unbelievable feat. Israel, wrote James B. Reston in *The New York Times*, "had the courage of *our* convictions." We were not, however, confronted with the awful alternative of survival or extinction. The Russians, who egged on their Arab clients, took a pasting the world over. They refused to come to the rescue of their clobbered protégés, falling back, instead, on breaking relations with the Israelis and unleashing violent epithets.

Our administration in Washington patted itself on the back. The Israelis had achieved an awesome victory, and we didn't have to become involved with material power of any kind. Nasser, to salvage himself, said the Americans really won it for Israel. Only Arabs— with the exception of hapless King Hussein of Jordan—believed Nasser. In a spirit of understanding, L.B.J. revealed he used the "hot line" between the White House and the Kremlin for the first time. Kosygin and the President agreed that they wouldn't get into a gunfight in the Middle East.

The Russians switched to kind words for the battered Arab regimes they refused to save in combat. Kosygin came to the UN and assailed the United States, which had done practically nothing, for assisting Israel. As for Israel, Kosygin called its leaders Nazis and demanded reparations for all the Soviet equipment destroyed. Quite a cynical charge from Kosygin, who was a minister in Stalin's government when the Nazi-Soviet pact was signed. That agreement paved the way for the Nazi extermination of six million Jews in Europe.

To cover up a nonexistent policy for the Middle East, L.B.J. came up with a program calling for peaceful negotiations and a development program designed to help all combatants. The fresh initiative for the U.S.S.R. to come and reason together was stretched out with handles. The Russians didn't like its shape. They wanted, without war, to fasten their own protectorate over Islam. In their power perspective the Israelis are of no consequence, except that of a transitory obstacle which stopped Soviet momentum in a revealing and humiliating manner.

The Russians will pursue these objectives again—indeed they have already begun to rebuild the Arabs' costly military programs. Thoughtful and patient Israelis, who spent their lives seeking a workable formula with the Russians under the handicap of two million co-religionist hostages, don't believe they can work out an accommodation with the Russians in the foreseeable future.

Even as Soviet Premier Kosygin appeared at the UN to provide balm for his shattered Arab clients, expert American voices clamored for a new approach toward the Russians. Barely had the dust of battle settled than James A. Wechsler in the New York *Post* called for a fresh *detente*. Wechsler, who broods and comments on facets of illiberalism, simply ignored his earlier, emotional appeal to assist Israel in the hours before the explosion. So did Joseph Kraft, who was even more distraught than Wechsler before the fighting.

Just as after the missile confrontation in Cuba, they contended, the opportunity was at hand for consensus with the U.S.S.R. In 1962, as after the Middle East episode in 1967, magnanimity toward the Russians and pragmatic togetherness were the goals. Red China was held up as the real reason why, not the turbulence of the Middle East. China successfully tested a hydrogen bomb during the clash of arms and blood-curdling UN recrimination. That event made accommodation with the Russians, declared the experts, imperative. On the government level, Ambassador Thompson argued for the new approach.

In the crisis that hung heavily over the United States because of Soviet missiles in Cuba, Thompson helped persuade the late President Kennedy to suggest fresh approaches to Nikita S. Khrushchev. His thesis prevailed as Communist China swept down from the mountains to maul the Indians and thereby show possession of power among Asian nations. At that time the Russians accepted the approach. But they concentrated immediately on improving their position in the Middle East. Interestingly, so did Red China, through modest arms deliveries to Arab states and judicious cash-and-credit arrangements devised by Premier Chou En-lai on flying visits.

Nevertheless, Chinese investments and their proclamation of pro-Arabism hardly dented the Soviet planned contributions. Yet China's spoiler role provided impetus for appeals by experts to link solid bridges between the United States and the U.S.S.R. as communication and cooperation for the future. Unheeded in the appeals by experts was the simple, rather cold-blooded fact that it takes at least two sides to make relaxation work. In the Middle East the Russians deliberately proved they considered the cold war placed in cold storage.

In external difficulties the Soviet Union always switches tactics. Examine contemporary affairs and see where, almost as in a plan, every five or seven years Soviet projections induce global tremors. There were, briefly considered: the blockade of Berlin, and Korea; the rising in Hungary and its ruthless suppression; the Cuban missile showdown; and, latterly, the blow-up in the Middle East.

A show of Soviet cordiality, however superficial, is always greeted by your experts as heralding a new Russian attitude. Recent history shows that Soviet tactics alter, but not the objectives. A personality as controversial and do-it-yourself as General de Gaulle was snubbed for practical purposes by the Russians. It followed after Kosygin talked to him on the way to the States. Ignoring popular pro-Israeli manifestations among the French, de Gaulle blamed Israel for making war. He also observed that American action in Vietnam was responsible for what occurred in the Middle East.

The Gaullist version of day-to-day history was remarkably similar to the Russians', who spurned his offer of a four-power conference. De Gaulle's own cabinet couldn't swallow the view. For the first time on an international issue he had difficulty stifling the objectors. Besides, such anti-Vietnam critics as Jean–Paul Sartre loudly disagreed with his analysis.

More important, Kosygin came to the UN—as it has since unfolded—for the express purpose of getting together with President Johnson. This was contained in messages to the White House. Kosygin meant to do his duty, first, to the Arabs. A formula for meeting, satisfactory to the Russians, had to be found. Immediately involved was Ambassador Thompson, summoned hastily back from Moscow. The charade of finding a suitable site, sort of a halfway house, was played out by the administration. In the excitement engendered by an off-again, on-again bilateral meeting, the predicament of the Middle East in general and Israel in particular became an impatient impediment.

All priority went to the stage-managed symmetry of the mid-1967 summit of L.B.J. and Kosygin. The quaint little New Jersey community of Glassboro was the midway point between the UN and Washington. A first meeting, with the principals wreathed in smiles, was extended to a second. Translations, after all, take up half the time. The fact that the meetings were held at all engendered a wave of euphoria. It was reminiscent of what we witnessed at the four-power summit in Geneva in 1955. Every participant, then, proclaimed good fellowship and peace. At the very same time, out of sight in Cairo, the Russians with Nasser laid the foundations for the arms deals that led to the 1956 Suez campaign and, a decade later, to the Israeli fight for survival. The Russians firmly believe, as their action and advice in the Arab world proved, that the pay-off is the battle for power.

In the last and grimmest episode the Israelis paid off—with something to spare. There is, however, no chance for a contrived Glassboro for them. They must traverse a long and booby-trapped route with no bridges to use; only a dogged determination to survive.

Chapter 16

AFRICA: PART THREE

†

THE antics and arrogance of most emerging nations, particularly
the African and the closely associated Middle Eastern, has long
been studiously ignored by the great powers. In this deferment of
reality the United States is as much to blame as any of the other
competitors. Our star-studded missions of regional experts, professional policy makers, and Presidential appointees, acted—still
do—so that no offense might be taken by the African. This was
partly a calculated reserve on the basis of color; partly, because
American policy is aimed at making the new states feel more pro
than anti-American.

Russian policy, given the head start of the indefinable "socialism"
to which it pays propaganda lip service, made some substantive
impact in Africa during the early sixties. The main Soviet objective
was entrenchment in the Arab world. Its instruments—men in the
field—didn't, however, care for the people and places to which
they were assigned. They were packed off to serve their state without much benefit of a *lingua franca,* French or English. Few feel
the weather bearable. Most find the local habits distasteful. The
combined reaction has been to take an overbearing attitude toward
Africans and African officialdom. Today Russians are generally regarded in Africa with some suspicion and growing antipathy. Their
fiasco in Egypt engendered contempt and rage.

Sooner than later most Soviet representatives in Africa do what
comes naturally out of their assignments. They begin to conspire,
to try to attract dissatisfied *outs* to plot against the *ins.* The Russians
do not hesitate, for example, to use one of their own physicians to
train a cadre, not for medicine, but for taking control of a health
service for future reference. To implement their objectives, they
pass around big and little bribes.

Avowed American intent is to blunt the "socialist" rallying cry of the Russians with useful aid projects, credits, and the Peace Corps. The Russians no longer even pretend to compete in these sectors. They try to reach into the center of power of a given regime, as they did in Ghana, and have the governments and overseers operate on Moscow time. The repeated American appeal to stop the Russians from filling a vacuum has little validity left. Soviet ambitions in Africa some years ago veered from assisting investment programs for development to planting networks that one day would be the hidden persuaders running any African government.

So far theirs is an indifferent success. This is due to the appearance of Red Chinese missions in the field and to the discovery by some African leaders that the Russians first, and the Chinese next want to get rid of them. Survival in politics, however humble, is an exacting rule. The result has been, particularly in East Africa, a Soviet-Chinese competition to get rid of one another. So obsessive is this campaign that the Americans are frequently overlooked or even ignored.

Red Chinese missions do what the Russians don't do and the Americans do somewhat haphazardly. They send out teams that live off the land in the African bush. They use the "color" line blatantly. It is simple and direct: Both the Russians and we, they say, are whites. The Chinese are colored. Therefore the Chinese interest is one of brotherhood. Simultaneously, the Red Chinese seek to build up a local takeover apparatus of their own. It is carried out in the name of "revolution." The cynicism is profound. Should it be a monarchy, as in poverty-prostrate Burundi (once a Belgian protectorate), the Chinese work with the royalists. The emphasis is on do-it-yourself with the success of Communist China coming to power as an example.

Money and gifts are spread, too. It isn't funneled, as is American assistance, through regular governmental channels. Nor is it the Soviet system of pinpointed bribery. The Chinese go out to the tribal villages, make friends with local chiefs or their heirs. They have some of their "technicians" stay on at the village. Simple indoctrination follows, along with the presentation of a simple machine, tea sets, and occasionally, currency with which to buy a commodity.

It took some time for our regional experts to divine what the Chinese were basically after in Africa. The shocking consensus is that it involves a long-range effort to dominate the continent totally and populate it with Chinese. These conclusions, waved aside imperiously by militant African politicians, are today also expressed by European Communists, assigned by their governments to Africa. The assessments of Red Chinese intentions have been circulated in many African capitals. They elicit varying reactions. A few have taken them seriously; most have not.

One of the authors was present when European Communists were baldly telling an African personality what they suspected of Chinese motives. A big fan circled lazily in the hotel lounge. Its blades screeched for lack of oil. The conversants were forced to pitch their arguments loud enough for them to reach the African on the other side of the table. In corners of the lounge sat polo-shirted Chinese, listening intently, if impassively, to the discussion. No timetable was given for the Chinese plan. It would just be patient step-by-step ascendancy. There was even consideration for setbacks. Chinese objectives, as explained, were first to gain footholds and then to shift their people into key areas.

The prominent African politician listened to the warnings. All he thought was that they were "interesting." He has since represented his country on a host of assignments, from economic conferences to the UN General Assembly. He lives exceedingly well when on a foreign mission. As with most emissaries from developing nations, he travels on a first-class ticket; American ambassadors can fly only economy class, unless they want to pay the difference. In any big city, especially New York (as the site of the UN), top members of African delegations are usually big spenders. The majority pretend that they wheel and deal in great global matters. Flattery, unbridled bribery, and intra-Africa-Asia competition make up the minds and votes of many delegates from emergent nations.

Yet the great powers, and those like France and Britain with a colonialist past, don't hesitate to play on the weaknesses. The flattery appears in public with affectionate gestures to a given African delegate. In semi-private, it is household parties where sophisticated men, like the late Adlai Stevenson, sit around on the floor with a group singing folk airs.

Real expertise on Africa, however, might be expected within special departments of the UN. After all, there are thirty-eight African states in the 121-nation General Assembly. In a matter of simple addition, add them to a dozen Communist delegations, which vote *pro forma* with almost anything African. Then, take variables from another twenty, plus twenty-four on-again, off-again Asians. The arithmetic usually comes to a two-thirds majority for the Afro-Asian group, which often casts its vote just like that, a bloc.

Secretary General U Thant, the one-time schoolteacher from Burma who succeeded Dag Hammarskjöld after a tragic plane crash in Africa, has shown little patience with, or knowledge of, Africa. As a former representative of a developing nation, U Thant might have been expected to acquire more first-hand information about Africa. In several meals with him, one of the authors discovered that U Thant's knowledge of Africa, its complexities, and personalities was unfortunately limited. He used the fashionable excuse that there were "progressive" Africans—Nkrumah might be difficult, but he was all-out for progress. Then, there were opponents of that progress, like Felix Hophuet-Boigny of the Ivory Coast.

The same misty concepts of African personalities prevail for U Thant as do for Westerners ready to forgive corruption, dictatorship, and misfeasance, if it is executed in the name of "socialism." When a crusty Swedish career officer complained to U Thant several times that his UN function as commander of peace-keeping forces was jeopardized by lack of genuine support, he was told to keep mum. Von Horn, as cautious a neutral as is his own country, was outraged. He resigned and wrote a four-hundred-page book on his experiences with the UN in key Near-East and African areas.

In his memoirs, entitled *Soldiers of Peace,* he indicted the UN as riddled with espionage and corruption. He specifically dissected areas—the Congo, former Palestine, and Yemen—where he commanded UN forces. The administrative department of the UN, charged Horn, had "foggy ideas about reality."

"It is filled," he added, "with a passion for formalism and manned by people who became a swarm of angry bees when their hive was threatened with criticism. . . . some UN employees had taken the job mainly to make money in suspicious ways: smuggling, black market deals, espionage, and corruption."

Other salient points made by Von Horn:

The Congo: "A complete mess, a completely amateur affair."

He also quotes the verdict of the late UN Secretary General, fellow-Swede Hammarskjöld: "Crazy."

Jerusalem: "Attractive Israeli girls were freed from military service to entertain guests from the United Nations. The enlistment for Israel's cause which took place between the sheets came second to systematic, organised corruption." Van Horn wrote that before he took up his Israeli UN command, Hammarskjöld told him to do all in his power to win the confidence of the Arabs. "But remember whatever you do you will never get complete confidence or co-operation from the Israeli side." Von Horn was not pro-Arab, either. He flails their intrigues and brands the UN operation in Yemen, where Nasser staged an invasion, as "a farce." Nasser is still there.

UN, New York: "The new member states revelled in the politically-inspired generosity of the big powers and had already discovered it paid off to act noisily, contemptuously and insolently. Everywhere there stood groups of eager Africans in animated discussion which vanished as soon as a white girl joined them. I saw it happen so many times, lonely white girls surrounded by a circle of shining, black faces, that it was difficult to forget reports of unscrupulous states which obtained sympathies among these delegates via politically-supported call girls."

Then, von Horn added a footnote to this togetherness by recalling that three girls, expelled by the police, reappeared in Warsaw.

Von Horn, to anyone who has ever met him, is by no stretch of the imagination a racist. Nor does he have the slightest ambitions to try and become a "political general." He set down what bothered him, but could not resist U Thant's appeal to go quietly so as to avoid "undesirable publicity." Limited as von Horn's examination of the UN may be, it was an honest account.

The fall-out came inside the three white-ruled territories of Africa. They seized on the von Horn book as proof of their lopsided, subjective claim that Africans are essentially unfit to administer countries, people, and policies.

This strange triumvirate, Rhodesia, Portugal through her East and West African domains in Mozambique and Angola, and South Africa are united in their own fight for survival. Geographically, in the southern section of Africa, they are defensively cohesive. To fend off all-African encroachment, these states practice economic interdependence. Determination to remain the primary white chiefs is their overriding goal. Each in their own way is racist. Their very existence and ability to challenge colored Africans is the real—and perhaps unique—factor that automatically unites all other Africans to oppose them in frustration.

Africa, on any other issue, is hopelessly disunited. Few states can agree on any external issue, except to demand the elimination of the three white-supremacy states that humiliate them by their challenging existence.

The apparently vanishing hope which was Rhodesia, for instance, survives quite successfully. On Armistice Day, November 11, 1965, it unilaterally declared independence of Britain. A regime run by an angular, lantern-jawed ex-RAF hero, Ian Smith, went off on its own. The last time that happened was when the American colonies revolted. There, the analogy ends. Britain, under a wheeler-dealer Labour party politician, who confuses sleight of hand with statesmanship, portly Prime Minister Harold Wilson, did little. He clamped on sanctions and got United States support. But sanctions, as exemplified so sadly by Mussolini's war against Ethiopia, are meaningless.

South Africa, ruled by its hateful policies of apartheid against the blacks, filled in whatever Rhodesia lacked due to the porous applications of sanctions. So did the Portugese-administered territories. All are adjacent to Rhodesia. The result is that 200,000 whites in Rhodesia rule a vast and inherently rich land that contains four million blacks. Just north of Rhodesia is Zambia, one of the newer African nations. It is governed by a moderate and highly educated African, President Kenneth Kaunda. At stake are the vast copper fields in Zambia and the hydroelectric installations just inside land-locked Rhodesia that are necessary to the production of copper.

Although American governmental behavior would be better suited tactically to simple condemnation of Smith's act, called UDI for short in Rhodesia, we agreed to the sanctions method. The Africans, increasingly frustrated, will have no recourse but to demand mandatory sanctions from the UN. Wilson has agreed to this as a last recourse. He will not dispatch troops to bring down Smith. But to implement mandatory sanctions means large-scale blockade. The only nation capable of even attempting to cut off South African and Portugese territories is the United States.

Instead of keeping quiet and putting on pressure where most useful, our experts gave a blank check to Wilson.

Led by "Soapy" Williams and even Arthur Schlesinger, Jr., who knows comparatively very little about anything African, we find ourselves painted into a tight corner. Should America demur, we will be reviled for bad faith by a Labour government that has mostly supported our role in Vietnam. If we agree, even partly, to provide the means for blockade, we will be in an act of undeclared war against one NATO ally, Portugal. Anything the United States furnishes, be it ships, planes, or military supplies, comes up for this determination: Who commands it? The Africans contend they must assume over-all command, as they do in the still-meaningless "liberation" units destined to rip through southern Africa. At worst, when mandatory sanctions have been exercised, the UN would take charge. After the previous global undertakings of the UN, no American President could possibly shift such vast stores of weaponry and policy to United Nations authority. He couldn't, that is, if he did not want to raise deadly criticism in the Congress.

The handcuffs and straitjackets we locked on our freedom of technique and action were fashioned by high officials who help make American policy. They, in turn, have been largely taken in by the demands, threats, or dexterity of African politicians. These same Africans, who claimed beginning about 1960 that this was their epoch, have been wrong in their estimates, inaccurate about their own influences, and tragically incorrect about the immediate future.

There are thirty-six African chiefs of state. In the early sixties they banded together in a group called "The Organization of African Unity." It is usually known by its initials, OAU. The idea behind its establishment was sensible. So different are views of the participating states, and so severe their jealousies, that the OAU is even a more practical forum than the UN for hammering out day-to-day coexistence.

Unfortunately it took only a few OAU sessions to prove to the majority that Nasser, Nkrumah, or Sekou Toure—often a combination of the three—tried to use the organization as their own. Disunity became the cynical byword for the OAU, even as caustically used by African members. A meeting in mid-November, 1966, just about finished whatever usefulness it might ever practice. It was preceded by the arrest in a Pan American airliner of a Guinean delegation bound for the meeting. The plane stopped in Ghana briefly on its way to Addis Ababa, the rarified Ethopian capital. Ghana authorities, smarting under Guinean protection of Nkrumah, held the traveling Guineans as hostages. Most of the work at the OAU conference was to effect the release of the Guineans. "An old tribal habit," was the supersophisticated crack made by a North African delegate to a Black African. That remark almost electrically made the conference rounds. Disunity was rampant. The only positive achievement was the release of the Guineans from Ghana.

The prospects of a shattered OAU even compelled Nasser to make an effort to hold it together. He strode into the huge dining hall built in 1896 by Menelik II of Ethiopia to house the rambunctious raw meat feasts of his elite units. Nasser entered, holding the tiny hand of his host, the Lion of Judah, Menelik's great nephew, Emperor Haile Selassie, frail, seventy-four-year-old representative of Africa's oldest nation and oldest dynasty. The handclasp was the overt sign of earnest efforts by the African left and right to hold together. But only sixteen states had their number one men in attendance. The other twenty were represented by ministers. Sekou Toure never went.

All the nations conferring, however, pointed up their inter-Africa divisions as well as the Balkanization of much of the continent by earlier colonial creations. What had been triumphantly hailed as "The Age of Africa" six years before—and believed by our own specialists, later promoted by government to experts—was on the threshold of darkness in division. Poverty, corruption, big-power intrusion, and mammoth ambition by outsized egos like Nasser's have made the African plight more pitiful—and dangerous. There are today twenty-four countries with a population of less than five million. Illiteracy is terribly prevalent and "developing" is only a word.

At that Addis Ababa conference, delegates bickered, indulged in mutual recrimination, and agreed in words only that somehow, some way South Africa and Rhodesia must be brought to heel. In reviewing the conference, Peter Webb, veteran chief Africa correspondent for *Newsweek,* observed: "It seems to me that Africa has got its priorities wrong. Its obsession with the white-dominated south has been allowed to overshadow grim economic realities, which if not tackled now on a continental basis, will bring disaster. There is a crisis of rising expectations stemming from the desire of Africa's 270 million people for a better life, and for the fulfilment of promises that were made to them at independence. To fulfil these promises needs every ounce of every African leader's efforts and fruitless resolutions at the OAU or the UN against Rhodesia and South Africa are simply a waste of time and energy."

In despair, Webb suggested a "continental basis" as a formula. This is also the proposal of Edward M. Korry, our ambassador to Ethiopia and architect of the *Korrygrams* mentioned earlier. Korry headed a team of experts that drafted a scheme for the salvation of Africa. It won State Department approval, just as "Soapy" Williams's former ideas once obtained enthusiastic consent. The Korry report, as distinguished from the *Korrygrams,* looks to Africa as a whole. It wants to harness resources of principal Western nations and channel them through a hard-headed, independent body such as the World Bank. Conclusion is predicated on viewing Africa as one and moving it forward by concentrating aid on major regional continental projects such as transport, communications, and power.

The Korry report is unrealistic. How would a Nasser commit himself selflessly to such a project? Who, among the majority Black Africans, would believe him, even if he agreed? Would a West African work in wholehearted cooperation with a North African, or even an East African and vice versa. Then there is the issue of aid from principal Western nations. Do our experts, guided by Korry, believe that France would gladly join? Or the business interests of West Germany? Or, even those in battered Britain?

Moreover, while this vast and grandiloquent project was getting approval from, say forty oddly assorted countries, what would Red China or the U.S.S.R. be doing? The Korry report seems obviously intended as a minor monument for its author. To ensure himself a place in African expertise, he often sought to belabor Bill Attwood, then his colleague in Kenya.

Attwood, who returned to the Cowles organization as top editorial director, once hand-picked Korry to succeed him as European correspondent based in Paris. A personally attractive man with a lovely wife and handsome family of three children, Attwood candidly regrets his Paris choice. He became exasperated, however, when Korry sent the first of his *Korrygrams* announcing his entry into the diplomatic service. A round-robin letter, in lieu of cards, was Korry's Christmas, 1962, revelation. In lieu of a reply, Attwood sent his own round-robin message. As a political appointee, Attwood dryly mentioned the fact that Korry never supported the winning candidate of the Presidential elections, John F. Kennedy. He eviscerated the sententious *Korrygram,* which most people in the press and public affairs received. The feud was on, often whizzing right into the White House. But Attwood had proved himself, taming Sekou Toure while he was on the spot in Guinea. His last post, in Kenya, was a triumph of patience, intelligence, and limitation to a specially sensitive place. It is a singularly remarkable achievement of United States understanding and hard work that bore fruit in Africa.

Born on Bastille Day, 1919, in Paris, Bill Attwood had the benefits of fine, formal education in the United States and a worldly atmosphere at home. After World War II service—he speaks fluent French so he was sent to the Far East, of course—Attwood became a newspaperman. As a foreign correspondent who traveled widely, he developed ideas of his own. When he returned to New York as an editor of *Look* magazine, Attwood became engaged in some of the hurly-burly of politics. In the 1956 campaign he was a speech writer for Adlai Stevenson. As with many others close to Stevenson, he was personally devoted, but felt the need for something more realistic in looking at the outside world.

Between the 1956 and 1960 political campaigns, Attwood edited, interviewed, and traveled extensively. His face-to-face talks with Fidel Castro are models of reflection and judgment that most of his eager colleagues would have done well to study before passing their own judgments. Attwood worked with President Kennedy in 1960. Because of his background and foreign language facility he could have taken up a few more glamorous posts than he did by asking for Guinea.

Near the end of his tour, by which time Sekou Toure was behaving toward the United States in a reasonable and practical manner, Attwood fell ill and nearly died. He was in the grip of a bad case of polio, at first wrongly diagnosed. Then came the long haul in Washington hospitals to come back to active life. With the constant attention of his wife, Simone, Attwood made it. He was no longer a vegetable and believed he had something to offer. Africa was very much on his mind, and he asked about Kenya.

At that time our relations with Kenya could scarcely have been worse. Virile but aged Jomo Kenyatta, known as "Chief Burning Spear" in the years of the Mau Mau rebellion against the British, was President. His government was shot through with pro-Russians and pro-Chinese. Kenyatta's most dangerous rival was his Vice President, Oginga Odinga, usually called "Double-O." Among the principal tribes rivalry was stoked to a white heat. Odinga, arrogantly confident about his own future ascension to power, drew large sums from the Russians and the Chinese.

To top off a bad situation, Kenyatta was compelled to call for British help—as a Commonwealth member—to quell mutinous signs in the fledgling armed forces. It never got as bad as the plight further south, in then Tanganyika (later Tanzania), where Dr. Nyerere fled and hid until the revolt was crushed. All the ingredients for an internal explosion were available in Kenya. The Americans were the most suspect outside force of all.

Attwood arrived and began building confidence from a crisis status. He sought first to make the United States at least equal with other foreign nations in Kenyatta's eyes. There were rebuffs and indignant fits of pique. But Attwood never tried to attract Kenyatta with pan-African concepts or even bigger global thoughts. He proved to Kenyatta's satisfaction that we were not out to undermine him. And Attwood made good on localized promises—schools, bridges, animal husbandry.

Progress was steady if not spectacular. Attwood was not interested in personal glory. That undoubtedly provided him with a surgical approach to the problem. He wanted to do what he could to make Kenya—just Kenya—more viable, more amenable. A cruel blow nearly finished his work. There was the Belgian paratroop drop in Stanleyville, in the eastern Congo. Missionaries were saved and Congolese rebels, wilder and more difficult than even the nationalist-cum-mercenary forces pitted against them.

Kenyatta blew his stack, because Africans were slain by soldiers of a former colonial power serviced by United States planes. Again, Attwood went to work as he had before. The Stanleyville affair was no plot for wider action, he explained. If Kenyatta rejected the humanitarian aspect, then he knew as well as anyone that the Congolese rebels were supplied and suborned by forces inimical to Kenyatta, too. Quietly, for months, the talks progressed. "Double-O" never lost an opportunity to snipe at Attwood. Our ambassador to Kenya ignored Odinga and kept fulfilling promises for projects as far ahead of schedule as possible.

Came the showdown. Security agents loyal to Kenyatta reported on assorted Communist subversive operations. Kenyatta wasted no time. He expelled Soviet, Red Chinese, and Czechoslovakian diplomats, as well as their agents who usually pose as journalists. Then he cracked down on "Double-O," who resigned and went into a twilight opposition. Young men long slurred by Odinga as American stooges, such as Tom Mboya, began to rise in influence within the Kenyatta government. We have the picture of Kenya clamping down on foreign Communists, but Tanzania providing a structure, for both the U.S.S.R. and China, from which to maneuver. Somewhat the same situation holds in the shaky Kenyan neighbor to the north, Somalia. Attwood was thanked by Kenyatta for the "unselfish" job he did. At the airport, when the family departed, a group of young Kenyans swarmed to the plane bearing placards that read: "Yankee, Don't Go Home."

His success should be studied as a pilot scheme for future emissaries we dispatch to Africa. Attwood stubbornly fought the tempting bait of becoming an expert. He stayed a reporter, an observer, who asked for nothing but coequality and an opportunity to prove that he could deliver certain commodities that were promised. He wrote a book about his African assignments which angered Kenyans for all it revealed. In effect, he smashed the self-help schemes of the Chinese and wrecked the bribery and subversive methods of the Russians. It was a young Kenyan delegate to an Afro-Asian "solidarity" conference who best summed up what Attwood achieved.

"We are not Marxist-Leninists, and most of us have never read a single line of 'Das Kapital,'" he declared. "So what interest do you have in our participating in your doctrinal quarrels? I have had enough, when I am eating a sandwich, of being accosted by someone who asks me what I think of Soviet positions, and when I am drinking coffee, by someone who questions me about the Chinese arguments. I would like to be able to eat in peace!"

That rebuttal, so plainly eloquent, goes for all attempts to insinuate forms of American ideology or latter-day personalized theories concerning civil rights in America. Senator Robert F. Kennedy, the late President's restless brother, stirs young people no matter where he appears. The mystique may be of golden youth, or the amazing impact made on young people around the world by the assassinated President. Bobby Kennedy's forays into the stadia of public diplomacy have been rousing and crowd-pleasing shows. Private diplomacy, as we mention later, has been an exercise in frustration and fiasco. But Bobby's public displays are also worrisome. He can leave. The enthusiastic crowds he addresses cannot.

This was never more poignantly proved than when Bobby went to South Africa in 1966. Thousands of students and black and white sympathizers joined him in chanting the civil rights song "We Shall Overcome." That was in Durban, where he also mounted the top of his car to sing and make little speeches. His use of an auto top is unique in conveying a thought or message abroad. Bobby first used it in Poland in 1964 when he was still United States Attorney General. His song then was "When Polish Eyes are Smiling." Splendid corn. But the Polish audiences, who respond enthusiastically to any American, aren't smiling and remain under the same Communist regime.

By appearing and addressing crowds in South Africa, Bobby Kennedy showed his distaste for the white supremacist rule. Without question, he moved the students at the University of Capetown. He spoke of the "excitement of danger" and the "appetite for adventure" to black and white youngsters. "It is your job," he asserted, "to strip the last remnants of that ancient, cruel belief from the civilization of man." On other occasions, Senator Bobby advocated that the struggle in South Africa be nonviolent. But that speech to the university in Capetown was as ill-advised as it was emotionally charged. Somehow, it overlooked the bitter fact that any serious demonstration against apartheid in South Africa is illegal.

It took *The Observer* of London—which by no means shrinks from coming to grips with apartheid—to remind the world that this sort of talk hadn't been heard since Sharpeville, 1960. Those riots took a toll of 72 killed and 184 wounded. Quite patently, *The Observer* correspondent in Capetown noted alarmingly that "all this is intolerable to the Prime Minister, who must now act quickly to check any repercussions."

For a man in the public eye of the world, Senator Kennedy spoke out with inexcusable irresponsibility. In South Africa he was on the side of right and dignity, just as thirteen years earlier he was the advocate of wrong and indignity when he served the late Senator Joe McCarthy and his inquisition. Senator Kennedy's journey through Africa without maps also produced some glittering nuggets of expertise. He is rapidly reaching a new format: The cult of the universal young expert. On his way home, Kennedy stopped in Addis Ababa to talk to an assemblage of African diplomats at the OAU. Although the organization was then badly splintered, Bobby appealed to its officials to take worldwide leadership in breaking the deadlock on nuclear arms control.

He told his audience that the great powers had failed in this task. "You must now take the lead and restore the flagging energies of governments and their negotiators," declared Senator Kennedy. Considering the abysmal and tragicomic record of new African states in misgovernment and nongovernment, it was a staggering suggestion. It didn't even reflect the unwillingness of superpowers to delegate to others language and guarantees for A-weapon controls. Probably the most concise view of this Kennedyism was an arch comment in *The Reporter* magazine. "The most charitable thing that can be said about this episode is that the Senator, in his eagerness to remain young, proved childish."

Far more realistic, although often held in contemptuous amusement by fellow-African leaders, is a Scotch-trained physician, Hastings Banda, turned President of Malawi. In British colonial times Malawi was known as Nyasaland. It is another poverty-stricken little African country, sandwiched between the white-ruled areas of southern Africa. Banda has belittled pan-African attempts—particularly those sponsored by Nasser or the dualism of Sekou Toure-Nkrumah—either to cooperate or to compel white rule to knuckle under.

A stubby man, edging seventy years of age, Banda has been derided as an African Uncle Tom or an imperialist clown. In his own domain, he showed how in survival—chief asset of any African leader—he needs no lessons from any other African leader. Banda expelled or jailed the ambitious younger men who wanted him as a figurehead. But he caused a collective cry of anger from most black Africans when he sneered at their ability to crush the three hated white-ruled states.

In November, 1965, Banda stood before the Malawi Parliament, visibly annoyed. It was just after Rhodesia's runaway regime declared independence. Threats to smash Rhodesia were plain crazy, said Banda. The black Africans vowing to do so had paper armies. "Remember, at this stage of our lives, ten white mercenaries will whip five thousand African soldiers," boomed Banda.

"Sanctions? Who has the money in Africa? Not the blacks. We need peace, education, and development, first."

Banda was saying, despite his detractors, that it is not the principle but the speed of African advance which is at issue. The experienced British writer and editorialist Colin Coote said it succinctly when he wrote: "The devoted advocates of the 'liberation' of Africa should realize the inevitability of gradualness. Otherwise they will find the formerly Dark Continent not blessed by a dawn but menaced by the night of a Dark Age such as once blacked out most of Europe for centuries." The premise is well worth the time of the new expert, the Africanist, to think about, before rendering judgment.

It hasn't been heeded. The Africanist and most African politicians rushed to the side of Nasser. Israel, to them, loomed as the main arm of the ever-handy bogey, "neo-colonialism." The new expert agreed with the fancied fear—without question and with full condemnation.

African expert opinion, rallying as it did around Nasser, had an unsettling impact on restless, bewildered, and stricken areas which comprise most of Asia and the Far East. An *ad hoc* association emerged between African and Asian leaderships since 1959. Most felt a togetherness born of poverty and suspicion. Instinctively, they were searching for a future and resented offers of assistance from old colonial masters and the United States, decried for its potential takeover powers.

In the years since our nuclear bombs demolished Hiroshima, the embers of discontent have glowed fiercely in the problem of colonial dismantlement. They took on many forms and colored sparks. More than in any other part of the developing world, leaders in Asia restoke the fire in the ashes of what they describe as colonialism. The word is used and abused in the sacred name of calls to nationalism, or to launch predatory raids over another frontier, or to maintain a guerrilla war. Americans, within that generation after 1945, have swiveled their interest from one side of the world to another with every cataclysm, and then turned their attention back again.

It has been toward Europe that the Americans have persistently turned after brief spells with Asia—briefer ones with Africa and Latin America. But the concentration of the world today is largely on far-off Vietnam. The reason is obvious. Americans are involved in a clash of arms in jungles, and in an arcane discussion at home for and against our role in South Vietnam, Never in American history have there been so many instant experts as there are about this pawed-over area and mauled people. Most are insistent, some are lucid, and few have the basic knowledge to demand the consent for which they offer their counsel. The whole sequence of explosion or forced alteration to induce a pattern for power has left us looking like spectators at a tennis game.

Chapter 17

ASIA AND THE FAR EAST:
PART ONE

❦

W^{E ARE} told about the players and where the leading conten-
ders are burning up the courts. It is a huge chunk of the
world, yet we find ourselves overwhelmed with the fustian and
treacle of expert advice. If we take the time and maintain a hard-
nosed attitude about the qualifications of those by whom most of
the advice is offered, we should arrive at a lean list of twenty-five
or thirty who have a right to be heard. Hundreds of others, presenting their examinations of Asian problems, enjoy only the privilege of observation. Since we are fascinated by expertise, whether
in machine tools or comment, we suffer these views, if not gladly,
then by accepted custom.

The inherent rights of Asia, it seems to us, are most often dis-
puted by Asians themselves. Americans, after a brief introspective
isolationist spell following World War II, applauded and supported
a massive economic transfusion for Europe known as the Marshall
Plan. It was the Old World we knew best. Therefore, interest in
the whole string of old countries predominated.

When India was granted independence by Britain, in a civilized
transfer of power, we swung away briefly from Europe to look at
some of the horrendous episodes that rocked the whole subconti-
nent. Administrative India was partitioned; one part becoming
the Republic of Pakistan. Hindus and Moslems slaughtered each
other. Apocalyptic famine stalked the torn up, have-not provinces.

We didn't spend much time, nor did publications give much
space to the turmoil between India and Pakistan. We paid very
little heed to the onrushing Chinese Communist armies soon to
expel Chiang Kai-shek from the mainland. Only a short time before, the Provisional Premier of France sent the first postwar rein-

forcements expeditiously to then-Indochina. His name was Charles de Gaulle. He emphasized the absolute need for France to re-establish her colonial presence especially in the Vietnam enclave of Indochina. De Gaulle enjoys supremacy as a political expert in the world today.

The Korean War, which ultimately brought Red China to the aid of the aggressor North Koreans, produced a certain quantity of military expertise. Issues, like who undercut Chiang and why, produced their ugly spate of Washington witch-hunting, epitomized by the late Senator Joseph McCarthy. One of the bright young assistants he had on his staff was Robert F. Kennedy, present-day junior Senator from New York.

Senator Bobby has undertaken to become an expert on Asian problems as well as those of Africa and the United States proper. He had no voice, except one of detached silence, when postwar Asia was in the throes of trying to come of age. Later in Indonesia Bobby thought he had made a fast deal to better the climate between President Sukarno and the United States. It was a classic in the confrontation of two experts. Sukarno, the super con-man, deflated the deal while Bobby was barely airborne, heading home to talk of triumph.

Indonesia is one of the sharpest cases of modern American expertise gone haywire. By the time the September, 1965, military move against Sukarno was executed, he was high on most preferred blacklists. But the average expert in Asia, belittling his personal vices and amatory acrobatics, got through. Sukarno seemed possessed of everlasting stamina as number one in Indonesia. The vast archipelago was even written off by most experts as a soon-to-be satrapy of Communist China.

When the military, under General Suharto, sprung the trap into which the huge Indonesian Communist party and the Sukarno entourage fell, the experts backtracked. At first they thought General Suharto—of whom almost nobody had heard—was not the real coup leader. Ex-Defense Minister Haris Nasution, who had lost his little daughter in a Communist raid, was much better known. Therefore, the experts reasoned, Nasution was the brains. It has turned out that Suharto was then and remains top man. Very belatedly, even then reluctantly, these same roving Asian experts agree that the deflation of Sukarno and the rollback of the Communist party was Red China's greatest single defeat in Asia. It could be broadened to include the entire Communist world. Then came long and somewhat hasty surveys of the slaughter of Communists. No accurate count can ever be made. Some estimates mention 400,000 dead.

That so gentle a people as the Indonesians could become so ferocious against their own fellows was a shock. To expect wounds to heal patiently and quietly where retaliation is the norm is as patently unrealistic as to expect instant parliamentary democracy in nations whose citizens never even knew of its existence. The assault on Communists in Asia—mixed certainly with personal settlement of old scores—commanded more attention and attendant bathos than did mass killings of Hindus and Moslems, let alone the brief Indian-Pakistan war.

Even now, when starvation threatens some Indian provinces, we are provided principally with the expert views of Chester Bowles, our ambassador. Big and shaggy of frame, Bowles has been interested in India ever since independence. He has twice been ambassador, which speaks well for his perseverance, if not for his acumen. Like so many with an intellectual bent outside India, he sees the seething country as the democratic answer to hegemonistic Communist China, brooding astride the northern frontiers of India. He has occasionally been annoyed by the posturing of Indian intellectuals who seize on anything "left" as an immediate panacea for relief. But Bowles urges patience and understanding of India, whether it be led by the late Prime Minister Jawaharlal Nehru or his daughter, Mrs. Indira Ghandi. The point perhaps might better be made another way: That Indians who lead and aspire to lead their country try to obtain a better insight into the United States.

Food and its scarcity remain the basic elements for news and comment in India. In a scathing survey published in *Commentary* magazine September, 1965, George Lichtheim tried to take *The New York Times* apart for its smug superficiality. He lit on some copy from India, written by J. Anthony Lukas. It was all about food prices being cut, sort of a boon for any Indian. In his tart comment on the Lukas article, Lichtheim—who apparently had done considerable research—thought the whole piece was slight. There was, wrote Lichtheim, "no indication of how much the price had risen previously, during the famine period, and whether its current drop had brought it back to 'normal.'"

Lichtheim's indictment of *The New York Times* is a sweeping one: "For the plain fact of the matter is that as a reliable source of information about the world outside America's borders, *The New York Times* is inadequate and misleading."

That happens to be almost—but not all—the news about the *Times* that is fit to print. Take the horrible example of reportage about India, which Lichtheim saw fit to dissect.

There was a three-year period, from 1955 to 1958, when the published information in the *Times* about India was unparalleled in its brilliance. A.M. (Abe) Rosenthal, one of the most gifted writers and minds ever in American journalism wrote, in those years, a living history of India. In the far-off northern hills, or in the steaming southern streets, Rosenthal transmitted an alive picture of India, her people, her problems—and her inner struggle to keep from flying apart. In his political assessments and interviews, Rosenthal pried the veneer off the professionally arrogant and angry disciple of Nehru, V.K. Krishna Menon. Nehru, the elder statesman of Asia, also was treated to Rosenthal's surgical examination.

Wherever he was subsequently assigned, Rosenthal illuminated the drably monotonous columns of *The New York Times* with his splendid journalism. Never an expert—a position he avoided assiduously—Rosenthal set standards so high that nobody on his paper has ever come close to them. The same might be said of most United States publications and television.

Rosenthal, a bespectacled, nervous man of medium height and of great compassion, was rewarded. He was made an editor in the New York office. Painfully, with agonizing slowness, he has been able to wrench some changes. The going has been difficult. Who, after all, can argue with a balance sheet in the black?

The meteor that was Rosenthal hasn't occurred again, either among *Times* correspondents or anyone else's. There have been competent people, malcontents, and astringent adulators. The only time the United States rushed a big contingent of reporters and camera crews to India was, naturally, when Red China swooped over the mountains in 1962. Preoccupied as the United States was with the missile crisis in Cuba, it is a wonder American public media sent out as many reporters as it did.

In 1961 we sent out what Washington assumed would be a one-man diplomatic band certain to make a constant impression on

India. He was altitudinous John Kenneth Galbraith, economist at Harvard, author, and adviser to Presidents. If any American envoy ever got a better sounding board than the one awaiting Galbraith in India, it has never been a matter of record. Somehow, he never went down well with the intellectual and ruling Indian elite. Mention his name there today, and a shrug is the reply. Perhaps they never appreciated his icy wit—or his economics.

For all of Galbraith's actual achievements in India, we might as well have sent a dress manufacturer with an able number two in tow. Ever since he departed India, Galbraith has spoken the lexicon of the expert about the world with one noteworthy exception, India. He writes and comments extensively about Europe, telling the British for instance, how fortunate they are. The Galbraith wit is exemplified in arch remarks like "spending on our divine mission in South Vietnam."

He has made himself in late 1966 a member in good standing of the universal experts with: "At no time did President Johnson stand back and take a look at the strategic needs of our position in Southeast Asia, which at any time in the last three years would certainly have required us to disengage ourselves from that area."

The first part of the observation is either facetious or plainly wrong. As an ex-ambassador, Galbraith must know there is a regular monthly regional assessment. It's for the President to review, take counsel, and alter should he so choose. Galbraith's flat declaration that if L.B.J. had leaned back and looked hard, he would have taken us out of Southeast Asia in a hurry is an unabashed, neo-isolationist remark. In its unvarnished arrogance, it defies any dissent, which many of Galbraith's younger staff, while he was ambassador, suffered in semisilence.

Galbraith has his opinions about Vietnam. But he knows next-to-nothing about it. His views, though, dovetail with those so often uttered by the late Nehru and his daughter. And they were both consistently inaccurate in judging Chinese nonintervention and the mammoth problems besetting their own country of 500 million.

Where we have cheerfully accepted near-ignorance and the platitudes of a better organized propaganda unit than in India, is the state of Pakistan. It would be more proper to say that it is two states, separated by a thousand miles of frontier with India. Within that wedge is a sharp instrument honed fine—the Indian-administered territory of Kashmir. Known to outsiders for its houseboats and as the birthplace of Nehru, Kashmir embodies the circumstantial evidence of hostility between the sovereign states created out of Britain's grant of independence. More education, proportionately, and kindred intellectual heart throbs made Americans infinitely more conscious of India than of Pakistan. Size has little to do with what absorbed our curiosity.

Our experts turned their backs on Pakistan because it was a military state under a ramrod-tough officer, Field Marshal Mohammed Ayub Khan. It had become, when John Foster Dulles was Secretary of State, a model ally in the framework of CENTO. The sight, to many, was a refreshing contrast to the niggling nonalignment of India, acclaimed by its outside intellectual supporters.

For four years, since the Chinese assault on India, Pakistan has been guided by a type of desperate and undefined neutralism. Interestingly, almost nobody who applauded India's neutralism will even nod favorably toward Pakistan. This may be because Pakistani statecraft rests on hopes of Red Chinese benevolence, primarily in armaments. Bereft of American aid in the agonizing seventeen days of September, 1965, Ayub Khan's regime turned pugnaciously to China for future help. The logic was frantically expedient. China is an enemy of India, which is hostile to Pakistan. Massive Soviet and American aid went to India in 1962, and then during the fighting with Pakistan.

The major modern Soviet diplomatic initiative since World War II was in Tashkent, the mediation between India and Pakistan. Yet the Pakistanis aren't terribly grateful. From Ayub Khan down, they don't believe that Soviet military aid to India is earmarked principally for defense against China.

For want of carefully acquired knowledge of Pakistan, our homegrown experts are inclined today to view the India-Pakistan mutual hate as something similar to the fury between the Arab world and Israel. It happens to offer an easy comparison, and with that, dismissal. A little examination shows how hollow this parallel concept really is. Pakistan, if need be, can acquire arms quickly from China. Not so Israel, from interested Western countries. Hindu versus Moslem is of a totally different character than Arab against Zionist.

Ayub, a man of clever maneuver, has relied on a balancing act ever since he shifted from being the model Western ally and made his arms deal with troubleshooters of Mao Tse-tung. By keeping an eye on malcontents—especially among retired army officers—Ayub tries to maintain a grip on the machinery of Pakistani political power. While a take-charge man, as he demonstrated in October, 1958, Ayub is by no means himself the political boss. That is his most glaring weakness which he is not at all loathe to discuss as he has done with the authors, among others. To keep on top of internal political twists and shifts of local allegiance, Ayub uses the balancing act. He reluctantly got rid of his most loyal henchman, the former governor of West Pakistan, usually called the Nawab of Kalabagh. This was to satisfy a triumvirate that sits for him when he is outside the country. The Nawab, a lifelong friend of Ayub, was dismissed with hundreds of loyal subordinates. They had, in their feudal manner, become embarrassing. By dismissing them, Ayub weakened his political hold. He had no other choice, or so he felt.

His internal opposition, anti-Chinese in their attitudes rather than pro-Western, is in quest of a formula to make their impact felt in the country. They cannot be active in politics because this is an arena barred to them as to others. A few, under vigilance, were permitted to warm up again politically in 1966–1967 with others scheduled for reappearance in 1968–1969. There is, to date, no real political program that could challenge Ayub seriously. The critics have been distributed around the country, where their splintered forces can do Ayub the least harm.

The main virus affecting the political longevity of Ayub Khan is his absolutely obstinate policy in resenting and countering every Indian wrong. Despite the experts, there has been more than an occasional Indian wrong. Begin with India's claim that Kashmir is Indian territory forever more. By opposing India at every step, Ayub fritters away his meager resources. Worse, he works himself into difficult positions as he did by going to China for military aid. Pakistan is a captive of circumstance. That doesn't lessen its importance in the world, or certainly, to us. America has ignored the country and its split personality, although it possesses the same potential for trouble and tragedy as does the all-German issue on the other side of the world.

Looking every inch the Sandhurst-trained officer he is, military mustache clipped as was his search for the right word at the correct time, Ayub Khan looked at the immediate future hopelessly. It was in London, after a state visit in November, 1966. Pakistan, he said, had not found security in Western-backed treaties like SEATO and CENTO. But his country wouldn't leave them. Staying in, of course, means that Pakistan wrecks the concept of the northern tier of alliance.

He talked to the authors, of Communist China. It was not with the fervor of a new believer. Ayub Khan is by no means a Communist or even a sympathizer. He was pondering over the rise of China as a world power. He wasn't even mindful of the phantasmagoria that Mao Tse-tung calls "the cultural revolution," which creates a permanent purge in China. Ayub Khan was obviously thinking in terms of atomic power for China, a new and awesome weaponry to challenge both the United States and Russia.

"It will take ten to fifteen years," he mused. "Until then this world is going to remain a terrible place indeed."

Unspoken, however, were the thoughts of Ayub Khan's political counselors, the men who switched to China for arms. They think in terms of obtaining nuclear weaponry from the Chinese to provide Pakistan with a deterrent against the atomic potential of India. In her anguish, famine-stricken, economically dislocated India wants to build an A-bomb fast. The reason is not so much the cost but defense against the day China exerts nuclear blackmail. Rather than say so outright—this is left to the scientists and the military—the Indian government threatens the possibility of a nonproliferation agreement. It demands a ban on underground tests plus signing by China, France, and Albania, countries that resolutely refuse to join the club.

Yet it is Hindu riots to protect cows from being consigned to slaughterhouses that get nearly all the headlines and all the serious review by experts on India. Virtually all the quests for internal and external influence are ignored, as if the stunted cattle could solve India's economic and social horrors. Similarly, our experts bite their thumbs indifferently at Pakistan, leaving Kiplingesque tales to relate stories of the Khyber Pass and maybe what happens on an occasional Pakistani Airlines flight to Peking.

Information about prevalent conditions and trends is fairly easy to come by with the use of a little patience, some footwork, and concentrated research. The same cannot be so easily accomplished in another, smaller Asian nation, also run by a military man. In Burma, with large and penetrable borders with India and China, General Ne Win invariably gets more favorable treatment from the experts than does Ayub Khan. He declares that he is a "socialist." Therefore, to so many of our experts dealing with developing countries, Ne Win is worth a measure of approval, even if he is a dictator.

Yet next to Vietnam—where a shooting war predominates— the Union of Burma is the most chaotic state in Asia. That is saying a lot in view of the deliberate international silence about it. The Burmese regime, run by General Ne Win, controls at best about half of the country by day and around one-third by night. Control is gained through military and police prevalence in a population of twenty-two million. Two competing Communist parties, which Red China is seeking to fuse into one, usually fight each other. But they make common cause to gang up on govern- ment security. Opposed to them and the government is a fierce separatist movement, which wants autonomy.

The tough, taciturn general who in 1962 arrested the entire cabinet, headed by Prime Minister U Nu, embarked on a special "Burmese road to socialism." That U Nu was left in the lurch by once-trusted aides, like UN Secretary General U Thant, never got any attention. The man in power, Ne Win, has been courted. Indeed, he went to Washington to visit President Johnson. The feat of getting him there, or so it appeared, delighted our Ambas- sador Henry Byroade. His previous achievements had been chalked up with Colonel Nasser, where all United States policies were re- viled. Byroade, though, remains a state department "expert" on underdeveloped countries.

In any case, Ne Win's programs have led to enormous shortages, dislocation of facilities, and rising xenophobia. Accredited diplo- mats in the pagoda-studded capital of Rangoon can't take side trips without much previous negotiation. Unsettled conditions are the reason. But these go unmentioned. A journalist, with rare excep- tion, cannot obtain a visa for better than an overnight stay. One of the exceptions has been Harrison Salisbury of *The New York Times*.

Through the years Salisbury has accentuated the "positive" as a resident correspondent in Moscow. He usually finds Americans and American policies easier to lampoon and criticize. In a relatively open society, this is easy. Salisbury's efforts have become known in the journalistic trade as "visa-writing." That is, don't be harsh and you get a visa again. His trip in the spring of 1966 was along the strung-out frontiers adjacent to China. The Russians, he concluded, were under the mad gun of the Chinese; the Americans in varying Asian nations, mostly PX buffoons. His was a benevolent assessment of Burma. With this expertise, it's useful to delve a bit deeper.

After reflecting lightly on a Burmese government headed for ruin, Salisbury saw Communist China as the biggest menace to the U.S.S.R. This difficult predicament made togetherness with the West an ultimate natural for the Soviet Union, Salisbury observed. Burma and its military ruler, General Ne Win, were struggling manfully to achieve something known as "Burmese socialism," which its regime hasn't yet defined. What Ne Win's ruinous policies did to Burma got skimpy treatment from Salisbury. The Burmese strongman, after all, was becoming a high-flying international personality. Following his visit to Mrs. Indira Ghandi in India, Ne Win made the trip to the States and balanced it off by receiving Marshal Chen-yi out of Peking. Unsuccessful with his domestic programs, Ne Win has done well with outside forces. The big power guessing game is confined to whether the Chinese might try to overrun Burma and seek to set up a stooge regime or simply stir the political pot more vigorously.

The idea of China taking over in a swift coup didn't appeal to Chinese geo-politicians even before the frenetic cultural revolution. They feel China would be less inclined to make such a move today. Why? The economic mess in which the nation flounders requires food stocks China simply doesn't have on hand. Pro-Soviet Communists assigned to Burma have shuddered at what they are supposed to help remold, in the name of economic planning. To get a line on what was in store for the future, Ne Win visited a swami in India. Nobody really knows today what that selfless type of seer, living humbly in a cave, suggested to Ne Win.

Most of the world that regards itself as responsible waited breathlessly on the outcome of the cave predictions. The Burmese pro-consul kept the divine revelations to himself. Between desultory talks with Mrs. Ghandi, he played golf. That had been declared a "people's game" in Burma, which makes it unique among so-called "socialist" regimes in the rest of the world. He did, however, go to see U Nu, the gentle Prime Minister he arrested. What would U Nu do if released?

"Jail you if I could as the head of a rebel government," was U Nu's reply.

On October 27, 1966, U Nu was released from four years of

detention by General Ne Win. The event was largely ignored. A little persistence produced interesting information. U Nu was suffering from hypertension. Released with him was U Ba Swe, former president of the opposition Anti-Fascist People's Freedom League (AFPFL). He was in pain from arteriosclerosis in both legs.

U Nu said that Ne Win promised the two men help if they needed treatment outside Burma. But he asserted clearly—and told Ne Win directly—that he could not reconcile himself to any form of seizure of power, especially when his government had been duly elected by the people. There had been no need for any *coup*.

"General Ne Win and myself each had different points of view regarding the federal issue," said U Nu. "Had I known his viewpoint two minutes before he staged the *coup d'etat,* the course of events would have turned out quite differently from what is obtaining today."

The courage and dignity with which U Nu made this comment and his absolute allegiance to parliamentary democracy drew no commending review from the experts on Asia. They didn't say anything at all. Ne Win, as chairman of the Revolutionary Council— these *coups* are always staged in the name of "revolution"—seized power because he was alarmed, he said, by economic deterioration and clamor for secession by some of the autonomy-minded states. In his own four years, Ne Win brought Burma to near-total disaster. But the owner of the most important voice, who had protested repeatedly in the past his loyalty and devotion to U Nu, never uttered a word about the *coup*.

He is U Thant, successor to the late Dag Hammarskjöld. U Thant had been appointed permanent Burmese delegate to the UN by U Nu, his sponsor in their homeland dating back to their days together as schoolteachers. When the *coup* was organized against U Nu, the chief Burmese delegate to the UN knew of the hostility against his old chief. He never warned him nor did he ever show any displeasure.

U Thant was regarded so highly as a protégé of U Nu that the deposed Prime Minister assigned him to Rangoon for several years as secretary for projects in the office of the Prime Minister. Then came the second most prominent job for a Burmese—that of permanent representative to the UN. That was in 1957, when U Thant was forty-eight years old. He succeeded to Hammarskjöld's post as a compromise, when the Russians under Khrushchev were demanding the revised three-way secretaryship that came to be known as a *troika*. Khrushchev thought—wrongly—that there was undue Western influence at the top in the world organization.

U Thant took over. Coincidentally, within three months his old, unselfish sponsor in Burma was in prison. U Thant, a professional neutral, displayed lopsided detachment. He ignored the plight of U Nu, and since 1963 he has ranged from icy to hostile toward any United States proposals for ending the war in Vietnam. He has trampled underfoot his own words about handling the UN post. He was trained, he said early in his tenure, "to achieve a certain degree of emotional equilibrium or detachment." The record shows he has acted exactly the opposite.

In his seemingly bland way, U Thant has shown publicly just how detachment can be distorted. At one press conference in New York, he observed: "As you all know, one of the great virtures of democracy is ability to change governments by peaceful constitutional processes and without resort to force—a feature which is completely absent in the Republic of Vietnam." He ignored, of course, Communist-ruled North Vietnam. Worse, he never even mentioned his own country and his old chief, languishing in jail through a *coup*.

In an editorial entitled "The Frailest of Them All" in *The Reporter,* Max Ascoli tore the hide off U Thant.

> One could go on quoting him but to little use. The man endlessly repeats himself about East and West, respects the changes in political structures that Communist violence has ruthlessly brought about, but hates the efforts, no matter how unselfish, that a country like ours is making to prevent or stop the Communist "wars of liberation." What Communism has achieved is accepted with detachment by this nice smiling man who dresses and talks like a Westerner. He did not disappoint Khrushchev, for he proved to be a one-man troika.

Nevertheless, when U Thant decided on a coy ploy about a second term at the top of the UN, appeals from the West that he stay on—strangely as vociferous as from the East—came in a spate. Strange phrases like "indispensable man" were employed by our press, the self-perpetuating experts of the UN, and the American representative, Arthur Goldberg. In the grand, bland manner,

U Thant kept his hand hidden. He consented in trying times to stay on for just a wee bit longer. Then he wasted no time at all, lambasting the United States role in Vietnam again. The United States must, he declared, stop its bombing of North Vietnam indefinitely. U Thant graciously accepted a new five-year term. There was never a word, of course, about U Nu.

In private, some of the most devastating appraisal of U Thant comes from the Japanese. They emerged from the twilight of postwar defeat to an apogee of international respectability the West Germans can only dream about. It may have been that nuclear weapons were used by a white power against Asians, or that rejuvenation like Japan's expunge, in Asian eyes, all previous sins of any gravity and inhumanity. But the Japanese, their diplomatic and commercial scope ever expanding, have taken a global reading repeatedly on U Thant. The conclusion is one of near-contempt, some ironic amusement, and a caustic Japanese comment relayed from hard-nosed Chinese Communists: "If there was someone, almost anyone but U Thant, we might take the UN a little more seriously."

The remark might seem facetious in an off-hand manner. Yet the Japanese are not noted for their off-the-cuff humor. As cynically as other members, they voted for U Thant. But as the most industrialized nation in Asia, Japan takes its own contacts most seriously. They become bigger and more important with the passage of time. This encompasses the Communist-run countries, especially in Asia. Japan's pro-Western government has sensitive soundings in China, and its trade with both halves of Vietnam mounts. Its imports from North Vietnam, principally coal, come to about twelve million dollars annually. Japanese exports to Ho Chi-minh's regime are around three to four million dollars a year. Japanese ships aren't used in the two-way trade: Russian, Polish, Bulgarian, and Greek-owned Cypriot and Maltese vessels are chartered.

In our expert reviews of Japan, on the public media and diplomatic levels, few of these details ever emerge. They are easily obtainable. So is information about trade with South Vietnam. In 1966 nearly one hundred million dollars was exported and only seven million dollars imported. Chicken feed, maybe, but the extent of Japan's accessibility to regions we cannot reach—the Russians and Chinese, in their separate ways are also held off—

make Japan a tremendously important listening post. The dialogues are unfortunately largely overlooked, unless some spectacular interview is held between an outstanding Japanese personality and a ranking Chinese in Peking. The brilliant exceptions to this practice have been by *The New York Times'* Rosenthal, while he was in Japan, and the Japanese-speaking United States Ambassador Edwin O. Reischauer, now back at Harvard.

The Japanese have launched their own feelers in a delicate, long-range liaison. It involves them and America, Japan and the U.S.S.R., and has already produced large commercial contacts between China and Japan. The eminence of Japan—a member in good standing of the UN, and honor that hasn't come to West or East Germany—enables its governments to probe on their own initiative. The imaginative boldness of the pro-American Japanese government in foreign fields has not sparked speculation from our Asian experts. It hasn't even provoked a side-glance from voluble critics of American policy in Asia, always ready to blame the United States for putting someone else up to a job.

There have also been Japanese official examinations into the possibilities of placing contingents at the service of UN peace-keeping forces. These studies have gone unnoticed because our Asian experts are all too wrapped up in the Vietnam war. Officials of the Self Defense Force (SDF), Japanese armed forces, attended UN seminars on peace-preserving work. Another, startling proposal has made the rounds of Japanese higher governmental offices. It looks to the possible time that the United States, which administers Okinawa, may one day ask Japan to assume the responsibility. Left-wing and pacifist protests bring these moves into the open. The supposedly deep and expert studies provided for our public have a certain exclusivity: they almost never mention them.

Another possibility—rather macabre for Japan—exists. Japan could easily become a nuclear power after 1967. Several reactors will soon be in operation. They produce plutonium as a by-product. That plutonium could be used to manufacture a stockpile of Nagasaki-type plutonium bombs. In addition, Japan's own four-stage rocket, which places a three-hundred-pound satellite in orbit 650 miles above the earth, puts the country close to the scale of our Minuteman missile. This rocket is the primary American thermonuclear deterrent. All of Japan's Prime Ministers have been interested in A-weapons. The present Premier Eisaku Sato told the Parliament that China was a real threat to Japan now that she had a nuclear armory. Sato's remarks were made openly, but they didn't affect commercial and unofficial diplomatic contacts with China. That made the revelations of the Premier more interesting.

Our experts, except for Reischauer in confidential memoranda, never touched its ramifications. They have been too obsessed with Vietnam and the fallout on Southeast Asia, as they see it. They see the largish army (around 50,000 troops) of the South Koreans as the result of enormous American pressure. General Chung Hee Park, an impassive authoritarian, doesn't acquiesce to pressure even if he needs United States funds for development.

Expert criticism of General Park—Lippmann has led the outcry on occasion—never takes into account two incontestable facts of life about South Korea: its rate of economic growth is proportionately three to five times higher than that of any Communist-run state, and North Korea sponsors an ugly, dangerous guerrilla intrusion. One infiltration operation occurred in an area visited hours before by President Johnson.

The whole campaign, which strangely has elicited little comment from the experts, began in the early winter of 1966. It was launched to terrorize the steady South Korean economic and political stability. Three-man teams, later raised to eight, carry automatic weapons, cash, and rations. They are trained to hit specific districts and make contact with relatives and former friends. When the mission is accomplished, they try to return northward. North Koreans encountered and killed in 1966 on these missions totaled 106. By the end of June, 1967, the figure was 143. Simultaneously, incidents mounted in like proportion in the demilitarized zone. Yet student demonstrations, when they flare today, command instant attention. Communist infiltration is largely ignored.

It was General Park's own idea to send troops to Vietnam. They are most effective in combat and in pacification. The fact that his is an authoritarian regime without the patina of "socialism" makes a voluntary South Korean contribution suspect in the eyes of many experts on Vietnam in particular and Asia in general.

These critics feel the same way about the more modest contingents dispatched by the Philippine government. Their critical explanation: A rather corrupt government seeking to distract attention at home. But it isn't as corrupt as, say, India. Then, they impale their arguments by pointing out that demonstrations, so easy to seize on as a matter of unrest, opposed using Philippine troops. There is a Philippine force, however, in Vietnam.

Toward the end of 1966 these same expert-critics were still groping for explanations of Australia and New Zealand supporting their Prime Ministers. The late Harold Holt chopped up his anti-Vietnam opposition and increased his majority. Right down to the elections, however, the demonstrations against Australian troop contributions were cited by experts as proof of Australian desire to become uninvolved. Keith Holyoake won handily in New Zealand, too, under the same critical handicaps.

These results should have shattered many of the experts. But drawing on the invulnerability despite inaccuracy of the most imposing expert of all, Walter Lippmann, they went back to why we should not be in Vietnam. This is a war and an involvement that has provoked more passion and verbal inaccuracy than any conflict in modern history. It has also produced more experts and expertise, some in a matter of days and weeks.

Chapter 18

ASIA AND THE FAR EAST:
PART TWO

A WAVE of the most deafening volume has washed over the churned-up territory of South Vietnam. Never in the comparatively brief history of the United States as a great power have so many immediate experts appeared in so small and violent an area with so much to say. They have been accompanied by the quick-buck carpetbaggers, the dedicated reformers—many very brave, indeed—and the shadowy political operators. By commission and omission what this great gaggle proposes or hints, provokes violent rebuttal, support, rephrasing and retreading, and great emotionalism.

Many of the best-known names, outside of government, are involved in demanding either withdrawal or escalation. Most have relied on the daily experts, those who appear with comments on TV or in the daily press, to support their demands. The war in Vietnam is by far the most extensively covered conflict in modern times and probably the worst explained ever. Personal ambitions color evaluations. Official suspicions distort aims. About the only people, with a few magnificent exceptions, who get things done without much griping and recrimination are the men who fight and die. Theirs, naturally, is a limited choice and target.

President Johnson, who inherited the build-up in Vietnam from the late President Kennedy, is the most reviled head of state since Lincoln. Had he decided to cut out the growing military confrontation with Communist forces in Vietnam, he probably today would have been denounced as an "appeaser" or an ignoramus who just didn't grasp what was at stake in Southeast Asia.

The most consistent critic of the United States role in Vietnam is Walter Lippmann. We have seen earlier how his judgments over nearly fifty years of commenting on the home and world scene have been awry, fantastically off the beam, and indicative of Lippmann's own peculiar, isolated beliefs in elite rule and judgment. Attracted to his lucid, simple style of presenting assessment as Jovian decrees are a group of congressmen, senators, and eager writers, who hope they may be regarded as proper successors.

There has also been a proliferation of White House ex-advisers. They left L.B.J. and wasted no time telling the world that they oppose our present-day policies in Vietnam. Foremost is Professor Arthur Schlesinger, Jr., whose work with Latin America was a resounding failure. The more imaginative, up-to-date leaders, like Peru's Belaunde and Chile's Frei, have spelled out their consternation with the driblets offered up by Schlesinger. While he remained within the White House, however, Schlesinger upheld administration policies in public debate. Once out, he flipped.

More glaring in its own way was the admission of speechwriter Richard Goodwin. After Kennedy's death he served Johnson. When he departed, Goodwin lashed out at Johnson's policies on Vietnam. To make his arguments more plausible, Goodwin said that he had written accounts of the Vietnam war some of which he believed and some of which he did not. If he did not subscribe, would it not have been more honorable for Goodwin to quit and say why?

Goodwin's fast footwork in affairs of state was matched by his advocacy of the Kennedys throughout the *Death of a President* uproar. Schlesinger and Goodwin are shimmering examples of men who, leaving or being expelled from positions of power, suddenly convert to ferocious critics of personalities and policies they once espoused. The turnabout is not unique in American political life. It is more sustained and, with the passage of time, more subjective. Men like Goodwin and Schlesinger, out of the magic circle of national and international influence, seek to sustain the momentum they formerly maintained by exercising public shock treatment.

In their particular cases, regarding Vietnam, they were more hawkish than most advisers to the late President Kennedy and L.B.J. Secretary of State Dean Rusk confided: "It's most peculiar. They (Schlesinger and Goodwin) were much more militant in making recommendations than McNamara and I. There were times when McNamara and I argued for a long time against their suggestions as inadvisable, overly dangerous, and even emotionally naive." Rusk, of course, has his own axe to grind. It's most unlikely that he would utter such a remark simply to generate a fresh controversy with ex-colleagues. He usually prefers to stay mum.

As leading pro-consuls in Bobby Kennedy's entourage, assisting actively in preparing the grand design for national power, Schlesinger, Goodwin, and the R.F.K. Cabinet-in-exile are guilty of a glaring operational error. Their recommendations, as we have been told by a disenchanted member of the "in" group, is based on personal evaluations and what they believe Bobby Kennedy wants to hear and should hear. In this arrogance of aloofness, they were catalysts in the wretched tug of war on the Manchester book. On Vietnam, Schlesinger put together his own book, *The Bitter Heritage*. A principal concern that emerges from his critical views is the fear that extremism may get out of hand with the continuance of war. He compared the possible mood to what came out of the Korean War, "something roughly comparable to the McCarthy phenomenon of 1950–54." It would have been more to the point had Schlesinger asked Bobby Kennedy for first-hand comment. After all, Senator Robert Kennedy served a stint with the McCarthy committee.

Lippmann, who has never been to Vietnam like so many of his writing and speaking fellow critics, has persistently predicted only debacle and defeat for us. On an extended trip to Europe the summer and fall of 1966, he came up with this thought on Vietnam: "For in this new world mission in which we are supposed to be leading mankind there is not a single independent state in Europe or in Asia which follows our lead."

Lippmann's current geography on the issue also was out of whack. Thailand, independent for one thousand years, happens to side with us. So do the Philippines and Australia and New Zealand, just as examples.

Let us consider countries whose leaders won't say it out in the open, but urge the American government not to make any major concession in South Vietnam. We have heard that appeal from some of the closest confidants of Mrs. Ghandi in India. She goes on record urging American withdrawal. That mollifies the intellectual elite of India. They believe in the "socialist" aim of Ho Chi-minh in North Vietnam and the National Liberation Front, more familiarly known as the Viet Cong.

The authors heard Lee Kuan Yew, the impatient, Cambridge-educated Prime Minister of Singapore, say the United States must resist Communist infiltration in Southeast Asia. That, to him, meant no withdrawal from South Vietnam. Lee told lean and intent William P. Bundy, Assistant Secretary of State for Far Eastern Affairs, the same thing. The Prime Minister of Singapore is not especially disposed to Americans. He claimed that the CIA tried to buy him in 1958. It still bothers him. Lee likes to think of himself as a practitioner of British Prime Minister Harold Wilson's own adaptation of "democratic socialism." But he is far more of an intellectual than Wilson. In Bill Bundy, he found an agreeable meeting of minds.

But Lee's argument for the United States staying in Vietnam has never got into an evaluation by Lippmann or his potential successor Joseph Kraft. A little, bespectacled man who devotes himself to causes such as the FLN in Algeria, Kraft, on his first trip to Vietnam, thumped hard the idea that we had no business out there. We don't know where Kraft, in his whirlwind tour, found his evidence. What we did learn was that a magazine article prepared by Kraft for *Harper's* was distorted and could have been written in Washington.

Like Robert Kleiman, editorial writer for *The New York Times*, who uses Vietnam as a personal fiefdom, Kraft exercises the peripatetic approach to the problem. In Kleiman's own personalized swift touch with the facts of Vietnam, he brought anguish to a serious fellow *Times* man, Seymour Topping. Kleiman simply transported his views—wrong war, let's get out—to Vietnam and used the dateline of Saigon. Topping, then chief correspondent for Southeast Asia and now foreign editor, thought seriously about resigning. Kleiman is an all-out liberal these days, after years of playing the conservative side when he was with *U. S. News & World Report*.

As George Lichtheim wrote gloomily in *Commentary* magazine, the foreign affairs coverage of *The New York Times* is, on balance, awful. He gave the paper brief credit for trying to get away from just using releases from the United States defense force and the embassy. This is enterprise. But Lichtheim didn't go far enough. The case of David Halberstam bears more scrutiny. Harvard-educated and an editor there, Halberstam came to Vietnam determined to make a name for himself. Ngo Dinh Diem, the mandarin-type President of South Vietnam, was an autocrat who didn't belong. Halberstam set out to reform South Vietnam. That had been tried in the recent past in Cuba. For coming to grips with Diem and his then-supporters of the United States Embassy and government, Halberstam enlisted a few other young reporters on the spot. They campaigned.

Muchraking of the old Lincoln Steffens school, after research and detail have produced evidence, is legitimate. Lending yourself to a predetermined cause is propaganda. The militant Buddhists who staged demonstrations and human burnings got everything they pursued, through Halberstam. The Halberstam "group" was the extension of local Buddhist machination to get rid of Diem and his ruling family clique. In their fervor, the Halberstamites never bothered trying to find out how much real influence the Buddhists possessed. This was only one of their major shortcomings. Halberstam departed from the *Times* for *Harper's* magazine—twelves issues annually.

In their zeal to reform South Vietnam into an overnight showplace of parliamentary practice like, say Sweden, the most violent critics paid little heed to Communist brutality. A reporter who set out to document this particular phase was Jay Mallin, for many years Caribbean correspondent, five of them in Cuba, for *Time* magazine. In a brief but hardhitting book, *Terror in Vietnam,* Mallin observes: "Terror is a weapon as real as a gun—and sometimes more deadly. For it can kill not only the body but the spirit of those lives it touches with fear."

Mallin systematically analyzes the Viet Cong's use of violence. He researched his inquiry on Vietnam by going there from the Caribbean. It is an investigation. He quotes Che Guevara, the tactical brain of Castro's revolution on terrorism, which he found so similar in Vietnam. "Violence," declared Guevara, "is the midwife of new societies."

For the Viet Cong, reflects Mallin, it has become "a highly developed, highly refined political weapon."

Vietnam became the classic arena for Communist practice of the technique of terror—a vile exercise that Halberstam and his reformers ignored or forgot. Narrowed down, this violence was inflicted by armed men on helpless civilians. It could be mining roads; machine-gunning buses; kidnaping villagers; burning homes; and murder or torture. The Viet Cong employs them all. It is, as Mallin writes, "brutality with a purpose": to destroy the morale of the Vietnamese citizenry and to discredit any government in Saigon. Halberstam and many of his successors are out only to see the dark side of any government in Saigon. They ignore the factors that caused the ordeal.

There were inevitable clashes between government personnel and Halberstam. Usually, government flaks are incensed when someone doesn't accept at face value what they disseminate. It got to be a personal vendetta between the two sides. So much so that fed-up correspondents, those who spend time and energy trying to ferret out fact from fancied grievance, called the debacle "Halberstam's war." Brought home, he wrote a series and shared a Pulitzer Prize for reporting. His journalistic writing talent, as one of Halberstam's editors remarked to the authors of this book, is "rather heavy-handed and often emotional and mawkish."

The Halberstam episode provided a precedent that a host of young correspondents have tried since to copy. Many have lashed out at the United States efforts to fight the undeclared war, pointed grandly to deficiencies about which they know little or nothing first-hand, and usually complained about facilities. Facilities for getting somewhere—a battlefront, for example—as well as logistical support are the best organized we have ever known. From jeeps to helicopters to reaching commanders in the field, as well as accommodation, information, and provision for carvanseries of television equipment, arrangements are unparalleled.

Generally, though, the coverage is wretched, particularly when it is compared with, say World War II or the Korean War. Military historian, S.L.A. ("Slam") Marshall wrote in *The New Leader* just how bad the coverage generally is. In the summer of 1966 a United States Army operation called "Paul Revere II," said Marshall, was the major one of the time. "It was larger than San Juan Hill and El Caney combined, bigger and more impressive than Pork Chop Hill, bloodier than Cantigny, and lasting as long as Belleau Wood." Yet, Marshall noted, it did not rate a single headline in any American newspaper.

Then Marshall, whose credentials as a military historian of the first order are unassailable, remarked that neglect of Paul Revere II, showed a basic flaw in reporting out of Vietnam. The overwhelming majority of reporters, stated Marshall, exhibit a "cynical faddishness" that had not characterized the reporting of any previous United States war. "Today's average correspondent," he observed, "prefers a piece that will make people squirm and agonize. The war is being covered primarily for all bleeding hearts and for Senator Fulbright, who casts about for a way to stop it by frightening and shocking the citizenry. It is not being reported for simple souls who would like to know how it is being fought and how good are the chances that the South Vietnamese and the American forces and their allies can bring off a military victory."

Marshall's is a lacerating treatment of the reportage, as he gets a little closer to the bone. He didn't find that many of his younger colleagues had much of the war reporter's enthusiasm for long and dangerous combat missions. Too many, he complained, resemble TV crews "who want blood on the moon every night." He wrote of quickie searches for sidebars and tangents. Then there are the off-beat stories which "fall into several familiar patterns, none of which promises a beat any longer, though collectively they are beaten to death. Any demonstration or riot is sure-fire copy. Then there is the thing-that-went-wrong story. Hapless civilians have been killed in every war fought by the United States but only in Vietnam, where they are far less common than in France during the invasion or in Korea, do they command front-page treatment every time."

Marshall, a retired brigadier general but a professional writer and a veteran observer, commented acidulously on correspondents' beefs. The attitude of most reporters toward military briefings in Saigon is that they are for the birds. Marshall has said this is non-sense. He has personally attended briefings over many campaigns, most of them involving non-American forces. He found a high level of intelligence among public information officers in Vietnam.

"The deplorable thing," he wrote, "is that young writers, too lazy to gather the facts themselves, sit around and sneer at all that is said. With the conference reeking of pseudo-sophistication and half-baked cynicism, perspective inevitably becomes blurred. The result is an accenting of the negative and trivial story that obscures the truly important.

"The pity is, a national will might polarize around this solid, shining and reassuring performance (*i.e.,* in Vietnam) if we were but permitted to view it."

When Slam Marshall's piece came out, the experts back

home were the first to roar back in print and in private. He was, the gist ran, simply running true to form as a member of the trade union of officers. In their criticism, they always ignore the accusation that theirs is a smart, closed club which brooks no rebuttal. Yet anyone who has attended the Saigon briefings—and been privy to many others in the years gone by in all parts of the world— agrees with Marshall. In Vietnam, ultra-sensitive souls, who felt Marshall was singling them out personally, wrote protest letters to the editor. They might have spent the time more profitably going after a piece of hard news.

There can be no defense of the editor back home who assigns a correspondent to the field, be it Vietnam or Venezuela, and tolerates preconceived judgments. He is responsible for creating an instant expert. The reporter should be recalled, and the editor compelled by associates to explain the mistake. Every thinking human has his and her built-in prejudices about someone or something. These elements are more apparent when commenting about a stated situation or personality. Conclusions and evaluations get across almost instantly to millions, via the newspapers, TV, and radio. There is, at the same time, ferocious competition from the correspondent to get it first and to make an impact.

This should not mean deliberate cultivation of self-aggrandizement. That has, unfortunately, become an obvious trend among many journalists. In a miasma, as is Vietnam, the tendency most often has been for reform. Part of the zeal can be attributed to contradictory declarations, from the Presidency on down. Another part is traceable to the inclination to seize on a glaring sensation and hammer it hard rather than exercise larger judgment predicated on common sense. Then an almost inherent feeling to do battle with assorted authorities, because they represent an establishment, takes over.

The result is competition and conflict between the authority and the reporter. It becomes divisive, frequently offensive, and too often conveys lopsided judgments. To attain a fairly constant equilibrium, the correspondent passing judgments that affect the attitudes of millions, the steadiness of the surgeon is required. Emotionalism must, even under tremendous subjective turmoil, be damped down. Difficult as it can be, concrete fact, rather than passing commentary on people and places, serves to enlighten and not confound. Doubts of why we ever went into Vietnam in the first place are valid in the context of reasoned discussion and debate. Arbitrary pleas for us to get out are not. The role of the correspondent is to present a given condition and the people responsible, not to summarily demand the retirement of someone or the abandonment of a policy.

This tendency to be arbitrary is symptomatic of the expert, not the reporter, observer, or even detached authority. It has recently been exemplified in a distasteful manner by Senator Fulbright when he promoted his book *The Arrogance of Power.*

Kenneth Crawford, in a column in *Newsweek,* February 6, 1967, took Fulbright apart for his remarks on a TV program. Fulbright insisted that Air Vice Marshal Ky should be bounced as Premier if he declined to promulgate peace negotiations with the Viet Cong. What if Ky refuses? Crawford quotes Senator Fulbright as saying: "Well, the present government, if they will not do what we tell them to do—which they are likely to do—then they can be easily changed. We put it in and they are our government . . . He (Ky) is there because we put him in."

As Crawford points out, we opposed Ky taking power. He made it because he commanded the South Vietnamese air force "when its potential was decisive and because the U.S., wisely or not, follows a policy of noninterference in Saigon politics. As top man in the ruling junta, Ky has shown a genius for saying the wrong thing (admiring Hitler) while doing the right thing (suppressing a minority Buddhist uprising by means Americans thought ill-advised, conducting a nationwide election and promising to step down in favor of a civilian government after another election)."

Fulbright's attitude is the arrogance of authority, drawn from his Senate position, and the arrogance of the expert. Crawford added this reflection: "Whatever the damage he has done Ky, it is probably less than Fulbright has done himself. His extreme position on Vietnam, the fuzziness of his defense of this position and his apparent indifference to the consequences of extravagant talk have unquestionably weakened the authority of his chairmanship. . . ."

Because of his uncertain grasp of the whole scope of the political-military-social morass in Vietnam, Fulbright might have adopted the counsel of silence and do-nothing. It was the formula he followed when the ugly Little Rock school integration fiasco exploded in his own state, and he chose to sit it out—in Britain. In foreign affairs, as often as in politics, doing nothing is expedient if amoral. In the last couple of years, because of our concentration on Vietnam, we have not become embroiled in the recasting of Western Europe or in the uneasy shifts in Eastern Europe.

Our detachment has not made the American role more understandable to foreigners, but it has wrung out the grudging concession of noninvolvement. The principal danger in this kind of innocence by disassociation is in the revivalist feeling that produces neo-isolationism. Ironically, we have been accused by experts repeatedly for wanting to be world policemen. What happened in Europe contradicts the charge. It was proved hollow, actually, as far back as the grim autumn of 1956, when we shied away from doing anything about the uprising in Hungary. At the same time we sided with the U.S.S.R. and against our NATO allies, France and Britain, in terminating the Suez campaign in Egypt.

This type of "noninvolvement" has the approval of experts like Lippmann and Fulbright. As a result, we have been the recipients of a type of insinuation-involvement by Europeans. France and Britain, allies we helped humiliate in 1956, have been pouring out counsel on what to do about Vietnam. The left-wing of the British Labour party advises and criticizes while the Labour government tries to look the other way. Sometimes, as in the case of de Gaulle, it is a brutal and self-seeking behest to stop the world and get off. In other cases it conflicts with Gaullist ideas and, like many querulous Asian-African regimes, urges us to stand firm and persist in a workable arrangement with which everyone can possibly live.

Books about Vietnam have tumbled off the presses—and will continue to do so for a long time—like autumn leaves. The experts have had announcements heralding their occult insights into the problem. Interestingly, the most rational, soundly backgrounded books have come from writers who modestly still insist that they are students of the scene, never experts. One is *New Yorker* writer Robert M. Shaplen, a rangy man with a gregarious nature and a profoundly deep political awareness. He has written many delightful, highly informative articles for *The New Yorker* about faraway corners of the Far East. He has also been an observer for more than twenty years of the crosscurrents that affect life and living in Vietnam. If there ever was an expert on Vietnam, Shaplen is one, but he shuns the concept of expertise as pervasively poisonous.

In his book, *The Lost Revolution,* Shaplen traces our course through the military and diplomatic jungles of what was once called Indochina. He saw and set down lost opportunities to thwart

Communist encroachment, especially in Vietnam. With a great deal of genuine sadness, Shaplen believes that many of our disappointments and defeats might well have been avoided. It is a highly complex story he has provided in detail. He is adamant in all his criticism of our deficiencies and setbacks in Vietnam: We cannot and should never terminate the war and withdraw as demanded by less modest experts.

But there was an expert, French-born and risen to professor at Howard University, who tried lustily to make a virtue of hindsight. Bernard B. Fall had admittedly been tougher-minded and more experienced than some of his countrymen who want us out of Vietnam this evening. One of his most recent books, *Vietnam Witness,* was rather disturbing because of its supreme egoism. The bibliography, for example, listed only Fall's own work. That alone covers four and a half pages. Fall did not come right out and say that the United States cannot do better than France, but he implied it strongly. What he seemed to overlook was what French politics had done about war and peace in Vietnam. Fall, obviously possessed of a major ego, claimed to have been accurate about everything he wrote since 1954. This is the hallmark of the unabashed expert.

The forty-year-old Fall, active as a teenager in the French resistance, was rather unique among experts. He sought regularly in his own field to update ideas for which he was responsible. This brought him fairly frequently to Vietnam and led to his death in a United States Marine operation on February 21, 1967. He died in Quang Tri Province, ten miles northwest of the old imperial city of Hue. The area in which Fall was slain is called "Street Without Joy." He wrote about it in his book of the same name. A peppery talker, who insisted that he be heard first, Fall had been arguing about de-escalating military operations and escalating political talks just before he died.

Because of his experience, Fall has been given attentive hearings in high policy making levels of the United States government. With it all, he had not made the impact that a British writer and professor, who frequently lectures in the States and is heard in Washington, has made. Professor P. J. ("Paddy") Honey speaks Vietnamese, has taught in the country, lived in Hanoi, and knows most of the upper echelon of the ruling Lao Dong (Communist) party in North Vietnam. Out of the infighting of American politics, an academician, Honey has no axe to grind. He shuns the word "expert" and has an amiable contempt for the experts who air their views and criticisms on Vietnam. His is an almost *sotto voce* commentary. Because of its low key it is possessed of a shattering quality.

On a TV broadcast, after American bombers raided near Hanoi, his interrogator demanded: "Wasn't it risky, let alone disgraceful, to bomb where so many people are concentrated?"

Replied Honey, after defining the area: "Vietnamese are no more stupid than you and I. The bombing was carried out over a stockpile area. Nobody lives there. To get to it you must cross a bridge after showing a special identity pass."

He has written a couple of books about Vietnam. They are in the nature of academic treatises, which is in character. One book, *Communism in North Vietnam,* is really the first full non-Communist account of the Ho regime and of the partitioned northern region. Professor Honey is not regarded by the experts as an authority. He is not one of them and therefore is relegated to the position of a nonpersonality. With a quiet chuckle, Honey simply asks to talk over the issues involved with the better-known experts. When that request is made, excuses are almost always found to avoid Professor Honey, even if he is a nonpersonality.

There is no shortage of associates or aspirant experts, if they are deemed acceptable by established, resident experts. High on the priority list today is Senator Bobby Kennedy. In a rather sensational reference—prepared, as every major Bobby declaration is, in advance—he proposed that Communist guerrillas in Vietnam be represented in whatever Saigon government is established after peace talks. Pretty much like U Thant. His view dropped Bobby into the hottest water of his early senatorial career. Wrote columnist Cyrus L. Sulzberger, whose views are diametrically opposite those of Kleiman and *The New York Times* editorial board: "Sen. Robert F. Kennedy proposes Communists be included in the Saigon government. It would be more honest to suggest abandoning Vietnam without even bothering to negotiate." The *Times* military affairs correspondent Hanson Baldwin wondered who could have fed such give-away ideas to Bobby. Sulzberger and Baldwin, long on experience, keep up a minority battle with a handful of others against fuzzy emotionalism on the paper.

Stung sharply by the Sulzberger needle, Bobby retorted that he was misinterpreted. He has since asserted that what faces us are three alternatives: a military triumph that would turn Vietnam into a desert; a withdrawal that would undercut the American position in Asia; and negotiations. Only negotiations, he observed, are worthy of consideration. Bobby added that if the United States is truly interested in peace talks, the Viet Cong must be offered a place at the conference table and the hope of something more than unconditional surrender.

To acquire some instant insight into global affairs—and also to avoid additional unpleasant political fallout from the Manchester book—R.F.K. took a fast trip to Europe early in 1967. It resulted in another fallout, this time with President Johnson. Secret diplomacy was the guideline in fresh probing with North Vietnam. Bobby divulged at Oxford University that the succeeding three or four weeks from the time he spoke would be critical in the search for peace. He talked to Prime Minister Harold Wilson, on the eve of Soviet Premier Aleksei Kosygin's week-long visit.

In Paris, where he conferred with General de Gaulle, Bobby's inexperience booby-trapped him. He was told by Etienne Manacih, director of Asian affairs, about a three-point North Vietnamese program. Senator Kennedy speaks no French. With him was a diplomat from our embassy in Paris, who is fluent in French and spent a long time in Vietnam. The North Vietnamese delegate in Paris and the French government denied the story, as it was leaked, that Bobby got a peace feeler. A few select foreign journalists, who spoke to R.F.K. at some length, are unanimous on this point: that he broadly hinted he had something special on Vietnam.

When he encountered L.B.J. in the White House, the purported peace feeler circulated the world. President Johnson, *Newsweek* magazine reported, denounced Bobby's intrusion into so delicate a dialogue. The leak, Bobby rejoined, might have come "from your State Department." *Newsweek* said L.B.J. replied: "It is your State Department, not mine." The President insisted that Bobby deny he received a peace feeler as he left the White House. The junior senator from New York did so. It was a rather gamy episode. Bobby, who often served as a special Secretary of State during his late brother's tenure of office, used the jet-propelled trip abroad for headline purposes. He was supposed to attend an international conference in Britain with six other senators. First, he informed the American Embassy in London that he wanted nothing special.

Once he got to Britain, Bobby demanded that a press conference be set up for him with American news media. Then he spent only half the time earmarked for participants at the conference. It put the noses of other senators who stuck to the ground-rules out of joint. Among them were Charles ("Chuck") Percy, Republican of Illinois, and Democrat Joseph Tydings from Maryland. That didn't dent Bobby. Because of his special position in American public life he had doors opened to him that normally are not easily passable even to United States senators. On a swift swing through Rome he also had an audience with Pope Paul VI. The calculated suggestion passed to selected and worldly Italian commentators was that Vietnam had been seriously pondered.

From Wilson, de Gaulle, and the Pope, Bobby's statesmanship was attached to the international scene afresh. His adviser-admirers back home allowed as how he had special information and channels. They seethed with anger and indignation over the L.B.J. brush-off. Senator Robert Kennedy's latest active entry into world affairs proved to Kennedy-watchers abroad his superficial touch with foreign issues. On his own, without his specialized advisers, as the authors were told in Paris, Bobby's views of international difficulties are naive and inadequate. "He is too impatient for what goes into negotiations. His instinct is to read a headline in any move and to look for a fast deal." It was a sharp and succinct comment and came from a personality who had a difficult but prominent part in Bobby's visit.

Kennedy's own stated position, somewhat revised from the original, is to allow the Viet Cong "to play a position in the government" after negotiations but under rigid international controls to prevent a resurgence of terrorism. In concept, the view is naive and a variation of an original Soviet suggestion of a three-way amalgam for South Vietnam as was applied in Laos. There, it doesn't work, since the Communist Pathet Lao won't even permit the neutralist Prime Minister Souvanna Phouma to tour territory under Communist control. Included is that bitterly provocative strip of territory used by North Vietnam to funnel supplies and reinforcements to its regular units and the Viet Cong fighting in the south. The world has come to know the strip by the name "Ho Chi-minh trail." Bobby recently even backtracked from his altered points of view. The fact that he did try out some views held by critical experts endeared him to dissident intellectuals and professional liberals. They hadn't been happy about Bobby, remembering his work with the McCarthy committee. His opposition to administration policy in Vietnam changed their minds about him.

He has not rebuffed these new devotees. The assessments of Bobby's efforts in this direction have been neatly summed up by writer Gore Vidal. "Bobby is now projecting a liberal image," said Vidal, "because politically it happens to be the smart thing to do. He's following a political course that could have been charted by a computer."

Other senators, notable for their opposition to the United States role in Vietnam, usually look for a lead from Senator Fulbright. As chairman of the Senate Foreign Relations Committee, Fulbright invariably wonders about the use of American power. He is a remarkably superficial man for one so steeped in foreign affairs for many years. Many of the Fulbright trial balloons come from Walter Lippmann, who congratulates the senator for being so reflective a legislator.

Fulbright's contributions to foreign affairs repose principally in his unhappiness. He has an ingrained habit—shared by the expert and self-important liberal—of thinking in terms of black and white with little or no care for rounded historical reasoning. Typical was a major Fulbright speech, later expanded into a book, *Old Myths and New Realities.* For someone who admitted to one author that he possessed what amounted to a smattering of ignorance about Communist affairs, the thesis was of most momentous nature. In short, his old myths were riveted on the incompatibility between the global ambitions of communism and the transcendent value of freedom. The new realities, according to Fulbright, see major shifts in the world ruled by Communist forces that can provide for accommodation—with freedom. Not even the most enthusiastic adherents of "building bridges" East to West would accept that concept as valid or even workable. The more fervent hope for opposite regimes to make life happier, action more elastic, and creativity less fettered. Providing freedom in the parliamentary democratic sense would mean the liquidation of self-perpetuating Communist regimes dedicated to preserving themselves.

In a trip to the U.S.S.R. in late autumn, 1966, Professor Marshall D. Shulman, for years a student and observer of Communist practices, was singled out by the Russians as a spy. Because Shulman patiently seeks to probe far below the surface, Soviet officialdom regards him as implacably hostile. He is an internationally known academician and professor of international politics at Harvard's Fletcher School of Law and Diplomacy. After the trip a couple of points made by Shulman, interrelated with Vietnam, were worthy of consideration by Fulbright and his friends. They didn't bother. Despite senatorial silence, these remarks stand out forcefully. Professor Shulman wrote:

> First, with overwhelming unanimity, there appears to be a total misreading of signals from Washington in that part of the world [Eastern Europe]. The intentions of the U.S. are universally interpreted within a framework which completely vitiates the administration's overtures toward an improvement of relations. The President's speeches on this point are simply not believed. Second, it is no longer possible to think that Vietnam is but a temporary interruption in the detente between the Soviet Union and the U.S. Even if the fighting in Vietnam were to stop today, it is doubtful that the world could go back to things as they were. The Soviet government appears at this moment to be weighing a choice between two lines of policy, *neither* [authors' italics] one of which is pointed toward a restoration of the pre-Vietnam relationship with the U.S.

The glib and reflex-fast reaction of the pro-Fulbright experts is to shun Shulman-type assessments. They fall back to their second line of favorite argument. It is the present Red Chinese upheaval inside the vast mainland, among 700 million people, that inhibits the U.S.S.R. from pressing for an end to war in Vietnam. The Chinese Red Guard and the clamor for a cultural revolution evoke gasps of sophisticated horror. These voices harp incessantly on the theme that Mao Tse-tung and his appointed number two, Marshal Lin Piao, put the Russians on a spot. The Soviets, so reason these experts, cannot be shown as worn-out "revolutionaries." Therefore, they must stand fast on demanding American withdrawal, while exploring all possibilities for accommodation with us.

The prattle of their contentions defies the facts of Soviet performance. Incidentally, it also ignores Marshall Shulman's careful quest for judgment. Again, the dire fault is in our posture—the experts declaim—and in American recklessness in wielding vast power as it suits us. The "divine mission," it has scathingly been characterized by Senator Fulbright. It led him in lectures at Johns Hopkins University to speak of the "Arrogance of Power." With near-mystical passion, Fulbright declared:

a great nation is peculiarly susceptible to the idea that its power is a sign of God's favor, conferring upon it a special responsibility for other nations—to make them richer and happier and wiser, to remake them, that is in its own shining image. Power confuses itself with virtue and it also tends to take itself for omnipotence. . . . It was approximately under this kind of infatuation—an exaggerated sense of power and an imaginary sense of mission—that the Athenians attacked Syracuse and Napoleon and then Hitler invaded Russia. . . . Gradually but unmistakably we are succumbing to the arrogance of power.

Fulbright's fervor didn't square with history. Henry Fairlie, an English writer observing the flow of political events in the United States, was shocked by Fulbright's distortions and double-talk. On the historical analogies Fairlie wondered why Fulbright didn't attempt more rounded erudition. Why didn't he, for example, also cover the Roman Empire, the Spanish Empire, and even the British Empire? None were selected, Fairlie observed, because they didn't suit Fulbright's seizure of history.

"Again and again, in fact, Rome tried to limit the boundaries of its empire, to draw a final line against the barbarians, to say 'thus far and no farther,' " wrote Fairlie. "Rome remains to this day the outstanding example of the very opposite of what Sen. Fulbright is trying to demonstrate: it was an empire which tried to stop, and when it found that impossible, tried to contract, and failed."

In an editorial, the Paris International New York *Herald Tribune* took issue with Fulbright's charges this way:

But there is another arrogance—the arrogance of dissent, the arrogance which inspires an individual or a group to a sense of righteousness which they seek to impose upon their fellows while at the same time exalting themselves above the common herd. Dissent is, as Sen. Fulbright asserts, both a right and a patriotic duty. There are few countries in this world which recognize that right and that duty to the same degee as the U.S. But dissent of itself is not necessarily right.

Those (who like Sen. Fulbright) compare their opposition to the war in Vietnam to the opposition of Abraham Lincoln, or of Henry David Thoreau, to the Mexican War should restudy their premises. Lincoln and Thoreau were objecting to the spread of a slave power of war. Which is the slave power in Vietnam? And those who equate the Viet Cong to David and the U.S. to Goliath might look beyond mere size. On which side is the army of the Lord? Those who fled from North Vietnam can provide some telling testimony. . . .

Certainly very few in places of authority have spoken of the war there with either recklessness or (to use Sen. Fulbright's phrase) with arrogance. But can the same be said for the other side—for Sen. Morse or for Sen. Fulbright himself? There can be an arrogance of dissent, just as there can be spiritual arrogance. It justifies itself by appeals to conscience and to a higher law. But the most convinced can be wrong and the most conscientious can be in error. As the Bible warns: "Be not righteous overmuch."

Senator Wayne Morse of Oregon has been at least more consistent in his criticisms. He seeks to be a latter-day George Norris, out of the grass roots. The trouble is that his arguments are predicated almost entirely in irrational emotionalism. The morality propounded in Fulbright's anti-Vietnam policy might have a more authentic ring if the senator from Arkansas ever had the dignified stature to support social reform in his own state, Arkansas. Many of his peculiar views are also voiced by the Senate Majority Leader Mike Mansfield from Montana. Here is an earnest, rather somber personality who often traipses on quick stopovers around the world. He apparently has discovered his own specialty. Mansfield usually prescribes how bloodily divided nations can be patched together. It is a wonderfully simplistic method, which might work in a pastoral community where herds wander and people are nomadic.

Senator Mansfield proposes that a general election be held in which all the inhabitants have their say, even those who have been segregated and manipulated by unchanging totalitarian regimes. He doesn't lay down any conditions except some sort of a reciprocal amnesty and an ambiguous UN supervision. All inhabitants will turn into citizens by casting their ballots, thus redeeming their right to freedom. During the last years of the Eisenhower Administration Mansfield also proposed a similar program to reunify East and West Germany.

More recently Mansfield, who regards General de Gaulle's views rather highly, advocated a substantial reduction of American forces in Europe. The timing of the Mansfield idea was interesting. It was disclosed about the same time that de Gaulle, in the capital of Cambodia, Pnompenh, demanded our forces leave Vietnam. The two declarations were strikingly similar and congenial. Moreover they were put out without any suggestion of reciprocity from the Communists. De Gaulle, who a generation before tried to restore the French colonial presence and failed, equated Vietnam with Algeria. The comparison usually finds favor with most experts and particularly those who subscribe to the Fulbright and Lippmann arguments. Lippmann invariably sees in de Gaulle's suggestions infinite wisdom.

Nevertheless, Vietnam and Algeria cannot in any way be equated on a realistic level. Algeria had been a colony incorporated into France as an administrative department, or thus, part of France. Vietnam, as part of Indochina, had for one hundred years been a French colony and was exploited to the hilt by France. In Vietnam the United States is not liquidating or founding any empire. American soldiers aren't even there to serve as crusaders against Asian communism. They are in Vietnam to block the overflow from the Communist north beyond the established boundaries. De Gaulle will not accept that premise. In fact most of de Gaulle's agents and operators in Asia, including business people with rubber estates, act as another enemy.

The Gaullist, anti-American policies so militantly pursued in Southeast Asia, also caused resentment among some Frenchmen. They show their distaste by supplying information to the Americans. But the Gaullist pursuit of policy often is macabre. Consider what the authors found in some areas where bitter fighting with the Viet Cong is virtually a round-the-clock routine. In at least three places we were able to locate, where the Americans managed to cling to outlying compounds, the French demanded payment for rubber trees at $700 apiece if we cut them down to command a clear field of fire. Viet Cong snipers make full camouflage use of the tree network. We spoke to young and courageous American doctors who operated on wounded men while under sniper fire from trees still uncut.

This particularly poignant episode reached the marble halls of Congress. It didn't get much further because Senator Fulbright was at it again, this time strictly in the framework of moral rectitude. He charged that "both literally and figuratively, Saigon has become an American brothel." He spoke with a sense of shock, he declared, about Vietnamese putting their wives or daughters to work as bar girls "or to peddle them to American soldiers as mistresses."

"As a result of the American influx," Fulbright thundered, "bar girls, pimps, bar owners, prostitutes, and taxi drivers have risen to the higher levels of the economic pyramid."

The unmistakable sound of the evangelist rather than the critical contemporary historian momentarily silenced Fulbright's supporting experts. Any social seaminess, inflated or recognizable, is usually of no interest to them. Power is the name of the game where they are concerned. Rebuttal came fast to Fulbright. When, in war, was there ever an absence of camp followers? Fulbright dropped the subject and came charging back into the arena of debate by talking of Vietnamese culture. Back in 1965 the authors asked if he read deeply into Vietnamese history. Not much, replied the senator; he hadn't had the time.

What the senator hastily abandoned—pimps and prostitutes—the French in Southeast Asia expanded and exploited. As people with a century of experience in the area and with their special worldliness, French trouble-shooting resorted to a twisted line. Added to their claims throughout Southeast Asia—that the Americans cannot win—they spread stories made more lurid ever since —that Americans intended to use Vietnamese women not only for their own pleasure but as hostages. The meaning to Southeast Asians was clear: Women often work harder than the menfolk. They also are symbolic of holding together the family unit, quite precious in a place like Vietnam. Holding women hostage would be tantamount to wrecking the family unit and would therefore be anti-Vietnamese.

Many French diplomats also took as an article of faith a remark made by their Foreign Minister Maurice Couve de Murville at a SEATO conference in Manila. Asked to endorse United States pledges, he refused. He observed that he understood what we were attempting to do in checking Communist subversion and infiltration. But, he added, France believed we would be unsuccessful; immediately thereafter French policy in all Indochina entered the active anti-American phase. Some Frenchmen even communicated to Communist officials American intentions and planned build-ups.

A Communist leader, though, lambasted Couve for one-sidedly blaming the war in Vietnam on the United States. In a meeting with Couve in Yugoslavia, President Tito said that China was as much or more to blame than the United States. True, China reviles the portly Yugoslav ruler as a revisionist of the worst kind and Tito rebukes the Chinese. But the Yugoslavs normally support "revolutionary" situations as a matter of faith. De Gaulle's views, interestingly enough, found less fertile ground with Tito than among experts here.

Even the Gaullist brand of new diplomacy could never come

close to matching a project, international in scope, dishonest in organization, and unprecedented in arrogance. This is known as Bertrand Russell's International War Crimes Tribunal. It had one immediate and salubrious effect: All that the "expert" witnesses produced was defused and de-escalated by their slanted testimony.

Chapter 19

ASIA AND THE FAR EAST:
PART THREE

T HE self-made Russell tribunal is without precedent in modern times. Lord Russell, in his middle nineties, has world renown as a philosopher, an unorthodox thinker, and dabbler in geo-politics. He recruited personalities for his tribunal to try President Johnson, his leading Cabinet Secretaries, and the United States administration, for war crimes in Vietnam. Russell's organizing committee originally presented its case for putting together a tribunal by citing others of the past: Professor John Dewey's, for example, on Stalinist-led Soviet sins.

The big difference between Russell's and the late Professor Dewey's is centered on the matter of truth. In the thirties Professor Dewey's supporters went to great lengths and self-sacrifice to obtain documentation and witnesses from all sides, including the hostile. It was intended as a scientific, not a propagandistic examination of the evidence. Moreover, it did not pretend that it could hold the U.S.S.R. guilty of crimes against humanity.

This—to hold the United States guilty of crimes against humanity—is precisely the aim of the Russell tribunal. Lord Russell, for his earlier coruscating brilliance, is purely a kook in political affairs. As an eminent adult—he was approaching seventy at the time—the good Lord urged the British people not to engage Hitler in war, but to surrender to Nazism. After World War II he urged the United States, with its monopoly of the atomic bomb, to drop it on Moscow. Later he conceived a vision of peace and has pursued his version in the weirdest manner. He has found the United States responsible for virtually all breaches of the peace. There is never attention called to Soviet expansionism and regime crackdowns on writers and artists, for example. Nor did the cruel

Chinese subjugation of Tibet merit his interest. These are only a few instances of omission.

His tribunal warrants some examination. It has gained support from predictable sources, the intellectuals and some experts who never see anything sinister in motives of anything that is left. For many years Russell has had as his left-hand man a young American, Ralph Schoenman. A little research into Schoenman's claims, as a student and thereafter, of militancy in the United States reveals no substantiation. At Princeton he was a campus radical. He drew little attention and drifted to Britain, where his overt devotion to the elderly Russell brought him into the "peace" entourage. Schoenman has bombarded governments and editorial offices with manifestos approved by Russell. In his work Schoenman also has met and been accepted by lifelong intellectuals in the genre of Jean-Paul Satre and Simone de Beauvoir.

Nothing as ambitious and pernicious as the tribunal ever materialized. Money for its operations was supposed to come from the Bertrand Russell Peace Foundation. The tribunal planned to have hearings for some months in Paris. But the Gaullist government wanted no part of such a spectacle. It pointed out that the statutes make it a crime to calumniate, in the tribunal manner, a head of state. The tribunal sponsors, however, made alternative arrangements. Then the grotesque plan—which had the all-out support of North Vietnam—ran into stiff and revealing resistance.

The rebuffs must be recorded because Russell's tribunal will acquire, as it now seeks, international respectability via propaganda. Heads of four sponsoring African governments resigned from the Peace Foundation, saying they were never consulted about the use of their names in connection with the tribunal. Tanzanian President Nyerere, today one of the more extreme African leaders, declared: "Lord Russell may not object to his name being used for other people's purposes. I do object to my name being so used. I also object to a serious matter like the Vietnam situation being dealt with by trickery and dishonesty." That was a most serious accusation from the chief of government the Russell sponsors believed was ultrasympathetic. Other African Presidents who publicly disassociated themselves from Russell were Kenneth Kaunda of Zambia and Leopold Senghor of Senegal. Emperor Haile Selassie, whose name was presented, resigned, too.

The authors went to a press conference in London where explanations were made about the disassociations. Lord Russell, who magnanimously said he invited President Johnson to defend himself, observed that intolerable pressure from the United States forced the resignations of various sponsors. Actually, any American pressure would prompt men like Nyerere to do just the opposite. In any case, Lord Russell and the Schoenman organizers pointed out with pride that their tribunal members remained intact. By inference this meant they were, in Russell's eye, inviolable. He held up the name of Stokely Carmichael, then head of the Student Non-Violent Coordinating Committee (SNCC), as a representative American on the tribunal.

Seldom has a press conference raised so many hackles. It also infuriated reporters who normally criticize American policy in Vietnam. In the chair was Vladimir (Vlado) Dedijer, Yugoslavian writer and beneficiary in the past of American university fees, subsidies and favors. The authors have known Dedijer for many years. A brave man who fought with Tito's partisans, he also sided with Milovan Djilas against Communist corruption. Dedijer suffered many personal and family misfortunes and tragedies. He returned to Yugoslavia from the States in 1965 because, as he told us, he refused to be "a professional emigre." Dedijer's own problem is an ego that needs constant inflation. It was played on in the name of Russell by Schoenman. "They kept telephoning me all the time," Dedijer remarked plaintively to us. "I just had to accept." The fact that his leader, Tito, was caustic to the French about being one-sided in their view of the United States and Vietnam made no impact on Dedijer. Once again, he thought, he seized a shaft of limelight. It pleased him.

The pitiful press conference sent some favorably disposed United States experts on Southeast Asia scuttling for cover. Theirs was the role of innocence by silent disassociation. The tribunal said that expenses for collecting evidence and the trial would be defrayed by a loan from the Bertrand Russell Foundation. Members expected to raise money through other private donations. Who would pay fares for North Vietnamese witnesses? Schoenman denied that he told the questioner a month earlier that the North Vietnam regime would pay. Then, he replied again to his interrogator, mysteriously: "The witnesses made available by Ho Chiminh will not be paid for by North Vietnam."

The proposals and aims of the tribunal moved even *The New*

York Times—so critical of what we do in Vietnam—to say editorially: "Mr. Nyerere hardly overstated the case. The men promoting this travesty in the name of Lord Russell have already convicted the U.S. in documents issued at a London press conference. It is the rankest hypocrisy to pretend that a 'tribunal' chosen by such men could deliver an 'impartial judgment.' Such a 'tribunal' will be treated for what it is—a propaganda demonstration."

Schoenman, who gravely led Lord Russell away without answering questions, has never himself replied to queries about the Viet Cong killing schoolteachers before their horror-stricken pupils as a lesson. The tribunal members have airily dismissed a catalogue of acts of terror and destruction wilfully executed by the Communist cadres in South Vietnam and those infiltrated down by the North. For that matter, even those experts who would recoil in disgust from plotted antics like those of the tribunal never mention these acts. The highest-level critical experts, from U Thant to Lippmann and Senator Fulbright, have studiously ignored this roll call of destruction.

When Russell's tribunal finally found a site to stage its mock trial—Stockholm, which assented by explanation of traditional neutrality, which Switzerland declined to invoke—all acts of terror and war were attributed only to the United States and South Vietnam. Not a single witness was allowed to testify against the Viet Cong and North Vietnam. Two American radio reporters were expelled from the proceedings without explanation. But North Vietnamese "witnesses" were permitted to discuss at length written charges they brought with them. There was not the briefest mention, even in the guise of reprisal, of Communist terror tactics.

It is not the purpose of this book to shake out most details of mass murder and terror visited by the Communists, north and south, in the name of nationalism and revolution. Suffice it to mention a few horrible reminders. Philip Geyelin, author-journalist formerly with *The Wall Street Journal* and now with the editorial page of the Washington *Post,* pointed out in September, 1965, that around 600,000 Vietnamese had been dislodged from their villages and hamlets—"most of them in the past six months—and driven toward the bigger towns and provincial capital in search of shelter, dependable food supplies or simply security from shot and shell and Viet Cong terrorism." Geyelin's details were not of any recondite nature nor were they weighted one way against another. Those facts, for that period, and any before or subsequent, are available.

The experts don't touch them and reflect only on how necessary it is for the United States to pull out of a "dirty war." They never look back to see how cadres of Communists and caches of arms and supplies were left behind after the 1954 Geneva agreements. Stress is placed only on the intrusion of the Americans, about how we have no right to be there. Nobody seems to question what justification critics have for assessing rights and wrongs. Observers like the authors can only wonder why it was that when the Diem regime was battered down in 1963, the Viet Cong didn't take over. The explanation is ridiculously simple: They tried. But they were beaten back by the South Vietnamese. At that time we weren't, *in toto,* more than a division strong.

Exhaustion of resources was inevitable. Had the United States not decided to reinforce its commitment, then there would be no need to talk of negotiation now. The United States would have been out of South Vietnam and undoubtedly in full retreat from all Southeast Asia. The anti-Sukarno reaction probably would not have happened. Instead of hand-wringing and phony compassion in the States, a full and ugly cry for inquiry might well be the pattern today. Those same experts whose voices never were heard in the McCarthy days would have withdrawn from demands to be heard.

The war, with all its tragedy, has thwarted the Communists from achieving a military takeover. They cannot push us out. What they can do is try for drawn-out nibbling, injurious techniques that sap the will of a government to wage combat—as it once did in Paris. The French Fourth Republic never was the embodiment of anything elected and implemented in Washington. To begin with, it was really born of defeat, no matter what fancy post-liberation label was attached. The Fifth Republic, embodied in de Gaulle, really cannot bear to have anyone else achieve something it failed to achieve. We easily forget that de Gaulle sowed the seeds of French defeat in Indochina.

Just as in 1965 the experts were nigh-gleeful in forecasting the expulsion of the scattered United States forces in Vietnam—they never reckoned that we would decide to stay and reinforce—so do they glibly predict disaster for our pacification programs. Pacifying the countryside means holding, staying, and securing territory so people can work and live in peace. The Viet Cong, contend the critical experts, are too entrenched. They run the peasantry and always will. It was about the same evaluation they provided for conduct of the purely military side of the war.

A beginning on pacification, winning people over to a sense of security, has been made. It has not been a gleaming week-old wonder. Nevertheless, it is the kind of program that Bob Shaplen approves and fervently hopes may work. This is the political phase one really, the special kind of silent war where there is no glory. Former Defense Secretary McNamara was unhappy with the pace. Like many of his fellow-Americans he wanted speedy results. A buildup of American military strength—controversial and costly— was urgent to implement programs of pacification. It was a political decision that provoked new criticism. Still, the command decision was taken by the President. Patience, an imponderable, was the next step.

There peeps through, however, the accomplishment now of little communities that show what can be done. Take the case Rowland Evans and Robert Novak cited in their column from An Nhon district. Hamlets in the area are specks on most overlay maps. A thirty-year-old Vietnamese, Vu Trong Hai, only graduated from a pacification school in September, 1965. His area is deep in Viet Cong territory. Yet in less than a year, Vu Trong Hai had the people in Vietnamese hamlets working for their own communities. They also passed information. There are innumerable hamlets like those Vu Trong Hai has secured. It also may require a long time for them to place their allegiance in dedicated men like Vu Trong Hai. He broke through, remember, where the experts abroad and in Saigon ridiculed the whole concept. As Evans and Novak reported, "Vu Trong Hai is the exceptional hero in Vietnam today." Try to remember, too, that there are thousands of men like Vu Trong Hai.

The French, as a colonial power attempting to reassert mastery, were never able to persuade many locals to join and support them. People they left behind in old Indochina, now Laos, Cambodia, and North and South Vietnam, are chiefly active in trying to sabotage American efforts and ideas in the whole area. Cambodia, hugging a long frontier with Vietnam and China, is an active anti-American proving ground for French projects. In their operations, they have a willing ally in the head of state Prince Norodom

Sihanouk, an absolutist at home, who claims neutrality and supports China and France in his own looking-glass political war.

Sihanouk, a volatile man with patrician tastes and a hobby playing the saxophone—the authors heard him play the blues for hours in his palace, while courtiers knelt with bowed heads—says the United States wants to swallow him. He demands we leave Vietnam. His profession as a neutralist is riddled with loopholes. North Vietnamese units cross over into Cambodian territory and use it as a sanctuary. Not at all true, cries Sihanouk. In the Mekong Delta area we went with some troops one sweltering afternoon toward the Cambodian border. We approached to within 1,000 yards. Boldly fluttering in an occasional breeze inside Cambodia was a Viet Cong flag. It hung over the site of a convalescence and refitting Viet Cong area command.

American forces have sometimes shot across the border when the enemy broke off and headed for the safety of Cambodia. Sihanouk and his French adherents decry these "violations." They never raise a protest when Communist reinforcements and commands use Cambodian territory to re-enter Vietnam. In their insistent denials, they also have enlisted the demurring voices of our outraged experts. This has become especially more emphatic since Sihanouk broke relations with the United States a few years ago. He is seen as a littler David trying to hold out against an invasion of Goliaths.

Senator Mansfield, on one of his speedy trips to far-off places, has talked to Sihanouk. He came away feeling that the poor prince was badly maligned. His encounter with Sihanouk helped Mansfield come up with a vastly amorphous neutrality proposal. It never got anywhere. Unlike Fulbright, Mansfield didn't press the plan; just put it away for the time being. While he was in Cambodia, the senator apparently never saw anything of Sihanouk's gray eminence, Charles Meyer. He is an old Asian hand, a veteran French intelligence operative, and more than a counselor to Sihanouk since French policy was reactivated by de Gaulle. This period covered the time of the demonstrations against United States and British embassies.

Half smiling, he conceded that he had something to do with the riots when we last saw him, face-to-face, at the abortive Afro-Asian nonaligned conference in Algiers in early summer of 1965. More important is his liaison between Sihanouk and China and as a go-between for the French government and Chinese trouble-shooters. Sihanouk is content to have Meyer run these sordid errands while he indulges in summitry with de Gaulle and the Communist Chinese. His pet project, with help from French advisers, was first unfolded in 1964. He envisaged a belt of neutral countries for Southeast Asia.

The countries in the Sihanouk plan, some nonaligned now, call for a specially neutralized Burma, Thailand, Laos, Cambodia, and South Vietnam. Confidentially he tells Asian visitors that South Vietnam should be incorporated into North. He never has suggested that North Vietnam be neutralized. But the plan had been made known to Mansfield, because Sihanouk always speaks about it, at home or in forums abroad. Thailand's government bristles at the Sihanouk project, but the Prince is always prone to apportion other people and their territory as he thinks suitable. He isn't too far from our own experts in a willingness to give away people and places that don't belong to them.

His views have become more fashionable for the critics and the experts today, as they see a fresh blessing in the type of neutralization Sihanouk espouses. Whenever Sihanouk denounces an incursion of Americans pursuing the Viet Cong, critical circles in Washington chortle: "We goofed again." Although Sihanouk has offered facilities to the International Control Commission (ICC)— Canada, India, and Poland—to inspect his disclaimers about the Viet Cong, the choice is strictly limited. He can hardly know how his tangled territory is being used in assorted spots. It is, at best, patrolled very thinly. But an explosive element has slipped into Sihanouk's quite special neutrality: In northern Tay Ninh province, barely a mile south of the Vietnam-Cambodia border, United States troops captured two Cambodians, members of a three-man team. They were the first Cambodian prisoners, and they were seized well inside Vietnamese territory.

Both men were wounded. A story written by William Tuohy in the Los Angeles Times attracted little play or notice. It pointed up, however, the calculated "neutralist" attitude of Prince Sihanouk, to whom de Gaulle paid a visit only a few months before the incident. On that triumphal staged tour, de Gaulle again demanded United States withdrawal from Vietnam and neutrality for the area. He conferred, too, with the accredited North Vietnamese chief of mission to Cambodia. A parallel—and equally unthinkable—situation would have been a visit by President Eisenhower to Tunis in 1960 to squeeze in a talk with a delegate of the FLN from Algeria. That was nearly two years before de Gaulle made his accommodation with the Algerians. He was President of France and the French were fighting in Algeria.

The case of the Cambodian prisoners has been soft-pedaled. With the third man, who escaped, they had been dispatched by their commander in a Cambodian outpost to reconnoiter. Americans, who returned their fire, wounded the two who were grabbed. Other fire-fighting incidents occur frequently with Cambodian teams who scout inside South Vietnamese territory. So far it has been fire-and-quick-retreat by the Cambodians when Americans seem to be coming too close to them. Sihanouk insists that we have a willful plan to violate his real estate. He addresses his complaints first to Red China, then to the French, and finally to the world.

Senator Mansfield, having met and talked to Sihanouk, worries aloud about the Prince's perplexity. There is no need for it. Sihanouk's plight, admittedly complicated by his country's geography, has led him to a form of neutrality usually applauded by Communist China. When there are conferences concerning the United States and our Asian associates, Sihanouk gratuitously proposes "counterconferences," which would convoke outright Communist regimes and pro-Communist ones. There is hardly any neutral element in those plans. He also went ahead with a weird athletic tournament, paid for almost in full by China. These were the "Ganeflo" launched originally by Indonesia's discredited Sukarno. They mean "Games of the Newly Emerging Forces." Among those forces entered were teams from the Palestine Liberation Army.

Sihanouk's country of five million is part of southwest old Indochina, wedged uncomfortably between little Laos to the north, Vietnam on the east, and pro-American Thailand on the northeast. There were "Free Khmer" (ancient name for Cambodia) terrorists in Cambodia until the break-up of Indochina. By his special neutrality, Prince Sihanouk managed to get them withdrawn or quiescent. Occasionally, they return to show they exist in Cambodia, a lovely country with magnificent ruins of an old civilization at Angor Wat. Only Sihanouk, his French advisers and immediate entourage, and the Chinese play at power politics. Cambodians, self-sufficient on their land, pay no attention.

Sihanouk invokes a legendary fear of Vietnamese expansionism. He pretends, as a power politician however modest should not, that Thailand is virtually as militant as South Vietnam. The Thais, declaims Sihanouk, are out to embroil him in the war in Vietnam. Thailand is mainly concerned to see that Sihanouk does not extend his neutrality into assistance to pro-Communist guerrillas slipping into its territory. At the same time, Sihanouk deliberately ignores Chinese and North Vietnamese violation of even the paper sovereignty of underpopulated Laos. A sliver of what once was Indochina—Laos and its 2,500,000 people—is in a perpetual state of chaos.

Back in the summer of 1962 a big power deal was made on the banks of somnolent Lac Leman in Geneva setting up the first troika government in history. A neutralist Premier, pipe-smoking French-educated Prince Souvanna Phouma, was installed. The Communist Pathet Lao, in name directed by his half-brother Prince Souphanouvong, had a third share in the regime as did the anti-Communists in southern Laos dependent on United States support. Only a few weeks after he took office, the Premier announced that the Communists had broken all their promises.

He was strictly forbidden to visit the provinces abutting Red China and North Vietnam. Pathet Lao forces were beefed up by the introduction of North Vietnamese units. Chinese advisers and technicians were profusely assigned to key districts in the northern territories. Their aims, in a very short time, became clear: To safeguard the trails used to send supplies south to guerrillas and regular North Vietnamese forces in South Vietnam and to keep the neutralist regime of Souvanna Phouma in a state of total disorder. Our experts never mention the problem.

The Premier, who frequently visits Paris, told us of the insuperable problem of just keeping his "neutralist" element afloat. American-supplied armed trainer jets are used by the Laotian government to try and show some sovereignty. They strafe trails and support neutralist forces under the command of a unique young officer. His name is Kong Le, and he led some coups against American-oriented regimes and Laotian units. After a few months of "troika" settlement, Kong Le found himself under repeated attack by the Pathet Lao.

"I have to fight back," said Kong Le. "The Pathet Lao aren't Laotians. They use Lao people to carry supplies. They are almost all Vietnamese from the North. From the way they operate, they are only interested in dominating Laos. This I will fight to the end."

In his sessions with de Gaulle, the urbane Prince-Premier has relayed Kong Le's views. De Gaulle remains frigidly indifferent. Kong Le, in the conditions of reality imposed upon him, concedes honestly that he cannot carry on the "neutralist" hopes he once cherished. "The Communists won't let the Premier or me do what we want and what we believe is best for such a small country as Laos," he said. In such an atmosphere, with pressures piling up, Kong Le's plea to be left alone goes unheard among our experts. The authors inquired one time of Senator Fulbright what our government—or he—thought might be done to help out a forthright man like Kong Le.

"Let's see," was the reply from our most eminent senator in charge of examining foreign relations. "Where is he from?" We supplied the answer, and the added observation from the senator was a drawling reflection: "Well, that is part of the whole problem in South Vietnam. First things, first. A decent settlement in Vietnam would practically take care of Laos in an automatic manner." His was such a simplistic interpretation that we turned to another senator, aged Ernest Gruening of Alaska. We braced him in the Senate dining room one early afternoon while he was there for a light lunch. Senator Gruening, who agrees with nearly every phase of foreign policy enunciated by Fulbright, charged that "we are the aggressors" in South Vietnam.

But in polite interrogation, it was clear within minutes that Senator Gruening knew little of Laos, of Kong Le, or of the little nation's peculiarly carved-up state. He became irascible, as a matter of fact, and grumbled that "Bill [Fulbright] knew exactly what he was talking about." Critics of Fulbright, commented the senator, are "hawks." We remarked equitably that we were "owls" in bird classification of war and peace in Vietnam. Looking at us suspiciously, Senator Gruening brought our little *tour d'horizon* to an abrupt end.

In leading an interrogation of U. Alexis Johnson, then Deputy Undersecretary of Political Affairs and today ambassador to Japan, Senator Fulbright ventured into a review of our relations with Thailand. This was the end of summer, 1966. Washington is brutally hot and oppressive in that season, and the session in the Congress had been long and tedious. Fulbright, most prominent expert in the chamber of the Foreign Relations Committee, declared that he believed the "real purpose" of the United States in Asia was to stay there indefinitely to counterbalance Communist China. If they could really believe as much, the people who lead the governments of India, Indonesia, Malaysia, the Philippines, Singapore, and Japan would be relieved. The Fulbright belief led him to his next logical sequence of thought. Since we meant, by his interpretations, to stay forever in Asia, then we were building up in Thailand. Therefore, according to the Fulbright reasoning, Thailand was certain to become the next Vietnam.

Support for Fulbright on that thesis formed quickly among the experts, who wrote and spoke their equal conviction. The build-up, from twelve thousand United States troops in December, 1965, to thirty thousand-plus by August, 1966, persuaded the critics of Johnson's policies that we were embarked on what amounted to them as a simple expansion of our role in Vietnam. Their off-the-cuff criticism totally ignored the history of Thailand, a Red Chinese avowed declaration to launch insurgency, and the Thai point of view that never made it anyone's colony. Through one thousand years, Thailand (known commonly as Siam) zigged and zagged. In World War II it was a nominal ally of Japan and contributed little but reluctance and trouble to the Japanese. Like the preponderant majority of Asian states, Thailand is far from a parliamentary democracy. The army generally delivers a marshal to run the affairs of state. The young monarchs are a handsome couple with attractive children, but the subordinate echelons of governments are handled by intelligent, worldly, younger people. Thailand and its thirty million people are in a process of gradual development, sneered at by experts like Fulbright.

Nevertheless, his TV examinations of United States-Thai togetherness showed that Fulbright hadn't done much homework. He overlooked the Communist Chinese-supported "Voice of the People of Thailand." The clandestine radio, operating in North Vietnam, promised to throw out the regime and the Americans and to establish guerrilla forces. It was a pledge made at the end of 1964. Within six months guerrillas were shooting down police in the northwest, close to northern Laos. There are fifty thousand or so Laotians, as well as a sprinkling of Vietnamese, in that corner. The area is depressed, and only after the Communist declaration of a "Thailand Patriotic Front" did the Thai government in Bangkok go into some action.

At the southern edge of Thailand, where the waist is narrow and comes close to Malaysia, more guerrillas have appeared. These are cadres who went into hiding after their war in Malaya proper was stalled and repelled. Leadership is Chinese, and their tactics are essentially those of the Viet Cong. It is easy to perceive the truth of the United States build-up in Thailand. Our striking air force fighters run many of the bombing raids over Vietnam from Thai fields. The Thais, in the original instance, approached the Americans to obtain agreement on this stage and what was to follow.

Even that doughty universal expert Harrison Salisbury was prudent about embracing the whole Fulbright view. He acknowledged, in *The New York Times,* staunch Thai independence and its homogeneity, which provided a strong central regime. "Thailand could become another Vietnam only if beset by a large-scale underground uprising or hostilities from across her borders. The potential for either seems limited." Then Salisbury, after noting huge American-built installations like Sattahop airbase with 11,500-foot runways, mused over the accusation that we might be planning to use them against China or as a fallback position if we pulled out of Vietnam.

"But a conservative assessment of the situation indicates these possibilities are remote," wrote Salisbury. "The Thais themselves say firmly why they would not provide a 'fallback' for the U.S. And they have been firm in their resolve to limit the actual number of U.S. troops and the amount of U.S. spending in order to avoid becoming an economic Vietnam with all its disastrous inflationary consequences."

The Salisbury assessment, to anyone who has spent time trying to unearth some of the stickier issues, is sober and sound enough. But Salisbury, whose expertise shares affinity with Fulbright's views, felt compelled to add: "The danger persists, however, of a creeping U.S. involvement in Thailand which might inexorably lead to consequences neither desired nor foreseen by either government. Light may be cast on these dark potentials by the Fulbright hearings." Sadly enough, Fulbright hearings on the record have provided light—for Fulbright's findings and counsel as an expert.

A bit of contemporary history might be in order. When the Communists took over in North Vietnam, the Thais began to think seriously of their own future. Their boundaries are shaped in a strategic triangle: Laos and Cambodia on the east; Burma on the west; and Malaysia due south. As long ago as a SEATO meeting in 1958 Thais warned their allies of Communist intentions to penetrate South Vietnam in a big and serious way. Their admonitions are on the record in imposing detail. Eliciting shrugs or only reassuring words in return, the Thais went to work to devise their own defenses.

With the Americans the accommodation has been one of advise and consent. It was not always so harmonious an arrangement. The Thai mind, more complicated than that of most Asians, can be almost impregnable. We had a series of inept or impatient ambassadors—either condescending diplomats and soldiers or gung-ho reformers. Today, the image of the Ugly American has practically disappeared. One of the ablest, yet most self-effacing, American diplomats steered the course for the United States. He is Graham Martin, a soft-spoken, steely minded man out of North Carolina, who is keenly conscious of Thai sensibilities. His awareness, has, in turn, been rewarded with subtle understanding and cooperation on nearly every level.

In opening the nation for development, as no other emerging nation ever has, Thailand also extends cooperation where it counts to some immediate neighbors. Take the Ubolrat Dam, recently opened. Hailed by the UN as a great achievement, the dam will provide electric power in the lower Mekong Basin to Cambodia, Laos, and South Vietnam, as well as to Thailand. Irrigation and potable water also will flow to the parched northeast, where China supports insurgency. Opening the outlying provinces is in the hands of some of the most talented men in Asia such as Thanat Khoman, foreign minister, and Pote Sarasin, former secretary of SEATO, who heads national development. A delicate balance exists between the civilian echelon, the military, and police, headed by Marshall Thanom Kittikachorn.

This is not the classic textbook government, undertaking a program of full prosperity based on the concepts of outside ideologists. This government is practical, sensible, and highly aware of what is required in Thailand today and tomorrow. This alone puts Thailand several leaps ahead of Mao Tse-tung, professional "liberation" thinkers in have-not Eastern Europe, and the critical, cynical experts. The Thai upper echelons don't hesitate to lay it on the line when they have something they believe needs saying forcefully. In March, 1966, at one of the most tense diplomatic encounters ever held in Asia, Thailand's foreign minister gave the Soviet ambassador a tongue-lashing that left the air-conditioned office as the steaming, tropical temperature outdoors.

Veteran Foreign Minister Thanat Khoman, mild of appearance and sharp of language, told Russian representative Mikhail Volkov that professed Soviet friendliness "means cutting our throats." Thanat, a graduate of the Sorbonne and a former ambassador to Washington and the UN, heard Volkov read from a document assailing Thai association with the United States. Volkov read that Thailand was in collusion with the Americans "in sponsoring aggression against Laos, Cambodia, and Vietnam." Thanat interrupted Volkov. The charges were totally false, he snapped. His country had the inalienable right to defend itself as it saw fit.

"It is the Soviet Union," declared Thanat, "that is one of the chief aggressors, by providing arms to Communists to kill Asians." Thanat's emphasis was on *Asians*. He went on to reprimand Volkov about what he saw as a deliberate attempt to frighten Thailand. The encounter attracted little notice in Washington. It was reported from Bangkok, where even Volkov conceded "much difficulty." Experts obviously discounted its importance. The point Thanat made about Asians went around all the independent Asian governments that help make a conference in Manila.

But Senator Fulbright and Senator Stephen Young, among his regular yes-men on foreign affairs, were quick to scoff in advance at the Manila conference. It would be, predicted Fulbright, "a cozy affair." He was writing it off, as would Lippmann, because the idea that the United States has any following and support in Asia is unreal to them. As Robert J. Donovan, a long-time reporter and chief of bureau in Washington for the *Herald Tribune* and then the Los Angeles *Times,* reported from Manila: "The critics were let down, the cynics amazed."

To the Manila talks came Thailand, South Vietnam, and South Korea, Australia and New Zealand, the host, the Philippines, and the United States. The Manila group, as Donovan and others noted, may eventually mean more to a country like Thailand than SEATO ever has. Philippine President Marcos, who a few months before presided over a formative Asian economic conference, increased his personal stature at the meeting. Except for the late Ramon Magsaysay, who smashed the Hukbalahap guerrilla movement and introduced gradualist reforms, Marcos is well on his way to being the best President ever in the Philippines.

These developments somehow never grasp the imagination or the attention of the experts. Out of Johnson's attendance at Manila and his trip around the Pacific and Southeast Asia, he convinced some critics—by no means all—that he wants to end the killing of Americans by Asians and vice versa. The Chinese claim that the Vietnam war is a struggle of Asians against "white imperialist aggression" got chopped up badly by L.B.J.'s presentation and proposals to Asians. The conclusion was not assessed by the experts. It was reached, most interestingly, by Asians in governments called neutral and committed our way. Their newspapers, if not their government leaders, said so publicly and tellingly.

All voices, however, have been loud and clear about the at-home problems prevalent in the have-not world: their population explosions and the corresponding inabilities to feed people. The shocking sight of emaciated children, national appeals for grain, for birth control, can be heard above the cacophony of demands and counterproposals on methods by which war in Vietnam—war in general—can and should be eliminated.

Only in the most dire circumstances, as with India's famine, are the cries for help heeded with some speed and efficiency from better-off nation states. Scientists, governmental agencies, and the UN produce reports replete with statistics. They convey a shocking picture, via statistical research, of the near-terminal cases of the have-nots. There are, alas, no experts in these fields to arouse universal interest and even continued compassion. There is no mileage in becoming a recognized authority on dwindling resources and ever-increasing human requirements.

Conflict has the awful, occasionally awesome appeal of glamour. Nothing glitters in any appraisal of squalor, enfeeblement by malnutrition, and the fatalistic, eye-rooted expression of despair. There are experts who assert that we should not attempt to be policemen around the world. In the next breath, they also declare that we cannot be expected to feed the world. What they ignore is the principal issue, namely people.

Chapter 20

CHINA

🔯

THE latest, most prominent nonstarter in the world of foreign affairs today is expert opinion on China. Its rise to respectability, in the spectrum of mass information and education, stems from the thrust into public view of the Soviet-Communist Chinese conflict. The obligato of recrimination—which Communists sharpen like surgical scalpels—produces a fascinated, globe-wide audience that automatically takes sides. In the West, it has become quite obvious that the Soviet Union is in the right in this battle; Communist China, all wrong. By choosing sides, without much reflection, particularly in the United States, we have rushed to a conclusion that the Soviets must be on our side.

After all, the argument runs, the Russians are under the Chinese gun; Mao Tse-tung is a bitter, aging man, determined to bring down the world with him. So, despite Soviet trappings of totalitarianism, Russians leaders have far more to lose in their growing-up inclinations than do the Chinese. Mao wants war; the Soviet leaders do not. *Ipso facto,* we support the U.S.S.R. It is a neatly and superficially prepared package that has staggering current acceptance. We must try to remember, for one thing, that the early revelations of a Sino-Soviet problem came from the Russians. They have ever since, through private diplomatic encounters and their propaganda services, circulated the first freshets of news about rampages by undisciplined young Red Guards, embarked on Mao's cultural clean-up on behalf of proletarianism.

Since the West learned many years ago never to accept Soviet information at face value, the inclination to do so about China is a puzzler. Part of the explanation may be a desire to tempt the U.S.S.R. at long last into some permanent peaceful accommodation. Another phase probably swings around American rejection even of information since the ascension to power of the Chinese

Communists on the mainland in 1949. The Chinese Communists proved their militant anti-Americanism by sending vast forces into Korea. Now, they are engaged with our enemies in North Vietnam in prolonging the war there. These are popular conceptions made more dramatic by Soviet maneuvers to challenge the Chinese. The fact that the U.S.S.R. and her Communist associates in Europe seek, each in proportion to resources, to support North Vietnam is waved away by the experts. Reason? What else can you expect the European Communists to do? They cannot, declare the experts, abandon even pretenses of aiding a comrade. Somehow, we never get the same understanding apologia.

Because we have more or less given Red China the back of our hand since 1949, ignoring Asia's giant to concentrate on Europe, we are stuck today with a huge assortment of experts. There are, for example, the "China watchers." They may sit in Hong Kong, geographically hugging the mainland with all the creature comforts and easy communications at hand. They also abound in great cities like New York, Washington, London, and of course, Moscow. This is a special brand of demonology that captivates the practitioner. The result is that men and women who normally try to keep a sense of stability are swept into the act. They don't offer erudite considerations. All they do is sign a petition that is inserted in a national newspaper as a paid advertisement. The two favorite outlets for the paid ads are *The New York Times* and the Washington *Post*. One such ad in the *Times*, assailing our China policy, prompted a page one lead news story by a ranking member of the paper's Washington Bureau. It was signed by a host of names.

The trouble in that episode was that most of the 198 signers, self-styled experts on China affairs, hadn't been closer than restaurants serving regional specialities. To counteract that full page advertisement, came another entitled "Liberals Support China Policy." Its theme was the unwise view of any two Chinas proposal which would include Formosa—and appealed against seating Communist China in the UN and according her any diplomatic recognition. To deflect any impact of the "liberal" petition, another advertisement appeared in the *Times*. It called for attention to Vietnam. Headed "Let Us Act Together to Bring Peace to Vietnam," it presented an exotic collection of names. Among them was Enrique Lister, Communist commander of Spanish civil war times; Friedrich Ebert, Mayor of East Berlin, and a member of the Bulgar parliament. The petitions are something any citizen has a right to sign. But they have become plain silly or greasy kid stuff shibboleths.

Examinations of the "China Problem," done in a penetratingly academic manner by long patient and true authorities—like Professor John K. Fairbank, A. Doak Barnett, and Brigadier General (retired) Samuel B. Griffith—don't seem to rub off on the experts. Theirs has been a special great leap forward. Some have adapted techniques which they used in the occult science of Kremlinology. Once the uproar became part of Soviet denunciation, these experts felt it necessary to examine China's qualities.

Then, there is the ubiquitous universal experts, headed by Lippmann, who writes about China's intentions. He has never delved into the history of the teeming nation of 750 million, nor has he ever made any particular study of Mao's methods and party behaviorisms. Lippmann has never spent any time in China. But that doesn't inhibit him from passing judgments.

A few other experts, critical of American policy, are writers like Edgar Snow and Felix Greene. It was Snow who made most Americans reading magazines conscious of the Communists in China with his prewar reports in the *Saturday Evening Post*. He lived in China and has also written books about Mao and the revolution. They are weighted with a mighty prejudice in favor of Communist rule in China. So are expert screeds written by Felix Greene, once a BBC announcer. He moved to the States and goes off on trips to China and, more recently, North Vietnam. He finds film presentations and lectures most profitable these days, particularly with a Stateside base. As a combined China-Vietnam expert, Greene has some special views which are worth noting. One of his keener observations, in the light of Red Chinese announcements, says:

"The mood of relaxed confidence which is so apparent to the visitor in China today comes, surprisingly, at a time when the people have come to realize that a major military confrontation with the U.S. is possible. The time and the place is the war in Vietnam. There is very little ballyhoo, no great military parades, no glorification of war. In fact I see more men in uniform in California than I did while travelling in China a few months ago. . . ."

That nugget of perception was published in September, 1966. The cry of Red Guard demonstrations was in full throat. Communist New China News Agency reports spoke of massed thousands either smashing old relics or demanding military action against the American imperialists. Still and televised photos from Chinese propaganda agencies showed marching youngsters in Peking and other big cities, under the vigil of instructors. Japanese reporters on the scene wrote of tremendous posters of a China girding for action. A film taken by Greene's old employer, the BBC, had a sequence of five-year-olds being trained in the use of small arms. Green saw more troops in California because he was never permitted to enter Chinese staging areas, but he doesn't think the omission worth a mention. No ballyhoo, indeed.

But the smattering of ignorance that permeates most of us today emerges from the divinations of the published and TV-taped China watcher. They first came of accepted age back in late 1964, although China watching had for years been the province of an interesting band of diplomats. These include some of the most perspicacious wits in the American and British foreign services. The Americans have developed a new post-Korea crop. They are steeped in Mandarin and the various dialects of China. Their study centers for language training are primarily on Taiwan (Formosa). After completion of language and prodigious history courses, they are assigned to Hong Kong or peripheral areas. Unpublicized and strictly absolute students of the scene across the way, they will answer questions when—and if—they are asked. Flanking these watchers are priests and missionaries, fluent in Mandarin and dialects.

Only in an extreme case will a present-day China watcher ever solicit an opinion from these unpublished, unwatched watchers. One of the most noteworthy exceptions is Joseph Alsop, for years immersed in the history, policies, and customs of Imperial, republican, and present-day China. A man of erudition and great personal courage, Joe Alsop makes instant enemies because of his shock at what seems to him to be flamboyance. His interests make him an amateur, in the French sense, more a connoisseur than an expert. It's a word from which he usually recoils. Alsop lived and worked in China and has frequently been to Asia. It was he who in 1962 reported the great famine in China that was snuffing out the existences of hundreds of thousands. Before that disaster, Alsop produced evidence to show how Mao's "Great Leap Forward" was plunging the nation and people into unrelieved disaster.

Presently, the China watcher—in the American reading public's eye—is exemplified by a stocky, little man around forty, named Robert Elegant. Of New York background, Elegant professes to have learned Mandarin in an Army school. He first showed his journeyman skills as a Hong Kong reporter for *Newsweek*. The magazine, after some years, sent him to Germany. He didn't like the transfer and returned to Hong Kong in 1965 for The Los Angeles *Times*. He makes very occasional trips outside the enclave. Elegant sifts material from the Chinese Communist press, talks to refugees he can encounter, and interprets the mainland scene as one of the chief China watchers.

His role is much like that of the expert who sat in Riga, Latvia, in the early twenties, assessing the early Soviet Union. There were reporters in the U.S.S.R. then, and admittedly, it is unique for an American journalist—unless he is someone like Snow—to obtain even a short-term tourist's visa for today's China. Sticking to his post in Hong Kong, Elegant has become a recognized, on-site expert China watcher. It has been a porous production: the anti-Communist anti-Chinese episode of Indonesia escaped his eagle eye. Moreover, mainland newspapers never mention any atomic build-up leading to nuclear explosions or guided missiles.

Swashbuckling Morris ("Two Gun") Cohen, once bodyguard to Sun Yat-sen and a business wheeler-dealer, could qualify as a China watcher. He is still on relatively good terms with regime authorities and was among prominent visitors near Mao Tse-tung at a Peking demonstration recently. More important, Cohen has been in China, can at least today converse with some higher-ups, and perhaps can even offer to serve as middleman in a business deal. In 1959, when the authors had a meal with Cohen in a London Chinese restaurant—the Good Earth—he predicted that China was on its way to building an atom bomb. How did he know? "They told me so in Peking," replied Cohen, indignant that anyone would question his perception. He was right, of course, which puts him way ahead of most watchers.

The Chinese, at a site in Sinkiang, did in 1964 detonate their first atomic device. Only two years intervened before they fired a guided missile with an attached nuclear warhead. Scientifically speaking, it was an impressive feat. The test caught us by surprise, but France, the other nuclear power that, with China, refused to sign the test-ban treaty, pretended differently. The handicap to that aplomb is affixed by a confident remark attributed to de

Gaulle. After he recognized Red China in 1964, de Gaulle thought aloud, to listeners, that on nuclear matters China was quite a few years behind France. It's precisely the other way around now. A scientist available to predict the nature of nuclear things to come in China was available in the United States until 1954. As did other reporters, we spoke to Tsien Hsen-shem. He had been in the States for twenty years, until permitted to return to China in 1954. Tsien was once head of the Jet Propulsion Laboratory at Pasadena, a talented scientist and research analyst. In 1950, a year after Mao's regime took over the mainland, he predicted that an atomic bomb would be priority for the Communists. When the test was successful, Mao was hailed in the streets. There was no mention of Tsien, so he eluded the scrutiny of the China watcher-experts. Yet it was the guiding scientific genius of Tsien that led to China's first hydrogen bomb test.

Our experts prefer to cull the names of Mao's lord lieutenants, to record his mighty swim down the Yangtse River, and to see how the hierarchy stands after criticisms. Thus we are exposed to a massive series of names after Mao and Premier Chou En-lai, the second-best-known of the Communists, but not the most important. Marshal Lin Piao, second to Mao and author of a treatise on do-it-yourself revolutions sweeping the world, holds pride of headline. Then, head of state Liu Shao-chi comes in for breathless re-evaluation almost daily. The same is true of disgraced Peng Chen, ex-mayor of Peking, and Teng Hsiao-p'ing, secretary general of the party. The names are tossed around glibly by the experts from their watching posts. Little is reported about what, indeed, happened to them or to their subordinate associates. It has become a massive, inconclusive whodunit with a bewildering series of characters whose names become a horizontal blur.

We can hold ourselves to blame for failing to at least keep a casual interest in the ups-and-downs of Red China and her associations with the outside world. Equally, the experts are responsible for so much of their daily irresponsibility. Elegant, in a verbose article toward the end of 1966, called Marshal Lin the loser in the first phase of the cultural revoltuion. He had an escape clause, a sort of "on the other hand," believing Lin would try to regroup. Anyway, Marshal Lin was at Mao's shoulder weeks later, and the experts were concluding that he had managed to stave off defeat. The China-watching gyrations, as published and shown regularly, have led to the perplexed query: "What's the name of this game?"

In less brash, more reflective terms, the "game" is spelled out by academic authorities—not experts—like Professors Barnett and Fairbank. Their credentials to write and speak of moods in China, about the personalities involved, and our own obsessions, are of the highest order. Professor Barnett has long been with the East Asian Institute at Columbia University. He was asked to appear before a hearing in Washington sponsored by Senator Fulbright. On March 8, 1966, Professor Barnett told the Senate committee:

> I would like, right at the start, to state my own belief that there is a need for basic changes in the over-all United States posture toward Communist China. For almost seventeen years we have pursued a policy that might best be characterized as one aimed at containment and isolation of Communist China. . . . I strongly believe that the time has come—even though the Unied States is now engaged in a bitter struggle in Vietnam—for our country to alter its posture toward Communist China and adopt a policy of *containment but not isolation* [authors' italics], a policy that would aim on the one hand at checking military or subversive threats and pressures emanating from Peking, but at the same time would aim at maximum contacts with and maximum involvement of the Chinese Communists in the international community.

A little later, Professor Barnett said this:

> Although there are many persons in the United States—in government, in universities, and elsewhere—who are relatively well informed about Communist China, there is no doubt that the American people as a whole know far too little about China, or about the problems of evolving effective policies to deal with it. At the same time, issues relating to China policy have been among the most emotional in American public life ever since the late 1940's. It is probably fair to say that there has been less responsible public discussion of China policy than of any other foreign policy issue of comparable importance.

After Chiang Kai-shek was driven from the mainland by the Communists, there was a violent uproar in the United States about how and why it happened. Millions of words poured out, accusing government policy planners, diplomats on the spot and many long since reassigned, and a string of advisers of bad judgment or even knowing betrayal. Thus, earnest and knowledgeable career officers were served up as public scapegoats. One was compelled to leave a ranking post in Germany—and his career—because of hysterical accusations that he committed follies in China. From Senator Fulbright, who invited Barnett, there was not a public protest on behalf of some reasoned judgment. It compares with his unfortunate flight to Britain at the time of stormy integration of schools in Little Rock, Arkansas.

Ignored in all the furor were the experts who wrote with favor about the triumph of Mao Tse-tung and saw in his ascension to power a purge of corruption and a new deal for the landless peasants. The terror that followed installation of Mao's rule was, at first, deemed overzealous excesses. This was followed by bewilderment, and soon, silence. Detached from the hurly-burly and the synthetic expertise, Professor Fairbank wrote: "Chinese Communist totalitarianism is going to be with us for the foreseeable future and we are going to have to live with it and learn to deal with it.

"Even if China should miraculously cease to be 'Communist,' it would still have to be 'totalitarian'; state and community would still dominate the individual. The freedom of the individual cannot be expected to develop there in our American sense of the term. No doubt we can accept this if the Chinese people can do so; we cannot undertake to 'liberate' them."

The high-flown preachment of liberation came to the test, of course, in Hungary in 1956. Of the uprising, Mao declared that "these events tugged" at the mainland of China. We looked the other way in Hungary and reneged on once-proffered hopes made in the name of General Eisenhower by the late John Foster Dulles. People, as Professor Fairbank suggests, liberate themselves in spite of the regime steamroller that may crush them repeatedly by force.

Fairbank is a scholar with more than thirty-five years of study and wide travel in China and elsewhere in the Far East. Professor Fairbank has been a member of the Harvard faculty since 1936 and served in top advisory councils on Chinese affairs. His analysis of Chinese behavior is based on years of study, human contact, and a prodigious background of history and people. Presently, Fairbank is more pessimistic than not on the possibilities of making any two-way street of Chinese-American relations.

His is not the assessment predicated on China watching as

gleaned from the Communist press of the mainland, or expert values produced via quick, guided tours. It is based primarily on people and how they react to given circumstances, which he knows far better than most who sit in considered judgment. Thus, he has said: "Toward China a balance of containment and contact—informational, commercial, cultural, and diplomatic—may take years to achieve. But one will avail little without the other."

A swarm of experts, in journalism and lecture fields, have sought to attach themselves to either Professor Barnett or Professor Fairbank. Some have tried to associate themselves with both. If they decide to come down on the side of one academician, then the other is deplored as "naive," or plain unsophisticated. Barnett and Fairbank, who don't regard the Chinese puzzle the same way in all essentials, have both seen no purpose served by supporting any publicly self-proclaimed expert on China. Theirs has been a lifelong active and patient study of China, not an instant fascination with temporary tactics and strategy. Unmindful of the din, they carry on in their own manner.

In a do-it-yourself way, Communist China has sought to nibble at the edges of her isolation. The results, in the outside world, have almost uniformly been disastrous. Most African states, for example, were in awe of China until Premier Chou En-lai paid a second visit in 1965. To the consternation of his awe-stricken hosts, Chou—regarded as the most urbane and sophisticated personality in the Chinese regime hierarchy—volunteered in public that he sensed revolution in the air. It was, he added, ripe in Africa. To African leaders of any political persuasion, this meant that China was gunning for them. Invitations for Chou to come visit were rescinded overnight by a galaxy of African governments. They were followed by a series of severances in diplomatic relations with China.

All around the world Red China was on the receiving end of a string of foreign policy rebuffs. Mao's mystique in the do-it-yourself revolutionary spirit had been infused in external policy without regard to local personalities or conditions.

It is infinitely simpler to check out the lines of Peking projects in the outside world than to examine speeches and editorials from the outside, looking in. For one thing, many local authorities, especially in developing nations, are inclined to talk about their dealings with Chinese Communist missions. People visited by

Chinese teams and troubleshooters in the boondocks of these countries also talk about their guests and show the type of presents they give. In Tanzania, for example, some charming tribal folk displayed with delight the blue-glazed eating bowls a touring team left as gifts a few days earlier. What were they asked? "Oh, they just wanted to know if we could shoot rifles," replied the son of a chief. "If we couldn't, they offered to teach us on visits they would make."

On a higher level, in Dar-es-Salaam, the Tanzanian capital, the authors were among those asked to a press conference at the embassy. A tray of soft drinks, including Coca-Cola, was passed around. So were Chinese cigarettes, called "Happiness." The conference was held in a cinema, which several Tanzanian colleagues told us they visited occasionally to "hear lectures about Mao Tsetung." Outside the hall barbed wire ran around the compound. Guards, in boiler suits, lounged in the sentry boxes. After a short wait, a bustling, slender man in a blue boiler suit rushed in and distributed mimeographed sheets. They said that reports of Red China's trade with the Union of South Africa having increased was an imperialist lie. The distributor mounted the podium, rapped for order and said: "Ladies and gentlemen, please dlink your dlinks and leave. There will be no questions."

An area where the Chinese Communists throughout the world have managed to struggle to something like even terms with the Russians is an intramural cloak-and-dagger feud. The reason some of their operations come to light is, again, because local governments and authorities in have-not areas are pleased to talk about them. The Chinese and the Russians brutally attempt to sabotage each other's agents. None of these antics can be winowed out by even the most dedicated China watching in Hong Kong. The competing Communists expose, usually with a sly suggestion to a foreign government, activities of individuals or groups believed to be on either a Soviet or a Chinese payroll. In this manner they have blown networks in Africa and Asia that have existed for several years. The Russians, for example, blew the whistle in the spring of 1965 on pro-Chinese Communists in Northern India. In revenge, the Chinese revealed an old Soviet espionage hand entrenched in Ceylon. He was bounced.

Most recently Chinese operations seem to have centered—from what they themselves suggested to favorably disposed European comrades—around the vast and sensitive frontiers with the U.S.S.R.

They weren't bashful about saying that they wanted to know if the Russians installed any medium-range missiles aimed at China. During the India-Pakistan hostilities, the Russians quietly passed word among Asians and Africans that they installed medium-range missiles to deflate any Chinese militancy. Information that Soviet strategy was so directed in behalf of India was passed along so that it reached Chinese agents.

As the Russians apparently anticipated, China's ultra-sensitivity provoked a Chinese espionage inquiry at great expense. As is customary with Communist regimes, even those on good terms, one side didn't simply ask the other if the reports were true. A stock Chinese technique in Asia and Africa now is to keep emphasizing the "color" link between themselves and the local citizens and the fact that most Russians seen in the areas are white. When an African or Asian shows interest in the argument, attempts are made to recruit him for the Chinese. In retaliation, East European Communist technicians report on what they believe are unseemly acts intended to damage the Russians. The whole routine is increasingly amusing to locals who regale visitors with the anecdotes. When the Sino-Soviet competition gets too stiff for local comfort, selected journalists and diplomats are summarily expelled.

These competitive convulsions, so integral a part of the conflict, do not merit the attention of the experts and the expert watchers. Higher considerations—global for that matter—are an expert's preoccupation. These apparently were uppermost in assessments drawn by Harrison Salisbury on his magic carpet tour of the periphery of China in the summer of 1966. He concluded that Red China treated the U.S.S.R. as an enemy and vice versa. Salisbury, the ranking expert on *The New York Times* for Soviet affairs, put together a new book on his latest findings. As usual, his pro-Soviet feelings show. But his competitor on the *Times* editorial board on Communist affairs, Harry Schwartz, ranged far with an article in New York, headed: "Soviet Preparing for a War With China?"

Schwartz, who does a lot of Soviet watching, wrote in his leaden manner of Soviet propaganda hailing Mao's regime as "fascist." The thought intrigued Schwartz, who added: "The background has been created, in short, so that if war with China should come it could be presented as an Asian analogue of the struggle against Nazi Germany."

Schwartz's expert theme is based on Soviet material, which

always seeks to serve its own purposes. The propaganda, which Schwartz labels as such, is deftly employed by the Russians to make them seem guiltless for the past as well as the present and future. None of these expert reports contains any mention of the fact that the only country to have increased its territorial aggrandizement with a sense of permanency in the twentieth century has been the Soviet Union.

It was the Washington *Post,* which frequently wears the label "liberal" proudly on its opinion pages, that became annoyed with the Soviet techniques as applied against China. ". . . As the climate in Peking has changed, so has the outlook in Moscow," an editorial ran. "The Russians are now engaged in an extensive campaign to put pressure on Mao and to make his political life as arduous as possible. They want to dislodge his rule." The editorial punctured unemotionally the Walter Mitty dreams, so current in the United States, that Red China today is the main bane of our existence. Where, for instance, have reports of Red Guards fighting each other in China originated first? Usually through the Soviet news agency Tass. From Peking, Tass has been quoted about rival Chinese groups rioting and shooting each other. These reports often tell of the clashing guards calling each other "Fascist." In Tass terms this is a curious epithet. It is what Soviet propaganda employs in hurling abuse at Mao Tse-tung.

Felix Greene, in his strident book *A Curtain of Ignorance* published by Doubleday in 1964, gets caught badly with his expert plans down. From his perch as an Englishman resident in the United States, who travels to China, Greene contends that the only way for a backward nation to advance is to do what the U.S.S.R. did. Never mind the human toll, he suggested, if industrialization is the objective. Of course, the question that quickly arises today is: Would he so dogmatically restate the argument for China as well as for most of Asia and Africa? But Greene in this book takes a hard-nosed look at American innocence and ignorance of China. He thought it ridiculous that the American press should have reported starvation conditions, mass discontent, and disinterest in many regions in 1960–1961.

Greene, touring China at the time, was obviously on the well-guided tourist track. Chinese military documents have been available for some time about those conditions. They contain orders directed to Chinese army commanders explaining how to cope with existing discontent in the ranks, caused by malnutrition and by reports of famine deaths in the home villages of peasant soldiers. As an expert on China, Greene could have obtained translations from the Hoover Institution at Stanford University. They are entitled *The Politics of the Chinese Red Army,* edited by J. Chester Cheng. Author-lecturer Greene managed to swallow many Red Chinese myths and propaganda bits. For instance, he wrote that it was the Communists who took the initiative against the Japanese, never Chiang Kai-shek. Generalissimo Chiang draws from Greene only opprobrium. On the matter of initiatives against Japan, Greene might have learned differently from an interesting authority—Mao Tse-tung. Mao made the correction in the selected works he consented to have published.

Professor Fairbank has through the years mentioned the official myth that Mao altered. But who wants an authority if an expert is around? Lately there have been some Western writers of repute who toured China and reported their impressions. Their impact, alas, has not been on a mass scale. But what they have to say is worthy of some thought. Take Harry Hamm, who writes on Communist affairs for the West German *Frankfurter Allgemeine Zeitung.* He contributed a short piece to the vast and fascinating picture book compiled by Swiss photographer Emil Schulthess (Viking). Hamm, a modest multi-lingual observer, contributed eleven pages on "Revolutionary China in Transition." Professor Fairbank described the Hamm contribution as "one of the most realistic brief appraisals yet available." Zeroing in on China's problems after giving a regime, for which he has little sympathy, credit for some achievements, Hamm specified four principal problems.

The first, population: "The density of China has become a nightmare." Second, accumulating capital out of agriculture proved unexpectedly difficult. So, industrialization had to slow down. Third, China's 90 per cent illiteracy of 1949 has only been reduced to 60 per cent in the villages and 20 per cent in urban areas. The burden of having to memorize Chinese characters is overwhelming as is providing teachers for one hundred million schoolchildren. Finally, wrote Hamm, "the teaching of Confucius is still alive in China . . . many signs make us suspect that the outward show of solidarity has little significance . . . the Communist cadres have no real hold on the masses." Hamm concluded that the "primacy

of domestic politics in China is more valid than in any other country in the world."

Felix Greene might note how different were Hamm's assessments
from his own. He might also note this remark from Professor Fairbank about Hamm's evaluations: "For Americans this plainly
means: don't get too excited over Peking's foreign policy bombast;
try to understand the Chinese domestic nightmare before you get
involved in making it worse. . . ."

Nevertheless, we remain beguiled, even entranced, by reports
of Chinese Communists kicking up ruckuses at Communist conferences. Taking sides, because experts persuade us that the Soviet
Union is the more reasonable protagonist, if not our putative ally,
we become aroused at the spectacle of Chinese denouncing Russians. There was even a memorable occasion in Sofia, Bulgaria's
unattractive capital, when the Chinese delegates were prevented
from speaking. A meeting of the Soviet-run World Federation of
Trade Unions (WFTU) was in session. Bulgar police, with the
active assistance of Western Communists, kept the Chinese from
the rostrum. They also thwarted China's allies, the Albanians
(population under two million). Noses were bloodied. Out stormed
the Chinese and the Albanians. In speaking to some of the more
discomfited Western Communists on their return home declared
flatly that the Russians rigged the outburst at the handful of
Chinese-Albanians.

A few weeks earlier in the same ramshackle city, the Russians
tried to exact agreement on a big convocation that would drum the
Chinese out of international comradeship. There were no Chinese,
or even Albanians, present. Preparatory steps had been taken so
that Russian leaders felt they could try out the ploy. Some East
European delegates present told the author afterward that when
objections to such a conference were raised, the Soviet delegates
tried to steamroller opposition. Romanians, who enjoy a cynical
and special in-between relationship with the Russians and Chinese,
stood firm along with some others. The Russians thereupon declared any interpretation of their call to a conference was fallacious.
Party leader Brezhnev went on a tour to see if he could drum up
fresh support, which came through loud and clear as a summons for
a world Communist summit. China's policy, asserted the Soviet
central committee, had entered a "new dangerous phase." To
whom?

One of the great and constant games of expert speculation, sparked by Lippmann, has been the nigh-inevitability of Communist Chinese entry into the war in Vietnam. His admonition has, naturally, been taken up by admiring fellow experts. Each time an American undertaking backfires—or meets resounding success—the warning can be heard that the Chinese are coming. Appeals have come for restraint, reduction, and withdrawal since 1964, and they have reached a crescendo that has held steady since 1965. A rough estimate of fifty thousand Chinese—troops and technicians—in North Vietnam has been made by such assorted sources as Indians, Yugoslavs, and the French. True, China's frontiers with North Vietnam straddle the borders. More modern Soviet hardware flows into North Vietnam in a month than does Chinese in a year. That service is excused for two reasons: The U.S.S.R. must help another Communist state and simultaneously blunt any influence Red China can exert on North Vietnam.

What has been ignored or disregarded in this case is the expansionism inherent in Ho Chi-Minh's own regime. A vaunted explanation of the experts is that North Vietnam remembers and resents the time, centuries ago, when China imposed hegemony. That's like saying the Soviet Union can convince people in the Russian republic to recall the slaughter and terror visited on their ancestors by the legions of Genghis Khan. The expansionist tendencies of the Northern regime have absolutely no Chinese connections.

China, on its own, is capable of annexing Tibet and imposing commissar rule. It had been a territory claimed in the past by the Chinese Nationalists as well. North Vietnam doesn't simply look due south to satisfy its appetite. Theirs is a quest to ultimately control little Laos and Cambodia, which with all Vietnam were once part of French-ruled Indochina. It was so declared back in 1954. North Vietnamese troops comprise most of the units called "Pathet Lao" that operate in Laos outside the trails used for supplying guerrillas and regulars in South Vietnam. In its own militant pursuit for regional hegemony—a point never mentioned by experts—North Vietnam wants its hands free to deal with the war in South Vietnam and simultaneously to totally undermine Laos. This is far more adventurous than Red China's policies. Red Chinese armies, even with the specter of Korea hovering about, are in no condition to handle frontiers with Russia, and a confrontation on the field in far-flung places of South Vietnam against American combat units. China's nuclear armory still does not possess the means of delivering the dreadful weapons. But the universal experts, like Lippmann, contend that the Chinese can handle both fronts so far apart and maybe even involve the U.S.S.R. in a war against us.

The nonsense they prattle is shattered by the reasoned, learned observations of General Griffith. After twenty-seven years of distinguished service in the United States Marine Corps, Griffith retired in 1956. Many of his assignments took him into personal association with China. Before World War II, for example, he was a language officer at the American Embassy in Peking. He served as a field officer in Tientsin and Tsingtao. In addition, Griffith is an academician of the first rank, having also obtained a doctorate in Chinese history from Oxford. He has written in detail of the Chinese People's Liberation Army, known for short as the PLA. It is, wrote Griffith, well trained and strong in manpower. At eighteen, 750,000 new recruits are inducted into the army every year. It is unique among the world's military establishments.

"In non-Communist sovereign states, the armed forces are generally apolitical; their primary mission is to prepare for wars, and when necessary, wage them," wrote General Griffith. "In Communist China, however, the PLA has been given two additional major missions. The first of these is to assist party political cadres to conduct propaganda and to mobilize the rural masses. The second is to engage actively in production."

Griffith's examination of the equipment, transport, and supporting aircraft and marine units available to the PLA led him to determine gravely: "This leaves us with a conclusion of the first magnitude. In terms of conventional military power, and ability to project it, the People's Republic is now, and for many years will remain, a veritable 'paper tiger.'" Further the convulsions that riddle internal China, as reported by Chinese party personalities themselves in public demonstrations, pit pro-Red Guardists and antis in a showdown with private armies. The People's Liberation Army, mainly on the sidelines to date, has shown in upper echelons decided favoritism for or against Marshal Lin Piao. Therefore, the freedom of action blithely attributed to the PLA to march in several directions at once is even more drastically hamstrung.

Perhaps more important is the danger to Mao Tse-tung's regime from within, the first time such a development on an even loosely organized scale has occurred. Stanley Karnow, roving Far East correspondent of the Washington *Post,* made this searching assessment. He listens, interviews, and uses the talents of a skilled observer, leaving China watching expert assessment to others.

Interestingly, the first revelation that Mao was confronted by peril from inside the country was reported by Joe Alsop. The universal experts archly pooh-poohed the summation as "Alsopian."

They return endlessly to their theme that Communist China must be installed in a seat at the UN without qualification. The facile explanation is that, by the magic inspired in the tall glass edifice on New York's Turtle Bay, Red China can be induced into a tamed, salon tabby. It hasn't happened to many, smaller states. Membership in the vast, trussed-up club hasn't any special interest presently for China. A separate and competitive organization, as once promoted by Sukarno, interested China's rulers far more. When Sukarno's wings were clipped, their attention vanished. When the voting goes against admission of China, sometimes with a few additional votes and occasionally on a hairline, hardly rubs off on the mainland. All it does is cause the experts prominent in Washington to lament the folly of our governmental ways.

They could do worse in such a subjective melancholia than to examine what Professor Fairbank reflected on in *Life* magazine, November, 1966. It was entitled "A Nation Imprisoned by Her History." The volume of problems confronting Mao, according to Fairbank, have roots that reach back more than two thousand years. He wrote:

> A curious contradiction haunts Chairman Mao's revolution: the more he seeks to make China new, the more he seems to fall back on old Chinese ways of doing it. Two thirds of a century ago, in the mid-summer madness of 1900, the Boxer bands who were officially commissioned to exterminate foreigners in North China were composed largely of peasant youth—and they pursued their ends with the same zeal displayed by Chairman Mao's officially commissioned "Red Guards" in their attack on all things foreign. But where the Boxers wanted to do away merely with Western influence in China, the Red Guards express a double frustration: they also want to wipe out China's "old ideas, old customs, old habits."
>
> Chairman Mao is struggling not only against Western influence but also against the hold of China's ancient past. First he is trying to revolutionize the world's biggest political unit. No one has ever before tried to govern 700 million people through a single unitary regime, let alone remake their whole way of life and thought. But this

is not all. In the second place, China happens to be the oldest political unit with a continuous tradition. Chinese history lists 25 dynasties. Where Mao stands today on the Gate of Heavenly Peace facing Red Square in Peking, dozens of Emperors, Sons of Heaven, ruled for hundreds of years, building up the monumental inertia of Chinese tradition. When Mao wants to strike down this tradition, he can only find methods used before. China's long history has him in quicksand—as he struggles, he becomes more immersed in the attitudes and dreams inherited from China's past.

None of Fairbank's assessment, based on first-hand knowledge and study over his entire adult life, ever seems to be taken into account by Lippmann and his cult. Never have they attempted in public print and through electronic journalism to evaluate the words of a substantial authority as opposed to their easy know-nothingism. The result for Americans at large has been a melancholy declamation to beware of offending China and to yield up, with nary a morbid thought, people and places that do not belong to us. Even a new H-bomb should not create that kind of melancholy indifference.

Chapter 21

LATIN AMERICA: PART ONE

☙

A N ABRASIVE personality, as upsetting to Americans as Mao Tse-tung but less mysterious because he is close to our mainland, is Dr. Fidel Castro. Astride Cuba, he remains in the average consciousness as a co-conspirator with the Russians for sneaking in missiles that brought us an eyeball-to-eyeball confrontation with the U.S.S.R. His communism is unorthodox, which has annoyed both Russia and Red China. They have complained about him, and Castro has lashed out at both of them for trying to use him and Cuba for their own objectives. Nevertheless the Soviet Union and China constantly seek to mollify Castro. Indeed the U.S.S.R. sent Premier Kosygin to visit with him, immediately after conclusion of the Kosygin-Johnson mini-summit at Glassboro, New Jersey. Castro is unorthodox, but he stays steadfastly a Communist. This is the other point Americans bear in mind.

On November 17, 1966, Havana Radio broadcast a boastful item—so it seemed to most Americans—saying that Cuba was setting up special schools to train Latin Americans, Asians, and Africans in guerrilla warfare. Claims of achievement and menace from Dr. Castro, Cuba's garrulous but tireless Prime Minister, had become a bore. The trouble has been that as far as policy-sifters, program architects, and men of state in the United States have been concerned, Latin America has been a bore.

As a nation and a people, we are historically more interested and obsessed with Europe or the Far East; with the balance of power in the Old World or with the threat of communism. The same is latterly true where the Far East is concerned. After Communist China won the mainland, thence achieved nuclear power and a split with the U.S.S.R. over control of foreign party apparatus, we emphasized the shifts in alliances and savage in-fighting. Although Latin America was drawn inexorably into all global ups and downs, the United States still deals with the problems of our next door neighbors as if they were very distant relatives.

There are more than 150 million of these Spanish and Portuguese-speaking neighbors. To them, in the last few years, must be added the newly independent, overcrowded, tiny island-countries of the Caribbean, where English is the *lingua franca*. The land and geographical mass sprawls a vast distance. Its people are mainly chafing in what is loosely known as a developing stage. In 150 years, the United States has raised gaudy, often well-meaning accommodation intended to protect Latin America—for us and for Latin Americans. Once proclaimed, the arrangements were casually left to be worked out later. When Fidel Castro and two thousand guerrillas came down from the Sierra Maestra mountains and took over Cuba, our complacency was rocked.

A Communist regime, sitting ninety miles off the southern tip of Florida, was epitomized by the bewhiskered Fidel Castro. The permanent type of Communist purge began and so did seeping land reform. Built into the Castro revolution were all the pernicious elements of Communist rule: the midnight-knock-on-the-door police vigil; the economic theories of Communist-run Europe, which even those countries were trying to abandon; and the ever-dreary yet vicious quest for "counterrevolutionaries."

Above all, Fidel Castro was exhibited when he took power in 1959, as the reform-minded David who slew that calcified Goliath of North America, the world's top superpower, the United States. Because mass communications ignored, except for the *opéra-bouffe coup d'etat* rhythm, Latin America, the cult of Lochinvar was devised for Castro. The regionalists and over-all experts in the State Department were caught with their plans down. Old-line Latin dictators like Fulgencio Batista seemed always to have the local situation, like Cuba's, well in hand. Our diplomats in Latin America, for the most part, were guilty not so much of miscalculation but of senescence and moldy contacts.

We were preoccupied outside the United States, first with Europe, the Atlantic alliance, the Soviet Union, and then de Gaulle. Communist China was still a cloud, maybe bigger than a man's hand, but not much more.

The impressions we obtained about how and why Castro, were provided by a few American reporters, most prominent of whom was Herbert L. Matthews, of *The New York Times*. An old hand at the craft of being a foreign correspondent, Matthews made his way to Castro in guerrilla times. He sent back reports of a dedicated man bent on bringing Cuba into the mid-twentieth century on the basis of social justice and equality. There was Castro, sort of a curve-ball-pitching (easily recognizable to any baseball fan) reformer. Matthews' image of him was instant. It got immediate acceptance among reform-minded people in the States and was blessed by the self-advertised intellectual-liberal as "progressive."

The decay of the Batista dictatorship and the corruption supervised by North American gangster overlords and their gambling fiefdoms also revolted many visitors from the States. The miserable have-not conditions of Cubans at large contrasted with the tinsel and glitter of the quick-buck structure of state, spawned a massive if inarticulate demand for change. Our own ambassador, financier, and conservative Republican Earl E. T. Smith stuck unswervingly to support of Batista. Detesting any surge towards change of an existing order came naturally to Smith. Thus, it wasn't difficult for him to abhor appeals for reform before it was too late. This was especially true in his loathing of Castro, who came down from the hills while Smith was American ambassador.

Smith didn't care for most of the professional staff assigned to him, especially the younger diplomatists. They seemed, in his view, rather ultraliberal or ignorant of the then Cuban facts of life. To Smith this meant supporting the existing regime of Batista. He, as ambassador, became the on-scene expert. It is, therefore, very strange that Smith was not only an old friend of the Kennedy family but was proposed by the late President to Switzerland as ambassador. The Swiss sniffed; their government, in a unique refusal, spurned Smith as an American emissary and asked us to send someone else. When that appointment was lost, Smith became a writer-lecturer on Cuba and subsequently a trustee of the John F. Kennedy Memorial Library.

It wasn't hard for Smith to continue as a regional expert, to show how right he'd been to warn against Castro. The criticism, of course, encompasses many one-time supporters of Fidel, who saw in his seizure of power a long overdue clean-up of life and living in the island. What they didn't envisage—and this includes ex-members of his first government—was the chop-up that came with a regime of the permanent purge. Cubans seemed satisfied generally. Only after the purges produced regular firing squads did disenchantment appear. It engulfed "Yankee" correspondents and commentators, who longed to see readjustment for Cuba on the basis of parliamentary practice.

Their problem was manifold: Political naivete, "Quiet American" aspirations, and expulsion from Cuba for any persistent digging and reporting tinged with criticism of the regime. The overhanging threat of expulsion from any totalitarian-run state always is a recurring problem for journalists. It never is for experts —they make judgments most often from their own base of operations.

Many of these minds, disillusioned with Castro or with their own vagaries, contended they never really heard that he was a Communist. Yes, his brother Raoul was known to be one and so was the saturnine tactical architect of the Cuban rebellion Dr. Ernesto ("Che") Guevara, originally an Argentine physician, who is now dead, slain in Bolivia. This kind of logic is inexplicable. If the immediate numbers two and three are avowed Communists, how then can the number one be uninfluenced?

We are not engaged here in dealing with the in-fighting and defection of elements that supported Castro in expelling Batista. The purpose is to show the fiction and misinformation that was circulated as the real measure of the man and situation.

Among a sizable number of others, one of the authors asked Castro quite early in his rule whether he was a Communist. "I believe implicitly in Communist practice as it is known," he replied without hesitation. For some time before this remark, not very startling to anyone who'd taken the time to ferret out something about Dr. Castro's beliefs in earlier discussions, Matthews remained adamant. To Matthews and his newspaper, Fidel Castro was the best phenomenon in Latin America for many generations. This led, in a short time, to some bitter conflict on the *Times* Olympian editorial board. While factionalism fired up on the paper, Matthews's own colleagues remembered cuttingly some of the wretched bloopers he had dropped in his career.

Perhaps Matthews is fascinated with the multifarious forms of authoritarianism. The *Times* loyally defended Matthews as a correspondent and until his retirement retained him as a distinguished member of its editorial board. For that, its clever advertising slogan —"I got my job through *The New York Times*"—has been turned around by critics to show Castro making it to employment the same way.

The Matthews voice is rather a whisper these days, if it's raised at all about Cuba. But Fidel Castro's voice and that of his immediate entourage is heard around the world. The only omission is Che Guevara's. He simply vanished to an unmarked grave. Castro, having paid comradely tribute to Che, doesn't seem to mind. He is the total center of attention. Why his challenges are mainly ignored today is a mystery. Is it that in the United States we are incapable of paying any real heed to Latin Americans, be they friends, critics, or enemies?

When Castro's radio in Havana announced its own schools for guerrilla warfare and subversion, it attracted bare minimum attention. The facts in existence for nearly two years before the broadcast were Cuba's infiltration into Africa, South America, and Asia. The African intrusion by Castro is one of the most amazing of all Communist world activities. Cuba, a have-not nation, has around five hundred troops and military specialists in Brazzaville (ex-French Congo). That's just across the crocodile-infested, sluggish Congo river from Leopoldville (ex-Belgian).

Little love exists between the two regimes on opposite sides of the river. Brazzaville, which has a big Red Chinese mission, keeps Castro Cubans as an elite guard for its regime. It all began in the summer of 1965. The fall of Ben Bella in Algiers prompted the Cuban Ambassador Servera Riveri to move with staff to Brazzaville. The transfer was worked out in advance with both Soviet *and* Chinese intermediaries. It's on the record. Examine Havana Radio monitoring reports. Propaganda? The State Department has voluminous records of East Europeans discussing this. The Yugoslavs, who compelled the Cuban delegation to a conference to park pistols outside the hall, were astounded by Castro in Africa.

In any case, Castro's people moved into the palace of President Mssamba-Debat. When an army *coup* was attempted against him in June, 1966, the special Cuban palace guard stopped it. Castro's regime, so poor remember, also offered two hundred scholarships to Brazzaville. These went to medical and agricultural students of a country whose population is only 800,000. In return, Castro was granted the option of reinforcing his praetorian guard, thousands of miles from Latin America. That isn't the end of the Castro story in underdeveloped Africa.

He was extremely busy in Ghana, too, with Nkrumah's approval. Yet what business has a self-acclaimed "revolutionary" regime, which has not put its own house in order, spending money far away? The best educated guess—from Latin Americans and Africans—is that Castro is determined to show that nothing can stop his own locomotive.

When the Cuban Embassy was closed in Ghana in September, 1966, some of its tentacular activities came to light. A substantial documented brief of the operations was supplied by Dr. Leonel Alonso. He had been charge d'affaires in Lebanon before defecting earlier that year. As a former minister to Ghana, 1961 and 1962, Dr. Alonso said that he was in the midst of a subversion campaign for "the whole of Africa." The timing is most interesting. Castro undertook a role in fomenting disorder in Africa only two years after reaching power in Cuba and before the missile crisis rocked the world. For some reason, Dr. Alonso's revelations about Cuban operations in Africa got the scantest possible publicity. Latin American experts had always contended that Castro's work in Africa was strictly show.

They also were dismissed with a fine wave of arrogant condescension by Dr. Arthur Schlesinger, Jr. Historian and counselor on Latin American developments to President Kennedy and for a time to President Johnson, Schlesinger had contempt for Castro's abilities. He knew comparatively very little of Latin America, indeed of the rest of the world (outside the United States), which he skims lightly. In his subjective assessment of life and living in faraway places, Dr. Schlesinger ignored the capacity of Castro to cause grief.

But Dr. Alonso was able to tell unemotionally of some of the more jarring episodes. He said that planeloads of subversive African elements from half-a-dozen countries were taken to Cuba. They were trained in guerrilla warfare and "liberation" tactics. In addition to stepping up activity in Brazzaville, Castro's regime decided to provide maximum support to the "liberation" movement in Portuguese Guinea. Castro, so supposedly absorbed with his own hemispheric affairs, regards that organization as one of the better-organized in Africa.

When trained units in early 1964 swooped into the somnolent island of Zanzibar, hard on Nyerere's Tanganyika, there was brief Western reaction. Mostly it was confined to the idea that the Sultan should have been deposed long before save for British protection. What was nearly ignored were declarations of thanks from some of the "revolutionaries." They thanked Castro for having harbored them and supplied them with the necessary hardware and cash to make their *coup* possible.

Castro has never relaxed in his objective to prove that he is the center of gravity for introducing his social justice into all Latin America. He has put men and money—no sign of loosening up yet—into Venezuela. There, one of the most decent governments of the hemisphere, that of Dr. Romulo Betancourt, had to fight for its life. Abductions of officials, including United States mission personnel, hailed a rule of terror. After years of misrule and corruption, Betancourt had succeeded in providing Venezuela with a proper format for its future.

The Communists would not stand idly by to see implementation of a national program to allow for human dignity and removal of many basic social and economic inequalities. They even tried—by the gun and the machete—to terrorize the national elections for a successor to Betancourt. That they failed is only a tribute to Betancourt's perseverance and the solid foundations he emplaced for Venezuelans at large. Still, Castro fiercely whips up demand for intrusion in other sister Latin American nations. Peru, which has an enlightened government under President Fernando Belaunde Terry, combats both last-ditch oligarchy influence and Communist guerrilla depredations.

In the January, 1966, Tri-Continental Solidarity conference in Havana, the Peruvian Communist party allowed that the Belaunde regime was making things tougher for Communists inside and outside Peru. The delegation discussed its plight at length with Castro and his leading ideologists. Then it came up in the conference with a remarkable formula, which the Czechoslovak party paper *Rude Pravo* quoted: "The Communist Party supports the guerrilla movement, although the Peruvian Communists do not consider that there is a revolutionary situation in the country."

This fitted neatly into Castro's triumphal prediction back in 1961. He prophesied at the time that the whole Andean Range in South America would be for revolutionaries what the Sierra Maestra had been for his Cuban movement. To that purpose Castro also diverted funds, specialists, and munitions. In the Andes, it has been virtually the opposite of the Castro prediction. Juan de Onis, a *New York Times* correspondent who is a reporter of hard facts rather than a rambling reformer, reported from Colombia that Latin-American counterinsurgency blunted Castro.

This was five years after Castro heralded his views of the future for the hemisphere. His contribution was enormous, considering Cuba's poverty.

"Self-style guerrilla forces of National Liberation—using Cuban tactics, often led by revolutionaries trained in Cuba and financed by Communist movements abroad—have been destroyed, as in Peru, or have been seriously crippled and are on the run, as in Colombia and Venezuela." De Onis, who made this assessment on the basis of digging, also pointed out that the Communists in Latin America will continue to employ guerrilla operations. They are bound, through sustained unrest, to compel thought to tend in the direction of putting an end to the trouble. In the end, by generally withdrawing and recoiling from the problem the field is wide open to intellectual expert advice, as it has been in Vietnam.

But the Latin American nations directly concerned have already proved that the Communist myth of inevitable victory for guerrillas is a propaganda tale. In midsummer of 1966, Castro delivered a long, discursive speech. It added up to an exhortation for fresh "revolutionary action." But the Latin American governments, afflicted with his Cuban financed, armed intruders proved on the twilight field of guerrilla war that they can cope adequately. What is baffling, however, is that so few expert, emotional, or fair-play voices ever protest in the United States against the avowed attempts by Castro to bring down other governments. These governments, moreover, have proved themselves infinitely more efficient than Castro's in clearing up centuries-old political and economic messes.

Nevertheless, their uphill work is sorely beset with having to defend themselves from subversion deliberately introduced from the outside. The Soviet Union, of course, has upheld all such armed operations as "justifiable wars of liberation." When the on-again, off-again East-West thaw appears, neither Khrushchev nor his successors ever have repudiated that rallying call of comrades. It is most instructive to examine just a few key places in Latin America where guerrilla warfare keeps aiming at a government that has given no offense to Castro. Take Colombia, as a starter. The military and police drastically reduced rural banditry, political and otherwise, in four years. The total Communist guerrilla strength at the end of 1966 was estimated at 150. But Colombian forces lost about 400 killed in that period, beginning in 1962. That was a few months after Castro made his prediction for the Andes.

One of the major counterinsurgency clashes in Colombia—which, alas, got little notice—occurred in midsummer, 1966. An army patrol suffered fifteen killed and fifteen wounded in an ambush. It was a trap set by a guerrilla band led by Pedro Marin. He is better known as *Tiro Fijo,* or Sure Shot. Starting out as a rural outlaw, Sure Shot, by his own declarations, is oriented to Castro. Some of his lieutenants have been trained in Cuba. Cases of automatic arms destined for him have been captured. They were of Czechoslovakian manufacture and had been transshipped via Cuba.

Some of the most spectacular and effective counterinsurgency has been achieved in Peru. In terrible terrain high in the Andes, Peruvian units in seven months smashed operations mounted by Cuban-trained guerrillas. The insurgents appeared in 1965. They were led in two bands, totalling around eighty. At their head was Luis de la Puente Uceda, a Marxist-minded lawyer. With him was Guillermo Lobaton, who studied political science at the Sorbonne in Paris. They also spent time in Havana as did some of the guerrillas who turned up with them in the Andes. Their operations followed the guerrilla textbook techniques of Che Guevara.

In remote regions the joint guerrilla leaders set up a network of camps. They bought supplies and some arms for which they deliberately paid handsome prices to impoverished peasants and Indians. The Indians were of the Campa tribe, disgruntled and dissident. After base camps were secure, the guerrillas attacked a rural police patrol. They gunned down seven policemen. The victims were totally innocent men, none of whom ever had been fingered for abuse. But the attack followed the text set down by Che Guevara.

Once word got back of the mass assault, Peruvian forces went into action. President Belaunde, quick to recognize that his program for gradual reform was at stake, made an emergency area in the mountains. Police and the military, in coordinated moves, sealed off the guerrilla-inflamed region. That was to deny outside support. Into the emergency belt filtered government intelligence agents. They persuaded local populations—without the pressure of reprisal—to simply avoid contact with the guerrillas.

Into the main mountainous area the elite Peruvian Ranger Battalion was summoned. It had been in counterinsurgency training for five years. The Rangers tracked down dispersing guerrillas. All told, Peruvian security lost thirty men. It keeps mum on how many guerrillas were seized or shot. The peasants, who know the mountains and men involved, say that both guerrilla leaders were killed. Most of their men were reported dead. Only a handful of prisoners were seen alive.

The United States is directly implicated, but only in the sense of helicopter supply and other military assistance hardware. Some United States technicians service the choppers. But the combat against guerrillas is strictly by Latin Americans. Peru, Venezuela, and Colombia, to name the leaders in the field, combine mobility, good field communications, intelligence, and specially trained anti-guerrilla units. They have benefitted, so some of their commanders said, from cost in lives and treasure in Vietnam, which is far from being just an infiltration struggle. Because of the homogeneity of the country under attack, its determined leadership, and gradualist reform, the government obtains sound intelligence. Armed forces are in quick contact with isolated rural communities. This is managed via social and economic improvement projects or civil action. The civil administration on a national scale runs the whole show.

Sooner than later, the issue of United States-supplied helicopters and technicians will become a testy problem. Oppositionists in a given country of Latin America are certain to contend we do it for a price—namely, exploitation and indebtedness of the ruling regime to Washington. It is quite likely in some cases to come, where the government, feeling secure, tells us to leave the helicopters but to pack up and leave. This particular source of military supply can only become something about which to barter for influence, blackmail, and the real ultimate objective, power.

There is no ready-made answer or guaranteed outcome. It can be distorted out of perspective, abused by the power elite, and even turned against us because of latent xenophobia. To eliminate this type of assistance at this stage also is no answer. Pledges cannot be frivolously made and removed in cavalier fashion. But the entire concept—once some basis of equitable stability is achieved—must be reviewed and certainly recast in terms of pragmatism and human frailty.

The United States must take another hard look at sociological, political, and economic winds of change sweeping key and poorer Latin American nations. Rocky regimes need more than military transfusions to keep alive. Closer than Peru to the site of Castro's own power, in Guatemala, Communist-run guerrillas are a serious menace again. Their takeover bid was repelled in 1954 when Jacobo Arbenz was forced to flee. For the successor regime, the United States government was accused of complicity and coopera- tion. The CIA was shown to have a big hand in the anti-Arbenz operations. They were successful. Yet only twelve years after Arbenz went off to nurse his savings accounts in Switzerland, the present government of Julio Cesar Mendez Montenegro is in grave trouble. Mendez is trying to fight the guerrillas with reforms and the entrenched old economic oligarchy fights reforms.

Thus, in tiny Guatemala—population under four million, half illiterate—the critical battle of the Alliance for Progress is already joined. When the Alliance was launched by President Kennedy in March, 1961, Fidel Castro's rise to power had as much to do with it as the age-old, cumulative economic and social inequalities. The United States switched in Latin America in the spring of 1961 to a diplomacy that incorporated the social revolution. It was not in support of a Latin American *status quo*. Castro managed to make of Latin America, to quote President Kennedy, "the most critical area in the world today." The Alliance for Progress was the most revolutionary foreign policy pronouncement affecting Latin America.

"The Soviet camp could no longer claim monopoly of concern for social change," wrote Dr. Federico G. Gil. He is professor of Political Science and Director of Latin American Studies at the University of North Carolina.

We became the champions of reform. But the step-by-step work in Latin America, the insistence on moderation and gradualism, enabled the monopolies and old-line oligarchies to undercut and divert the alliance's work. Unfortunately, the glamour, even with a multibillion-dollar new Alliance, was not in Latin America. Only when revolts flared or named politicians were threatened by a real or fancied *junta* was our attention diverted—slightly. As a nation, we looked outside either to Europe, or to the Far East with primary attention on Vietnam.

Emphasis on the war in Vietnam is a normal, human concentra- tion. But newspapers, radio, TV, and our Congress in Washington did little to at least correct the distorted image of emerging Latin America to the outside world. What effect can a world "expert" like Senator Fulbright stir at a TV-illuminated hearing on counter-insurgency in Peru? It just isn't jazzy enough. Since TV and newspaper expertise on Latin America are still counted as a white-gloved honor guard, we get background and comment only about a fiasco, but not about what made it one. It is quite remarkable that a British Labour government bill like a wage freeze can command literally fifty times the space and comment in the United States that is given to the upheaval in Guatemala. At worst, the coming showdown may sabotage the Alliance for Progress in Central America. The best we can hope for presently is a Communist slowdown there.

President Kennedy launched the Alliance as a cooperative effort. The United States pledged its financial resources to raise life and living standards in Latin America. Its scope, as set out in 1961, is vast. To cooperate, every Latin American nation must also help itself. How? By introducing the necessary structural reforms to raise standards.

Guatemala needed money badly in the winter of 1966. If anything, it is in more desperate shape today. A government program to tax gross incomes hit propertied groups. The money President Mendez sought to raise was modest even in a poor country like Guatemala: Around fifty to sixty million dollars annually. The total would cover investment funds to meet the minimum Alliance target of 2.5 per cent net growth a year. New taxation would cover about one-fifth of the amount; the remainder to come from abroad in loans and investment capital in the country.

What happened? The tiny slice of Guatemalan society that represents money balked. The whole tax plan, it shouted, was an imposition. In the United States, certainly in Western Europe, this defiance would certainly provoke government action with the broadest possible base of mass support. The pro-Communist Arbenz regime, removed with United States active assistance, had not intended to provide the oligarchy in Guatemala with a blank check. Certainly, the Alliance for Progress expressly warned against such semifeudal concepts.

But the wealth-producing elements showered the country and peoples abroad with propaganda. The material pretended to show that what Mendez tried to do was Communist-inspired. Here is where the ultraconservatives always manage, in their blind anger, to serve a Castro machine. Necessary structural reform is anathema to them. The authors once heard their views expressed by Barry Goldwater at a small luncheon. In the serious manner he has, Goldwater observed that military *juntas* were a good thing. They represented stability. Maybe they did, in a transitory way, about thirty-odd years ago. Winds of change blow strongly in Latin America, too. But the pilot case for the Alliance in Guatemala teeters precariously. When the Mendez government took office in the summer of 1966 there were strong accusations that it was Communist-oriented.

Governments brought back after the ouster of Arbenz were not distinguished in grappling with the internal problem. They just bought time for the class with cash. It is scarcely the way in which to build support and strength to combat Communist subversion among a have-not people. The glittering examples of Betancourt in Venezuela and Belaunde in Peru—with built-in oligarchies to protest policies—showed the empirical path to reform.

The Guatemalan government tried the gesture of reconciliation with underground guerrilla forces. It failed quickly because the leaders of the antigovernment movement believe they can take over, reasonably soon. So Mendez called on the military to fight them. At the same time, he pushed reforms in what, for Guatemala, is a vast area. There are two columns opposing him: one represented by the guerrillas abetted by Castro, the other by the antireform oligarchy. The third column, on which the future of Guatemala rests, is the still-uncommitted mass of Guatemalans. They still watch—and wait.

This drama, spun out so painfully, has passed largely unnoticed by our experts, inside and outside government. They also were remarkable for their silence on a high-level church meeting that could be the turning point of awakening Roman Catholic church interest in Latin American changes. For a week in early autumn, the Latin American Episcopal Council—*Celam,* by its Spanish initials—met at Mar del Plata in Argentina. Its participants, prelates from the hemisphere, were rather studiously ignored. Perhaps the kindest reason was that Mar del Plata is 250 miles south of Buenos Aires. Moreover, the conference organizers successfully resisted efforts by military strongman, General Juan Carlos Ongania, to have himself closely associated.

In 1955 Celam came into existence as an effective force. It was created through the strenuous efforts of perhaps the two most dynamic bishops of the Southern Hemisphere—Dom Helder Camara, Archbishop of Olinda and Recife in Brazil, and Monsignor Manuel Larrain, from Chile. The Monsignor, unfortunately, died earlier in 1966 in an automobile accident. Dom Helder Camara has been undeterred for years in calling attention to the sprawling area of underprivilege, poverty, and disease to which he spiritually ministers. In that festering, fermenting territorial district locally bred and Castro-assisted discontent is easily provoked.

Despite his and his late associate's efforts, Celam did not appear to be moving fast enough for the new spirit in the Vatican. The reason for delay was in the stubbornness of the conservative priests, standing by established interests. So blinkered was their outlook that Pope Paul, in November, 1965, exhorted the Latin American bishops to take a more active part in the process of social change in the hemisphere. As a result, a special meeting of Celam was summoned. Its debated theme was "The active presence of the church in the development and integration of Latin America." Although invited, the Cuban hierarchy sent no representatives. But bishops from nineteen nations attended. The meeting was amazingly realistic. Yet, despite a veil of privacy, little of the conference resolutions and attitudes was ever reported and reviewed. Such information was easy enough to acquire—from several of the participants and from the Vatican. In the United States, where there should have been some detailed comment and background from even church papers, the conference, which reached historic conclusions, received rather sparse treatment.

A final declaration of the meeting was: "The Latin American episcopate considers that the integration of Latin America . . . constitutes an indispensable instrument for the harmonious development of the region. . . . The integration which we desire and support must be the fruit of a genuine effort in each of our countries to integrate the marginalized sectors [meaning *the poor*], in all countries to enable them to participate in the political, cultural, and economic life which contemporary civilization ought to give them."

Without knowing where it derived, Guatemalan propertied people dismissed the conclusion as "Communist propaganda." But another passage in the conferring bishops declaration said: "The necessity of organizing dynamic production and just distribution at Latin America's present stage of growth demands a profound overhaul of the socio-economic structure at three levels: individual property, companies and corporations, and the state." The bishops added tersely: "Integration and development are complementary and inseparable factors, and that development is the modern name for peace."

In toto, the conclusions reached by the bishops are revolutionary in gradualist form. They provide additional proof of a growing alliance between priests and technocrats of modern mental design. The challenge is clear. It is thrown down to the present authority of military-supported technocrats in Brazil and the Argentine. The ideas advocated by the conference underwrite the concepts of Dom Helder Camara. His theme, hated by conservative Latin American Catholics, contends that Latin America's quasi-feudal poor should and must be made conscious of their plight—and the reasons for it. Strong medicine.

To reinforce the bishops' conference position, Dom Candido Padim was appointed head of the educational department of Celam. He had been appointed in 1962 in Brazil as episcopal representative to Catholic youth movements. When he was found to be consistently siding with the students, Dom Candido was withdrawn. The pressure came from the government and conservative clerical groups. He was "difficult" because he supported economic and social reform as a first measure to deflect Communist infiltration.

Both Brazilian prelates and their advocates are highly suspect by Brazilian leaders. They are a military government that continues to call itself "the revolution." In a methodical manner it concentrates on institutionalizing itself so that a civilian political machine could emerge. Then it could run Brazil for twenty years. The principal instrument of consolidation is the official National Renovating Alliance party. It is called ARENA, rather symbolic of the free-for-all of politics in Brazilian life. When General Artur da Costa e Silva was elected in the near-winter of 1966, nobody paid any attention. It was a foregone conclusion it would happen.

Fatalistic resignation has been part of the scenery in Latin America too long. Silva, the kind of tough career officer the Brazilian army breeds, took over from another officer. He is Marshal Humberto Castelo Branco, elfin in looks, but steely in style. Branco seized control early in 1964, when the country seemed on the rock of despair and disintegration. His was a *coup,* in the venerated name of "revolution." Essentially it was a reaction to incompetence, flaccid leftist-leanings, and indecision by then President Joao Goulart. Before him there had been a strange, unhappy man Janio, Quadros, who, fed up, abdicated through resignation.

Almost all the preceding generation had been dominated by the dictator Getulio Vargas. Even an early successor, now a darling of our coterie of writing Latinists, Juscelino Kubitschek, was elected President as a Vargas man. The army, intervening strategically, rid Brazil of both sponsor and protégé. Vargas committed suicide. Kubitschek sits in Portugal, sending home guided missives of democratic hope and thought.

As the largest and most populous state in South America— around sixty-eight million people—Brazil has persistently been paid less attention than, say Belgium or Holland. Rio de Janeiro is no longer the capital, but "Rio" has a certain magical draw. Dances and fiestas get confused with the mention of Brazil, except for nuts. Even the new capital at Brasilia is barely known to many of our sterling Congressional members who say they steep themselves in foreign affairs. Worse, only the *coup d'etat,* bringing in Castelo Branco, and a rumble in the poverty-prostrated Northeast get some instant expertise in our press and television.

Broadly speaking, the Castelo Branco "revolution" won favor in Washington. At the time almost anything but Fidel Castro would have achieved the same. Brazil was in the throes of galloping inflation and monstrous maladministration. The *coup* regime, pledging an ultimate return to civil government, also promised to curb inflation and root out Communism and corruption. The step to authoritarianism was firm and short. Old political parties were banned. Political rights, like those of ex-President Kubitschek, were denied for ten years.

But inflation has been whittled down. It has been chopped from an annual level of 144 per cent during Goulart's time to about 35 per cent in 1966. Simultaneously, the gross national product has climbed, reaching about 6 per cent at the end of 1966. Reforms have been pursued in banking and taxation which have benefitted the national revenue immensely. A huge public works program has been undertaken to assist the entire nation. Its principal, and laudable, effort is in the ferociously poor Northwest. After that, nobody ever suggests what lies ahead.

None of these (stolid but vital) alterations is in the nature of a glamour project. It doesn't get the pitiless examination of our official and advisory experts as would denial of certain civil rights, always overlooked in the search for "liberalization" in Communist-ruled countries. Infrequent but most useful assessments are provided by regional specialists like Nicholas Raymond and Winthrop Carty, editors of *Vision*. They are not involved with the demonology of the continent but only in what happened and why. Automatically, this realistic approach excludes them from acceptance into the circle of experts.

Chapter 22

LATIN AMERICA: PART TWO

J UAN DOMINGO PERON, paunchily comfortable now that he is
well launched into his seventies, dreams nostalgically from exile
on a plain in Spain about bouncing back to power. The triumphal
return, of course, is to the Argentine. For ten years Peron and his
chic late consort, Eva Duarte Peron, ran Argentina—nearly into
the ground. Peron, remarried to another young, attractive lady,
Isabellita, seems to be the center of all major upheavals in his
old homeland. So much so, as a matter of fact, that every military
takeover and threat to civil government stirs the bogey of Peron
charging back from exile.

It was, so the military assured its mismanaged nation, to prevent
Peron and Peronism that President Arturo Illia and his civil administration were booted. On June 29, 1966, Illia was removed from
office. He had been charged with corruption. If so, he personally
wasn't guilty. Shattered, Illia now depends on handouts from
friends. The brassy exile, Peron lives with a huge retinue in a villa.
He manages in the style, to which he became accustomed as the
Argentine dictator, from mammoth funds stashed in Switzerland.

Not only was Illia's administration corrupt, thundered the military, but he was plotting with Peronists to make a deal for their
support. Illia, in desperation, was talking to some of Peron's supporters in the trade unions. The military, which forced out Peron
back in 1955, also had been engaged in clandestine talks with the
same elements. Pro-Peronists, nevertheless, approved the military
takeover. This *coup* used slogans from "revolution" to civilian
administration with military support. Into power was swept be-
mustached, retired General Juan Carlos Ongania. Surprisingly,
because of Peronist acceptance, the new general leader attracted
overwhelming public approval. He dismantled all constitutional
forms swiftly.

There was absolutely no fuss in the takeover. After the bloody intramural conflict of the military in 1962–1963, Ongania had the total support of all the once-fratricidal armed forces chief. He said he would introduce strong measures. Today he is accepted as a "strong man." Argentine people, from childhood, are taught to believe that their country is one of the richest in the world. It probably should be, but always descends into an economic tailspin.

Then United States policy, backed by the expert determinism of a group of self-perpetuating experts on the area, rushed in with a loan, credits—and support for the military. (These experts were led by Tom Mann, a career diplomat who became an L.B.J. favorite and an assistant Secretary of State.) The irony is that the official United States operational view of Argentina is diametrically contrary to the aspirations and recommendations laid down by the Alliance for Progress. It puts a crimp into ideas and work in Peru and Chile, for example. In the occasional note taken of hemispheric affairs by our national magazines, *Time* and *Newsweek,* it's ho-hum, another military *junta.* But, the regime in Argentina has more solidity than any of the previous ones. So, the assessment runs and General Ongania heads unhindered into autocracy. The whole episode was ignited by our writing experts. On the diplomatic front, the experts only saw stability.

Yet it isn't terribly different from directions taken by Peron. The major difference is nearly a generation, and the techniques vary. The threadbare arguments offered in behalf of support for the Ongania regime is that all civilian governments in Argentina in man's memory terminated in fiasco and economic ruin. It is the same argument that can easily be applied to military directorates, even when they use the tissue-thin excuse of civilian government with military support. Interestingly, it was the embodiment of an idea the corpulent old dictator, Peron, lofted from his luxury villa in suburban Madrid.

The trouble with Peron's plan was that it was grabbed in Buenos Aires by another general. After all, who in the outside world ever heard of any other Argentine officer except Peron? All our own experts on the country, our mass publications, and our Latin America affairs counselors always dug up Peron as a horrible example. At his command post in the big villa, Peron dreamed of becoming the de Gaulle of not only Argentina but Latin America. The old Peronist organization, the amorphous labor groups he called "shirtless," has a fresh, young leader. His name is Augosto Vandor. When he was a marine corporal, Vandor had a charming nickname, "The Wolf."

Either through miscalculation or cynical belief that the plot wouldn't work—Vandor himself gave the latter idea currency—Peron in early 1965 was persuaded to try to return in triumph. He didn't get very far and nearly endangered his safe sanctuary with Spanish dictator Generalissimo Franco. Rid of Peron for good, the Peronists could maneuver for themselves at home. Through the largest union association, the Confederacion Géneral del Trabajo (CGT), Peronist manipulators like Vandor made their contacts. Also they deliberately left striking dock workers in the lurch.

Power was what the Peronist leaders, shorn happily of Peron, wanted. Either a share or recognition of support. Little of this wheeling dealing has, alas, ever been made public. Peronists, when Ongania took over, chortled that they liked generals, whether it was Peron or anyone else. As a starter they got admirals, too. Ongania named generals and admirals to sixteen of the twenty-two provincial governorships. Subordinate officers, colonels and majors, were appointed to a big proportion of other key administrative jobs.

An excuse offered for Ongania's sort of staff appointments, after he dissolved national and state parliaments and abolished political parties, was that he didn't have a wide acquaintance with civilians. His outside-the-army contacts were with the Church. Those were almost entirely the rock-ribbed, do-nothing clerics criticized by the Celam conference in Argentina four months after Ongania took control. The drive toward autocracy in Argentina also leads to the never-never land of the corporate state. Evidence is beginning to build up in this direction. There is no Communist internal menace of any substantive nature which Ongania has admitted. Argentina is fortunate in that respect. At the rate Ongania is setting the ground rules, he will create a Communist bogey, real or fancied.

Instead of reconciling all elements, which he pledged, Ongania appointed some strange personalities to places of ultrasensitive trust. One of the most notorious has been Dr. Enrique Martinez Paz. Minister of the interior, he aroused much world suspicion and scared locals stiff. Martinez received nationalist toughs of the *sub-rosa* organization that calls itself "Tacuara." It has a sordid record of vicious Jew-baiting. With pockets of old but well-heeled Nazis—Eichmann was found in Argentina—Tacuara never has to worry for funds and advice. Ongania sought to reassure the Chief Rabbi of Argentina. He said the government was not anti-Semitic. Then he sent personal greetings to the Jewish community for the Jewish New Year. In Egypt Nasser also visits a synagogue but employs Nazis on missile projects designed to destroy Israel. Argentine Jews are more disturbed today than at any time since Peronists staged anti-Semitic riots with the benevolence of their sainted leader.

Peronists, who see Jews as leading architects of Argentina's economic difficulties, have hastened publicly to show on what good terms they are with Ongania. The government, of course, wants a single responsible organization that represents labor. A parallel development would be setting one up for management. That, too, is in the Ongania tactical book. Moreover, since Ongania banned politics, he requires a friendly labor set-up. Virtually all Peronist labor leaders are politicians.

"By talking with them, Ongania is talking with the most powerful political force in the country," wrote Mrs. Gladys Delmas. Her perceptive editorials are heard over the Canadian Broadcasting Company. She travels widely in Latin America but except for an occasional literate piece in smaller and more sober United States periodicals, her work is known only to Canadian audiences. Anyway, to make the first giant stride towards a *modus vivendi* with the Peronists, Ongania took a little of his imposed lid off inflation. He gave the metal workers a big raise. Industry obtained a huge credit to pay it. And who was there to sign in the President's office? Vandor, "The Wolf," even wearing an unhabitual necktie for the occasion.

The result has been that Argentine labor ignores other trade union demands. It has gone so far as to turn its back against the decree that, in effect, outlaws strikes. These have been the acts that tame labor served for Mussolini and are part of the fiction, in Communist regimes, that workers cannot strike against themselves. Handmaiden to the approach to corporate-state rule is the enthusiastic regime acknowledgment of nationalism. It always existed in a loose fashion in the Argentine. Now Ongania's administrators set about to cultivate and use it as their own weapon.

Resurgent, organized nationalism, as Mrs. Delmas has pointed out, has led to a campaign for Argentina to withdraw from the Latin American Free Trade Area. The danger in such a wrecking operation also is a deep divergence settling into the Alliance for Progress. Argentine nationalists are active today, declaring they are opposed to the sharing roles that economic integration implies. They demand an independent industrial complex—within their own frontiers. This also underlines a nationalist jealousy, which grows and centers on Brazil. The nationalist concern, spoken openly by the Ongania regime, worries about being outbid by Brazil. It is talk that openly mentions the status of big power. If this happened in Europe, expert articles would appear, and the State Department immediately questioned. There has been hardly a mention in this case.

Yet the glamour again does not repose in the factual examination of what the Ongania operation is all about. The expert Latinists have obviously decided that turmoil can't occur soon in Argentina. Peronist leaders have made their own deal with the regime. Besides, by definition, experts and their intellectual advisers inevitably accept authority, particularly the authoritarian type. This was largely behind the outcry of commingled passion and indignation over our intervention in the Dominican Republic.

In the last ten years the Dominican Republic, which shares the Caribbean island of Hispaniola with prostrate, incredibly poor, and voodoo-ridden Haiti, has been a special grail for self-important American liberals and their expert apologists. It began in the last years before the pint-sized, long-time dictator Rafael Trujillo was assassinated. A New York lawyer, whose name for years headed the causes of civil liberties, undertook an inquiry to exonerate Trujillo of the charges of abduction and assassination of an exile. Morris L. Ernst headed the inquiry. It must have been a very expensive kind of investigation as well as long and complicated. What happened? Trujillo got a bill of health from the Ernst findings. The fact that Ernst even lent himself to being retained by Trujillo's public relations firm was excused by his supporters on the grounds that he was motivated by humanitarian, objective facts. When Franklin D. Roosevelt, Jr., Liberal party candidate for New York governor in 1966, was on the Trujillo payroll, there were some sneers. His shocked colleagues on the professional liberal line suggested sanctimoniously that Roosevelt, Jr., did it—for money.

What followed in turbulent post-Trujillo days—after the cruel, little dictator was assassinated—became rival partisan movements. Into the power vacuum, experts and even homegrown civil rights reformers flocked. Trujillo had been slain only a few months after what has become known in contemporary history as the Bay of Pigs fiasco. Castro, the defiant Marxist David, crowed triumphantly in Cuba. Another dictatorship, but not endowed with the laurel wreath of "left," had been removed in rather nearby Santo Domingo.

Trujillo was gone. Democracy was on its way. A white-haired academician, Juan Bosch, became the first post-Trujillo constitutional President. He was acclaimed by the experts. Bosch was possessed of a cluttered but often agile intellect. His reflections, therefore, endeared him to expertise reform, which airily dismissed nearly five hundred years of misrule, despotism, and the infiltration work of Castro and his henchmen. He also had been in exile thirty-two years. Bosch was a resounding failure. He was a nice guy, but he simply did not know how to cope with the problems that swarmed over the Dominican Republic.

Years of exile had left Bosch in a twilight world of unreality. He had in Puerto Rico, for instance, spent countless hours discussing with peripatetic intellectual ailments inherent in his homeland and Latin America, generally. Bosch and his interlocutors were playing the power game so dearly cherished by intellectual experts: Implementing by a turn of phrase reforms they conceived without regard to the realities of the resources and the countryside.

Exile, too, had produced an errant Machiavellian quality in Bosch. He looked upon intrigue—still does—as a means of maintaining the necessary balance of power. Any other representative of a power structure—principally that of the United States—he fancied would just as soon try to out-intrigue him, Thus, Bosch never has understood that the Kennedy-appointed ambassador to the Dominican Republic, John Bartlow Martin, earnestly wanted to cooperate with him. Martin, a magazine writer of meticulous reportorial qualities, never could hit it off with Bosch. The then-Dominican President's suspicions and intrigues always skirted down-to-earth issues.

In his book *Overtaken by Events,* Martin said, somewhat sadly, that Bosch's maneuvers and "very real failures to meet the people's needs" invited the counterscheming military to stage a *coup.* Out went Bosch, back to exile in Puerto Rico. But the *coup* by no means solved the plight of the upside-down island republic. Bosch had, in his intrigues with a combination of political and military forces, left behind pockets of power bent on seizing control. Within these combustible caches were agents infiltrated from Cuba. In 1965 the anti-*coup* forces laid down a shooting challenge. Regime power reacted. Street fighting became the practice and the United States reacted.

There ensued a series of strange events, in back-stage maneuvers. Leading the proclaimed "progressive" pro-Bosch forces was Colonel Francisco Caamano Deno. He insisted that his forces were "constitutionalist." His number two was a rather glamorous officer, a frogman, Lieutenant Colonel Ramon Montes Aarache. They insisted that the right wing—in Latin America even more than elsewhere, right-wing and left-wing are frequently employed as opposition accusations—provoked civil war. The evidence is that the Dominican Republic's churned-up population of 3,500,-000 was caught up by a Caamano bid for power.

To prevent a Castro-type takeover plus a bloodbath the United States sent in Marines and infantry and kept warships off the Dominican Coast. In Washington, the ineffable chairman of the Senate Foreign Relations Committee and our legislative universal expert, Senator Fulbright, was outraged. The administration, he allowed, was guilty of "overreaction." That was also the gist of hastily-assembled assessments by two flying journalistic experts. They represented a curious combination, Tad Szulc, Polish-born, Latin American-reared correspondent of *The New York Times,* now in Spain, and Barnard Collier, an almost doll-like, articulate Latin affairs reporter for the now-defunct New York *Herald Tribune.* Collier has since gone to the *Times*—as a correspondent in Latin America. Presently he is in New York.

It had always been an accepted matter of tradition and competition that *Herald Tribune* correspondents and those of the *Times* do not engage in journalistic togetherness. For the old *Trib* it was a matter of survival in gathering news to avoid such a combination. The idea always had been for a *Trib* reporter to try and get as much as possible on his own. Then, by better judgment and infinitely superior journalistic writing, he would outdistance the competition. This time, the practice went awry. Szulc and Collier worked together.

They also undertook, on their own initiatives, to visit Bosch in his exile. Why? To try and persuade him that only his return to the riddled Dominican Republic could there be any assurance that tranquility would be restored and the healing process might begin. That this was absolutely no partisan business of any correspondent is inherent in the craft of reporting. Then they journeyed back to the scene of turmoil, and their reports conflicted, to say the least, with much of what was going on. But they were, at home, regarded as experts.

Martin had been persuaded by President Johnson to go back for a while as a special emissary. The Organization of American States (OAS) had met in deliberation and agreed to exercise task-force supervision of factional fighting forces. Both Szulc and Collier, hipped on "progressivism," found only reason in Caamano and sinister motives in any opposing elements, including those of the United States. As serious correspondents, neither ever had any time for or acceptance of a pro-Communist line. But they disliked intensely what they believed was an avowed United States objective to restore to power corrupt and old-fashioned *junta* set-ups.

This was far from the case in the tumultuous mix-up of the Dominican Republic, and in recent years in much of Latin America. Clinging steadfastly to their pro-Bosch determinations, Szulc and Collier went all out to prove their points. They were, to critics at home and abroad of United States policy, "experts." In pillorying United States efforts, including mediation, Szulc called Caamano a well-meaning nationalist. Ex-diplomat Martin, in his book, declared: "I had met no man who I thought might became a Dominican Castro—until I met Caamano. He was winning a revolution from below. He had few political advisers in Santo Domingo at that time but Communists."

Charges of "Communists" were shrugged off by the anti-Communist *Times* and *Tribune* experts as a threadbare attempt to stave off nationalism. They also ignored, in early spring of 1965, the boast of East European mouthpieces about twenty Communist-trained Dominican nationals who were rushed back to work with the Caamano advisory groups. The agents, out of Czechoslovakia and all under the age of thirty, are thought to be still undercover in the Dominican Republic. If the revolt was crushed or dissipated, as it was, they had instructions to estabish an underground network for future use. The papers they carried at the time were assorted Dominican, Haitian, and Cuban passports.

Their training grounds had been ancient Charles University in Prague. They were all subsidized with scholarships, housing, and spending money, beginning in 1963. The university, once a mighty citadel of European learning, under Communist rule has special faculties for Latin American, Asian, African, and Arab students. Africans have occasionally got out of hand in protests against authority. The Latin American student body has, with the exception of the Cubans, carefully avoided public limelight or even university publicity.

Some of those who slipped into the Dominican Republic from Prague were also known to have participated effectively but briefly in revolutionary action with Castro Cubans at Zanzibar in 1964. One of the more outrageous ironies in the assignment of the Czechoslovakian-trained Dominicans was their well-heeled finances for travel: big rolls of United States $100 bills. This was spotted in Mexico City, which some of them used as a transit stopover. Cuban students, who rushed in Prague and other East European communities to volunteer for service in Santo Domingo, were told firmly but politely that their services were not required. They were, to a point, but only for propaganda, which included films of comradely demonstrations and lines of students waving clenched fists.

In the debates that keened fiercely over Washington, almost no attention was paid to the travels of the wrecking squads from Prague. When Colonel Caamano turned up in London as military attaché, after the four-month civil war tailed off in the Dominican Republic, he was supremely confident he'd be recalled. An election would be held and his chosen civilian leader, Bosch, would be elected. So he told us and listed thirty-four "controversial" personalities who were sent off to Dominican diplomatic missions around the world.

During a fairly long talk, in which he modestly talked of his own ambitions—"I will not tolerate an OAS peace force"—Caamano said that the United States was his single greatest source of disillusionment, Why? The United States, in league with a tame OAS and the right wing, were conspiring to prevent elections. That, declared the colonel, was certain to trigger off another civil war. The new explosion, in his confident view, would "embroil" all progressive forces in Latin America. Caamano was wrong on a lot of counts. Elections were held; the favored Bosch was trounced. A moderate conservative, Joaquin Balaguer, was elected President. On balance the vote was unfettered and the only threats came from the Caamono cohorts. "We'll be back," they warned.

Their threat should not be ignored. By the same token the so-called "constitutionalists" want a settlement only on their terms. To the experts like Szulc and Collier, who adopted a side and proceeded to report only that view, former Ambassador Martin has this to say: "I have no doubt whatsoever that there was a real danger of a Communist takeover. Given the circumstances at the time, President Johnson had no choice but to send the troops."

Had Johnson dallied, Martin wrote, Castro-motivated people "would have spread the rebellion throughout the republic and in the end established a Communist-dominated government." Today the last United States soldier has long since gone from the Dominican Republic. The antediluvian right wing, so harshly deprecated by the experts, are scattered. Notably General Elias Wessin y Wessin, the officer who spearheaded the supposed right, has about as little influence from exile abroad. Caamano does, though. His loyal and fervent supporters, many underground, coordinate their work—which is to work against and ultimately overthrow the Belaguer government.

Success in that objective would almost certainly induce another triumph in the eastern portion of Hispaniola, where the wretched Republic of Haiti writhes in the grip of maniacal dictatorshop. A physician, Francois Duvalier, exercising terror and torture runs a benighted, mainly illiterate—85 per cent—country of four million impossibly poor and superstition-wracked people. His private janissaries, called the Tonton Macoute (creole for "bogeyman"), keep the nation in squirming subjugation. Whenever they need extra cash, the Tonton Macoute simply extort money from communities they select.

Elected as a "liberal" in 1957, Dr. Duvalier, called "Papa Doc" to show that he is a man of the people, wrecked the miserable country beyond belief. There is probably today, even in the most backward or deliberately repressed areas of the world, no stretch of real estate in so bad shape as is Haiti. The French were approached by some of Papa Doc's intermediaries a few years ago, after he had himself appointed President for life. Since Haiti had once been a French colony and French was a *lingua franca* for the educated, Duvalier thought he might interest General de Gaulle.

His reasoning was starkly simple. France was embarked on an independent course, which often dislocated American interests. He, Papa Doc, was similarly engaged. Besides, there was an old identity of French culture. Coldly rebuffed—some French diplomats reported that the burden of taking on Haiti was a crime against humanity—Duvalier went on a rampage. He sent his Tonton Macoute out on "reprisal" expeditions. They machine-gunned hundreds of innocent people in their grass and tin hovels. When their ammunition was expended, they attacked families with machetes. Why? Papa Doc had been undermined by people circulating "malicious rumors."

A nation of absolutely have-not mulattoes and Negroes, Haiti is usually known to the outside world only for its weird traditions of voodoo rites. It's about the only facet of life Duvalier permits to go unhindered, and that only until something crops up against him.

The tragedy is that educated Haitians have shown little talent for governing themselves. Correspondingly, through the last hundred years no responsible American government—the United States leading all the rest—has shown any inclination to ameliorate the plight of Haiti.

Late in 1966, the United States approved resumption of economic aid after having withheld it for two years. The original grant was small, less than $1,500,000. More was supposed to follow but has been held up for a good reason. Papa Doc always has managed to get his hands on the lion's share. This he squanders recklessly.

The Duvalier record, for a country Haiti's size, is without parallel for deliberate abrogation of human rights. But none of our experts on Latin America have deemed Haiti sufficiently important for analysis. In the grip of degradation, only when it becomes the center of explosive global attraction will Haiti elicit the instant expertise of our own Latinists.

There is quite another and a tantalizing story deep in the southern hemisphere in a narrow strip of western coastline. It is the story of seven million people who make up Chile. A peaceful revolution, rather terraced gradualism, is converting the country into acceptable egalitarianism. If permitted to develop along the lines pursued by intent and patient President Eduardo Frei, Chile can achieve the middle way that has stamped itself indelibly on Scandinavian countries of the same size. Frei, a Christian Democrat, was elected in 1964. His far-left and far-right opposition combined frequently to undermine him and hold up legislation. His regularized revolution has been conditioned by a minority Christian Democratic representation in the Senate.

Most recently, Frei began making solid inroads into the upper house majority. Pursuit of his Chileanization program enabled the government to buy a minority interest in one of the country's largest copper mines. He has prudently gone about dividing huge land-holdings, many badly mismanaged, into small holdings, but individually owned. In every case where his government encountered roadblocks to legislation, Frei refused to stoop to appeals that he go out to the streets or call on mob demonstrations. In that way, his centrist policies—in much of Latin America they are suspiciously labeled "left"—take the steam out of all Frei opposition. He forced a coalition of the Liberals and Conservatives. Their chief cry is hatred of wretched Bolivia. On the other side of the spectrum, the alliance of Communists and Socialists disagree openly on how to take on Frei's Christian Democrats.

Our experts rarely comment on what Frei has achieved. He has taken away their most potent appeals with all his Christian Democratic internal programs of reform.

A veteran Swiss observer of Communist and Marxist doctrine, Ernst Halperin, approves after long study, on the spot, of Frei's evolutionary methods. Experienced *Neue Zurcher Zeitung* and West German correspondent, Halperin watched and wrote for years about Eastern Europe. The last few years he has concentrated on Latin America, including Cuba, which he visited several times. Halperin amassed the first-hand background and subjective study to comment on Communist trends.

What recently anguished him as did other foreign views was the fresh, crazy-quilt arms race that thundered over Latin America. Both Chile and Peru went after British jet fighters. To top them, as a potential Latin giant, Brazil negotiates with West Germany for about four times the total of the other two countries. The arms trend clashes head-on with a campaign for economic and social reform to lead toward stabilized parliamentary democracy.

The fact that Frei in Chile and Belaunde of Peru, two of the leading gradualist personalities, are in the arms race is disturbing. Why? First, they deny any such competition. All they say they desire is to replace outmoded and unsafe aircraft. In private, though, they have conceded that domestic pressures by their own military and by outside forces—mainly those of the United States—prompted the race. This blame on the United States brings up the whole question of our defense policies concerning Latin America.

The criticism boils down to this: Often ambivalent, the United States maneuvers to maintain Latin forces as a bulwark against Communist subversion and yet to keep those forces out of politics. Frei-Belaunde criticism points to the little-known deal in mid-1965 when the Argentine navy and then the air force began negotiations to buy French Mystere jets. Our Air Force promptly entered the picture. Its argument, known as "controlled escalation," holds that if the United States provided key arms to Latin America, we could maintain greater control over their use and proliferation than we could with purchases from third parties.

Contracts torn from their hands, British and French governments complained bitterly and started a price war as well. There were ironic comments from the European continent about a "sudden United States excess of pacifism."

The military aircraft deals with Europeans have been denounced by Vice President Humphrey and Senator Bobby Kennedy in withering terms. Secretary of State Rusk has been more cautious. He didn't see any pell-mell arms race as yet, but he said the United States wanted to see a "balance of arms." His prudence centers around the aspiration that quite soon there could be an "Inter-American Force," which could be rushed to quell attempted Communist takeovers such as the one launched in the Dominican Republic.

The point is that where defense is essential, none of the Latin American governments can afford ultrasophisticated military hardware without siphoning off large funds from Alliance for Progress reforms. Even in the totalitarian set-up of Fidel Castro, Communist armaments have to be paid for, in cash or kind. His peasantry will be harvesting its sugar quotas for years to come to meet payments for Soviet Union and allied regimes arms deliveries.

Despite their reasons for getting into a jet fighter competition, Frei and Belaunde dismayed emulators and supporters outside their own countries by their acquiescence in the name of expediency. For at least a year, however, all these maneuvers went publicly unnoticed and unpublicized by United States experts. Even when they finally attracted notice, it was most perfunctory. Bobby Kennedy remains the leading critic in the United States. His arguments in the Senate are based almost entirely on high-minded cliches about militarism.

Aside from this potentially pernicious move into armaments,

Frei has achieved glittering results in every other sector. He also controls the Chilean student federation. That makes his the only Latin American government with a majority of students behind it. The Castro regime claims the same. But all Communist governments contend that the students are unanimously behind them. Even twenty-four hours before the uprising exploded in Hungary, that miserable regime claimed student support, which melted the following day. Student unrest in Latin America is very much part of the political scene. We almost never hear of it unless, as in Ecuador in March of 1966, student enmity leads to the overthrow of a traditional military *junta*.

Striving themselves to put the Latin American house in order, delegates of twenty-one countries in Mexico City on February 14, 1967, signed a nuclear-free-zone treaty. It preceded by far the nonproliferation pact about which nuclear powers like the United States, the U.S.S.R., and the United Kingdom propose and counter-offer. The treaty, to be sure, involved states that have no A-weapons. Both the Soviet Union and the United States warned the contracting governments that the nuclear explosions required for excavation, or for extracting oil or natural gas, could be carried out only with devices that would be potential weapons. In other words, no peaceful blasts could be permitted.

Whenever a nonproliferation treaty becomes operational as a result of deliberations and disarmament discussions in Geneva, there is certain to be overwhelming assent from the Latin Americans. They proved—with the exception of Cuba, which preferred to be absent—that the impetus for nonproliferation can come from nonnuclear nations, too.

In an immediate follow-up, Latin American nations conferred in Buenos Aires on a Common Market project. The precedent they used was not Europe's Common Market, but the Common Market in Central America. That had made steady, upward progress in spite of glaring deficiencies in resources and trained manpower. United States material assistance, whether directly to the new market or through the Alliance for Progress, is required for the foreseeable future. In the wider quest for coordinated social progress, land reform, and the easing of import barriers, there can be a cut-off point in that kind of aid. Short of actual armed subversion, Communist encroachments can therefore be truncated.

Communism is one of the major unsettling factors that provoke unrest in nearly all of Latin America's two hundred universities. It has, however, declined rather precipitously as the combustible factor. The Castro variety is, except in Cuba, about over. It waned beginning back in 1961. Communists then lost the control of the Latin American association of university students that they had won in 1959. Ever since they have suffered badly and were mangled by the Chinese-Soviet conflict. In Peru, for example, a pro-Chinese faction won and the pro-Russians slipped to third. In between rose a formidable non-Communist opposition.

In Latin America political activity is rooted in a tradition of student radicalism, which North Americans only realize in their indignation at demonstrations and egg-throwing antics. Economic backwardness and traditional suspicion of United States intentions keeps stirring up restiveness. What has become of uppermost importance, however, is the hard life students encounter. The majority, incidentally, still come from middle-class families. At most, only 10 per cent of Latin American undergraduates are of working-class backgrounds. Yet at least half find they must work for a living to put themselves through college. Scholarships are sparse indeed. Where they turn up, scholarships come to thirty-five dollars a month. Then, conditions are monstrously overcroweded. Technical students, with the exception of facilities in Mexico, Brazil, Venezuela, and Argentina, must go abroad to pursue up-to-date work in their fields.

It is a massive brain drain, which none of the Latin American countries can afford. Castro tries hard to keep the drain from becoming a hemorrhage. Cubans, who can make it out of the country legally, are more infrequently physicians, engineers, and technicians of assorted kinds. The regime acts to keep them inside the country much as many are suspect, as did the East Germans when they built the Wall to isolate East from West Berlin to help dam up the brain drain.

Human and power factors at work like these are hardly as spectacular as, say post-morteming, as soon as possible, about something more immediately momentous, like the missile crisis in Cuba or the disappearance of Che Guevara. We have had expertise at length, in books or long accounts of the Kennedy administration, of the emplacement and withdrawal of Soviet missiles. These accounts have been within the context of instant history. Some are even articulately presented. But all have the quality of a fast movie scenario that must be placed before the public in a breathless fashion, lest a competitor appear. One day, maybe a generation from now, we may have a detailed, documented account. We haven't been privy to such a presentation yet.

The tragedy, particularly in the sixties, is our unwillingness to become as interested in Latin America on a national scale as we are in the rest of the world. As a matter of national interest, let alone survival, our indifference is rivaled only by the distorted demonology of experts in Latin America. Despite aid plans and intramural defense conferences, we usually tut-tut the economic-political-social disorder south of our border. We try to take the sting out of current, compelling reminders that we must pay constant attention, by taking casual comfort in the growth of our own society.

Chapter 23

THE RELUCTANT IMPERIALISTS

🍾

IN THE six war years (1939–1945) the United States of America succeeded in doubling both its industrial and its agricultural production. At the same time production in Europe, and particularly in Germany, declined. This contrast between the increase of production on one side of the Atlantic and the decrease on the other provided both the basis and the cause, the means and the need for the Marshall Plan. To correct the course of the Carthaginian peace, the American government took the unprecedented step of creating a standing fund within the national defense budget for "Government and Relief in Occupied Areas," the GARIOA Fund.

This was almost immediately followed by the Marshall Plan, which embraced the whole of devastated Europe, including England, as the Plan's official title, the European Recovery Program (ERP), showed. In the greatest and most comprehensive economic aid program ever conceived and implemented, the American government in the ten years from 1949 to 1959 infused well over three billion dollars into the West German and West Berlin economies alone. More than this, an entire range of German-American governmental organizations supplementary to GARIOA and the ERP, such as the Commission for the Promotion of German Exports, sprang into being.

These organizations, which represented a considerable investment of American experience and expertise, were complemented by similar governmental institutions on the German side. Indeed, the Germans went so far as to create a federal ministry for the Marshall Plan (the Greeks created their Ministry of Co-ordination for the same purpose). The result was a degree of intergovernmental cooperation in the economic field unprecedented in peace time (and the laying of foundations for the extraordinary degree of economic interdependence—heavily weighted, of course, on the

American side—that has since developed between the donor and the various receiving countries). Another result was a chain of economic and political events such as the creation of the economic unit "Bizonia" and the introduction of the West German currency reform. It covered West Berlin and thus precipitated the Berlin blockade. This in turn spurred the formation of the Federal Republic and split Germany between East and West.

But the essential nature of the Marshall Plan was that it treated and dealt with the whole of Western Europe—including West Germany and West Berlin—as an economic unit. In short the Marshall Plan established foundations for the economic integration of Western Europe and the inclusion of Western Europe in the American economic system. This was why the Soviets, who instead insisted on the "shopping list" approach (a series of bilateral, country-to-country aid programs), rejected the Marshall Plan. The U.S.S.R. charged that the integral European aspect of the plan, the intent to extend aid only within the framework of a coordinated European program, would constitute "interference in the affairs of sovereign states" and the established pattern of bilateral trade agreements.

The Marshall Plan was the greatest of those radical corrections that take place in American foreign policy as soon as it becomes unmistakably evident that the course currently pursued is disastrously wrong. The *divida et impera* theory, as applied to Germany and particularly as practiced by the four sovereign powers, proved far too costly in the economics of the modern industrialized society of mass production for mass consumption. It is noteworthy that the United States did not make the same mistake in its occupation of Japan: it prevented the Soviets from as much as setting foot on the islands. We ultimately signed a peace treaty with Japan, scorning Russia's refusal to participate in the peace conference—a fact which the Soviets (who have still not concluded a peace treaty with Japan) tried to bring to bear while threatening to sign a separate peace treaty with East Germany.

Moreover, what went for Germany went all the more for Europe, of which—as it was gradually rediscovered—Germany was the center piece. Thus, via the dictate of economic necessity the notion of Europe as an economic and political unity was born. Undoubtedly, as a Dutch diplomat has remarked, there was also "the vague uneasiness and even irritation about the fragmentation of the old world and the genuine desire to transplant the American image to the shattered European countries." If this sounds like an oblique description of a refined form of imperialism it is for good reason. What disturbed the Soviets far more than the imminent resurgence of Germany was the spectacular emergence of America as the overwhelming dominance in a vast new global context, the Atlantic (and Pacific) Community. For the Soviets, the heralding of the American Century was merely another way of heralding the American imperium. What disturbed and confounded the Communists, particularly the Soviets, more than anything else was the technological, and more specifically and recently the electronic, revolution. The progressive aspect of capitalist technology—"capitalist" in the literal sense that it requires enormous capital investment—has knocked the socially progressive character of communism unrecognizably awry.

The capitalist technological revolution, as Joseph Schumpeter has described it, "has driven both the liberal and conservative ideologies before it." As a result, conservatives and liberals have virtually reversed their positions in regard to the great corporations in particular and big business in general.

Hofstetter cites a survey, "Big Business as the People See It," undertaken by the Institute of Social Research of the University of Michigan in 1951. The survey indicated that the ambivalent American attitude (regard for bigness, fear of power, regard for individualism and competition) had been "largely resolved in favor of the big business organizations."

Big business, according to the survey, is now commonly regarded as a good employer. Little concern was expressed about the power of big business over workers and still less about the influence of big business on government. Much stronger feeling was shown against the labor unions than against big business. Small business used to be what Theodore Yntema called "a symbol of opportunity, enterprise, innovation, and achievement—of an independent way of life." It has now been driven to the sidelines, where it tries to maintain itself often enough by mounting its own attacks on the competitive principle.

In the United States and elsewhere, Hofstetter sums up, liberal intellectuals now cock a suspicious eye at the small businessman, if not as a potential stronghold of support for fascist movements, then at least "as the backbone of the reactionary wing of the Republican party."

On the other hand, "An occasional big-business leader may stand out for his enlightenment and urbanity, as compared with the small businessman, who more often than not proves to be a refractory anti-union employer, a parochial and archaic opponent of liberal ideas, a supporter of vigilante groups and of right wing cranks."

Hofstetter also cites an article in *Fortune,* a survey of "The Class of '49." "The Class of '49," the editors reported, "wants to work for somebody else—preferably somebody big. No longer is small business the promised land. As for the idea of going into business for oneself, the idea is so seldom expressed as to seem an anachronism."

The arguments put forward in the dock by the cartelists in the Nuremberg I. G. Farben trial bear a striking resemblance to the opinions expressed by the Class of '49, while the case made by the prosecution under "I.G. Joe" DuBois is identical with the alarm sounded by the American muckrakers at the turn of the century. Hofstetter concedes that Roosevelt's antitrust-inspired TNEC investigation "was from a pragmatic point of view a fiasco." Antitrust, he noted, was "essentially a political rather than an economic enterprise and Thurman Arnold's "experiment can be judged, at least from one angle of vision, a substantial failure." Pleading, as Hofstetter does, that the Antitrust Division's successes in affecting business conduct make up for its inability to reverse business concentration, is another way of saying that the acceptance of institutionalized antitrust activity was contingent upon the acceptance of the cartel as the basis of big business organization.

Hofstetter's parting observation that the antitrust movement "is not the first reform . . . whose effectiveness depended less upon a broad movement of militant mass sentiment than upon the activities of a small group of influential and deeply concerned specialists" provokes this reminder: The Antitrust Department in Washington is probably by far and away the most frustrated and disgruntled "small group of influential and deeply concerned specialists" in American government.

Of equal significance is the collapse of the Stalinist command economy long-term planning based on Leninist objectivism. "For the victory of the Socialist form of society over capitalism," pronounced Lenin, "work productivity will be the ultimately decisive factor." With this fiat, production became the first commandment of Marx. Hence the perpetual Communist obsession with the increase of production in general. There is a permanent Soviet fixation on giantism—on heavy industry, on the Stalinist system of highly centralized, nonspecialized planning—which sets the same broad quantitative norms for all selected fields of production. It derived partly from the need to increase radically the basic industrial plant of a backward nation. In large part it also derived from the dominant crudeness of a people that tolerated the sloughing off and liquidation or banishment of its various elites. But forcing industrial expansion by a strict system of priorities has categorically predetermined the neglect of entire areas of the economy. The principle of the system is basically that of the breakthrough in military strategy—the concentration of overwhelming force at one or a few selected points to the commensurate neglect of the field as a whole.

Specifically, the object of the exercise was to neglect those areas that could best endure neglect over a longer period of time so as to maximize heavy industrial production while minimizing plant and equipment renewal, relying on spot repairs to maintain existing assets in service and production. Retirement rates of productive fixed assets were extraordinarily low throughout most of the 1950's in Eastern Europe. In Czechoslovakia, for example, less than 1 per cent was replaced by new equipment. East Germany was almost equally remiss.

The chief victim of the selective neglect was the service sectors of the economy in general, where capital investment would not in any case show direct results, and transport in particular. Billions upon billions of dollars were spent in building new plants and machines that, because of bottle-necks in the service sectors, could not be put into production until years after their completion. The direct result of this was the poor quality of product and the consequent high incidence of rejects.

Combined with the rigid central planning system that studiously ignores consumer interests and needs, this has produced a vast backlog of unsalable products. One of the great contributing factors to the collapse of the Stalinist command economy has been a widespread refusal to buy. "A crucial oversight of the Communist state," said a Slovak writer, "was the failure to codify a penalty for sales resistance." Meanwhile, despite attempts at economic reform—Libermanism, Langism, *et al.*—the ponderous dilapidated machinery of state enterprise creaks implacably on, churning out huge quantities of outmoded or inferior articles which can never be sold or which, if any are sold, merely ensure that none of the products from the same country will be sold in future. Moreover, the failure to provide timely renewal or large-scale modernization, especially of railroads, rolling stock, roads, and storage space (more than ever because of the enormous backlogs of unsalable products) has resulted in scarcities and a near total lack of reserves. This has made the system and the planning it requires all the more susceptible to sudden stoppages of supplies due to breakdowns.

Quite apart from the studied neglect of so many areas of the economy and the resultant accumulation of obsolete plant, unfinished products, and inefficient services that is the dark side of the command economy, the very concentrations on the positive side have placed intolerable strains on the "favored" sectors, such as the industrial-construction and machine industries. The United Nations Economic Survey of Europe for 1962 estimated the value of unfinished investments in Czechoslovakia, East Germany, and Hungary at one year's gross fixed investment.

The underlying cause of communism's uneconomic economy is the principle of making all measures directly or indirectly dependent on political considerations and making these, in turn, directly or indirectly dependent on ideological considerations. The most striking example of this approach is the traditional Communist compulsion to collectivize agriculture. The ideological fetish of collectivization became an *ersatz* for capital investment in agriculture. This was neglected for so long that when it became clear to even the most fanatic ideologue that considerable capital investment in agriculture was imperative, that actual need for investment had meanwhile increased geometrically to truly astronomical proportions. The result is that the very considerable amounts now being invested throughout the block bring only piddling results. The functionary leaders have remained one step behind the pace of events.

One of the greatest ironies in the Communist economic dilemma is the fact that the much-heralded younger-generation *apparatchik,* whose accession to positions of power was anticipated as the turning point in the economic fortunes of the experiment, has turned out to be more hide-bound by doctrine than his Old Guard predecessors—precisely because he grew up without the bourgeois basis of comparison. Perhaps even more ironic, the one departure from doctrine that the young *apparatchik* has managed to negotiate in the quest for reliable cost accounting, namely the insight that masking production costs must cease if a profit system is to be developed, runs directly counter to the essentially hortatory function of the Communist use of statistics and the quota system in long and short-term planning.

The flaw in the doctrine is traceable to its source: Lenin's dictum that reality for a Marxist is not what is but what should be, and that the first gigantic step toward achievement of the goal is the proclamation and insistence that what should be actually *is*. This is why for years the planning commissions of the various Communist countries have made such a hash of planning. More often than not they have simply included the unfulfilled section of the previous plan in the new one, thus raising the quota of each successive plan only to have the entire structure before the expiration of the five- or seven-year period.

Ever since 1963 a heated discussion has been in progress between party functionaries and economists over how to retrieve the economies of the various Communist countries from their collective plight. The collapse of the Stalinist command economy throughout Eastern Europe (except in maverick and industrially primitive Romania) in 1962 was a far more serious and important event than the de-Stalinization announced at the Twentieth Congress by Khrushchev, six years before. The significance, psychological as well as material, of the failure of Stalinism in the economic field for the East has been compared with that of the Crash of 1929 for the West. In fact, it is far greater. This controversy is a reflection of the controversy in the arts and sciences.

Broadly speaking, the same groups—intellectuals against party hacks at all levels—are involved in both struggles; the basic issue is the same. What is at stake is the concept of economic centralism and hence central control by the party, just as central, party direction and control of writers, artists, and scientists is the nub of the Socialist Realism controversy. It is this aspect of communism— the control problem—that has made the Stalinist command economy and Socialist Realism the respective economic and "cultural" equivalents of martial law. It is the control problem—how do you decentralize without losing control?—that has stopped and altered various attempts at reform, be they economic, political, or cultural reform.

The upshot of both these developments—the run-away technological revolution and the collapse of the command economy—is that the capitalist world, predominated by the United States, has far outstripped the Communist world in the economic field. The most important aspect of this result is the interconnection of the free world economic network and the United States military expenditure programs, *i.e.,* maintenance of American military bases abroad and military aid programs to allies. The fact that the great bulk of American foreign aid has consisted of military assistance in weapons, weapons systems and services, coupled with the fact of huge investments in men, money, and materiel necessary to maintain over one-hundred overseas bases, foreordained the nature of the American commitment abroad and the foreign policy designed to support it. The cause of the predominantly military aspect of the American commitment abroad is the unbroken series of Communist acts of aggression or war beginning with Greek Civil War in 1946 and extending through the blockade of Berlin, the Korean War, the French-Indochina War, the Berlin Ultimatum, the Berlin Wall, and the Vietnam war.

A signal mistake of the American government was the decision to negotiate on the basis of the old wartime alliance with the Soviets, and hence *without* the Germans, rather than on the basis of the new postwar alliance, NATO, *i.e., with* the Germans— among the other allies *against* the Soviets. The attempt to fall back on the old alliance with the Soviets as a basis of negotiations inevitably looked like an attempt to make a deal with the Soviets at the expense of the Germans—and not only the Germans. The failure of the Western Allies to contest the construction of the Berlin Wall shattered the magnetic field between Bonn and Berlin, split West Germany, and ruptured the postwar alliance. Since the Christian Democrats were the party of NATO, the passivity of their allies at the final phase of the national election campaign cost Adenauer his absolute majority and forced his government into coalition with the erratic Free Democrats. The resultant pivotal position of the latter made possible the holiday-pass agreements between the Berlin Senate and the Communist regime of East Germany. It also ushered in the Social Democratic party's policy of "small steps" or "change through closer relations" with the East German Communist regime in defiance of Bonn. The SPD was able to implement this policy because its leader, Willy Brandt, was also the mayor of Berlin.

The French refused to negotiate over Berlin, as Britain and the

United States were intent on doing, and thus produced a split in the Western side of the old wartime alliance. When the British and Americans reconfirmed the policy of relaxation in the face of the Wall at the NATO conference in December, 1961, half of the Adenauer government turned to the French, who agreed to represent German interests in all four power councils—if necessary by refusing to attend. In this spirit France went on to refuse to take part in the disarmament conference in the spring of 1962 or to sign the test ban treaty in 1963. De Gaulle also was determined to pursue his nuclear force. Germany, given one day's notice in advance by the United States, signed in silent fury because of international and moral pressure. For the French, the fact and rationale of the Anglo-American acceptance of the Berlin Wall were decisive confirmation that NATO was hardly less restrictive for France than for Germany, and that France in order to break free would have to reverse the process of integration. Accordingly, de Gaulle chose to withdraw from NATO in order to pursue his own "European" policy, and he evicted the Alliance from French soil.

By the same token, the political leaders of all three parties represented in the German Bundestag regard the United States government's avowed intention of signing an antiproliferation treaty with the Soviet Union as yet another deliberate, and this time definitive, step in the direction of re-establishing the wartime alliance with the Soviet Union in the form of a security system on the basis of the *status quo*.

A week before the NATO conference in December, 1962, the United States announced its intention to cancel the Skybolt guided missile program. This decision has been described by a leading American diplomat as the worst mistake America has made since the Second World War. It threw the Alliance in to an uproar on the eve of the Nassau meeting between President Kennedy and Prime Minister Harold Macmillan. It converted that meeting, which had been called to review the world situation after Cuba, into a discussion of nuclear strategy and its effect on the Alliance. The Nassau agreement stipulated supply by America to Britain of Polaris missiles instead of Skybolt, an air to ground missile to be carried by jet bombers.

The implications of this unilateral decision were enormous: It meant of one thing that Britain, having no carrier rocket system (the development of the Blue Streak had been scrapped in favor of Skybolt), had no independent nuclear deterrent except their obsolescent bombers until their adapted Polaris system became operational in 1968. Meanwhile British Polaris forces were to be integrated into NATO and "targeted in accordance with NATO plans." The stipulation seemed to spell the doom of the British independent nuclear deterrent. The Nassau agreement so enraged de Gaulle that he deliberately thwarted another favorite American project—the entry of Great Britain into the Common Market. The Nassau agreement did something else. For the first time, the Nassau communique called nuclear weapons the "shield" and conventional weapons "the sword." This was the great strategical switch from the massive deterrence of Admiral Radford to the flexible response of Maxwell Taylor's Uncertain Trumpet.

It had the effect—immediately seized upon out of an age-old apprehensiveness—of demoting the Europeans to the status of the docile infantry of an overlord whose nuclear armor enables him invariably to impose his lordly will.

The most curious and telling aspect of the Skybolt fiasco was that it came as the result of the cost accounting approach to international affairs. McNamara decided to scrap Skybolt in order to reduce the defense budget in advance of appearing before the Senate Appropriations Committee. Since the current budget, featuring Skybolt, had six months to run until the end of the fiscal year, holding Skybolt over would have meant continuance of the astronomical expenditures involved for another eighteen months.

McNamara had made his decision affecting the American "buy" of Skybolt, having found for its discontinuance as "nonessential." However, the British "buy" was prorated at a cost that depended in large part on the much larger American "buy." Since the American "buy" had fallen away, this meant that the price to the British would have been increased considerably. However, instead of consulting with the British minister of defense and giving him the alternative of buying at the increased price, McNamara simply junked the project without consultation and presented him with a fait accompli. And this at a time when the British Conservative government was struggling desperately with the national economic situation. The Americans expected the British to get out of the nuclear business as a result—that is, after a period of making do with the obsolescent V-bombers with their smaller warheads—of flying them "till their wings fell off."

Instead, the British came straight back with a request for the next best thing ("What do we do now?"). Thus the "Skybolt Decision" involved a gross misjudgment of the British national character, a judgment that was colored by the American hope that the British would simply get out of the strategical nuclear business. This hope was part of the larger United States government determination to achieve a nonproliferation agreement with the Soviet Union—the "Soviet-American strategical nuclear condominium."

The odd but significant thing about the Skybolt decision is that it was a purely military decision—and a cost-accounting one at that —that was allowed to override all other considerations. The decision was correct from McNamara's point of view, but it should have been carefully screened and changed by the State Department.

More than one telegram was sent to the State Department from American ambassadors abroad pointing out the disastrous consequences that were bound to come if the Skybolt decision were allowed to stand. One ambassador insisted that even at a cost of billions of dollars the Skybolt program should be kept going—not for military reasons (it was agreed that militarily the project was impracticable), but for political and diplomatic reasons. "If it was absolutely necessary to scrap Skybolt," said the ambassador after the event, "then at least it should not have been scrapped at that time—when negotiations for Britain's entry into the Common Market were at a crucial stage. However, once the blow had fallen, the United States should have put all possible pressure on Britain to pool its nuclear capacity with that of France. That way the day might still have been saved."

This was what should have been done at Nassau. Instead, the Secretary of State was not even present at the Nassau meeting. The point is that as the American global position has evolved since the Second World War, the most important official in the formulation and conduct of foreign policy after the President is not the Secretary of State, but the Secretary of Defense. The reasons for this shift of competence are not to be found in the forcefulness of Robert McNamara or in the carefully cultivated phlegma of Dean Rusk ("In negotiation tedium is an asset").

The primacy of the Department of Defense in American foreign policy is the result of the fact that the American global position is built on a system of military alliances in an age in which the development of nuclear weapons has revolutionized both military and foreign policy concepts. It is ironic that the State Department came into its own as a result of the Second World War, only to discover itself obsolescent. The obsolescence of the State Department as the instrument for conducting the nation's foreign affairs is the principal reason for the increasing prominence of the Central Intelligence Agency.

The CIA has been gradually superseding the Department ever since the end of the Second World War, chiefly because the work of maintaining the American global position—not to say "empire"— against the attempted incursions of communism cannot be done by traditional diplomacy. The nature of the Central Intelligence Agency has necessarily changed to the point where it has become the foreign political action arm of the United States government. An accurate designation of the CIA would be FPAA (Foreign Political Action Arm).

The primacy of military considerations in a nuclear age has created the rarest and most attenuated species of expert—the nuclear strategist, such as Henry Kissinger, Robert Bowie, Hermann Kahn, Carl Dibble, *et al.* As new vocabulary has been invented to meet the conceptual need with words like "first strike," "second strike," "overkill," and a flurry of abbreviations, ICBM, MRBM and, to date the most ominous abbreviation of all—MLF.

The idea of the Multi-Lateral Force (MLF) was to skirt the problem of sovereignty by creating a nuclear pool, which all members of NATO could join. The use of the force—a number of surface craft equipped with Polaris missiles and manned by mixed crews from the various member nations of NATO—was to remain under American control to be exercised by veto.

"Le propre de l'arme atomique," said Maurice Couve de Murville, "est que c'est national." (The essential characteristic of the atomic weapon is that it is national.) The great complicating factor of the nuclear age, however, is that the statement reversed is equally true: le propre de nationalism est l'arme atomique—the essential characteristic of sovereignty is a national nuclear force. It was this consideration that prompted Charles de Gaulle to create a French nuclear force at astronomic expense, thereby incidentally thwarting the American drive for a nuclear "hold" in the form of an atomic test ban to be followed by a nonproliferation treaty. Despite concerted American cajoling and argumentation to the effect that France simply did not possess the wealth necessary to sustain a meaningful nuclear program, de Gaulle went ahead.

Ironically, the Multi-Lateral Force idea was assigned to the

expert, Robert Bowie, in an attempt to demonstrate that the project was unfeasible. This demonstration was expected to be so convincing that it would serve as evidence in support of the American
contention that strict international control over the development
and acquisition of nuclear weapons was imperative. In short, the
MLF project was envisaged as part of a coordinated disarmament
program, the basis of which was to be the nonproliferation treaty.
Instead, Bowie in his ratiocinations convinced himself and a number
of people in high places in the State Department (but *not* in the
Pentagon—the project as perverted became anathema to the Department of Defense) that the MLF was not only feasible but
highly desirable. There followed the extraordinary spectacle of half
of the American foreign policy establishment trying to convince the
Allies that the realization of the MLF was a foregone conclusion,
while the other half thundered against the idea and its advocates.

In the end, after alienating the French still further, the project
had to be abruptly withdrawn, to the intense chagrin of the Germans. They were in part persuaded to believe that the project would
solve the problem of Germany's nuclear needs and the world's fear
of the same. Also, German and other disgruntlement at the now-
you-see-it-now-you-don't aspect of American "cooperative" nuclear
policy has generated a degree of resistance to the nonproliferation
treaty that makes the realization of that project highly questionable.
Both Italy and India also have misgivings.

Precisely the same considerations were operative on the American side in the German Starfighter scandal. The only reason the
Bonn government purchased, at enormous and continuing expense,
some seven hundred of the F-104 fighter-bombers was as an investment in nuclear integration. The burdening of the aircraft with
320 pounds of extra electronic equipment for its role as an atomic
bomb carrier (making it probably the heaviest and most complicated single-seat aircraft in operation) has in good part caused
the death of some forty pilots, the destruction of more than seventy
aircraft, and the damaging of some two hundred and fifty more.
But what really bothered the Germans was McNamara's urging, in
the spring and summer of 1966, that the planes be limited to the
use of conventional weapons.

"After having implemented the directives of NATO and adapted
our armaments accordingly," said Heinrich Krone, chairman of the
National Defense Council in the Erhard government, "we are now

being advised to convert the largest possible part of our most important nuclear weapons carrier, the F-104 squadrons, to conventional armament." Such advice is regarded by the Germans as the most ominous sign of all. When nuclearization became the touchstone of integration, by the same token denuclearization became coterminous with disintegration, particularly since the denuclearization is regarded as "equating with a thinning out or an armaments-control measure." Once again it was the atmosphere of unilateral disengagement without consultation that was unpleasantly reminiscent.

Like the Skybolt fiasco, the Starfighter scandal had its cost-accounting consideration. By far the most galling aspect of the crisis for the Germans was Washington's insistence that Bonn spend 1.3 billion dollars (the extent of its arrears in the offset purchase agreement) in the United States by July 1, 1967. The welter of advice, suggestions, proposals, and resolutions from Washington gave the strong impression that prompt payment by way of offset arms purchases and the continued presence of United States troops in Germany were closely related. "If the U.S.A. makes the number of its troops on the continent dependent on payment for this protective burden," said *Die Welt,* "the sense of military defense contributions by the European countries comes into question again."

The reluctance of European NATO members to meet their commitments in defense contributions is at least in good part derivative from their dissatisfaction with the conventional military roles assigned to them by the Washington casting office. The Alliance had long since begun to look like a division of competence by design. As such it was reminiscent of the division of competence by design undertaken among the service branches in the Austro-Hungarian Empire, with the artillery—in this case the strategic nuclear strike forces being strictly reserved to the American contingent within the Grand Alliance.

What rankled the Germans most was McNamara's insistence that the 1.3-billion-dollar procurement orders be exclusively for arms—for the moment precisely what the Germans do not need. Franz-Josef Strauss suggested that the Bonn government go ahead and buy the arms and then dump them in the North Sea. Said Strauss: "That way, we would satisfy our American friends and at the same time demonstrate our peaceful intentions to the world." But the fact that the economics of the American global position is overshadowed by military procurement and armament-selling programs is actually one of the horns of a secondary dilemma. The basic dilemma is one of choice. The choice is between the two alliances it has straddled for the last nineteen years. The Western or the wartime—which is to be given preference?

The straddle position of American strategic doctrine accounts at once for the militarist posture of the American global presence and the persistent American effort to escape from the one alliance into the other, former, wartime, world alliance. There are two remnants of the wartime alliance, both of which are being assiduously kept alive by the Americans and the Soviets: the Four Power Statute for Berlin, and by extension Germany, and the United Nations Organization. The Four Power Statute for Berlin is 95 per cent memorial dedication and 5 per cent reality, the whole of which serves as a linchpin of the makeshift complementary security structure for Germany. The United Nations Organization serves much the same purpose for the world at large.

But the primary significance for Americans is that it was meant to provide an escape hatch from American greatness, nuclear supremacy, economic predominance, etc., etc. "Morality," wrote Charles Dickens, "seems to be a transatlantic monopoly." The traditional high moral strain in the American attitude toward everything, itself far more than merely the lineal descendant of the New England Puritan ethic, preordained the growing apprehension against increasing power. To avoid responsibility, not only for the iniquitous possession of global power, but also for the imperialist stigma that attaches to the administration of such power, an attempt was made with the founding of the United Nations Organizations to delegate the authority that derived from it. In this respect the United Nations Organization was meant to be a more or less gracious parliamentary facade for the Soviet-American nuclear condominium. Franklin D. Roosevelt was realist enough to see that the two pillars of the international organization would have to be the United States of America and the Soviet Union.

The "stability" of the UNO is exclusively attributable to the fact that, for a shifting variety of reasons, to date neither country has seen fit to withdraw its supporting pillar. But there is another, far more important relationship of the United States to the United Nations. In a sense, the latter is an extension of the former—in a sense, the United States are the United Nations in microcosm.

The foreign ethnic heritages in American life are tremendous. An unpublished census study starting with a base of 135,000,000 white citizens out of a total of 151,000,000 Americans in 1950 showed that 126,000,000 of these came from the immigration quota countries of origin. After the basic "Anglo-Saxon" stock (English, Scots, Welsh, and Ulstermen) numbering 52,000,000, or one third of the whole, came Americans of German descent numbering 21,000,000, followed by an estimated 14,000,000 Americans of Irish descent. In fourth place were the Americans of Italian descent with 7,000,000; Americans of Scandinavian descent came fifth with 6,000,000; in sixth place were the Americans of Polish descent with 5,000,000. The other heritages of the American nation made up the rest—Russian, Spanish, Greek, Czechoslovakian, Hungarian, Dutch, etc. These heritages cannot in any sense be regarded as national minorities. They are rather the opposite. They are delegate populations from their countries of origin, integrated into a supra-national ethic that happened to be harbored geographically on the continent of North America. This was the original and enduring sense of the New World—a homeland for humanity at large, as couched in the inscription on the base of the Statue of Liberty in New York harbor, facing the open sea.

The American nation is not ethnic in any conventional sense. Sociologists have noted that it is the lack of ethnic grounding of Americans that is responsible for their quest of status. But the American nation is ethical in every conceivable sense. The all-important point of reference for America is that the *ethos* has replaced the *ethnos*. The informing spirit of the nation is the ethic. This is why morality and idealism are the insistent strains in the American tradition, beginning with the Puritans, who came to find a place where the ethic—in their case a religious ethic—could flourish. For the ethic is the stuff—and it is the only stuff—that binds the nation together: it is not only the basis of national identification, it is in fact the national identity itself.

Until the Second World War, while America remained in splendid isolation—a great power among several great powers— the fact that the new nation was composed of a large variety of foreign heritages made comparatively little difference. But when America burst into global supremacy as a result of World War II, its multiheritage make-up compounded its involvement abroad. The need for armies and staffs of occupation areas and foreign bases brought forth and highlighted the phenomenon of the reimmigrant. On the 1960 census one-fifth of the American nation is listed as either foreign born or of foreign or mixed-foreign parentage. Fifteen per cent of the population is categorized as "native speakers of foreign languages." This constituted the reservoir of foreign language talent—the bilingual Americans—from which the various branches of the American foreign service—Army, Navy, State Department, Department of Defense, and the Intelligence community —have been forced to draw. The reimmigrants—especially the German-Americans (more especially the German-Jewish-Americans), the Italo-Americans and the Greek-Americans—have vastly helped and just as often vastly complicated and hindered the implementing of American foreign policy.

Much of the trouble here lies at the very source of the American idea: What is "American policy"? What is "American"? Who is a better judge of what is and is not "American" than the immigrant who chose (or whose father chose) America as his ideal home rather than the native who owes his title to the concatenated accidents of birth? Who is better equipped to grasp and interpret the idea? Who the more expert in the application of the "American Way" in a foreign country than the reimmigrant who knows both equally well? Here is a type of expert peculiar to the American scene, an experience-trained and linguistically equipped representative of two countries each to the other. But the burden of representation is weighted in favor of America, the reimmigrant becoming a purveyor par excellence of American influence abroad.

Until 1964 a foreign-born American could not return to spend five years (in the aggregate, not consecutively) without losing his American citizenship, unless he succeeded in having a private bill passed in Congress stipulating his exemption. In order to have a congressman sponsor his bill the applicant had to show cause, *i.e.,* that his work in his country of origin was in furtherance of, if not important to, the American national interest—or set forth compelling compassionate reasons for his continued presence there. This State Department regulation—it was never a law—was finally contested by a Mrs. Angelika Schneider, a native of Rimsting, Bavaria, on the grounds that it violated the principle of equality before the law (which, of course, it clearly did). It was forthwith declared unconstitutional and rescinded.

The most spectacular example of the reimmigrant's wreaking havoc with American foreign policy is the case of Andreas Papandreou in the Greek constitutional crisis that began in early 1963 and ended in the military *coup* in the spring of 1967. Andreas Papandreou—the son of George Papandreou, who was leader of the Center Union party and became Premier in 1963—left Greece in 1939 to avoid arrest as a member of a leftist student organization working for the overthrow of the dictator John Metaxas. He took a Ph.D. in economics at Harvard, served in the United States Navy during the Second World War, taught at the University of Minnesota (where he also joined the staff of then Senator Hubert Humphrey), and ultimately became chairman of the Department of Economics at the University of California. In 1959 he received a fellowship sponsored by the Guggenheim and Rockefeller Foundations, at the behest of the Greek government under the conservative leader Constantine Karamanlis, to set up the Center of Economic Research in Athens.

Once the center was established it was financed by a combined grant from the Ford and Rockefeller Foundations and annual counterpart funds from the American Embassy in Athens. Andreas returned to California in January, 1961, but was back in Greece in the fall of the same year to manage the center. He became involved in Greek politics through his father, who was then leader of the opposition, and returned definitively to Greece (after another trip to California) in 1963, when his father became Premier. He campaigned in his father's old constituency and was elected to parliament. Shortly thereafter he was given the cabinet post of alternate minister of coordination, a ministry created in 1950 on the recommendation of American authorities in the interest of a more efficient distribution of American aid.

When young Papandreou entered Greek politics, his opponents seized on his American citizenship and his evident reluctance to renounce it, and proclaimed that his oath of allegiance to the United States had included a pledge to bear arms against Greece. There ensued a strange vacillation in Andreas' behavior. He informed United States Embassy officials that a new era in Greek-American relations had dawned with his return to Greece as an American citizen whose father was Premier. Later, when his candidacy for Parliament automatically voided his citizenship, he failed to renounce it formally, and his passport had to be secured by an official of the American Consulate. At the same time he reacted publicly to the charge of Americanism by becoming the most Greek of the Greeks and more anti-American than the local anti-Americans, a posture that soon drew him to the attention of the extreme left. He was billed by the left (always in search of a front runner) as a personal friend of President Kennedy and the hope of Greek youth against the entrenched forces of reaction. Andreas' increasing involvement with the left dovetailed ominously with his father's radical-liberal policies, particularly his efforts to wrest the nerve centers of power, the Central Intelligence Service and the army, from the control of rightists in the government.

Andreas Papandreou, who was wont to describe himself as a "Stevensonian Democrat," returned to Greece with an American wife, Margaret—a graduate of the University of Minnesota School of Journalism—and his four native American children. The entry and subsequent conduct of the Stevensonian Democrat in Greek politics was something to behold. Andreas felt constrained to side with Archbishop Makarios on the Cyprus issue, that is against the Greek government, against the NATO Alliance (chiefly, the United States), and against the hero of the Greek liberation of Cyprus from the British, Digennis—General George Grivas. But most important, Andreas' stand on the Cyprus issue turned out to be against the most important spiritual-psychological factor in Greek life, namely, the Big Idea, ἡ μεγάλη ἰδέα. In Greek life there is no need to ask what the Big Idea is. Every child knows that the Big Idea, born with the fall of Constantinople in 1453, is to liberate all Greeks from the Turkish (or foreign) yoke. But Andreas Papandreou had apparently forgotten what it was or at least what its full significance was. In Greece, the Big Idea invariably triggers a five-centuries-old emotional reflex that sets every Greek in motion —without discussion, for the Big Idea brooks no discussion.

During his one-and-a-half-year tenure as Premier, George Papandreou engineered the transfer of 2,506 army officers, considered to be rightist appointees, out of the Athens area. The formation—then in progress—of an army contingent for Cyprus provided a convenient excuse. The influx into Cyprus of officers known to be loyal to the right pleased General Grivas, who was in charge of the Greek army's Cyprus operation, but displeased Archbishop Makarios, the president of Cyprus. At the prompting of Andreas, the senior Papandreou then reversed his policy and began sending leftist officers to Cyprus—among them members of the small ASPIDA organization, whose aim was the severing of Greece's military alliance with the West. This pleased Makarios but displeased Grivas, who subsequently wrote a report exposing the ASPIDA conspiracy and implicating Andreas.

It was Andreas' implication in the ASPIDA conspiracy that ultimately brought down the Greek government and paved the way for the military *coup*. In the ASPIDA conspiracy trial, in March of 1967, an Athenian court found fifteen officers guilty of plotting against the state and the monarchy. In accordance with the findings of the court, the public prosecutor prepared charges of high treason against Andreas Papandreou. The prosecutor made application to Parliament for the lifting of the immunity of Andreas and another deputy. Meanwhile George Papandreou's Center Union proposed an amendment to the election law to extend the legal immunity of members after the dissolution of parliament. As it was (and remained: the proposal was not adopted) the immunity of members continued for only four weeks after dissolution. This would leave two weeks before elections during which members of parliament were liable to arrest.

When parliament was dissolved on April 14, the operative date became, not May 28 (the date set for elections), but May 12, the date of expiration of Andreas Papandreou's parliamentary immunity. The prospects were thus virtually nil that Andreas Papandreou would wait that long for the privilege of trying conclusions in custody, or that the rightist elements in the army and the state would wait still longer and leave the first move to the Papandreous or risk an electoral victory by the Papandreous only to intervene thereafter. There was almost bound to be some sort of military or at least paramilitary move (there was widespread rumor that sixty thousand rifles had been brought in and cached in the Athens area by the leftists). The only pertinent question was when the *coup* would take place. The question was answered within the week.

In the early morning hours of April 21 the Greek army rounded up some six thousand persons, including the leaders of all political parties except Spyros Markezinis of the Progressive party, who felt humiliated at his exclusion. Within a week after the *coup* Andreas Papandreou was arraigned on charges of high treason. Thus not only the "private" reimmigrants such as Andreas Papandreou and his group of six Greek-American economists at the Center of Economic Research (the group ultimately split down the middle for and against Andreas) but also the "career" Greek-Americans as it were—personnel of the American Army in Greece (technicians, liaison officers, etc.) staff members of the American Embassy, and the CIA contingent in Athens—inevitably became involved in Greek politics (Greek politics likewise becoming involved in American policy) as never before.

It was clear that the complications and repercussions of the case would not end with the trial and sentence of Andreas Papandreou. On the day of the *coup* literally hundreds of American academicians, many of them friends and former colleagues of Andreas, persuaded John Kenneth Galbraith to plead for direct Presidential intervention (the President reportedly did so intervene through Ambassador Talbot) on the theory that the *Putschists* would execute Andreas forthwith. As it quickly developed, the *Putschists,* being anti-Communists and hence dependent on American goodwill and particularly on American tourists (who make up exactly half of the Greek tourist trade—the largest single source of the Greek national income) were in no position to execute anybody. But the most disturbing aspect of the Papandreou case is that it has worked the extension of the great and enduring struggle of the American conservative with the American liberal into the purely national context of Greece.

The American conservatives— as embodied by the American government and official and commercial involvement in Greece — are for the first time confronted openly by the American liberals, mobilized in the cause of Andreas Papandreou, not only in the sense of the younger Papandreou's personal safety (there are now some two thousand American academicians organized in a "Save Andy Papandreou!" movement), but also in the sense of vigorous advocacy of everything Papandreou stood for in Greece, *i.e.,* a withdrawal of Greece from NATO, the liberation of Greece from American political influence, plus the complementing of American financial aid with Soviet aid. In short, the Papandreou case brought Greece into the same field of force that harbors the Vietnam debate where the liberals, particularly the academic community, are in open rebellion against the American government. Andreas Papandreou was amnestied and released from prison late in 1967. He was deported in mid-January 1968.

The greatest collective reimmigrant cause in history is of course Zionism, since the goal of the movement was realized in the partition of Palestine and the subsequent foundation of the state of Israel. The American-Jewish community (anti-Zionist as well as Zionist) is particularly important because of its very complicated relationship to Israel. American Jews comprise almost half of world Jewry, and yet they constitute perhaps the smallest segment of the Israeli population—fewer American Jews have heeded the call of the in-gathering than any other national community, a very sore point with Israeli authorities. But the American-Jewish Committee has contributed more financial aid to Israel than all other donors taken together.

The American Jew, like all other Americans, has embraced and been absorbed by the ethic. But his conscience with regard to Israel—both as an American and as a Jew—is bothering him. Hence his concern for Israel is particularly strong. For the American ethic was the midwife at the birth of Israel. The Nazi persecution of the Jews was the underlying cause of the emergence of the state of Israel. With the crushing of Nazi Germany, American moral indignation prompted initial and continuing government support for the Jewish nation-state. So much so that the United States has emerged as the chief foreign sponsor of the state of Israel.

American sponsorship of the state of Israel has brought American foreign policy to the virtually hopeless pass between the basic commitment by the ethic to the integrity of the Jewish homeland and the rising tide of Arab nationalism, itself in large part the result of the forceful expulsion of the Palestinian Arabs by the Jews. America is thus caught square in the middle of the Arab-Israeli life and death struggle. In all probability the Arab-Israeli issue is simply insoluble. The Palestinian refugees cannot be resettled because their status as refugees has become their *raison d'etre,* to be jealously guarded for the political leverage it will provide for the eventual homecoming. In short, the resolving of the Jewish moral issue begot the moral counterissue of the Palestinian cast-outs and resulted in the fixed confrontation between the two.

Perhaps it was out of a sense of indignant frustration and rekindled resentment against the original culprit (in our time, that is) that the American government pressured the German Federal Republic to front as a principal arms supplier to Israel after the Sinai campaign and the Suez intervention. Both Germany's moral obligation to Israel and its traditional noncolonial friendship with the Arabs came into play to make Germany appear positively and negatively as the best candidate for the ticklish job.

The failure to present the arms agreement with Israel to the German parliament for approval, instead of merely informing two parliamentary members of each party retroactively, cannot be legitimately criticized. Such a move would almost certainly have been regarded by both the Americans and the Israelis as a shift to torpedo the undertaking and parliamentary approval was extremely unlikely.

Thus the project was ill-conceived by all parties to it; but no such project could have been well conceived. As always, German considerations—such as they were—were based on the perennial expectation of minor miracles, *i.e.,* maximum support from their chief Ally in any eventuality. The German expectation was based on the fact that the chief Ally was itself the *spiritus rector* of the project. In the end all that was accomplished was the exposure of the Alliance's politically weakest member: the exposure of the arms deal cost the German Federal Republic its diplomatic relations with ten Arab countries. The American government clucked disapprovingly but did nothing more: indeed, it was not in a position to do very much more.

A good many professional participants in international events consider that America's failure to support Britain and France (and by logical extension Israel) in the Suez intervention was the first and decisive step in the direction of undoing the Alliance. This opinion is not often expressed publicly in America because it opposes the dictates of the ethic. It was (yet again) the ethic, as embodied in the idea if not the reality of the General Assembly of the United Nations, that made the American reaction to the Suez intervention (coinciding as it did so tragically with the Hungarian uprising) all but inevitable. It is, in the last analysis, virtually unthinkable that the United States should not have taken the stand it did on Suez. Not that America received any noticeable credit or prestige for siding with the United Nations and the Soviet Union against its Allies.

Such credit as the United States received can be measured only negatively by imagining the avalanche of censure and opprobrium that would have been precipitated if America had sided with the interventionists. The principal mistake of American policy in the region preceded Suez. Generally, this was the failure to extend as much aid and offer as much cooperation to Egypt as possible during the period of consolidation of the Nasser regime. Specifically, this was the failure of John Foster Dulles to arrange and proceed with the financing and construction of the Aswan Dam. Dulles' sudden withdrawal, in July of 1956, of the American offer at almost the last moment in a fit of pique was diplomatically inexcusable and politically disastrous. Both the positive and negative results of the act were tremendous: not only did it fail to bring Egypt into the American sphere of economic and political influence (by providing for massive American engagement in a construction project that would last two decades and more) but it precipitated the "resolution adopted by the Council of Ministers for the nationalization of the Suez Canal Company" which at once caused the Suez crisis and catapulted Egypt into the arms of the Soviets. John Foster Dulles was Secretary of State in a sense in which few men were Secretaries of State before him and none since. No American practitioner of foreign policy has blundered more spectacularly than Dulles did in his decision to retract the American offer to construct the Aswan Dam.

The nature and gravity of Dulles' failure becomes clear when it is realized that the "aggressiveness" in the American system is economic. The only means the system has of extending itself is by the basically beneficial process of economically involving new areas through aid and trade and then institutionalizing the process through the establishment of international corporate identities headquartered in America and such instruments as the General Agreements of Tariffs and Trade, the International Monetary Fund, the International Bank for Reconstruction and Development, etc. This is the only dynamism proper to the system. It is why the political action is almost exclusively devoted to warding off charges of "economic imperialism," the invasion of American investment capital, the "brain drain," etc., and the frustration of local, leftist revolutionary forces set in motion or adopted by the Communists. In strict political terms this amounts to a holding action—to conserve what American business genius has succeeded in establishing.

The haunting question, then, is one put by Charles A. Beard in his introduction to *The Enduring Federalist*. He asked, rather hopefully: "Is the American system of federal and representative government to endure through the ages and be used as a model for a world union intended to maintain peace among the nations?"

Until the distortion that so largely is attributable to the experts is corrected, the old left, the new left, the true left, will brand the majority of Americans "the good Germans." Why? For having the unsophisticated gracelessness to support their government. Or, as Dr. Martin Luther King remarked: for being "on the wrong side of the revolution."

"This need," declared King to an audience of Vietnam critics, "to maintain social stability for our investments abroad, accounts for the counterrevolutionary action of American forces."

His charge was curiously reminiscent of Franz von Papen's defense of Imperial Germany. Papen claimed that the Kaiser's Germany in World War I had only the aim of securing and protecting her markets abroad. Ours is the role of the diffident imperialists, who seek through generosity and frequent compassion to blur the image. We don't care for the position. But there is no retreat from it without defaulting to the massive, crude obscurantist force of communism, which inherently is brutally imperialist. Our experts have seen in that force just the difficulties that come with growing pains. But the sacred cause of that force is not, and cannot be, co-existence *with* us, but no-existence *for* us.

INDEX